Society of Others

Society of Others

*Kinship and Mourning
in a West Papuan Place*

Rupert Stasch

UNIVERSITY OF CALIFORNIA PRESS
Berkeley · Los Angeles · London

University of California Press, one of the most distinguished university presses in the United States, enriches
lives around the world by advancing scholarship in the
humanities, social sciences, and natural sciences. Its activities are supported by the UC Press Foundation and by
philanthropic contributions from individuals and institutions. For more information, visit www.ucpress.edu.

University of California Press
Berkeley and Los Angeles, California

University of California Press, Ltd.
London, England

Library of Congress Cataloging-in-Publication Data

Stasch, Rupert.
  Society of others : kinship and mourning in a West
Papuan place / Rupert Stasch.
    p. cm.
  Includes bibliographical references and index.
  ISBN 978-0-520-25685-9 (cloth, alk. paper)—
  ISBN 978-0-520-25686-6 (pbk., alk. paper)
  1. Ethnology—Indonesia—Papua.   2. Kinship—
Indonesia—Papua.   3. Mourning customs—
Indonesia—Papua.   4. Ethnopsychology—Indonesia—
Papua.   5. Papua (Indonesia) —Social life and
customs   I. Title.
GN635.I65S73   2009
305.89'912—dc22   2008040618

Manufactured in the United States of America

17   16   15   14   13   12   11   10   09
10 9 8 7 6 5 4 3 2 1

This book is printed on Natures Book, which contains
30% post-consumer waste and meets the minimum
requirements of ANSI/NISO z39.48-1992 (R 1997) (*Permanence of Paper*).

Laura Hendrickson

Contents

Illustrations

Acknowledgments

My first steps in the work leading to this book were taken more than fifteen years ago. The book now exists thanks to the generosity of many persons and institutions who have helped me at different points since then, and it is a pleasure to be able to thank some of them here.

Valerio Valeri encouraged my interest in working in West Papua at an early stage. He, Michael Silverstein, and Nancy Munn lastingly influenced many of my anthropological sensibilities. Ira Bashkow, Anne Lorimer, Kathy Rupp, Alan Rumsey, Mike Cookson, and Danilyn Rutherford have similarly been great teachers and friends. Since 1997 I have had the good fortune to be in steady conversation with Joel Robbins, whose ideas and encouragement have meant a tremendous amount to me and to this work. Other persons who have given much-appreciated feedback on draft materials or in various ways offered valuable suggestions and intellectual models include Francesca Merlan, Bambi Schieffelin, Ward Keeler, John Wolff, Manuela Carneiro da Cunha, Marshall Sahlins, Terry Turner, Terri Silvio, Hoon Song, Courtney Handman, Janet Hoskins, Webb Keane, Tanya Luhrmann, Paul Manning, Rob Moore, Dan Jorgensen, Don Gardner, Tom Boellstorff, Bill Maurer, Julia Alper, Anne Ch'ien, Greg Downey, Mark Mosko, Stéphane Breton, Pascale Bonnemère, Pierre Lemonnier, Daniel de Coppet, Maurice Godelier, Denis Monnerie, Chris Ballard, Ian Keen, Jaap Timmer, Tom Goodman, Andy Kipnis, Kathy Robinson, Timo Kaartinen, Jukka Siikala, Karen Armstrong, John Gray, Magnus Fiskesjö, Fred Henry, Karen Sykes,

David Akin, and James Faubion. I have benefited greatly also from the intelligence, curiosity, and enthusiasm of my students at Reed College, where I was privileged to teach from 1998 to 2008. The many faculty colleagues at Reed whose comments and support have importantly shaped this work's development include Rob Brightman, Gail Kelly, Paul Silverstein, John Haviland, Charlene Makley, Wally Englert, Nora McLaughlin, Lisa Steinman, Libby Drumm, Doug Fix, Jackie Dirks, Ellen Stauder, Colin Diver, Peter Steinberger, Jon Bialecki, Alex Hrycak, and David Garrett. Research assistants at Reed who aided directly in the preparation of this book include Elly Blue, Ryan Wilcoxen, Kate Miller, Lauren Keeler, Vanessa Garrido, Gwen White, Ariana Paulson, Paul Manson, Kendall Taggart, and Jess Burgess.

Parts of this work have been presented at the University of Chicago, Reed College, the University of Helsinki, the Australian National University, Johannes Gutenberg University, the École des Hautes Études en Sciences Sociales, meetings of the American Anthropological Association, and meetings of the Association for Social Anthropology in Oceania. My thinking benefited very much from the generous comments of participants in those events. At the University of California Press, Stan Holwitz has been an enthusiastic supporter, Cindy Fulton has carefully guided the book through production, and Sheila Berg has greatly improved its readability. Bambi Schieffelin and Bill Hanks generously read the whole manuscript at a late stage and offered extensive, very helpful advice about the details, as well as the big picture.

This study is based on eighteen months of fieldwork in the Korowai area carried out between 1995 and 2007. Leading up to my main research in 1995–96, Leontine Visser and Paul Taylor were among the persons who helped me learn about practical aspects of the possibility of fieldwork in Papua. Paul pointed me toward the Korowai area and also toward Gerrit van Enk and Lourens de Vries's book manuscript, *The Korowai of Irian Jaya: Their Language in Its Cultural Context* (subsequently published in 1997). To Gert and Lourens themselves, I am deeply indebted, not only for all their Korowai-related writings (based on periods of mission-related residence in Yaniruma village between 1982 and 1991) but also for their hospitality in the Netherlands in 1999 and their acts of generosity from afar.

My fieldwork from September 1995 to August 1996 was sponsored by Universitas Cenderawasih (UNCEN) in Abepura, the Indonesian Institute of Sciences (LIPI) in Jakarta, and the American-Indonesian Exchange Foundation (AMINEF), also in Jakarta. Naffi Sanggenafa and

Frans Wospakrik at UNCEN and Nelly Paliama at AMINEF helped me in highly significant ways, as did Jos Mansoben at UNCEN in connection with my 2001 trip. In 1995–96 Paula Makabory and John Moore gave generous logistical help from their office on the UNCEN campus. In 1995–96 and during short return visits in 1997, 2001, 2002, and 2007, I depended very much on the aid and patience of the pilots and other personnel of several missionary aviation organizations based in Sentani or Wamena: Yajasi (three flights), Helimission (one), AMA (one), and MAF (eleven). I have also benefited repeatedly since 2001 from the kindness, hospitality, and interest of Peter Jan and Maaike de Vries, who now live in the Korowai area as Bible translators. Bram Rumere helped me in major ways when I first arrived in Yaniruma in 1995, and Buta Yaluwo was similarly generous to me across many years. My activities over the years have also received patient and enthusiastic support from the Kombai man Banio and his family, Amos Yalehatu and his family, Pak Guru Kabak (now Kepala Distrik), and the other Papuan families from the Digul watershed or the highlands who make their homes in Yaniruma. I owe much to all the Korowai and Kombai men who hold the office of kepala desa or rukun tetangga ("RT") in the villages of Yaniruma, Manggel, Mabül, Yafufla, Sinimburu, Mbasman, and Mbaigun. Tourism professionals with links to the Korowai area who have aided me significantly at different times include Kornelius Kembaren, Magnus Andersson, Bob Palege, and Jill Paley.

The preparations, fieldwork, and writing that led to this book were supported financially by the National Science Foundation, the Consortium for the Teaching of Indonesian, the University of Chicago, Fulbright-IIE, the Wenner-Gren Foundation for Anthropological Research, the Charlotte W. Newcombe Foundation, the Henry Luce Foundation (through a fellowship in Southeast Asian Studies in the RSPAS Department of Anthropology at the Australian National University), the National Endowment for the Humanities, the Graves Awards in the Humanities, and Reed College.

This book's major subjects include Korowai speech; the uncentralized, ownership-divided Korowai landscape; and the intense politics and emotion of paying, giving, or sharing objects on that landscape. All these were sources of steady personal difficulty and pleasure for me during my fieldwork. The single person who helped me the most in these areas, with enduring good humor, is Wayap Dambol. I also owe a huge debt to Fenelun Malongai; Fina Lexayu; Lutel Malonxatun; Xabel Malonxatun; Gia Xelexatun, her four sons, and her husband, Silom Dambol; Kombeon

Nambul; Betüdal Dayo and her husband, Xanduop Dambol; Kuali Wafüop; Sapuru (Labulun) Sendex; Nailop Xawex and her sister Mofu; Bolum Ngoxoni and his wife, Mamul; Yakop Dayo; the Dalxatun Dayo siblings (including Yameap) and their spouses; Mbex Ngoxoni; Dofux Xomai Xajaxatun; Ndaxi Dayo; the brothers Lüma and Gaxlel Dayo; Gaxlel's wife, Baibulan Ngoxoni; Kelekele Dayo; Filale Bafiga and his family; Xeliex Lamenxatun; Daxale Xalixatun *(nembainum);* Ela Malongai; and the Yaxipxatun Nandup siblings and their spouses and children. I have lived for short or long periods in about fifty Korowai houses, located on thirty-five clan places and in five villages. About 250 men and 230 women have sat with me for private interviews (the women usually in pairs or in the company of a child). Some persons spoke with me in this manner as many as a dozen times. I continue to be astonished by the diverse and thoughtful ways in which Korowai hosts, companions, and interviewees accommodated my awkward presence in their lives. It is above all else their intelligence and kindness that has led to whatever is of value between these covers.

Nemayox, ifexa mbuku, afe nuptonda. Nufe mbam. Nufe kolufoanop fundam bexelepteboda. Nu kolufoaup bedaibaleda. Pa gexenepto nexulmelun manopobatedo woleol aubale. Amodo ifexa mbuku, afe ango gexenepa woleol aubatexaülop. Nufe mofu walüpabül.

My parents, Mary and Nick Stasch, put me on the course that led here and supported me on the way. Jed Stasch, Asia Henderson, Danielle and Taylor Aglipay, Amy Stasch, Kurt Harris, and Trevor Harris have also been big parts of this process. I owe many thanks to Pat, Don, Julia, and Andy Hendrickson for their enthusiasm and warmth.

I have learned the most, in life and scholarship, from Laura Hendrickson. My anthropological ideas have been heavily influenced by following closely her work, and her critical insight and steadfast support have enriched all parts of this text.

Note on Language

The values of letters I use to write Korowai speech probably do not need special clarification, with the following exceptions. I use [x] to represent a velar fricative (like the sound written as [kh] in Indonesian). I use [ə] to represent a mid-central unrounded vowel (like the first sound in English *about*), which occurs only in unstressed syllables. The consonant written as [f] is bilabial rather than labiodental. I use [j] to represent a voiced palatal stop.

Korowai speech appears in italics. In the few places where I cite Indonesian words, these are underlined.

In places where it might be useful for readers to see morpheme boundaries within single Korowai words (such as between two parts of a compound), I separate the different meaningful parts of the words by hyphens. In other places, where the hyphens are more likely to be distracting than informative, I do not break single words up in this way. When I cite an uninflected verb root, I put a hyphen at the end to indicate that the form is always accompanied in speech by suffixes. I also put hyphens at the beginning or end of other kinds of bound morphemes cited in isolation, to indicate that they do not occur in speech as self-standing words.

In photograph captions and in my acknowledgments, I identify specific Korowai persons by binomials consisting of a personal name followed by a clan name. Korowai do not combine personal names and clan names in this way, except as a new, occasional practice associated with writing, government institutions, and commerce.

Introduction

Otherness as a Relation

This book examines the ways in which Korowai people of West Papua, Indonesia, make qualities of otherness the central focus of their social relations. According to a dominant strand of Western thought, people's social unity is based on their similarity and their shared experiences. The most authentic, valued, and intimate social bonds of life are ones that most approach an ideal of pure identification. In popular stereotypes "tribal" people hold a special place in this understanding: they are whole human populations whose main social experience consists of undifferentiated unity of consciousness, following from their enduring, intimate copresence in the same living spaces. One of this book's goals is to discredit this model of social bonds.

Korowai number just a few thousand persons, but they are known to tens of millions of Westerners as iconic "tribal" people, through articles about them in *National Geographic* and many other magazines and through television shows about them broadcast on a wide variety of networks.[1] Korowai live dispersed across several hundred square miles of lowland tropical forest. They grow and gather their own food, and they manage their social relations through egalitarian processes of direct give-and-take rather than political offices and a legal bureaucracy. Other attributes that media professionals have fixed on as making Korowai a perfect fit with Westerners' stereotypes of "primitive" humanity are their spectacular "treehouses" (figure 1), their limited possession of factory-made commodities such as cotton clothing, and their practice of cannibalism. As for cultural features interesting to anthropologists, Korowai society is kinship based, in the sense that people almost universally address each other in conversation by kinship terms. All Korowai belong to named landowning groups, with group membership determined by paternity, a pattern putting them in classic social anthropological terrain of subsumption of persons and events to the undifferentiated corporate unity of agnatic descent groups (after Maine 1861).

Yet for all the ways Korowai ought to be an excellent match with the stereotype of social bonds of unity founded on identification and shared face-to-face experience, their lived reality is quite the opposite. Much like the social experience of city dwellers in industrial, mass-mediated societies, Korowai lives are dominated by the perception that their society consists of large numbers of unreliable, largely anonymous others. Often these others are referred to generically by such labels as "strangers," "far-away people," or "angry people." Otherness is a main category by which Korowai themselves talk about social relations. Korowai speakers routinely describe specific persons in their world as being "other, strange" *(yani)*. Like an urban population, the Korowai population is not a face-to-face community. Korowai routinely encounter persons, places, and social processes they know little about, and they are aware of the existence of other people whom they have never met but whose presence in the world affects their lives. Despite calling everyone they meet by kinship terms, Korowai also often say that a specific person is "not a relative." Speakers also bluntly say of themselves, "I have no relatives." Even Korowai understandings of face-to-face interaction include statements that sharing the same space, besides making people unitary, can cause them to fight. Tellingly, Korowai contrast their own social condition with what they see as the undifferentiated consciousness of city dwellers. They say that in their own population, different people's thoughts are heterogeneous, resulting in much social conflict, whereas town people are obviously unified in their consciousness: they coordinate their actions on a huge scale, without constantly disagreeing.

If otherness is normal Korowai social experience, then what is a more accurate way to conceptualize social relations, in place of the model of unity rooted in sameness? I argue in this book that Korowai define their social engagements around ways in which they are strange to each other. Boundaries of otherness are points of unity between people. Perhaps all human relations have this paradoxical organization. Yet Korowai people's specific ways of living out the paradox offer an

Figure 1. House and banana garden of Melanux Waüo and Gayumale Wafüop, 2001. The woman Melanux can be made out as a small figure at middle left, stepping from a lower ladder onto the main ladder pole.

unusual opportunity for asking anew: What are social ties? What is the place of otherness in them?

This study examines some of the many otherness-dominated social relations important in Korowai day-to-day experience. The main finding I develop is that in Korowai people's reflexive sensibilities about social relations, a social bond conjoins qualities of otherness and involvement. This tense conjunction of mismatched qualities is the substance of people's links to each other. What is interesting about Korowai preoccupation with figures of otherness is not the element of otherness alone but the ways in which Korowai pose otherness *as* a relation—as a quality through and around which people are mutually close.

PATTERNS OF SEPARATION

A focus on otherness runs through all areas of Korowai social experience. By mentioning just a few specific examples of relations in which qualities of otherness are points of people's close social engagement, I can give a preliminary sense of why I have made otherness this work's central subject.

Most Korowai houses stand with their floors about fifteen feet above ground, supported by topped tree trunks. This remarkable architecture is itself a gesture of separation, dramatically setting domestic space apart from the surrounding world (figure 2). Even more impressive than houses' height, though, is the distance between them. Korowai build their houses standing alone or in pairs, often about a mile from the next occupied house clearing. Korowai explain residential dispersion, and the landownership system that organizes it, as a method of maintaining autonomy and equality. By living far apart on separately owned land, people avoid getting in the way of one another's activities or being subject to other people's political control. Yet dispersion and ownership also set the constructive terms of people's actual bonds. Korowai relate to each other *as* geographically separate people who own separate lands and are intensely averse to social hierarchy. This importance of spatial otherness as itself a basis of people's relatedness is apparent, for example, in prominent practices of visiting, during which persons related as "owner" and "guest" engage in delicate, valued close interactions across a divide of geographic belonging.

As for the vertical separateness of houses from the surrounding land, Korowai build their dwellings high above the ground for many reasons, but the most prominent is that they fear attacks by two categories of

Figure 2. The woman Kuali Wafüop carrying a container of water while entering the house of Kelekele Dayo. Kelekele's clanmate Lüma is seated on the house's balcony at left.

monsters: the "demons" that humans become after death and the "witches" within the Korowai population thought to cause all deaths. People organize many aspects of their daily lives around trying to stay separated from these monsters. Korowai people's concern with these beings is again typical of the general way that their worlds are populated by figures of otherness. Yet in speech and in the vivid imagery of the monsters' characteristics, the categories "demon" *(laleo)* and "witch" *(xaxua)* are paired in close contrast to the category "human" *(yanop)*. The "demon" category in particular is an intimate counterpart to humanity. The demon figure's deformations of human characteristics are points of unity with the concept "human" and points of social connection by which humans go on relating to dead relatives.

Kinship relations between living people, too, are dominantly organized along lines of otherness-based unity. Bearing children and forming bonds of attachment with them is the creative heart of Korowai kinship. Yet newborn babies begin life categorized as repulsively demonic, not human, and parents form positive bonds with their children by relating to them across this divide. Korowai accounts of intense attachment between parents and even mature children focus on disparities between them: the ways that children are at once signs of their parents and markedly separate from them in body and time. Many other specific kinship relations similarly involve paired persons whose main qualities of relatedness consist of strangeness and separation. Bonds between maternal uncles and sister's children are among the most emotionally poignant kinship relations in most people's lives, but these bonds are by definition between persons who belong to different clans, own different lands, and live apart. The relatives' separateness is part of their intimacy. Another prominent kinship bond is that between mother-in-law and son-in-law. Yet this pair's main relational practice is sensory avoidance. A mother-in-law and son-in-law approach each other in the space of bodily interaction much as Korowai at large approach each other in the space of landownership: every encounter is a dance of close involvement in which participants carefully signal the ways in which they are mutually other.

It is one thing to assert very generally that Korowai take otherness as a relation and something else to show concretely how this is so, to define and exemplify "otherness" in anthropologically meaningful ways, or to come to grips explicitly with further theoretical understandings of the nature of Korowai cultural process that are implied in the idea of otherness-focused social relations. Below I lay some groundwork for my pursuit of these deeper goals. I begin with a look at ways in which the stereotype of social relations of pure identification is not just a popular model but also one promoted by anthropologists and other scholars. I then outline the existence of alternative traditions of scholarly thought that have understood unity and otherness as dialectically interdependent. Finally, I sketch out several narrower lines of theoretical concern that this book pursues, building on those alternative traditions.

AGAINST GEMEINSCHAFT

The idea of a human social relation of pure mutual identification has held considerable currency across the history of modern anthropology. I can clarify this book's goals partly by locating the idea of "otherness as a relation" in opposition to this contrasting tradition of thought. An important reference point in the tradition is the German sociologist Ferdinand Tönnies's famous concept *Gemeinschaft*.

In 1877 Tönnies drew a contrast between two types of human social relation, termed *Gemeinschaft* and *Gesellschaft*. He defined *Gemeinschaft* (often translated as "community") as a population united by "a perfect unity of wills" (1957 [1887]: 37). This unity follows spontaneously from living close together in the same space, being kin, and sharing the same social experience. For Tönnies, typical *Gemeinschaft* relations included bonds between mother and child, husband and wife, and brother and sister, as well as between speakers of a common language or between common owners of "fields, forest, and pasture" (pp. 34, 37). Tönnies contrasted *Gemeinschaft* with *Gesellschaft*, or social relations that people enter into by virtue of calculating instrumentally that those relations are in their independently held interests. "One goes into Gesellschaft as one goes into a strange country," he wrote (p. 34). The typology had a critical edge: it denigrated modern urban social conditions of Tönnies's own place and time by juxtaposing those conditions with an idyllic alternative possibility of communitarian oneness. In developing this model, Tönnies was influenced by bodies of thought such as Hobbes's contract theory and Nietzsche's vision of social unity in Dionysian abandon, but he also found crucial inspiration in ethnography and comparative jurisprudence, particularly in Henry Maine's 1861 book, *Ancient Law* (see Tönnies 1957 [1887]: 181–83; Tönnies 1971 [1912]: 34; Mitzman 1973: 71–72, 83–84; Liebersohn 1988: 18–39; Harris 2001: xxi–xxvii). The idea of *Gemeinschaft* bears strong affinities with Maine's model of agnatic groups as person-subsuming permanent collectivities, as well as his notion of the "village community" (1871).

Gemeinschaft went on to become one of the most influential theoretical categories in the history of the social sciences. Tönnies's typology directly influenced Durkheim, who transposed it into his own famous typology of two kinds of social relations, now using the label "mechanical solidarity" for unity based on identity of consciousness.[2] The cluster of ideas articulated by Maine, Tönnies, and Durkheim in their models of noncontractualist social relations was foundational to the entire structural-functionalist paradigm in British anthropology. In the United States, Redfield (e.g., 1940) renovated the *Gemeinschaft* concept in his notion of "the folk society," Shils (1957) renovated it as "primordial ties," and other transformations of the category figured importantly in the sociology of Talcott Parsons. More generally, there are elements of *Gemeinschaft* thinking in a great deal of twentieth-century anthropological and sociological work oriented around the category "community" and also in the classic idea of the "village study" as a mode of ethnographic inquiry.

Under other names, the model of social bonds based on pure identification has recurrently informed anthropological studies of kinship. In highly influential statements about forty years ago, Fortes (1969) posited "amity" as the axiomatic moral orientation of kin toward each other, Sahlins (1972 [1965]) posited a correlation between unconditional giving on the one hand and kinship and residential closeness on the other, and Schneider (1980 [1968]: 50) posited "love" or "enduring, diffuse solidarity" as the defining quality of family relations in the United States. A more recent iteration of the idea is Carsten's equation of kinship with "shared experience" (2004). Another small but sharp example of *Gemeinschaft*'s ongoing theoretical life is Bird-David's model of hunter-gatherer sociality as relational unity based on intimate sharing of space, things, and actions (1999: 72–73, 78, 88).

Important traces of the *Gemeinschaft* idea can be seen also in widespread, even second-nature anthropological understanding of "face-to-face" social relations as being fundamentally special, and perhaps more solidary, than other kinds of links. Outside anthropology, Anderson's (1991) well-known account of the rise of nationalist imagined communities seems to imply an alternative nonimaginative face-to-face community from which imagined communities are a departure, one typical example of *Gemeinschaft*'s wide shadow existence in scholarship on mass societies. The popular sterotypy of "tribal" and "family" sociality as undifferentiated, space-based unity of consciousness is not a fact of popular history alone but has been shaped and bolstered by the work of intellectuals.

One major anthropological trend that might seem to be a direct rejection of the *Gemeinschaft* stereotype is the antiprimitivizing reform movement that in recent decades has sought to divest anthropology of a vision of "people and places" as its assumed, naturalized subject matter. One strand in this movement has been heightened discomfort with making anthropological generalizations about the cultural orders by which sets of people live their lives, in part based on the perception that populations of people are *not* internally unitary and homogeneous in their cultural lives, such that to generalize about their cultural distinctiveness would be to participate in a false *Gemeinschaft* stereotype. A complementary strand of the movement has been a turn away from studying the internal organization of small spatial and temporal scales of people's social lives toward studying the articulation of local social practices with larger spatiotemporal scales of cultural, political, and economic force. Here too the reform movement rejects the idea of an isolated, self-contained, and self-identical community, in favor of a notion that any "local" scene of human activity is not culturally autarkic but is constituted by its links to external, nonlocal orders of cultural process. In a charter text, for example, Gupta and Ferguson urged anthropology to leave behind its past "assumed isomorphism of space, place, and culture" (1992: 7; see also Boellstorff 2002, specifically on Indonesia).

A turn to large scales of cultural and historical articulation is undeniably valuable. Often, though, it has been premised on the untenable view that to study "local" or "endogenous" social processes as such would be to study *Gemeinschaft,* or communities of pure identification based on unmediated copresence in the same place of living. In this way, the turn tacitly affirms *Gemeinschaft* as an imaginable form of human cultural order in the very act of rejecting it as an object of study. A more accurate anthropology is one that studies otherness as an internal feature of local social relations and local social practices, in addition to studying the ways in which people's social lives are structured by nonlocal institutions and cultural influences. I show in detail in this book that Korowai places and social relations are not even isomorphic with themselves and that this nonisomorphism is of foundational importance to the shape of Korowai social experience.

A related trouble is the reform movement's partial entanglement in a one-sided "epistemology of intimacy" that Keane (2003) suggests has been central to main currents of anthropological thought across the past several decades. Here a vision of authentic human sociality as undifferentiated unity of consciousness informs not just anthropologists' definitions of what they study but also their definitions of their own knowledge-relations to those subjects. A case in point is Johannes Fabian's *Time and the Other: How Anthropology Makes Its Object* (1983), a groundbreaking reformist work that reproduces displaced *Gemeinschaft* stereotypy in an especially stark way. Fabian criticizes anthropologists for epistemological and textual practices of temporally separating the worlds of the people we study from the world in which we ourselves live, think, work, and write. In formulating this criticism, Fabian himself denies otherness, specifically otherness of time. He endorses a *Gemeinschaft*-style understanding of human sociality, to the effect that when people interact with each other, such as in anthropological fieldwork, they occupy positions of pure temporal unity. He introduces this premise through the idea of "intersubjective time": "To recognize *Intersubjective Time* would seem to preclude any sort of distancing almost by definition. After all, phenomenologists tried to demonstrate with their analyses that social interaction presupposes intersubjectivity, which in turn is inconceivable without assuming that the participants involved are coeval, i.e., share the same time" (Fabian 1983: 30, original emphasis; see also p. 42).

Fabian traces his idea of intersubjective time to Alfred Schutz (Fabian 1983: 24). However, Schutz's actual explorations of the relation between intersubjectivity and temporality are more complex. Fabian uses the term *allochronism,* or otherness of time, to describe anthropologists' wrongful othering of their subjects, at odds with the actual intersubjective practice of research. Schutz, by contrast, emphasizes that subjectivity and intersubjectivity are allochronic as a matter of course. People's consciousness at any time is composed of temporally complex orientations to other moments of time beyond the present, as well as orientations to their face-to-face temporal copresence. Interacting persons both share and do not share time with each other. Before another person, an actor is intersubjectively engaged with that person's otherness of memory, otherness of present tempo, and otherness of expected future, just as in relating to oneself a person is allochronically engaged with disparities between "now" and diverse other times relevant to one's being (e.g., Schutz 1944: 502; 1945: 374; 1967 [1932]).[3]

Rather than deny otherness of time, or cultural otherness generally, a more adequate way to dissolve misplaced borders between anthropologists' worlds and the communities they study is to engage intellectually with the ways people are involved with otherness in their own lives, including their experiences of otherness when interacting with consociates in a shared place and time. This involves a shift in the epistemology of cultural analysis similar to what Santner identifies as a crucial moment in the ethics of personal intersubjectivity, namely, the recognition that "what makes the Other *other* is not his or her spatial exteriority with respect to my being but the fact that he or she is *strange*, is a *stranger;* and not only to me but also to him- or herself, is the bearer of an internal alterity" (2001: 9; original emphasis). This book is an ethnography of the internal alterity of Korowai social relations.

ALTERNATIVE TRADITIONS:
THE BOOM IN OTHERNESS STUDIES

Alongside the *Gemeinschaft* tradition, which assimilates copresence in a single space and time to unmediated relational unity, there are long-running and growing traditions of thought that directly recognize otherness as an integral, central feature of social bonds. These traditions offer the possibility of overtly approaching society as a system of estrangements, separations, and disidentifications, as well as a system of solidarities.

The desire for bonds of unmediated unity of consciousness owes a lot to German romanticism's philosophic and aesthetic revolt against forms of human alienation entailed in economic and technological modernity. Yet other modern thinkers have offered accounts of alienness as an integral quality of social experience. Although fundamentally varied in findings and implications, the philosophical systems of such figures as Hegel, Husserl, Heidegger, Sartre, and Levinas are well known for according alterity a constitutive role in human consciousness and in social bonds rather than only a peripheral or corrosive role. In the social sciences, routine descriptive terms such as *interaction, intersubjective,* or *social* itself (in particular, in its Durkheimian and Weberian resonances) are to some degree shorthand evocations of a theoretical vision to the effect that disparities *between* humans are exactly the paths of their relatedness. In this vein, one specific counterpoint to Tönnies's romanticism from within the classic German sociological canon is Georg Simmel's understanding that *every* human relation can be analyzed as a "unity of nearness and remoteness" (1950 [1908]: 402).

There are also numerous precedents in the existing ethnographic literature for a focus on otherness as central and constitutive in people's sociocultural lives. Many of the precedents to which my interpretations in this study are most indebted are specifically about demographically small, nonurban societies. I earlier singled out work on kinship as an area of ongoing *Gemeinschaft*-leaning theoretical sensibilities, but Peletz (2001) documents a long history of anthropological concern with "ambivalence" as an integral aspect of kin relations. Anthropological research in Indonesia and Melanesia has been especially notable for making cultures of alterity a main theoretical concern. In the past several decades, scholars working in these regions have produced numerous major ethnographic works analyzing ways in which otherness is at the center of people's sociocultural lives (e.g., Munn 1986; Tsing 1993; Keane 1997; Nourse 1999; Spyer 2000; Rutherford 2003; Bashkow 2006).[4] Amazonia is another region where many ethnographers have found otherness, rather than pure identity-based unity, culturally pivotal to specific people's practices of social relating (e.g., Lepri 2005). Myers's (1986) well-known book on Pintupi practices of reconciling contradictory values of "autonomy" and "relatedness" is an additional example of an ethnographic work that can be read as a study of otherness-focused social bonds: it is a study of how certain Aboriginal Australian people make political otherness (in the form of egalitarian emphasis on personal autonomy) itself a medium of social connection (cf. McDowell 1990; Schieffelin 1990).

One short anthropological work that sets out a model of otherness-focused social relations with particular forcefulness is Viveiros de Castro's essay on "otherness as a constitutive relation" (2001: 27) in kinship processes of Amazonian societies. Viveiros de Castro begins from the observation that Amazonian "native sociologies . . . muster a motley crowd of Others, non-human as well as human" (p. 23). To explain these societies' appearance as a "crowd of Others," Viveiros de Castro postulates that in Amazonian social relations otherness is a quality that is unmarked or "given," whereas identity is a quality that is marked or "made." Being strangers is a normal, culturally central and valued face of Amazonian social relating. Or as he puts it in an overtly Dumontian idiom, in Amazonian sociality "difference precedes and encompasses identity" (p. 25).

This formulation can usefully be set alongside another Dumont-influenced ethnographic model, coming out of research in the Melanesian region, where Korowai are located. Dumont is well known for having suggested that societies are organized around hierarchically encompassing values, or definitions of what matters most to people.

Robbins (1994, 2004) draws on this idea in generalizing that a major aspect of the cultural distinctiveness of people of Melanesia is that social relations are their dominant focus of value. Other important elements in life, such as single persons' own identity, tend to be defined in terms of the more valued phenomenon of relations *between* people. I document in this book that Korowai people too have a strongly "relationalist" sensibility along these lines but also that they heavily emphasize otherness as a constitutive feature of the valued social relations. Viveiros de Castro, in formulating his own thesis about Amazonian social relating independently of Robbins (but sharing debts to the work of Wagner and Strathern), suggests that when "difference . . . encompasses identity," rather than the reverse, this alters the very nature of a structure of hierarchical encompassment:

> In the hands of Dumont, encompassment defines the characteristic of a Totality . . . in which differences are nested within a superordinate holistic unity. . . . Difference not only occupies the inner space of the "whole," but it is also inferior to the whole. The general emphasis of Amazonian ethnology on the cosmologically constitutive role of alterity, in contrast, refers to a regime in which encompassment does not produce or manifest a superior metaphysical unity. There is no higher-order identity between difference and identity, just difference all the way. . . . The Amazonian hierarchical synthesis is disjunctive, not conjunctive. (Viveiros de Castro 2001: 27)

The basic idea of a "disjunctive" social connection is one useful characterization of my subject matter throughout this study. I examine social bonds that are composed of simultaneous qualities of nearness and remoteness (as Simmel put it), without the element of otherness being reducible to an otherness-free higher relational quality of stable identification.

My interpretations of Korowai social processes in this book are very squarely within the tradition of otherness-thematizing ethnographic studies just outlined. This book has a more ambivalent relation, though, to the more prominent trend of contemporary scholarship on relations of otherness that can be loosely called the "Orientalism consensus." For at least a quarter century otherness has been a booming theme in scholarly writing about culture. A good deal of this otherwise varied body of academic output has in common the basic notion that people define themselves in their engagement with negative others and that processes of negative othering function to produce structures of political subordination and superordination by which some people occupy positions of power and socially recognized value and others are excluded from those positions.[5] This is a second-nature insight for many scholars today, for good reason: the model is often accurate. Certainly some Korowai social processes involve violent, exclusionary forms of othering, such as the categorization of certain men within the Korowai population as nonhuman witches. The Orientalism consensus is also salutary for the attention it has drawn to othering as a socioculturally constitutive process: the model posits that relations of otherness make people what they are and that these relations are the central sites where social orders and systems of value are produced.

Yet the question of the political organization of relations of otherness is empirical and needs to stay empirically open rather than theoretically closed (Bashkow 2006: 239–44). Some others are defined wholly by fantasy projections of the persons to whom they are other, but there are also others who exercise control over how they are defined or participate complexly in a mutual dialogue of otherness. Some processes of othering are pejorative; some are celebratory. Some processes are exclusionary; some have effects of drawing others *into* relations, as well as excluding them. The Orientalism consensus's vision is one in which analysts *do* posit a "superior metaphysical unity" (to borrow a formulation from Viveiros de Castro, as quoted above): the unity of power and the unity of the empowered self who covertly projects its own inverted negative and positive properties as its other's fantasized attributes. For the Korowai cultural practices I examine, this vision offers only occasional insights. Not just on the political level but on all levels there remains a question—not subtly addressed by the Orientalism consensus—of what a particular relation of otherness actually is, as a relation *of otherness*. How is it built? Of what does it consist?

MEDIA OF CONJOINED OTHERNESS AND INTIMACY

To this point I have described this book as a study of relations of otherness in Korowai life, showing how otherness is not antithetical to social connection and social closeness but an integral aspect of social involvement. In the remainder of this introduction, I go a little further specifying the *kind* of cultural process that I take as my subject. I do so by briefly outlining three more specific facets of Korowai otherness-focused social relating that will be steady concerns of the empirical chapters that follow. These are the concrete media of people's social "nearness and remoteness"; the temporality of relations; and reflexivity, or the sense in which otherness-focused relating is what can be called an "indigenous pragmatics" of social bonds.

Is otherness in social relations one thing or many? Paradoxically, "other" often works in scholarship as a homogenizing category.[6] One reason the category is so susceptible to meaning everything (and thus nothing) is that it is intrinsically relational to a context. Of the senses of *other* formulated in the *Oxford English Dictionary*, the one that scholars are generally concerned with is, "That which is the counterpart or converse of something specified or implied[;] . . . that which is not the self or subject; that which lies outside or is excluded from the group with which one identifies oneself."[7] The phrase "something specified or implied" highlights the heavily indexical quality of *other*. When not anchored in a context, the category becomes highly abstract and malleable. Otherness cannot be a very meaningful theoretical or ethnographic topic by itself. Any phenomenon of otherness raises the question, *otherness* in relation to what? In this respect, a simple roll call of different kinds of others in one cultural milieu—the "motley crowd" of Korowai others—would not be in itself anthropologically insightful.

To move toward specific methodological expectations about how to study otherness in the Korowai context, I find it useful to formulate a more expanded definition of *other*. First, at a classificatory level, when someone experiences something as other, this involves a perception of difference. There is a kind of disparity between the experiencer and the object. In some relevant way, they are not the same. Second, this disparity is not only a matter of similarity versus difference but also a matter of proximity and distance. A judgment of otherness involves seeing something as different from oneself at a level of logical types, but this judgment also involves a sense of combined separateness and contiguity in space, time, and world. Third and finally, there is an affective, evaluative, or self-reflexive component to otherness, bearing on the experiencer's definitions of his or her own being. Classifying an object as other not only involves perceiving it as being different and disparate from oneself; it also involves being attracted, repulsed, shaken, or otherwise moved by the difference. Here the relational, connective aspect of otherness has more to it than just classification and distance. Something that is other is strange. To engage with what is other is to participate in some sort of reflexive questioning, definition, or redefinition of one's familiar world-apprehending categories and one's sense of position in a categorial order.

Social otherness is a more complex variation on otherness generally. Social otherness exists when a person experiences as different and strange not just any object, but an acting being. This other being is thought to have some kind of consciousness of itself and surrounding events. The other being's consciousness is part of that being's otherness, part of what is different, separate, and strange about him or her. "Social otherness" foregrounds a crucial element of routine human intersubjectivity: the forms of separateness and strangeness that lie between persons who are conscious of each other's consciousness.[8]

Mindful that otherness is not a free-floating phenomenon but a judgment born out of larger processes of intersubjective involvement, I seek in this book to keep the topic of otherness closely tied to specific media, framing contexts, and contrasting possibilities in relation to which that otherness is experienced. This orientation is reflected in my main argument, to the effect that qualities of otherness are for Korowai a focus of social connection. The orientation is also reflected in another main organizing goal of this study, namely, to analyze the character of social relations through a focus on the media in which those relations exist.

Social bonds exist through concrete channels of communicative contact and separateness. The Korowai pattern of making otherness a basis of social connection plays out across an elaborate array of these different media. My main method for analyzing Korowai social relations in this book is to decompose those relations into concrete communicative media, including gifts of food, or acts of withholding; other forms of giving, sharing, caring, taking, or killing; residential locations; dwelling designs; histories of bodily connection, such as a history of one person having gestated, birthed, and raised another; travel practices; acts of touch or sight and other specific modes of physical, sensory contact; facial gestures, such as smiles or laughter; kinship terms and other expressions by which people refer to each other linguistically; the language people speak; the land they own; and allusions to past events or plans for future ones. An ethnographic approach focusing on the concrete media of people's contact helps give specificity to *otherness* as an interpretive category in several ways. It identifies particular areas of activity in which qualities of social otherness are created and anchored, breaking the subject into manageable starting places. It also leads toward differentiation of varied kinds of others in people's lives, defined by different degrees and kinds of otherness. For example, Korowai concepts of ownership, kinship, and morality prominently organize people's worlds as a spectrum, from zones of close familiarity to ones of radical estrangement.

Most important, a mediation-focused understanding of social bonds aligns well with the idea that a social relation is a "disjunctive synthesis" of otherness and intimacy. Throughout this book I show how Korowai themselves reflexively dwell on specific relational media as being points of both separation and involvement between persons. I also trace how social relations exist in multiple media at once, such that people are differently close and distant on the relations' different dimensions. Often a relation is centrally defined by a mismatched joining of intimacy in one medium and otherness in a different medium, or by a more complex pattern of mismatches and coordinations across the multiple media in which the bond exists.

RELATIONS MADE IN ACTIONS:
TEMPORALITY AS A MEDIUM OF OTHERNESS

The media of social contact and disparity examined in this book are diverse, but I often focus on space and time, following the pioneering work of Munn (1986). Reasons for the focus on space will become clear in the next chapter, which examines how thoroughly landownership organizes people's social world as a field of otherness. Here I want to underline how patterns of the *temporality* of social relations are a major concern.

Korowai often take events as the truth of bonds. They know relations by the actions that signify and create them. For example, in a style of person reference I discuss in chapter 2, two people call each other by a reciprocal nickname pointing back to an idiosyncratic event the pair once experienced together, such as a bodily mishap. Similarly, Korowai often say of two formerly unacquainted people that they have "become relatives," through specific face-to-face encounters and acts of giving. Examining these and many other practices, I show that the close link between relational categories and relational actions goes both directions: Korowai know relations by events, and they search for relational meanings in events.

One way I conceptualize the close interplay between a pattern of otherness-focused social relating and a sensibility that finds relations to be made by events is to describe temporality itself as a wellspring of relational otherness. Often the otherness at the core of a relation consists specifically of a mismatch between different *temporal* levels of people's relation, such as when persons who do not have a history of belonging are in close interactional contact or when persons with a history of living together are separated in the present. The Korowai pattern of seeking the truth of social relations in events of disruption stands out very sharply in people's approaches to marriage and to mourning, the respective topics of this book's last two ethnographic chapters. There are many other contexts, though, in which people's understanding of a relation is colored by the differences of history that preceded their current relational status, or by the possibility that their relation will later become something different from what it currently seems. For relations with strangers to be a major focus of people's social lives means that people's bonds consist of investigations of the otherness of those around them. Two persons do not know where they stand with each other. A relation is defined by participants' reflexive set toward events, as the emerging, immanent truth of what the relation is. The openness of temporal process, or the nonidentity of any given present with itself, maps onto the openness and internal disparities of a social bond. Temporalized in this way, the interpretive perception that relations are defined as tense combinations of otherness and intimacy, or even repulsion and attraction, can help us understand another prominent Korowai social pattern, namely, that people's evaluations of their bonds are often quite volatile. A relation is a kind of edge at the meeting point of multiple other relational states. Ways that other times are part of a present time help make people's mutual belonging unstable and plural. By focusing this study on people's activities of relating across margins of combined intimacy and strangeness (and thus keeping the subject of otherness tied to a context rather than imagining it as a self-standing fact), I hope to give an account of how Korowai find it normal to move swiftly between quite disparate understandings of relations they are in.

My concern at this point, though, is not to describe or interpret Korowai people's interest in events and the temporality of relations but only to draw attention to this interest as a recurring issue I deal with across different ethnographic subjects. I argue in this book that contingency, change, loss, and creation are not peripheral to people's understanding of social relations but internal to those understandings. I also try to address questions of *how* specifically people conceive contingency, what forms of loss or creation they engage in socially, and what specific ways they make experiences of loss or creation integral to the definitions of their bonds.

KOROWAI REFLEXIVITY: AN INDIGENOUS SEMIOTICS OF SOCIAL RELATING

The theme of reflexivity is the final element I want to add to the outline of the kind of object this book examines. Concerns with otherness, with media of contact and separateness, and with temporality that are so prominent in Korowai practices of social relating are not just a property of Korowai actions but also a reflexive sensibility *about* social actions. I sometimes refer to the sensibility as an "indigenous semiotics" or "indigenous pragmatics" of social relating. Stating what these expressions mean is a way in which I can give a sense of the importance of recognizing reflexivity as an aspect of the Korowai patterns of practice analyzed in this study.

By describing the sensibility as "indigenous," I mean only that it is culturally distinctive and that it is reflexively held by Korowai themselves as a stance toward their own lives. The sensibility could also be described simply as "vernacular." Meanwhile, calling Korowai people's otherness-focused sensibility a "semiotics" and a "pragmatics" is a way to register how overtly Korowai understand social bonds as matters of signification. The pattern of taking events as the defining signs of a relation is one aspect of this. Another aspect I describe is a tendency to define persons by traces they have created, such as their children, their plants, or other objects different from them but metonymic of their action.

These terms also index a general paradigmatic orientation from which this book is written, namely, semiotic and linguistic anthropology. This paradigm understands human sociocultural life to be composed of processes of signification and takes the central questions of how signification is ordered to be irreducibly questions of pragmatics, or sign use.[9] People live by systems of semiotic categories and codes, which do not exist autonomously of their use in signifying acts at particular places or times. Semiotic systems are affected by acts of use, are defined or redefined by acts of use, and are categorizations and encodings *of* use, through and through.

It makes sense to speak of Korowai people's otherness-focused relational sensibility as specifically an indigenous pragmatics, because part of this sensibility's distinctiveness is that Korowai themselves take as the crucial site where semiotic order exists the application of semiotic categories in action: the categories' application to objects, to persons in relation with each other, and to persons doing the actual semiotic categorization. The emphasis on application of categories in action becomes apparent, for example, in Korowai people's consistent reflexive concern with the transgression of semiotic rules. Breaking rules is not just something that happens incidentally in the course of living by those rules but is an active possibility that people dwell on and perform. The patterns I have already outlined of Korowai people's close attention to *medium* and *time* as aspects of social relating are also faces of their understanding that actual use of semiotic categories is the crux of cultural process. Korowai do not take media of signification as transparent windows through which messages of some other order are conveyed. Rather, as part of acts of signification and interpretation, Korowai focus attention on ways in which the specific properties of media themselves facilitate or derail communicative possibilities. *How* something is signified supports and conditions *what* is signified. So too a focus on temporality as an integral feature of social bonds amounts to a concern with time-based, time-saturated aspects of signification and categorization. Korowai ways of making events into the definition of social bonds are also ways of portraying temporality as an internal dimension of relational categories rather than conceptualizing these categories as existing transcendentally, apart from time. Here categories through which people represent and know their relations are not felt to be only selfsame logical types. The types are intrinsically open to what is outside of them, such as past, future, or alternative present categorizations, other coexisting semiotic orders, and the specificity of a particular time, place, or object.

The evidence for characterizing Korowai concerns with otherness as an indigenous pragmatics of social relating is set out across this study's empirical chapters. Here I have only meant to sketch the broad shape of this subject so that it will be more easily recognizable in the concrete forms we encounter it.

OUTLINE OF CHAPTERS

My account of Korowai otherness-focused social relating is organized as follows. In chapter 1 I analyze the Korowai social landscape as a field of otherness, in which activities of dwelling, moving, and laboring on land are the concrete forms of people's social relations. This discussion is centered on people's relations of landownership, residence, geographic separation, and interlocal travel. I describe landownership as a major medium through which Korowai live out a basic social problematic of autonomy, separation, and boundary-traversing relatedness.

Chapter 2 examines a pattern of pairing and avoidance that Korowai enact across many different areas of life activity. People often take pairs as the basic units by which entities exist. To identify, know, and define a person or thing, they look to the person or object's dyadic counterpart. Routinely, though, paired entities are unified with each other in part by contrast and incompatibility, along lines similar to the dyad "human" and "demonic dead" already touched on in this introduction. The chapter establishes the further cross-cutting salience in Korowai life of *separation* as a mode of relatedness, beyond the patterns of specifically geographic separation examined in chapter 1.

Chapters 3, 4, and 5 are concerned with processes of kinship. The first half of Chapter 3 sketches the importance of maternal uncle relationships and describes how principles of this relationship play out across people's overall worlds of kin. Maternal uncle relations are strongly geographic, in ways that both follow and modify the lines of the landownership system's deep imprint on social life. My discussion traces how uncle relations make geography co-mediative with social connections of gender, bodily genesis, care, coresidence, and generational succession. In the second half of chapter 3, I move from specific kin categories to the category "relative" in general. Practical Korowai patterns of applying and enacting kin categories make visible people's understanding of social bonds as ongoing, contingent creations of belonging with strangers.

Chapter 4 concerns children and their relations with parents or other caring relatives. It develops this book's larger finding that Korowai approach persons as signs: here, signs of the present and its complex relation to other times. I explore how children are understood as figures of futurity and the present's transience but also as signs of past relational histories. I examine people's emphasis on the alienness of a child on its entry into others' lives and their concern with intersubjective attachment to children as a social quality that comes newly into existence across time, through actions of care.

Chapter 5 similarly explores different temporal and social levels of a single kind of relation, here the relation of marriage. I analyze marriage as a practice of systematic mismatches of closeness and strangeness. At levels ranging from spouses' shared living to events by which marriages come into existence to the politics of affinal relations, Korowai marriages are practices of testing how disruptive contact between people who do not belong together can be a substantial kind of social connection.

Chapter 6 examines understandings of death and practices of mourning. Like other people, Korowai take death as a major kind of event around which to define and know what social relations are. I look closely at people's concern with the monstrous demons that humans become after death and at bereavement practices focused on the dead as remembered interactants. These latter practices include quiet, personal acts of food renunciation, as well as stridently public acts of demanding payment from others to ameliorate grief and anger. The same sensibilities about otherness, events, and impingement as bases of connection that Korowai adhere to in their conduct of social relations between living persons are apparent also in relations with the dead. Conversely, the chapter documents something of the presence of death in all social relations and the cultural salience of mourning as a figure of social action at large.

ON KOROWAI AUTARKY IN THE WEST PAPUAN CONTEXT

In taking as a priority the study of the internal alterity of Korowai social relations, this book follows certain patterns that many anthropologists today disavow. One is that I have written the book largely in the ethnographic present, not because Korowai are "timeless," but because I have trouble representing their lives (as I was exposed to them between 1995 and 2007) as not being contemporary with my writing. A more problematic pattern I follow is that, for reasons of space and interpretive priority, I do not put at the center of this book the many ways in which Korowai are involved with exogenous foreigners, and I say relatively little about the important question of Korowai people's place in the broader history of Papua.

This troubled history is well known in its broad outlines (see Vlasblom 2004 for one synthesis). In the nineteenth century the Netherlands claimed sovereignty over the western half of the island of New Guinea, as the eastern extreme of its larger Dutch East Indies colony. The Dutch East Indies ceased to exist after World War II, when a Java-centered revolutionary movement won national independence and created the archipelagic state of Indonesia. Defying the revolutionaries' demands, the Netherlands retained control of West New Guinea. In the 1950s, under pressure to justify its rule, the Dutch colonial administration made its first major efforts to extend institutional reach to its claimed colonial subjects. Colonial state formation was at this time a slow business, due to physical and social challenges of movement across the landscape, only modest extractive prospects, and extreme linguistic and cultural diversity. (There are 1.5 million indigenous people in the western half of New Guinea—an area the size of California—speaking about 270 local languages.) By late 1962 Cold War politics had led the United States to support Indonesian nationalists' ongoing campaign to possess the territory as part of their state. Indonesia gained control in 1963. Today about 800,000 settlers from elsewhere in Indonesia live in the territory, mostly in towns, where they are numerically dominant. Ever since Indonesian takeover, Papua's burning issue has been Indonesian economic, military, and political domination of Papuans and Papuan nationalist opposition to Indonesian rule.

One effect of this troubled political history has been that little social scientific research has been carried out in the territory. My main fieldwork with Korowai speakers took place in 1995–96, during a relatively brief period when foreign scientists could secure permission for research in Papua by the same process as permission could be received for research elsewhere in Indonesia. At that time and during my later return visits, Korowai people's political situation was highly exceptional. Their location far from centers of governance, transport, and resource extraction meant that, in comparison to many other Papuan communities, they had been only recently and tenuously subject to the powers of the Indonesian state and settlers. Exogenous institutions and cultural patterns are major presences in Korowai people's lives today. Yet the overall situation of *relative* cultural and political autarky is such that otherness as a quality of relations between Korowai persons themselves, within the geography of Korowai lands, stands out as an important, intricate subject of inquiry in its own right. At later points I touch on ways that Korowai engagement with Indonesian people and institutions has followed patterns typical of Korowai modes of otherness-focused social relating generally. Overall, though, Korowai people's place in a broader Papuan geopolitical context is something I have chosen to discuss in studies complementary to this one, at the length it deserves.[10]

In leaving those subjects at the periphery of this book, I do not mean to endorse media representations that make Korowai out to be exemplars of the Western popular primitivist stereotype of a "tribe" of people who are "isolated," "uncontacted," "intact," or "pure." These portrayals are fantasy projections of the cultural worlds of Westerners, not accurate representations of the lives of Korowai people or anyone else. Thus I agree fundamentally with Fabian's project to dissolve misplaced borders between anthropologists' knowledge communities and the communities they study. However, this book takes its own approach to discrediting primitivist stereotypy. It is not enough to integrate other people in exogenous histories. A crucial further step is to engage with other people's own experiences of otherness in historical process. The fantasy of "uncontacted" people is in part an image of people who are not involved with humans strange to themselves. This book repudiates that image by detailing Korowai people's elaborate experience of foreignness as an internal feature of their own most basic, familiar practices of social life. To do this is to illustrate how people of New Guinea, far from ever having been "uncontacted," are long-standing masters of contact across boundaries of otherness.

CHAPTER I

A Dispersed Society

Place Ownership and the Crossing of Spatial Margins

A basic feature of Korowai people's social world is that their landscape is divided into a patchwork of territories owned by named patriclans. Almost all interaction is strongly inflected by questions of who is an owner of specific places and who is not. When I once asked a friend named Fenelun the purpose of landownership, he said the institution exists so that a man can live on his land, marry, raise children, and go about producing and procuring food without other people getting angry at him. Many other Korowai answered questions about landownership in similar terms. They said that if people were to build, dwell, hunt, trap, garden, and eat on the same land, then they would consume each other's property, have affairs with each other's spouses, criticize each other, and fight. To avoid conflicts, everyone should have separate places to live and different streams, sago palms, garden clearings, pandanus trees, and other resources to exploit.

Such statements straightforwardly link landownership to spatial dispersion. Often it is more than a half-hour walk from one occupied clearing to the nearest neighboring houses. This separateness is organized by the clan territory system. The statements also tie ownership and dispersion alike to a more basic value, political autonomy. Actors will violate one another's rights over desirable possessions if they are not separated by a spatial buffer. Korowai see their system of landownership as a system of self-determination.

People's ways of categorizing space and acting in it are central to the making and defining of social life. Korowai take an intensely space-focused approach to social relations. I argue in this chapter that Korowai spatial practice shapes people's lives as a matter of otherness-focused social relating. My description of the Korowai landscape here is a description of an otherness-structured social world. At the same time, it is a description of Korowai people's acute, constant concern with qualities of *belonging* in relation to what is around them. What I document is that Korowai spatial categories and spatial practices are systematically two-edged. They at once define boundaries of otherness between people and link people together across these boundaries of otherness. Belonging and otherness are mutually interdependent and irreducible.

Landownership defines the character of the Korowai polity and social relationships in it. This spatial institution's structuring of residential dispersion and its support of political autonomy are major channels by which the institution is simultaneously separative and connective. Fenelun's account of ownership might suggest that ownership is purely separative: people own different lands in order to step out of relations altogether. We will see instead that what ownership does is institutionalize an otherness-first configuration of social relating. Ownership sets the space-traversing, autonomy-affirming terms of people's mutual involvement. The Korowai landownership world is a world of connections that people make across boundaries of strangeness, drawing the familiar and strange together.

PLACES OF BELONGING

After emerging from the highland mountain chains, New Guinea's southern rivers cross a ninety-thousand-square-mile lowland plain. The Korowai lands lie in the northwest corner of this plain, near the mountains and far from the coast, in the upper watersheds of the Eilanden and the Ndeiram Kabur Rivers (see map 1). The tall, multilayered forest between these rivers is broken only by smaller waterways, banana gardens that Korowai clear around their houses, and stands of sago palms, which are shorter and sparser than stands of woody trees and which flourish on low, occasionally inundated ground near the rivers and at the origins of small streams. Korowai see important variations of topography and vegetation across all parts of the land, but they portray waterways in particular as cuts of distinctiveness in the forest terrain. Streams are the only land features that bear proper names. Alongside stream names, categories such as upstream and downstream are even more important in people's ways of orienting themselves on the land, in

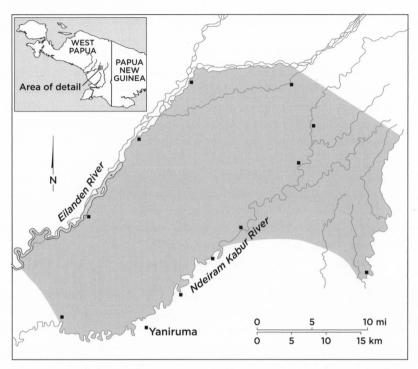

WEST
PAPUA

PAPUA
NEW
GUINEA

Area of detail

N

Eilanden River

Ndeiram Kabur River

Yaniruma

0		5		10 mi
0	5	10		15 km

Map 1. Korowai lands, shaded. Squares indicate locations of current villages.

their talk about spatial locations, and in their talk about links between different locations. Because of heavy but erratic rainfall and flat relief, streams fluctuate dramatically in size, something people also monitor with great day-to-day interest.

Even more prominently than the landscape is divided and unified by streams, it is divided and unified by ownership. The day-to-day consequentiality of landownership is well illustrated by pressures I experienced during my fieldwork. There was always an intense politics regarding where I was staying on the land. It would have been almost unthinkable for me to travel to any place without its owners' agreement. Owners were the people most burdened by my presence, and they were also the persons with whom I most needed to establish valued relations of mutual recognition, such as through gifts. In addition to raising questions of my obligations to owners, their gains from me, and their moral accommodation of me, my physical location shaped nonowning people's access to me. How someone else stood in relation to owners affected whether that person would come into my presence at all and what conversations and material transactions would occur between us.

Landownership tightly joins three categories: "place," "clan," and "owner." A place (*bolüp;* Ind. dusun) is usually a contiguous, irregularly shaped segment of land, typically about a square mile in expanse. A place is by definition the territory of a particular named clan, and all clans have places. Korowai ubiquitously speak of different parts of the landscape by combining clan names with the term *bolüp*. For example, *dambol-bolüp* is "place of Dambol." The term *clan (gun)* itself also means "species, type," an indication of the strong sense that a clan identity is a *type* of human. To anchor the definition of themselves as different kinds of humans, Korowai look above all to the landscape and its different places. Korowai talk about clan-owned places constantly in their lives, such as when they discuss where they or other people are on the landscape or when they deliberate over actions they might undertake and their reasons for doing so. Newcomers who arrive in the Korowai area with any ability and concern to communicate linguistically with Korowai about their lives quickly become aware of the land's division into these owned territories.

A person generally grows up as a member of the clan of his or her father, so I call the groups patriclans. (I also refer to clan places as "patrimonial" land, taking patrimony here in the sense of "paternally inherited estate.") Clans are small, averaging about ten living members. Many are represented by just one or two persons; others are extinct. Clanmates are often oriented toward one another more by being owners of the same land than by notions of common ancestry, or other facts unrelated to land. Clanmates own their land and its resources together, though particular persons exercise exclusive ownership over garden plants, animal traps, buildings, sago palms, or other objects they have made or stewarded.

Just as concepts of clan and place contain each other, so too a concept of belonging is present in the concept of land. The word *bolüp* "place" ubiquitously occurs as a grammatically possessed item, prefixed by possessive pronouns. The concept of owning is also expressed by the word *giom-anop* "owners." The men, women, and children of a patriclan are all "place owners" *(bolüp giom-anop)* of the clan's land. Like English *own, proper,* and *property,* Korowai *giom* joins a sense of dominion over the owned object with a sense of the owned object being proper to a person, a qualifying condition of his or her being. *Belonging* is an English category aptly conveying this bidirectionality. Places belong to people, and people belong in relation to those places. The inseparability of land and belonging is also why I translate *bolüp* as "place." Alternatives include "estate," "land," "country," or "home," but "place" best unites the idea of a piece of land with the idea of belonging. Korowai sometimes speak of a clan territory as their "truly own place" *(bolüp giom-xajan)* to distinguish it from other land that counts as their own in weaker ways. This is a statement more about the "ownness" or "properness" of the object to a person than about a person's dominion over the object. To be a place owner is to be known and anchored by that place. Consistent with this unity of landowning and human identity, places are inalienable. New persons can be included as owners of land, and existing owners can die out or move away from their land, leading to the ownership relation being forgotten. At a given time, many specific clan territories are in an ambiguous transitional status of being remembered by some persons as actually the land of a certain extinct clan but known by others as without qualification the place of some clan that has in actuality only taken over that land in a recent generation. But while there is some long-term fluidity in relations between clans and land, owners cannot at one moment sell or give away land. Until recently the idea was hardly imagined. On hearing about land commodification elsewhere, Korowai have now formed an explicit consensus that land should not be sold, because any person's alienation of land would lead everyone toward universal landlessness. This is typical of their sense of the incommensurable worth of clan places.

In these ways, owning land is like having a body or a voice. A place is a kind of second body, a footing in the world by means of which a person acts expressively toward others or stays carefully separate from them. Yet while Korowai use the category "place" *(bolüp)* to shape their existences around a dominant, constant concern with belonging in relation to physical segments of land, here as in other areas of life owners' relation with land consists of complex back-and-forth interaction and shifting alignments, not seamless unity. Being an owner is distinct from people's actions in their first bodies, even as bodily action and landownership affect each other. To illustrate how gaps between owners and their places are central to ownership experience, I examine briefly two overlapping areas of owners' bodily practices in relation to their land: resource exploitation and residence. The salience of these activities is clear in Fenelun's and other people's portrayals of landownership as allowing people to live on land and procure food from it without getting into fights. Yet the interaction of landownership with food-getting and dwelling is more ambiguous than is indicated by Fenelun's and other people's accounts of landownership as a social buffer.

Korowai understand transformative action on land to be a basic element of the ownership relation. When stating what their land is, people talk about their sites of dwelling and food getting. A clan place consists of fallow garden clearings, stewarded tree resources, other historical sites of human presence, and specific small streams the owners dam and bail during dry weather to get fish. Walking across land, Korowai routinely remark on scenes of past human actions, such as grave sites, places where a pig was killed, birthplaces, feast sites, abandoned pathways, and logs felled by specific persons. Owners are especially prone to speak of sites of exploitation when their links to land are questioned. One major way in which owners reshape land is by planting and tending sago palms, the source of a starch flour that is people's staple food. Sago groves are the greatest material repositories of value in Korowai life, and important landmarks. Many groves exist only because humans cleared forest and planted sago sprigs (cf. Ellen 2006). Even groves that are not wholly anthropogenic are heavily affected by owners' care. The cliché "Sago groves will be killed by the world!" expresses common knowledge that groves shrink when humans neglect them. The statement is also typical of broader Korowai tendencies to describe the world as a hostile scene of existence.

Korowai understandings thus emphasize that people demonstrate ownership of land through action on it and through mixing their labor with it, in a manner reminiscent of the ideas of Locke. If persons have left their land to live elsewhere, their co-owners or other relatives might urge them to return, to keep the ownership relation active. Once when I was talking with a man about cultural change, he expressed the hope that two of his four children would grow up attending school and living in a village and that the other two would live in the forest on his clan-owned land, "lest the place's paths grow over with trees and that good place itself be taken over by other people." Persons often speak idiomatically of a place having become "cold" when its owners have died out or moved away. Following a death, the disappearance of pathways, gardens, houses, and other traces of a deceased person's presence on the land is a main focus of the bereaved's efforts to define their loss.

In this focus on transformative labor, ownership relations have a two-sided and even contradictory character. A place is available to owners as a total surrounding life-space. (The word *lamol* "world" is often used as a substitute for *bolüp* "place" to refer to clan territories.)

Figure 3. Four women pounding sago in late 2001: Ngengel Nandup, Safunax Lefilxai, Layam Nambul, and Kwandil Xawex. The pounded pith is next washed and filtered to separate the edible starch from inedible fibers.

Exploitation by owners is land's telos and part of land's very definition. Clan places are "good" *(manop)*, as resource bases and sites of human occupation. The owned place gives people their food, while owners are seen by themselves and others in the marks they make on their land. Yet exploitation-focused talk also highlights the difference owners make to land. The land is separate from them, and their ownership is an active, contingent practice of transformation. Owners could die out or move away, ownership could lapse, but the land would exist nonetheless. Owners take from land, give to it, and inscribe their presences on it. If they do not do so, the land grows and degrades into other shapes than it has when owners are present. The inscriptive relation of owners to land is a relation of unity that is known through resistances and other possibilities besides unity, such as the lamentable absence of owners from land due to death.

Tellingly, Korowai often remark spontaneously that "the earth eats people" *(wolaxolol yanop nole)* and that they are fearful of the land as a consequence. This is an allusion to the disappearance of dead people's bodies into the earth in burial, and the statement does not have anything directly to do with landownership. Even so, the statement and the sense of fear it expresses are characteristic of the unease that is one face of people's relation to the landscape on which they live. The sharpest aspect of land's strangeness to its owners, though, is the presence on most clan places of "taboo sites" *(wotop),* often centered on stream junctions. People's main orientation to a taboo site consists of day-to-day awareness that they should not exploit the site or travel through it, lest occult beings be angered and cause deaths. Until the recent intrusion of missionaries, tourists, and other foreigners on the landscape, Korowai regularly offered pig fat to occult beings at the sites. Performing these sacrifices, people stringently observed a prohibition against nonlandowning strangers being present on the land, because landowners face extreme danger in their relations with ill-tempered *wotop* beings, and the presence of outside interlopers would endanger the landowners even more. Here too we see a pattern of intimacy and otherness: stewardship of taboo sites is fundamental to landowner status, yet landowners stand in risky, volatile antagonism to their own land. While clan land is by definition a place for resource exploitation, this exploitation is transformative and transgressive, and owners' relations to land are partly ties of danger.

There are many levels at which landownership and land-focused belonging are the concrete form of Korowai society, such that to describe social relations is to describe landownership and vice versa. However, another aspect of Korowai people's intensely spatialized modes of living and defining their social bonds, distinct from landownership and interacting complexly with it, is the question of where people physically *are* on the land. One important mode of physical presence on land is residence. The activity of "living" *(bau-;* also *babo-* "stay, sit")* in particular houses, on particular clan places, and with particular other people is a salient fact of Korowai persons' worlds in their own representations. Expressions such as "house people" *(xaim-anop),* "housemates" *(xaim-lelip-anop;* lit., "same house people"), or "live together" *(lelip bau-)* are prominent in people's talk about their lives. Dwelling at a specific place, or sharing a roof or even hearth with specific people, is itself a practice of belonging, at least notionally. To state where someone is living, or with whom a person is living, is in Korowai understanding to state value-laden definitions of who the person is and what social relations that person is living out as the most important ones of his or her daily activities. What land a person *owns* matters a lot to Korowai, but where the person *is* also matters.

For a lot of people a lot of the time, ownership and residence coincide: persons live on their own patrimonial places. Alongside other forms of physical action on land, dwelling on places is a main way in which Korowai enact their ownership. Presence on land is a practice of human-land unity, taken by Korowai to be emblematic of the owner-ship relation. They live on owned land because they are comfortable and politically secure there, even as dwelling somewhere can itself assert and reaffirm ownership of that place.

Yet if Korowai society is a world of landownership and of belonging-imbued experiences of dwelling on owned land, it is also a world of movement. Korowai travel avidly, and their lives and social networks are histories of motion. People's practices of movement take them very frequently across landownership boundaries and into situations of dwelling at a distance from their own patrimonial land, on the land of other people. One of my main goals in describing specific practices of travel and residential mobility throughout this book is to show how dwelling and movement are mutually implicated correlates, rather than mutually exclusive opposites, and more generally to show that there is an internal relation between practices of people living on land of their own and people living on places where their sense of belonging is lim-ited or tenuous. There are many levels at which being apart from owned land, and being physically present on nonowned land, is a normal event in the Korowai landownership system and an important part of people's overall experiences of belonging in relation to place. In the next section and farther along in this chapter, I look at people's experiences of polit-ical vulnerability in relation to other people's land and the practices of transient visiting and hospitality by which Korowai routinely create social bonds across divides of geographic otherness. At this preliminary point I only want to indicate very broadly some ways that *residential* relations to land also pervasively run against the grain of landownership-determined belonging, in addition to at other times aligning harmo-niously with that belonging.

One way in which living away from owned land is systematically built into the landownership institution is that clans are exogamous. Mar-riage, as a relation of shared living between men and women, is by defi-nition an interlocal social process drawing together people who belong at different places. Although Korowai follow many different principles and desires in deciding where to live, a general expectation is that men, children, and unmarried women will live on their own patrimonial places and married women will live at the places of their husbands. Some couples live at the wife's place for lengthy periods or even their whole married lives, and most couples commute a great deal between their respective territories, but overall it is typically women who relocate so that spouses can live together. Households vary enormously in composition, but it is common for a house to have at least one married couple among its core occupants, such as a middle-aged couple with children. Landownership geography and people's conceptions of what a "house" is are in this way deeply interconnected with gender and sexuality. This co-mediation of space and gender is not something Korowai see as needing overt discussion. When I have asked why women move while men remain on patrimonial land, the most that male and female interlocutors alike have usually said is that this is so women will bear children and clans will continue to have people. To Korowai, patrilineal inheritance of land, patrilineal inheritance of group membership, virilocal residence, and patriarchy (or men exercising greater power than women in having other people's lives organized around their wants) go together as reciprocal sequiturs. People do not generally step back to question or explain the whole tautological and teleological package.

The concrete effects of exogamy and virilocality in the shape of people's spatial lives are diverse. One major effect is that these norms, when followed, put women in a systematically different kind of relation to land from the basic one of living on one's own patrimonial place. Sometimes, or in some respects, this puts women in a straightforward situation of vulnerability and dispossession. They do not belong at the place they are living (a husband's place), and so they do not feel comfortable there and do not have clear rights to the land's resources; meanwhile, they are separated from their own land, where they would be comfortable and secure, and their prerogatives of ownership in relation to that land and specific resources on it might even be diminished in practice by the words and actions of other place owners (though in theory women remain owners on their natal land until death). But there are often highly affirmative sides to the extrapatrimonial geography of outmarried women's lives. These women frequently come to enjoy relations of ownership and ownership-like belonging in relation to their husbands' land. Sometimes women are quite pleased to leave patrimonial land and the people there well behind and to strike out somewhere new. At other times the residential and resource-exploitative relation to natal land remains strong: married women and their husbands live near the land anyway, they return regularly for feasts and other major events, and they steadily tread the path between the two places. People on all sides of a marriage may find this interlocal bond an entrée to attractive forms of partial belonging in relation to land other than patrimony-based ownership. For example, while a woman's children do not inherit rights of ownership in her place or its existing resources, they can still stand in complex relations of belonging in relation to that place. Through their mother's history of movement, these children may be in close touch with maternal clan places that are not strictly their own and may feel vividly at home on that land when visiting it in passing or when staying on it for long periods of their lives.

While the norm of residence on one's own clan territory (and virilocal residence for married couples) shapes a great deal of actual practice, the norm is far from universally enacted. Persons living at odds with these expectations are present in almost any house setting. Many couples live at the woman's place rather than the man's, or at some other place altogether. Unmarried people also often find reasons to live at other places than their patrimonial ones (e.g., children who grow up at another place after the death of their father or elderly widows or widowers who move to other relatives' land for companionship), and they sometimes become comfortable there. About half of males and one-third of females live on their own clan places at any time. Presence on a land of patrimonial belonging is accompanied and known by its alternatives: by experience of living differently oneself or by intimately sharing lives with immigrants on one's own patrimonial land. A specific term for relatives of other places who live with landowners for a sustained period is *laboxdun-anop*, literally, "accompanying people, joiners." Immigrants can come to be called "owners" in conversation, thanks to closeness with the patrimonial owners and long-term presence on the land. Owners themselves can also become estranged from patrimonial land—because clanmates there are hostile, because of bored annoyance with the land's characteristics, or because other owners are all dead and the few surviving persons no longer feel emotionally secure and settled living alone on their clan land.

Not only are there a lot of people living elsewhere than their own or (in the case of married women) their husband's patrimonial land at a given time; another major feature of the social landscape is the rapidity with which people shift from one overall residential arrangement to another across their lives. This rapidity is well illustrated by the household arrangements among people resident on one clan territory, the Dambol place three miles north of Yaniruma, across the five-year interval from 1996 to 2001. In the mid-1990s there were two households on Dambol land, usually living near each other in a single clearing. The core residents were two late-middle-aged Dambol brothers named

Silom and Xanduop, their three living wives, and their eight unmarried
living children. Silom had three other children who were married and
living elsewhere. One married son was staying mainly at his wife's
place, one son and his wife alternated between Silom's house and the
wife's land, and one daughter lived with her husband on borderlands
between Dambol territory and her husband's adjacent place. The
Dambol households were also home to Silom and Xanduop's "uncle"
(their mother's brother's son), whose wife and only child had died, leaving his nephews as his only close relatives.

By 2001 this uncle had died. Silom's own death that year made the
future of his widow's separate household uncertain, even as that household was newly alive with the chatter of three orphaned non-Dambol
children who had moved in with her. Silom's eldest son was now living
at the Dambol place rather than his wife's place, and this couple was
now the core of a third household. Xanduop was alive, but his two
wives had both died, and his house had become the residence of five
non-Dambol newcomers. These were (1) the aged new wife of Xanduop's first son to marry; (2) another old woman who came to her kinsman Xanduop's house as a neutral space where she could live separately
from her husband, with whom she was in conflict over polygyny; (3) a
widow who came with her children to evade the marital advances of
one of her dead husband's relatives; (4) the orphaned brother of one of
Xanduop's dead wives, who had come to live with the children of his
dead sister, escape his ill-tempered clanmates, and join in marriage with
Xanduop's niece; and (5) the niece herself, who was a member of a geographically adjacent clan and who had been socially intimate with the
Dambol households before moving into her uncle's house. Also in the
intervening years, the Dambol-based people had at one point built
houses on the land of nearby people who needed help with a feast and
at another point carried out a feast on their own land. During the
preparations for their own feast, they were joined for several months by
whole households of relatives from other clan places. Across all these
years many people of the Dambol households also alternated between
the Dambol clan place and a house they maintained in Yaniruma village
a couple of hours distant.

Idiosyncratic in its particulars, this small sequence of residential
comings-and-goings at the Dambol place over a few years is nonetheless
typical of the fitful quickness with which many Korowai persons'
dwelling arrangements change from one time of life to the next. At least
as remarkable, though, is the quickness with which Korowai also move

from one house to the next on a day-to-day basis. In 2002 I met a newly married man whom I had known well on first coming to the Korowai area in 1995 but had not seen again in the intervening years. When I asked, "What are you doing these days?" his simple answer was, "Going back and forth." He was referring to his and his wife's movements between a village house, another house at his own clan place about five miles north of the village, and still another house on the land of some relatives of another clan. In describing travel as his main life activity, the man could have been speaking for numerous other people who reside in several households at once. For example, some mother-daughter pairs shuttle back and forth together between houses on the clan places of their respective husbands. Many unmarried young men are constantly on the move. Even families or other networks of people who live fairly continuously on one clan place will often have more than one dwelling that they currently occupy at different localities on that place. Almost all people shift sleeping places at least once every five days or so, whether as a temporary visit to others' houses or as a residential alternation to a different house of their own. A house that is completely empty one night might see the arrival of a young married couple and their child, then the following night shelter twenty of their kin, and then a night later be home to just the main couple and a few close relatives. Korowai houses, and the clan territories on which they stand, are spaces of arrival and departure as much as staying. In one telling idiom, people sometimes refer to their clan places as their *gix* "harbor," meaning a place on the land they come back to between times away elsewhere, much as a canoe is regularly beached at rest at a specific site on a riverbank between waterborne trips. Korowai experience the idea of landownership not only through living on their land at a given time but also through traveling to or from the land, through memories and expectations of visiting the land or dwelling on it, through turning over in conversation or in bodily practice the possibility of living away from owned land, through forming ties to places not previously their own, through making nonowners feel at home, or through otherwise straddling different sides of an ownership boundary. The landownership institution leads people to feel at home when dwelling and moving on certain stretches of territory, but the crossing of ownership boundaries is integral to people's experience of their lives as organized around land-focused belonging.[1]

A last broad way that I want to mention in which land-focused belonging is relational to its alternatives is that the definition of what land counts as a person's own is also fluid and a matter of contingent processes of persuasion and alignment. For example, clans with adjacent territories sometimes define themselves as having "the same place" *(bolüp-lelip)*, but in other contexts they spell out their distinct territories. A small episode, again from the Dambol households, tellingly illustrates the context dependency of owner standing. Across his adult life Silom stood in a relation of reciprocal hospitality with a man of another clan named Bolum, the brother of Silom's deceased first wife. In 2001, when Silom was still living, Bolum became a target of angry compensation demands on the part of a youth of another clan because the youth had wanted to marry one of Bolum's daughters, but the woman married someone else. The Dambol houses stood close to the Dambol place's border with the youth's place, and the youth's clan and Dambol are often said to share "the same place" on the basis of being neighboring clans. One afternoon when the youth was in Silom's house, Bolum and his family arrived for a visit. The youth left the house in silent rage and from another house sent demands for compensation. In response Bolum and his family left for their own place, despite the house owner Silom's objections and reassurances. Later, overhearing reports of the youth's statement that Bolum should not travel on his place until he paid him, Silom wryly retorted to the absent youth, "This is not your place. Your place is downstream." The youth claimed an expansive definition of his "place." Behind the youth's back, Silom affirmed a more restricted threshold of ownership. Here, as in many other situations, owner status arises most clearly in encounters between people who belong more and people who belong less, on a spectrum of possible states of identification and estrangement in relation to land.

SOCIETY AS A FIELD OF OTHERNESS: EGALITARIANISM AND BOUNDARY CROSSING

The pattern that a life structured around land-focused belonging is also structured around estrangement is even clearer when we move more fully from trying to consider the relation between owners and land in artificial isolation to giving central attention to relations between different people across the landscape. One of my points in looking at this level of the interlocal landownership institution is to document that Korowai dominantly experience society as a field of otherness. People imagine their social world as consisting of a population of strangers, they experience specific relations as built mainly around qualities of otherness, and they locate different relations by how they compare to each other on measures of nearness versus distance. My additional goal, though, is to show that in this field of otherness distance and edginess are connective as well as separative. Korowai understand boundaries of interlocal otherness to imply and demand engagement between people separated by these boundaries.

Korowai experience their world as a field of otherness on many dimensions, but space is an especially prominent one. One reflection of people's imagining their social world to be a field of otherness is the frequency with which they use words meaning "other" and "stranger" (or their opposites) to talk about their social relations. Korowai routinely describe specific persons in their lives as "other, strange" *(yani)* to themselves or as "together, identical, unitary" *(lelip)* with themselves, and they frequently refer to specific persons as "strangers" *(yani-yanop)* or as "intimates, together people, associates" *(lelip-anop)*. Intimates and strangers are the categories that matter in Korowai reckonings of where they stand in the social world. But people often specifically portray social unity or strangeness as a matter of geography. The words *yani-bolüp-anop* "person of another place" and *ləxinga-anop* "faraway person" are commonly used synonyms for "stranger," while *bolüp-lelip-anop* "same place people" is a common synonym for "together people."

Before turning to the role of landownership in organizing people's world as a field of otherness, I want to offer three simpler illustrations, from domains other than ownership, of the general kinds of points I will be making in that discussion. The first illustration is the statement "Upstreamers are angry" *(kolufo xenga),* which is one formulaic item in a wider range of common Korowai turns of speech describing the world as populated by hostile strangers. The statement is typical in portraying the world as populated specifically by *geographic* others. "Upstreamers" *(kolufo)* live distantly east or northeast from the speaker, higher up the courses of the region's two rivers. People assert the stereotype of angry upstreamers when explaining those others' past violent actions or when urging relatives to avoid contact with them. Tellingly, the cliché centers on a shifter. Persons described as "upstreamers" by someone else will themselves deny that they are upstreamers and instead use the same term *(kolufo)* to refer to people still farther upstream. Being "angry" is similarly here a shifting attribute of people who are geographically strange *to the position of a given speaker.* The stereotype of angry upstreamers is also typical in the way it blends multiple modes of otherness. The cliché describes upstreamers as epistemologically strange by portraying them

as indefinite, generic people on the speaker's outer horizons. "Angry"
also means "violent, hostile, fierce, sharp, wicked," and it describes both
an emotion and a quality of action and demeanor: for Korowai, "anger"
is what people do, not an interior state removed from activity. Thus the
cliché portrays upstreamers as culturally and interactionally strange:
their character is that they act violently and unreasonably. The statement
also asserts political otherness: cooperating socially with upstreamers as
equals is impossible. This kind of bundling together of geography, emotion, knowledge, interactional morality, culture, and power is a major
feature of Korowai experience of spatial otherness.

The two other illustrations of the pattern of geographic otherness
highlight the tendency for otherness to be connective. One is a pattern of
fighting. A feature of persons' sense that they are surrounded by a world
of hostile strangers is that even antagonism is a *relation*. People are
engrossed by connections to enemies and by their own sense of living on
an overall landscape of unreliable others. As an idiom of negative relations, "anger" often involves intense relational engagement. Persons
locked in conflict over theft, killing, or marriage sometimes proceed by
the commonly felt compulsion to transform their antagonism into a positive relation through sequences of demand, payment, and sharing. This
is the "reciprocity" in what Sahlins (1972 [1965]) termed "negative reciprocity."[2] Even murders may lead to marriages that join together as
mutually supportive kin people who were bitter enemies only months
before. A minor event from my own experience was typical of the positive potentials of enmity. In 2002 a man sought me out to say I should
sleep in his house, rather than someone else's, when I came to the area
where he lived. He said I should do so because some years earlier he had
expressed anger at me and his nephew for coming to his land, when we
mistakenly thought I was welcome there. He cited the earlier interaction
as a history that joined us more strongly than I was linked to other people in his vicinity. The overall pattern of seeing conflict as relational
exemplifies the way that Korowai take social connection and estrangement to be correlates rather than opposites.

A pattern of ethnic self-designation similarly illustrates how belonging in a place and involvement with strange peripheries are two sides of
a coin. The geographic extent of the Korowai dialect chain exceeds any
speaker's own travel experiences, and stable social categories larger
than patriclans are not prominent in people's talk. Yet Korowai do
sometimes speak of themselves as an overall category of humans, in
contrast to other people. One ethnic self-designation is *kolufo,* which

also means "upstreamers" and which is the source of the internationally known name *Korowai*. The term's use as an ethnic self-designation probably derives from its more basic use as an other-designating shifter. This association of the meanings "upstreamer" and "Korowai people" in one word is symptomatic of the importance of perspectival relations between self and distant other in Korowai understandings of who they are (cf. LeRoy 1985: 28–29; Welsch 1994: 88–90). The more common Korowai self-designation, though, is *bolü-anop* "place people." This word is ordinarily used as a synonym for *bolüp giom-anop* "place own-ers," in the sense of owners of a clan territory. Its use as an ethnic self-designation is based on a larger-scale sense of "place." Drawing a contrast with lands of non-Korowai people, speakers refer to the total-ity of Korowai lands as "the Korowai place" *(kolufo-bolüp)*. The ethnic self-designation *bolü-anop* "place people, place owners" is based on a model of the tight linking of language, land, and category of human being (Stasch 2007). A language and a category of people are both ter-ritorial entities. Asked why they call themselves "place people," Korowai often say it is because they all speak the Korowai language ("place language," *bolü-an-aup*), as if this fact of linguistic affiliation is reason enough for the land-focused ethnonym.

Speakers also say that the "place people" designation is based on being surrounded by peripheral strangers. Korowai regularly answered my questions about the ethnonym's rationale by noting that they live midway between other people and locations: between two neighboring ethnolinguistic populations, two bounding rivers, or two faraway cities. As one woman said about the designation, "It's because at the margins are people of other languages." In this understanding, to be defined by the land one owns is to live between other places to which one is mar-ginal. People sometimes refer to a clan-owned territory as *nə-ngaüm-ngaüm* "my boundaries, limits, margins." A person's clan place *is* the person's "limits." Belonging in relation to places involves mindfulness regarding surrounding peripheries that are not one's own but that are part of one's world.

Landownership is perhaps the single biggest cultural force making Korowai experience of social strangeness strongly geography focused and geography organized. Landownership spatializes social and ethical life. It does so by defining persons by their places, by making the divide between owners and nonowners salient across all action, and by organ-izing the geographic dispersion that is such a consequential feature of people's everyday social experience. In my fieldwork activities I was

highly aware of *not being in the presence* of the society I was involved
with. I lived only in the western Korowai lands, staying most of the time
with single or paired small households. The narrow spatial horizons to
what I was directly hearing or seeing at a given time are among the reasons that this book is an intrinsically partial, provisional effort. Yet in
often learning about events, people, and practices at second hand, I
experienced the dispersed social landscape in many of the same ways
Korowai do. The book in this sense takes as its subject the ways in
which separation-based uncertainty and partiality of knowledge are a
routine concern of people's lives and an integral feature of social bonds.

The institution of landownership structures people's social world as
a geographic field of otherness on many dimensions. For example, owners are very much connected to their land as a "territory of knowledge"
(Århem 1998). They know their land's features, the names of its
streams, and the histories of its use. The strangeness of other people's
places rests in part in lack of knowledge of that land. People's situations
of specifically epistemological belonging and estrangement in relation
to the heterogeneous landscape stood out most obviously to me when I
traveled with Korowai from one place to another. Here is one excerpt
from my notes after walking a long distance with four men who were
themselves from different regions of the landscape and had different
backgrounds of geographic knowledge:

> One lesson of the day was the intensity of the question of knowledge of
> pathways and the differentiatedness of the landscape in the form of path-
> ways and features along them. All along there were shifts among our group
> in which persons were familiar with local pathways, and lots of collective
> discussion of uncertainty about pathways. We cooked lunch 1:00–2:30
> across Mabül stream from the house of a Sendex man, and he showed us
> the path onward for a ways. Then when he stopped to return to his house,
> he gave us detailed descriptions of pathway features for the next couple
> miles. A lot of mention of species of "trunks" [i.e., standing trees] that our
> path would pass at specific transition points, such as hardwood or palm
> species. Also a *balep-siop* [pounded-out end of a thorned sago log] that we
> did in fact walk over. There were many times when we wondered if we had
> taken a wrong turn.

Another common event is for a traveler to ask a more knowledgeable
companion about whether people in the area swim in or drink from specific streams or whether these streams are off-limits due to being "taboo
sites" *(wotop)*. People's lack of knowledge of areas of the landscape
where they are not owners is intertwined with their emotional, political,
and physical wariness of those places.

To make concrete the point that landownership is particularly responsible for the strongly spatial cast of Korowai social life, I turn now to a sketch of the ways in which landownership works as a system of specifically *political* otherness: ways, in other words, in which landownership saturates social space with concerns of equality, autonomy, dependency, and subjection. My goal is to show how people's involvement with local spaces of belonging is implicated in a larger system of interlocal social relating and how that larger interlocal system is implicated in local spaces of belonging. The point I develop here is in this way parallel to my point about the "place people" ethnonym. Landownership is a particular organization of involvement with alien peripheries, not merely a way to have a home.

To specify what I mean by "political otherness," I need to make explicit how landownership stands in fundamental contradiction to a similarly taken-for-granted feature of Korowai people's lives, egalitarianism. Korowai egalitarianism consists of aversion to anyone controlling others' actions by authoritarian domination and discomfort with anyone being wealthier or better than others. Social relations are felt to be valuable and livable only to the extent that the participants are equals.[3] Prominent patterns of egalitarianism in Korowai social practice include that there are no indigenous long-term leadership offices; that any accumulation of wealth is usually quickly dispersed, under pressure of requests and demands; that a relation in which people's material gifts are reciprocal and commensurate is felt to be satisfying while asymmetry (*xolodoptanux* "one way only") is annoying and immoral; that acquaintances interrupt each other or take conversational turns with little regard for hierarchies of age, kinship, or gender; and that adults try to influence children by persuasion rather than command. Perhaps most significantly, Korowai models of personhood emphasize political autonomy. One common autonomy-asserting statement is, "He has his own mind" or "She has her own mind," which speakers utter when asked to explain or predict another person's actions. The statement is a blunt disavowal of the power to know other people's motives and of the power to control their decisions (Stasch 2008a).

Korowai egalitarianism does not mean that people's lives are free of inequality but only that inequality is a *problem* to them. Egalitarianism is here a partial and contradictory social principle, generating complex and troubled social experience, including acts of bodily violence, theft, and coercion. Such acts often follow from shortcomings of egalitarian recognition of others' autonomy as a path for fostering social coordination.

People's desires toward others (e.g., their desires for others' possessions, or for others' cooperation and intimacy) can regularly exceed their actual influence on those others so acutely that someone commits a deeply inegalitarian act.

In this broader context landownership both solves and creates problems of egalitarian living. Ownership puts people on an equal, autonomous footing by giving them independent resource bases, as is emphasized by people's "social buffer" explanations of the institution. Yet landownership is also exclusionary. In relation to any part of the landscape, some people are owners and others are not (Hallowell 1955: 239; Rigsby 1998: 23). As egalitarians, Korowai are acutely sensitive to the asymmetry between owners and nonowners. Owners' prerogatives in relation to land are generally not discussed as a highly codified, explicit body of rules but are immanent in people's constant sensitivity to who has owner standing, to whether owners are being appropriately recognized and deferred to by others, and to whether nonowners are doing anything that makes them vulnerable to being reminded out loud of their lack of standing. Telling someone he is "not an owner" in relation to the place where he stands or sits is an extreme breach of decorum, but it regularly occurs in disputes. Even in the absence of open conflict, contradictions between landownership and egalitarianism are felt in day-to-day interaction.

Keeping away from other people's places is one method for coexisting under these conditions. If a relation violates egalitarianism Korowai often physically stay clear of that relation. They avoid other people's power by avoiding their land. Sensitivity about owners' power supports a tendency for people who live far apart to be mutually fearful strangers and for people who live on shared or neighboring places to be moral and emotional "together people." Their relatively equal mutual standing across their histories of interaction helps them to be comfortable in each other's presence.

Yet boundaries of ownership difference also work as boundaries of contact. Different people own different places, but they hold in common similar *concepts* of "place" and "owner." The collective stake in ownership principles is exemplified by the pattern that other nonowning people sometimes exhort owners to act as they should in relation to their land. Bystanders might, for example, make a rhetorical case that absent landowners should return to their place and put on a feast that surrounding people will attend as guests. To have a land base is to be engaged also with the perspective of other people and to build up an intersubjective reciprocity of perspectives in which one's own standing and actions as landowner depend on the understandings and actions of those others (cf. Robbins 2003). The same institution both locates persons as belonging to specific places and locates them as living on a wider landscape of owned places to which they do not belong. Separate living is one face of people's lives, but ownership boundaries also set the terms of people's intense interactional and mental contact across geographic distances and across asymmetries of belonging in relation to place.

OWNERS AND GUESTS

Interaction between hosts and guests is a paradigmatic activity of involvement across ownership boundaries. This is a site where people seize on the connective potentials of political otherness as the very content of their social lives. In this section I look at evidence that Korowai themselves understand host-guest interaction as centered on the interaction's own contradictions of closeness across political divides and that this is what makes the interaction simultaneously fraught and valued. I look at host-guest interaction here both because of how it makes concrete some of the points about landownership outlined so far in this chapter and because it is a good entrée to another important aspect of the Korowai landscape I need to introduce the look and feel of houses. Before turning to details of Korowai host-guest encounters, though, I want to clarify in abstract terms the model I am putting forward of a "connective" aspect of boundaries of otherness. I do so by drawing links to two broad theoretical precedents for this model.

The first precedent lies in studies of grammatical shifters (after Silverstein 1976). Many linguistic modes of categorizing space, for example, depend for their meaningfulness on aspects of the context of category use, such as the bodily position of speakers and addressees, or the positions of speakers, addressees, and referents in relation to orienting landforms (Hanks 1990; Levinson 2003). Korowai expressions for "upstream" and "downstream" are a case in point: whether a referent is "upstream" or "downstream" depends not only on where the referent is but also on where it and the speakers are in relation to each other, and in relation to a waterway that is the deictic ground of the referential act. Something upstream in one conversation can be downstream in another.

The concepts of place *(bolüp)* and place-focused belonging are shifter-like. I earlier compared owning land to having a body. Unlike direct embodiment-based linguistic shifters, owning land is not a form of categorization concerned with mere spatial presence and perception, such as the physical location of people, land, and objects. The referent a speaker calls "my place" does not change with changes in where the speaker is standing, at least not as radically and directly as the referent of "upstream" changes.[4] Ownership is a perspectival category less in the order of physical position and physical perception than in the order of ontology: not *where* land and people are in relation to each other but *what* they are in relation to each other. Owning land involves a perduring emotional, moral, political, and epistemological position, the position of being at home in relation to the land and being recurrently present on it over the long run, regardless of whether one is present on it at a given moment.

The parallel between Korowai landownership and perspective-based linguistic categories resembles a parallel drawn by Viveiros de Castro (1998, 2004) in his work on Amerindian cosmological models, according to which animals experience the same world as humans do but see that world differently than humans. Viveiros de Castro compares this perspective dependency of perceptual experience to kinship terms:

> Kinship terms are relational pointers; they belong to the class of nouns that define something in terms of its relation to something else. . . . Concepts like fish or tree, on the other hand, are proper, self-contained substantives: they are applied to an object by virtue of its intrinsic properties. Now, what seems to be happening in Amerindian perspectivism is that substances named by substantives like *fish, snake, hammock,* or *beer* are somehow used as if they were relational pointers, something halfway between a noun and a pronoun, a substantive and a deictic. . . . You are a father only because there is another person whose father you are. Fatherhood is a relation, while fishiness is an intrinsic property of fish. In Amerindian perspectivism, however, something is a fish only by virtue of someone else whose fish it is. (2004: 472–73; original emphasis)

In a similar way, a Korowai clan territory is a place of belonging *for somebody*.[5] Place ownership transposes subjective perspectives into the land. A segment of land is a body-external medium in relation to which persons feel particular familiarity and compatibility.

Benveniste (1971 [1956]), in his famous analysis of first- and second-person referring forms like the pronouns *I* and *you*, emphasized that these forms encode aspects of a situation of language use. Like other shifters, they depend for their meaning on perspectival aspects of a specific event of language use, and they are thus an indissoluble unity of *langue* and *parole* (in the terms of Saussure's unsustainable distinction).

Benveniste emphasized further that in this way pronominal forms are points of integration between the perspectival experiences of different people and between personal perspectives and linguistic code generally (1971 [1958]: 224–25). One aspect of this is what Rumsey (2003) terms "perspective swapping": in occupying the alternating positions of "I" and "you" in the course of a conversation, a person is in contact with other people's experience of the same perspectival positions. This pattern of joining of otherness and contact stands out even more vividly in Viveiros de Castro's above-noted adaptation of the model of linguistic shifters to Amerindian cosmological thought. In his account the whole force of the Amerindian cosmological models lies in their relativization of the position of humans. Here, to occupy a perspectival home is also to be densely involved with other perspectives strange to oneself. A perspective consists of what is peripheral to a being, not just the being's familiar place for looking outward at peripheral horizons.

The image of society as a field of otherness has often been summarized by anthropologists diagrammatically, in the form of a series of concentric circles that represent degrees of social distance outward from a perspectival center (e.g., Evans-Pritchard 1940; Middleton 1960: 238; Sahlins 1972 [1965]; Århem 1981b: 71; Taylor 1985: 168). These diagrams describe the remarkable fact that in some human communities a spectrum of increasing strangeness is some people's *primary* image of what society is. This contrasts with images of a unitary social totality or a commanding social center held by people whose lives are organized around state regimes. However, it is easy to read concentric-circle diagrams as implying that strangers and estrangement are less important to people's lives than are familiars and familiarity. This would be a serious mistake (Viveiros de Castro 2001: 25, 30, 41 n. 14). The effect of perspectival cultural forms—like Amerindian beliefs about animals, or the Korowai concept of an owned place—is above all to organize social experience in otherness-charged terms. The image of a spectrum of degrees of estrangement, as the definition of society, construes all social relations in that field (wherever they lie on the spectrum) as relations of strangeness. Otherness is the defining metric of the social field. Korowai landownership, at least, puts at the center of social life a model of persons in perspectivally situated positions engaging with the alterity of what lies on their surrounding peripheries.

A second theoretical tradition that offers an orientation to the model of Korowai landownership I am forwarding is Simmel's frequent pattern of describing human social relations as a unity of opposite qualities. In a newspaper article titled "Bridge and Door," for example, Simmel takes as his subject the activities of "separating" and "connecting":

> One of these activities is always the presupposition of the other. By choosing two items from the undisturbed store of natural things in order to designate them as "separate," we have already related them to one another in our consciousness, we have emphasized these two together against whatever lies between them. And conversely, we can only sense those things to be related which we have previously somehow isolated from one another; things must first be separated from one another in order to be together. Practically as well as logically, it would be meaningless to connect that which was not separated, and indeed that which also remains separated in some sense. The formula according to which both types of activity come together in human undertakings, whether the connectedness or the separation is felt to be what was naturally ordained and the respective alternative is felt to be our task, is something which can guide all our activity. In the immediate as well as the symbolic sense, in the physical as well as the intellectual sense, we are at any moment those who separate the connected or connect the separate. (1997 [1909]: 171; cf. Certeau 1984: 126–29)

Elsewhere, Simmel develops similar claims in an idiom of "boundaries." He writes that humans live between boundaries, that we know ourselves by boundaries, and that "we *are* boundaries" (1971 [1918]: 353, original emphasis). He asserts that knowledge of oneself as bounded crucially involves knowledge of what is beyond one's boundaries: "For only whoever stands outside his boundary in some sense knows that he stands within it, that is, knows it as a boundary" (p. 355). Viveiros de Castro's account of Amerindian perspectivism describes a structure of this kind: the boundary between humans and animals is a boundary of extreme otherness, but it is also a boundary that puts humans in close engagement with the otherness of the beings from whom they are separated.

In a broadly comparable way, Korowai landownership organizes people's mutual separateness but is also a particular organization of the terms of their contact. Margins of otherness are subjects of people's practical acts and forms in which people's practical acts unfold. It is in the nature of boundaries as Korowai understand them that possibilities of involvement with what is across a boundary are part of that boundary itself.[6]

The idea of boundaries having the double quality of being separative and connective can also be put in a language of "crossing." Boundary crossing is an apt image because it suggests the idea of a person engaged in practical action of movement, oriented reflexively toward the margins he or she lives within and across. The social landscape I describe in this chapter is a space of boundaries and boundary crossings. People cross conceptual margins in actual concrete events of bodily movement. They also cross these margins linguistically and intellectually, even when not crossing them in body. For Korowai, "To practice space is . . . *to be other and to move toward the other*" (Certeau 1984: 110, original emphasis).[7]

Interaction between hosts and guests is an area where we can see crossing of ownership boundaries lived out practically. This interaction exemplifies how Korowai systematically join together qualities of otherness and close involvement as the positive substance of social bonds. The category "guest" is very prominent in the day-to-day politics of spatial life. In speech, "owner" *(giomanop)* and "guest" *(xuolanop)* are paradigmatically contrastive terms. These roles are usually defined in relation to a house. Korowai speak of "house owners" *(xaim giomanop)* almost as much as they speak of "place owners" *(bolüp giomanop)*. Persons who build a house are by definition its owners. Coresident spouses, children, parents, siblings, or other close relatives of builders are also readily categorized as owners, even if they did not help with construction. At least one of the focal adult owners of a house is typically also an owner of the place on which the house stands. Houses are smaller, denser sites of the same questions of belonging and estrangement posed by landownership on a broader spatial scale. Being a house owner involves being politically and sensuously at home in a space, as well as at home with others sharing that space. Guests are nonowners of a house who are in it temporarily.[8] Approaching house space initially through the "guest" category, we can appreciate how strongly houses are charged with questions of boundaries, belonging, and people's mutual involvement across separations.

"Guest" is a paradoxical category describing a category mismatch— the presence in a space of belonging of someone who does not belong there.[9] Visiting and hospitality are avid Korowai pursuits. People embrace the collisions and reconfigurations of mismatched categories that arise in visits. They travel across the land to visit others for many different reasons, all generally involving the desire for engagement with unfamiliar lives. Often people visit to pass on news, express opinions, or make plans. Guests might come to talk about a death, a work party, or a marital intrigue. People who live separately are highly aware that they do not know what others elsewhere are thinking, doing, or saying. There is thus a basic link between mobility and talk. People also visit to trade, to give or receive gifts or payments, and to seek the services of healers or other specialists. Korowai frequently explain travel in terms of curiosity to see new people and places. Above all, people travel to *be with* relatives, despite residential separation: as one man put it in explaining his presence to house owners soon after arrival, "I have not carried words [i.e., a specific political controversy]. I just wanted to come so we could chat together, and then I'll go."

The tenor of interaction between visitors and owners varies according to their relational history. Some guests are well known to house people; others are more alien to a household they visit. Yet almost all host-guest encounters are systematically contradictory in their interactional logic. One reflection of Korowai people's egalitarianism and their deep valuing of social connection as an intrinsic good is that people take mere physical copresence as a social state of some consequence. Korowai usually feel that it is extremely important to be interpersonally polite and harmonious. In a situation of host-guest encounter, two sets of people are in each other's presence, and this alone creates and confirms a sense of connection between them. But their presence to each other also focuses attention on their mutual strangeness.

Guests' presence is an interruption in the time that housemates are steadily at home together and separate from others. When guests describe their presence somewhere as "transitory" *(laux)*, they are highlighting that their time there is not self-contained but part of a trajectory of movement. The time is a marked period, when they are beyond boundaries that they will cross back over on return to a place where they are not transitory. Visits also have a temporal quality of unexpectedness. Often owners do not know visitors are coming until they hear them singing or whistling as they approach; this is a deliberate way to dispel any air of furtiveness. (Korowai men and women sing, or call out musically, a great deal across many different contexts of daily life, both for aesthetic motives and as a way to publicize their presence and position amid the dense vegetation of the forest.) House people might even learn of guests' arrival only on seeing them enter the house clearing or seeing them rise into view already on the house's veranda. Owners now often place a tin can upside down on the pointed top of their house's ladder so the can will clatter lightly when someone is ascending the pole. Symptomatic of owners' valuing of guests' visits and their reflexivity about their lack of foreknowledge of visits, they often wonder spontaneously whether guests might be coming, and they interpret certain bird calls and dream events as omens of strangers' arrival. In one convention, dreaming of a domestic pig portends arrival of guests from nearby, whereas dreaming of a wild pig portends the arrival of guests from far away. This is typical of the way otherness is the crux of host-guest relations: animality and wildness are here figures of successive degrees of social distance and interactional riskiness.

The mismatch of proximity and distance that guests embody is highly visible in the interactional tensions surrounding guests' entrance into domestic space. House owners express and address this tension by falling silent, particularly when the guests who have arrived are not routine daily visitors. If owners talk at all they only talk quietly among themselves about other topics, even though they are usually curious about why the guests have come. It is up to the guests to initiate conversation and give news. Guests often wait some minutes before doing so. Meanwhile, house owners speak through their food stores and hearths. They hasten to roast sago and press it on the guests, or they give the guests other food on hand. Sometimes owners' passing of food to guests is the first positive sign by which the parties acknowledge each other's presence.

In these sensitive transitional interactions, Korowai confront contradictions between egalitarianism and the prerogatives of ownership. By not speaking first and not remarking on the guests' arrival, owners defer to guests' autonomy. Travel is motivated by the intentions of guests themselves, and owners do not obstruct or dictate what guests are doing. During the entire course of a visit, owners do not speak about whether guests will stay overnight (not even to invite them to do so), because it is not the owners' place to determine what guests will do. The interactional stakes are high in the first place, though, because owners *do* have the prerogative to determine what goes on in their houses. Guests put themselves in a position of vulnerability by entering a space where they do not belong. They worry about their status there. Together, guests and owners tiptoe around the asymmetry between them. People avoid traveling to houses of marked strangers, out of a deep fear of feeling socially out of place and being directly or indirectly rebuked for their presence. Most people describe themselves as having few regular travel destinations. Even when visiting houses of close relatives, guests do not take for granted where they stand with the house people. Welcoming silence is the best way owners can avoid any hint of impinging on guests in this situation of vulnerability. Occasionally an owner does tell a newly arrived guest not to come to his or her house, prompting the guest to leave. This is an extraordinary breach of decorum and occurs only rarely, when travelers badly misjudge the state of their social relations. That it does occur testifies to insecurities beneath the respectful silence normally prompted by guests' sudden

arrival (cf. Shryock 2004: 37 and citations there). People let bodily copresence and expectant silence get them through the initial mismatch
between guests and house space.

By giving food, house owners extend to guests forms of caring typical
of domestic intimacy. A house is in major part the cooking and eating
that goes on in it. Between owners and guests, as between housemates,
giving and sharing of cooked food are practices of making close contact
with one another's subjectivities by providing bodily sustenance and
pleasure. Often guests are presented with a comical flood of roasted sago
cakes and other snacks offered by the various house occupants. When a
traveling party is large, owners work efficiently at roasting batch after
batch of food to feed all visitors. Through bodily gestures and halting
verbal interjections, guests express surprise and reluctance about the
gifts pressed on them. In part the force of this giving follows from the
fact that guests *are* weary and hungry from hard walking, if they have
come far. Travelers endure fatigue, foot wounds, chilling rain, mud, dangerous stream crossings, confusing paths, and uncertainty about whether
they will reach shelter by nightfall. By giving travelers food, owners
answer to guests' dependence on others for bodily help and partially
recategorize the new arrivals from intruders to persons who belong. The
more plentiful the gifts, the more delight the givers are expressing. If
house owners do not move to prepare sago at all, this is taken as an overt
statement that the owners do not want the guests in their house. Such a
sequence of events is again a rare, severe breach of social amity but does
occur. To ward off an extreme social rupture, owners who do not have
food on hand or who do not want to share what they have hidden away
are careful to tell guests apologetically that they entirely lack sago.

A convention of leave-taking also makes visible the contradictions
in guests' presence. It is another mark of Korowai egalitarianism and
extreme sensitivity to acts of boundary-crossing demands on other people
that in Korowai discourse there are no routine verbal greetings (akin to
English "Hello," "Good morning," or "How are you?") and no conventional valedictions uttered on parting. People navigate transitions of copresence silently or by nonritualized conversational openings. When guests
leave a house they often do so in nonchalant silence, similar to the silence
of arrival. However, there is one regular conversational routine that guests
and owners often perform when parting after a long visit. The departing
guests say that the house people are going to fall ill. The house owners
deny they will fall ill and in turn suggest that the guests will get sick. This
the guests also deny, and walk away. The logic here parallels health-

focused valedictions cross-culturally, such as "Take care!" or "Drive carefully!" except that Korowai express concern for others through worry about what will befall them rather than through exhorting them to be well. They count on the other party to complete the conversation with a reassuring denial.[10] To explain these parting conversations, people say that sharing domestic space with residential strangers is medically dangerous. One concern is that when strangers sleep overnight together, the house owners or guests might be invisibly assaulted by a male witch among the other people. But there is a more general range of ways in which people think it is possible to get sick by being too much in the company of residential strangers. Even when no one is showing signs of illness, Korowai are sensitive to the potential that someone in a visiting or hosting party *could* later fall ill and die. Following such a death, the person's relatives would scan the deceased's recent history of interaction with strangers for possible causes of the sickness. These relatives could retrospectively read silence at a time of parting as a sign of malice and blame the silent people for the death. By speaking up about fears of future sickness, guests and owners express care for each other.

Rituals of transition reflect anxieties that are felt over the whole time that mutually unfamiliar people share domestic space. Throughout visits, guests strike poses of restraint that signal worry over the space, food, and attention they are taking up. They even voice aloud their concerns about whether owners want them there. For example, at a house where I was once staying, a nephew of two owners showed up one morning to retrieve a steel ax he had accidentally left behind the day before. The house residents were butchering a wild pig, and they enthusiastically brought the visitor into their activities. Some time into his visit, the nephew mused aloud that he had been anxious about coming, because guests are not supposed to come day after day but should only visit once in a while. His hosts assured him they were not thinking this at all.

There is much more to say about variations in how at ease different guests and owners put each other through conversation, food-sharing, and other media. Here I have only sought to make clear that people's interactions in host-guest encounters are highly reflexive: the focus of these interactions is the interacting people's own ambiguous relational standing with each other. Participants carefully scan the interactional signs for messages about that relational standing. This reflexive sensitivity is fueled by the double quality of host-guest interaction, in which people recognize each other as sharers of an intimate space while also marking each other's strangeness and the guests' lack of ownership status. In hospitality,

Korowai create unstable but pleasurable structures of belonging and togetherness of a transient kind, across disparities of ownership.

I have focused on interaction within the time of a single encounter, but Korowai also evaluate visiting as something done repetitively. A visit has histories and futures of other visits. People take *reciprocity* of visiting, in particular, as a measure of the quality of relatives' bonds. A pattern of mutually entering each other's houses creates egalitarian relatedness across inegalitarian ownership divides. Across cycles of reciprocal visiting, persons alternate their roles as powerful "owner" and vulnerable "guest," like the shifting adoption of roles of "I" and "you" in a conversation. Whether existing stably across reciprocal visits or in a more emergent way during one encounter, though, the force of a bond between people of different places rests in the risks and vulnerabilities they *overcome* together by relating across the spatial and ownership divide between them.

CONNECTION AND SEPARATION IN PHYSICAL QUALITIES OF HOUSES

The physical features of Korowai houses also illustrate how a quality of belonging is a central concern of Korowai people's spatial lives, densely intertwined with their concern with boundaries of otherness. Forms of bodily copresence and sharing that prototypically occur in house space are basic to Korowai experience of being "together" *(lelip)*. In houses people do most of the resting, sleeping, cooking, eating, healing, and talking of their lives. These are activities that depend on and create feelings of belonging. People carefully plan their movements so they will never stay in a house alone, even for a single night, a hint of how thoroughly houses are defined as spaces of shared living. Yet while dwellings signify and foster closeness, there are numerous ways in which close connections between persons in houses are based on boundaries of otherness and on houses' links to what lies beyond them. Dwellings can be read in much the same way Simmel reads doors, in the essay from which I earlier quoted. A house is an ambivalent "boundary point" (Simmel 1997 [1909]: 172) of simultaneous isolation from surrounding spaces and integration with them, and a boundary point of simultaneous belonging and estrangement between persons.

Forms of belonging felt in domestic space, besides being shaped and organized by the social boundaries between those who are owners and those who are not, are also organized by the tangible, visible boundaries built into houses. The most obvious of these is the severe architectural separateness of houses from the surrounding world. Korowai build dwellings in many shapes and sizes, but the variations fall into two categories. A *xaim* stands high above the ground, supported by topped tree trunks. A *xaü* stands at ground level with the earth as its floor, or it is built a bit above the ground, atop a felled log. About two-thirds of dwellings are of the high type, and people generally regard high houses as superior to ground-level ones. Vegetal materials out of which houses are built dry quickly, so houses stand out sharply as brown bodies against the green of gardens and forest. To build a high house, people select a patch of forest with one or more good standing trees available as a foundation, build scaffolds, top all trees within the house's planned outline, add extra posts, build the floor platform at the level of the topped tree trunks, and then build walls and a roof on this base. Men usually do the work of assembling house parts, but women often undertake some of the heavy labor of gathering materials.

The height of Korowai houses is extraordinary. Extending into the present the colonial promotion of "treehouse" photographs as iconic of New Guinea people and their supposed primitiveness (Quanchi 1994: 112–30; 1999), travelers to the Korowai area have seized on tall houses as objects of particular desire and fascination. Tour guides and mass media professionals often portray single, spectacularly tall structures, up to a hundred feet above ground, as representative (e.g., Steinmetz 1996), but these houses are unusual. They are now typically built by youths for clubhouse camaraderie or for tourism income but not for use as living spaces, because they are hard to enter and are quickly blown apart by wind. However, Korowai do take moderate heights of about fifteen feet above ground as a normal feature of domestic life. Tellingly, a single verb means both "climb" and "enter," and the "climb" meaning is more basic. To enter is by definition to climb.

Korowai are well aware that elevated houses are harder to build than ground-level ones and that living in them on a day-to-day basis is laborious. As I noted in the introduction, people's greatest motive for living high above ground is the fear that otherwise they will be attacked by two kinds of monsters: the demonic dead *(laleo)* who prowl about as walking corpses in search of reunion with their relatives and male "witches" *(xaxua)* in the Korowai population who compulsively and invisibly eat other people's bodies, causing all deaths. Korowai are acutely anxious about these monsters' presence in their lives. A good indication of the monsters' day-to-day prominence is house elevation

Figure 4. Sel Nambul carrying the carcass of a domestic pig into a house, 2001.

itself. All across the land the physical height of houses is a direct expression of people's fear of the demons humans become after dying and the witches who cause humans to die.

In Korowai understanding, house space thus materially embodies not just questions of mutual political impingement but also questions of life and death. In chapter 6 I detail how ideas about demons are exemplary of Korowai cultural concern with alterity as a focus of social life. Here I only wish to make the basic point that *separation* is the goal of house architecture. People live high above the ground in an effort to draw a boundary between domestic space and beings connected with death. As with other projects of separation, this height marks the centrality of feared others to people's domestic lives as much as it keeps those others out.

House height also creates *sensory* qualities of separation. To enter and exit houses, people climb notched poles hung from one or both of a dwelling's ends. The poles are not fixed at the bottom, and owners often swing a pole's base to one side and tie it off when they leave their house so as to discourage others from entering. During a night of unusual fears, house occupants can tie back the top of their entry pole, leaving the ladder's base suspended beyond the reach of anyone on the ground. But in a more constant way, the vertical climb into a high house strengthens the sense of separation between domestic space and the world, more powerfully than a horizontal transition can do. Seen from the edge of a clearing or from another house in the same garden, domestic space has a quality of stagelike flotation, at a remove from what is beneath and behind it. To clamber up into someone's house is to enter a space apart from the surrounding land. The moment when a person's head and then body rise above floor level at a house's end is visually dramatic, for the climber as for anyone inside.

Clearings around houses also foster a sense of separation. They range from ten to one hundred yards across, and their openness and brightness contrasts with the close visual horizons that surround people almost everywhere else on the land. People open clearings in order to grow bananas and other foods, as well as to be able to view the land, the forest wall, and the sky. People often site houses so that a stand of a specific very tall, slender palm species will be at the clearing's edge because they appreciate looking across and up at the swaying fronds of these palms. Korowai also associate visual openness with security. They push back the forest margin to make it difficult for witches, demons, or human prowlers *(gawaanop)* to approach houses furtively. The physical openness of a clearing, like house height, concretely indexes people's perception that their world is populated by hostile others.

These gestures of separation from the surrounding world support the forms of social closeness that occur inside houses. House height, clearings, and the distance between houses throw housemates' domestic intimacy into contrastive relief and free housemates from the presence of

Figure 5. House in a newly opened clearing, bordered at left by a sago stand. The word for "clearing" means literally "logs."

more people, allowing them to give their food and attention to each other. Yet domestic enclosures are also systematically permeable to the surrounding world. Houses have ladders and doorways, and clearings have paths leading into surrounding forest. House residents themselves climb in and out of dwellings repeatedly in their daily rounds of looking for food, attending to their bodies, gathering water and wood, and traveling to other places. Within a house even close relatives stage questions of separation and contact by keeping their bodies, articles, and food apart, or by running them together.

The internal organization of house space, like the relation between house and surrounding world, is also focused on otherness and boundary crossing. Elevated houses have two roof slopes and a rectangular layout. The roof peak runs along the middle of the house's length, at a height of eight or nine feet above the floor. High houses vary in size, but the largest are roughly twenty feet wide and thirty feet long. Elevated houses usually have an open or semiopen veranda at one or both gable ends. These outer verandas are divided from a house's middle chamber by a lateral panel wall, and people enter the internal chamber through doorways where the lateral wall approaches the house's sidewalls (figure 6). Near these sidewalls the house's ceiling is at its lowest, so adults must bend down to pass through the doorways. The inside of a house is less bright and breezy than the verandas, and the enclosed interior is also slightly more marked as a space of separate belonging. Unfamiliar visitors to a house sometimes never enter beyond the veranda but remain seated in the outer spaces. Clay hearths in houses' floors are centers around which people roast food, warm themselves, sleep, and talk. A medium-sized house might have four hearths in the internal chamber and one or two on each veranda.

House space is strongly associated with shared eating. The sight of a house's ceiling is one indication of how much a house and the social bonds of its residents are defined by the giving, cooking, and consuming of food. Rather than throw bones away, Korowai habitually insert them in the roof thatch of the house in which the animal was eaten. House ceilings are arrayed with mammal and bird bones, turtle shells, carefully reassembled snake vertebrae, and whole fish skeletons. Large bones such as pig skulls, pig leg bones, and cassowary pelvises are often suspended directly over veranda hearths, where they blacken. In this way a house's interior becomes a museum of the meals eaten there. The longer a house has been dwelt in, the more cluttered the ceiling grows with animal parts, and the blacker it becomes with soot. Looking at a house interior, one sees the duration of residents' presence there.

Asked why they put meal traces in ceilings, Korowai say it is so "other people will see the prosperity" (yani-yanop folul imoxate). House occupants understand food bounty as what is "good, prosperous" (folul) in domestic life. They think of guests, or here generically "other people," as an audience whose reactions of wonder at displayed bones confirm the desirability of that domestic life. This is an example of outsiders being important to housemates' social closeness—here housemates' understanding of one another as literal companions, persons who eat together. The difference between veranda and enclosed interior and the difference between those who have eaten an animal meal in a house and those who only see traces of that meal later begin to hint that a house interior is itself subtly composed of internal boundaries, similar to the boundaries between house and surrounding world. The hearths of a house are also sites of complexly orchestrated solidarities and separations. By sharing a hearth or passing food cooked on one hearth to someone elsewhere in a house, people within a house create links of closeness, just as by observing formal or informal commensal separations the residents create qualities of otherness even between persons sharing the same roof.

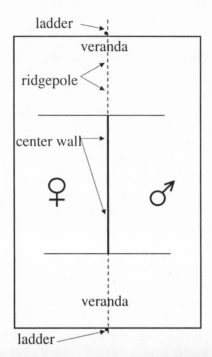

ladder

veranda

ridgepole

center wall

♀ ♂

veranda

ladder

Figure 6. Floor plan of a high house.

Figure 7. Meal traces tucked in one part of the ceiling of the house of Alemun Yengel and Baxuom Xayaanop. Among the pictured objects are fish skulls, fish skeletons, a pig leg bone, eighty crayfish carapaces, and leaf wrappers in which meals were cooked. The nylon fishing line at middle left has been stretched out for unkinking.

The most obvious separative boundary within house space is a solid panel wall dividing houses into gendered halves. This "middle wall" *(walüp damon)* runs underneath the roof peak, splitting a house's interior symmetrically into two sides. People give three reasons for the division: men's fear of contact with menses, the need for mother-in-law and son-in-law pairs to avoid each other's sight, and concern of house owners to prevent men and women from forming mutual sexual attraction through sight or propositioning each other by touch. In practice, small children and some elders move between the sides with little restraint. Visitors observe the gendering of space more thoroughly than house owners, and men among house residents tend to cross onto women's sides more readily than the reverse. Particular persons, couples, or households have their own styles of emphasizing or deemphasizing boundaries. Whatever the variations in stringency, this splitting of houses into masculine and feminine halves puts at the center of domestic space a gesture of separation similar to that built into house height and dispersed living. People refer to the two sides of a house as "men's place" and "women's place," using the same word *bolüp* "territory, place" that is more ubiquitously used to speak of clan-owned segments of land. This is a good indication of how the regions of a house are saturated by concerns of belonging centered on gender categories, parallel to saturation of the earth's regions by concerns of belonging centered on clanship. When owners describe a "middle wall" as intended to block people from forming sexual desires, they often portray this as an issue of keeping male visitors from trying to initiate affairs with house-dwelling women. Spatial divides of gender within a house are in part transpositions of boundaries between that house and the wider, sexually politicized landscape. But the architectural division also means that even relations between close coresident kin are conducted through the marking of people's mutual strangeness, especially their otherness of gender.

Thus far, in outlining ways in which the physical features of houses give material form to dialectically intertwined social projects of unity and separateness, I have focused on ways in which a house is a scene of social closeness made out of spatial boundaries and people's movements across them. Yet these aspects of houses overlap with patterns of house duration, abandonment, and remembrance. In other words, as part of their character as physical structures, houses are also very literally temporal events, composed of a complex set of links to and separations from other times. Houses vividly illustrate the directness with which Korowai spatialize time and see objects as temporal.

A major physical feature of houses is their transience. About a year after they are built, houses begin to sway, leak, and break too much to live in, at which point owners abandon them in favor of new dwellings. Any single house is a transitional phase in its occupants' orbit from one residence to the next. Thanks to this periodicity, houses are used as units of time reckoning, and they provide the main armature of temporal succession around which people locate other events. Rainfall and other environmental facts are not markedly seasonal, such that Korowai do not make much use of atmospherically based "year" categories in speaking about time. Rather, speakers routinely quantify duration using the unit "house falling apart" (*xaim-demun,* from the infinitive of *demi-* "fall apart"). A length of time is measured by the number of houses that fell apart across it. Similarly, people often say "the time of this house" *(i-xaim-alüp)* to situate an event as contemporary rather than long ago, and they speak of the "era" *(-alüp)* of specific previous houses to locate events historically. Residents remember each house they have lived in by the species name of its main supporting tree. The simplest way I could elicit an ordered account of the births, marriages, deaths, killings, feasts, and other major events that had shaped a certain person's life was to organize our conversation around the sequence of houses in which he or she had lived. Many adults can list fifty or more houses they have lived in. As they list each house, speakers readily mention the people with whom they shared domestic space and the life-changing transitions that occurred during their time there. People live the events of their lives *as* the spaces where those events occurred. A sequence of houses is a geographic memory palace of life events. The metonymic standing of houses as signs of whole times of social relating underscores that houses are foundational scenes of living. The space of a house and the forms of belonging created in it are basic to people's understanding of what it is to *be,* historically and socially, in the first place.

Anna Tsing, learning from Meratus people in Kalimantan, similarly collected "swidden biographies," or "narrations of the consecutive swidden sites of each household" (2005: 201). Tsing's interlocutors readily told their lives to her in these terms "because the narration of personal history through the landscape has been [for them] an ordinary genre for speaking about one's past" (201; see also Schieffelin 1976: 142 n. 5; Rosaldo 1980: 42; Wagner 1986: 21; Fox 1997). These modes of knowledge and narration construe forest spaces *as* people's social relations. The concatenation of spaces in sequences of living means that a forest location and the social state of people's lives at that location are not self-contained, but coexist with histories and futures of other places and social states different from the present one. Tsing uses the apt expression "shadow communities" to describe the way forest society is lived temporally as well as spatially. People stop living together, they move around, and they let some bonds attenuate while firming up others. Yet histories of past affiliation and co-living remain in consciousness as shadows, bearing on the present as its alternatives and underpinnings. Any residential present consists partly of its intertemporal links to other arrangements of living. Houses are their own times, but they are also temporally permeable, in coordination with their permeability in space. People living in a house are often preoccupied with their separation from dead former coresidents and might work strenuously to commemorate those dead or stay apart from them. More generally, people's practices of moving between different houses and households, visiting houses temporarily, and building houses in different locations or on different clan places are often allochronic activities of contact with other times or separation from those times. Through house-crossing motion, people are in contact with the time of an earlier history of parents raising a child, the time of a now-deceased woman's displacement from her natal kinspeople to her husband's place where she bore many children, or the time of a past gift or injury now being recompensed. A house is not only internally diachronic, in displaying meal traces or other signs of the length and character of its occupation; it also bears a diachrony of external links to other spaces and times. Houses' temporality is another way that these dwellings point beyond themselves to work as social boundaries of otherness that are at once enclosing and connective.

VILLAGE FORMATION AND THE
EXPANDED RANGE OF STRANGERS

This chapter has documented Korowai people's otherness-focused, relationship-focused approaches to the practice of space. I have argued that Korowai spatial experience is permeated by social qualities of belonging and otherness and that the boundaries across which people experience each other as mutually strange are also points of relatedness. Developing this theme with reference to place ownership and houses, I have indicated that to understand these kinds of spatial forms we must look also at the ways in which spaces themselves are diachronic and intertemporal. What an owned place or a house interior *is* rests partly in the temporal trajectory in which that space exists (such as histories of

generational succession or emigration and return in relation to a clan territory, or sequences of past and future houses with different config-
urations of living coresidents in relation to a current house). Another
important but quite different level of geographic intertemporality—or
geography embodying history—consists of changes that have unfolded
across the Korowai lands since about 1980, following involvement with
new social forces and new strangers. These processes illustrate further
the finding that Korowai take space as a medium of otherness-focused
relating and that this involves expecting spaces to be sites of change and
abandonment, as well as identification.

The new cultural forms Korowai are now involved with include
Christianity, Indonesian state institutions, international primitivist
tourism, and monetized trade in factory-made exogenous commodities.
An adequate examination of current intercultural processes would take
a book of its own. Here I focus on people's involvement with a new residential form, the permanent, aggregated village. Villages are the single
most consequential cultural phenomenon of the new epoch because they
engage Korowai life on its own primary terms, the terms of geography.

Village formation has followed patterns widely precedented across
the southern lowlands of New Guinea over the past seventy-five years.
In this region, as elsewhere, state authorities, religious organizations,
companies, and traders have considered people's aggregation at fixed
residential sites a necessary condition for having effective social links
with them. In the hard-to-reach Korowai region, it was the Dutch
Calvinist missionaries of the Mission of Reformed Churches (Zendings
Gereformeerde Kerken) and their Papuan assistants who, in the late
1970s, entered into sustained interaction with Korowai in their own
lands and initiated the creation of villages in the region (de Vries 1983;
Bakker 1996; van Enk and de Vries 1997). By the late 1980s the mission center of Yaniruma consisted of a central lane of two expatriate
residences and a dozen other metal-roofed, sawn-lumber buildings,
surrounded by three lanes of forest-material houses built by local families: one lane of Korowai houses and two lanes of Kombai ones (figure
8). More than twenty other villages have also been formed in the
region at different times. Most villages are sited near rivers and in border regions near the edges of Korowai landownership. All villages have
taken their names from adjacent streams, another indication of the
prominence of waterways in Korowai experience of geography. Many
villages were brief experiments, but about twelve are occupied today
(see map 1). A village lane might consist of between five and thirty

Figure 8. Yaniruma village, looking east, 2007. The Korowai houses are along the dogleg lane at left above the airstrip, parallel to the central lane of metal-roofed buildings.

houses in diverse states of partial construction, fresh completion, disrepair, or abandonment.

The Dutch missionary families left Yaniruma in about 1990. One missionary, Gerrit van Enk, learned to speak Korowai, and he and the linguist Lourens de Vries coauthored a monograph on Korowai language and culture (van Enk and de Vries 1997). A Papuan-staffed sister church now oversees the mission-established physical facilities. Several families of nonlocal Papuans connected to the church or to the Yaniruma airstrip, originating from the highlands or from the upper Digul watershed to the east of the Korowai area, live full-time in Yaniruma or sometimes in other southern villages. More recently, Papuan church workers originating from the highlands, serving with two other Protestant denominations, have begun to live in newer villages in the eastern and northeastern Korowai region. In part because of the occasional Cessna flights to Yaniruma by mission aviation organizations, this village has remained a major conduit of involvement with foreign people, institutions, objects, and spatial practices. Indonesian government personnel have generally visited Korowai villages only transiently, and they have rarely traveled to forested clan lands. Since 1992 about five of the largest settlements have been made official "villages" (<u>desa</u>) in the government's administrative hierarchy. Village governments are subordinate to regional administrative centers (<u>kecamatan</u>) several days' travel to the southeast or southwest (though as of 2007 Yaniruma itself was beginning to be made a <u>kecamatan</u>). In the period of my research the villagers' connections to the administrative centers were maintained through local bureaucratic office-holders' occasional travel to the centers. Travel to these distant centers for purposes of shopping in trade stores has become an increasingly routine activity for village-oriented Korowai men and women alike. Itinerant non-Papuan traders have also occasionally lived in villages for extended periods, drawn by a regional boom in the extraction of eaglewood (Ind. <u>kayu gaharu</u>), an internationally valuable aromatic resin deposit found in some fungus-infected specimens of a particular tree (see Momberg, Puri, and Jessup 2000; Gunn et al. 2004; Sekretariat Keadilan dan Perdamaian 2004). Most prominently, in the 1990s tourists from Europe, North America, and Japan began visiting Korowai and Kombai lands, to meet and photograph people who fit their stereotypes of primitive humanity. It is a paradox of economic and cultural globalization that Korowai live on the extreme fringes of motorized transport and mass-commodity trade, yet for exactly this reason hundreds of tourists come to them each year, creating opportunities for lucrative short-term cash income unavailable in most other places in rural West Papua.

Korowai people's ambivalent orientations toward villages provide additional evidence in support of the point that dispersion is a method of egalitarian social life. A village is exactly what Korowai say is socially unworkable when they explain (about their traditional practice of living far apart) that if they lived together in one location they would not be able to procure food and raise families in peace but instead would get in frequent fights. As these routinely invoked rationales for residential dispersion would predict, villages are in actuality often fractured by conflicts over theft, sexual affairs, and deaths. Even when no obvious feuds are unfolding, people often say that villages are uncomfortable because people in them are so visible and answerable to each other. Village houses are built in a foreign style, with closable doors, windowless walls, and little exterior veranda space. These architectural features are techniques for limiting visual and physical openness, but walls are much less effective at impeding access than the old system of place ownership and physical distance.[11] Food, for example, is one common focus of difficulty. In matters of food, as in matters of geography, there is an extreme directness in how people perceive relational truths of autonomy and belonging to be at stake in material facts. The expression "It's not your eating, I'm going to eat it" *(gəlunda, nəlep)* is a standard critical description of the village-associated pattern of people indiscriminately entering one another's houses, such that owners lose control over who sees their food and are compelled to share it. Conversely, the statement "They don't give to me" is a reason people frequently cite for why they have left a village behind after a period of trying to live in it. For a person to be in the presence of others who have food or other good objects while being left out of the circle of possession and enjoyment is a humiliating and relation-denying experience, by the same token that being given to is pleasurable and relation-affirming. When people live together in one place, it perturbs an already delicate economy of interpersonal access, recognition, and exclusion. More people are in each other's presence more of the time. Matters are made worse by food's greater scarcity in villages, due to depletion of surrounding resources and the long distances between village sites and people's patrimonially owned sago groves.

The sense that villages contradict received understandings of how to live socially in space is summed up by the contrast Korowai draw between "village" and "forest" as entire cultural environments. The main word used for "forest" is *du-lebul* "tree trunks," evoking the image of people walking and working amid the bases of tall hardwoods and their large buttress roots. The main words for "village" are *xampung* and *kelaja,* borrowed from Indonesian <u>kampung</u> "village" and <u>kerja</u> "work." (The jump from "work" to "village" followed early experience of land clearing and grass cutting as the defining activity of village space.) Korowai often speak of themselves as "forest people," in contrast to foreign "village people." Alternatively, speakers identify some Korowai as "village persons" or as regular travelers to "village side" and others as "forest people." The coexistence of "village" and "forest" as whole contrastive arrangements of living is a central preoccupation of Korowai consciousness today.

The antipathy between the village form and received approaches to space is also evident in the fact that villages are usually empty. Absence of people is Korowai villages' most striking characteristic. Almost everyone who maintains a village house also owns at least one house far away on clan land, or regularly stays far away with forest-dwelling relatives. Residents usually sleep in villages just one or a few nights at a time, between periods of living on clan places. Even when sleeping in a village, residents leave these spaces behind for most of each day. People's major orientations toward villages include avoiding them, staying in them only briefly, leaving them after a few months or years, or collectively abandoning whole village sites.

Yet the idea that villages invert existing Korowai sensibilities about space is only part of the story. I have argued earlier that in Korowai people's distinctive sensibilities about social boundaries, judgments of spatial strangeness are also points of social involvement. Bending a term associated with Foucault (1986), we might say that heterotopia is a native Korowai way of life. If so, then villages as a strange type of space might not have only a negative relation to received ways of making and using geography but could also fit positively into people's routine projects of crossing boundaries of estrangement. Village living is the antithesis of Korowai people's historical system, but being involved with one's antithesis *was* Korowai people's system. This is another way to understand the phenomenon of the empty village and people's treatment of villages as places of coming and going. Mobility is an endogenous Korowai way to make connections across boundaries of spatial otherness. Many people have readily adapted techniques of mobility to include the alien spatial form of the permanent, aggregated village in their lives. Paradoxically, village formation has *increased* residential mobility. Villages add more sites to people's rounds of spatial alternation, and they add another type of episode to people's lifelong sequences of living arrangements.

Even if villages are often empty, they exist. Korowai have avidly participated in village formation. While expatriate missionaries or Papuan church workers have had a direct hand in the founding of certain villages, the opening and long-term occupation of a village has only ever occurred if Korowai found the idea persuasive. Numerous villages have been founded with no outsiders' encouragement. Many Korowai approve of the idea of living together collectively in one permanent place. People sometimes use village positions to criticize forest life, rather than the reverse, even on criteria such as food and morality. In an image of reconciling forest dispersion and village aggregation, one person mused to me that people should build a village lane down the middle of the entire length of the Korowai lands, so they could all live on their own clan territories but also be joined in the aesthetic and political unity of a single open residential space. This compromise is not physically feasible, but in a figurative sense it is exactly what Korowai have done by forming villages in different areas, by alternating between village and forest houses, by practicing kinship-based divisions of residential labor (in which one relative maintains a forest house and the other a village house), and by otherwise closely involving themselves with the charged boundary *between* village and forest.

On this argument, the Korowai sensibility of otherness-focused social relating has a major role in shaping cultural change. The sensibility also means that there is no absolute distinction between endogenous and exogenous cultural forces (cf. Rumsey 2006). People's endogenous cultural pattern is one of seizing on what is marked as exogenous and engaging closely with it in modes of hostility, embrace, or ambivalent crossover and return.

This pattern is also apparent in other strands of Korowai intercultural engagement with new historical presences across the past three decades. For example, in practical involvement with actual foreign *persons,* Korowai have dominantly portrayed these foreigners as strange and repulsive. This is clear from their use of the word *demon (laleo)* as a label for all new strangers who have come to Korowai lands in recent times, including whites, Indonesians, and nonlocal Papuans. Sometimes speakers have applied this label in a mode of literal, full identification of foreigners with the malignant walking dead. Increasingly, some speakers describe the usage as "merely idiomatic" *(mofu filo-),* and *laleo* is coming to have two explicitly distinct senses, "dead nonhuman monsters" versus "foreign humans." Yet the two senses resonate figuratively, and "merely idiomatic" usages participate in an intertextual series with more literal-minded ones.[12] What the word signifies, even in its most ironic uses, is repulsive monstrosity. To Korowai, a first principle of the world is that humans and demons are supposed to stay mutually separate. Advent of the demonic dead among living humans is a long-standing image of apocalypse. People sometimes refer to the epoch before foreigners' intrusion as "when the world was good," by contrast with the present "bad" epoch. The most basic way in which the world has gone bad is the violation of humans' separateness from monsters through village formation and associated traffic of unfamiliar people and technologies into the land.

However, in the categorial logic of the human-demon duality (which I explore more carefully in chapter 6), repulsiveness also involves closeness. "Demon" is an intimate other to "human," even more than "village" is an intimate other to "forest." In addition to calling foreign persons "demons," Korowai use "demon" as a prefix for forming hundreds of compound words designating new material artifacts. Rice is "demonic sago," metal roofing is "demonic thatch," and so on. Speakers also use "human" *(yanop, mayox)* as a prefix to form compounds such as "human sago" or "human thatch," referring to endogenous cultural objects. This pattern portrays demonism as a deformed but coherent cultural ensemble, parallel to the human ensemble. By categorizing outsiders as demonic, Korowai fit the outsiders into their own sensibilities about the sublime value of shock and their expectations that other beings will occupy a social existence parallel and inverse to their own. In beliefs about demons as after-death monsters that predate the use of "demon" to speak of foreigners, Korowai portray the dead as an ethnoterritorial group. The dead have their own "demon place" *(laleo-bolüp),* far downstream from Korowai lands. (This is typical of people's geography-led approach to defining persons and events: even monsters are defined by a "place," and death is a territory on the land.) Calling new outsiders "demons" is a way to categorize them as ethnic others comparable to the human ethnic others at the edges of the Korowai lands. The demons come from farther away in geography and in category of being. They are beyond the pale of humanity but still recognizable as a territorial population.

Consistent with this way in which the concepts of human and demon are at once closely joined and mutually strange, ties with foreigners have in actual practice been marked by mercurial ambivalence. In the first twenty-five years of church presence in the area, only a handful of Korowai converted to the new religion, due to the stringency of Calvinism's requirements for baptism and many people's construal of Christian theology as being both parallel to and incompatible with their existing cosmological narratives. At the same time, missionary families have affected some persons' lives very intensely and are widely portrayed as major agents in collective history. Single events of interaction and mutual giving with outsiders are often remembered as poignantly valuable. Many Korowai are especially enthusiastic about interaction with tourists. Today "tourist" *(turis-anop)* is a major ethnic category. People talk avidly about past tourist visits or potential future ones. Yet they also find tourism intensely frustrating and see tourists themselves as frightening, bizarre actors. Tourists and other new foreigners have become subjects of aesthetic fascination *because* they are so strange.

Another area of intercultural involvement that has unfolded as a process of simultaneous othering and appropriation is the embrace of foreign commodities such as shorts, T-shirts, skirts, steel axes, machetes, pots, knives, plastic bowls and bottles, plastic bags, soap, shag tobacco, fishing tackle, swimming goggles, fish spears, and matches, as well as foodstuffs such as rice, instant noodles, and cooking oil. Although these "demonic articles" *(laleo-misafi)* are thin on the ground, they are integral to Korowai lives. Many people's enthusiasm for village living is based on association of villages with access to these articles. Traffic in the new commodities has been central to people's efforts to understand and engage with foreigners. Missionaries and other outsiders entered Korowai lives first by material gifts and trades. Korowai initially found the foreign objects shocking and fearful, and most articles retain an other-worldly aura even when their use is routinized, but the foreign commodities have broadly changed from objects of repulsion to objects of intense desire. The coexistence of intense valuing of imported goods with ongoing expressions of millennialist fear of them is characteristic of the mobility and contradictoriness of Korowai people's approaches to what is radically other.

Beneath the sea change toward desire for foreign commodities, though, there are important undercurrents of continuity. Whether repulsive or attractive, the objects are attention-grabbing, and their otherness makes them so. The value of foreign objects draws on a broader Korowai disposition, linked to egalitarianism, to express identity by putting oneself down and others up. For example, the meteoric rise of Korowai enthusiasm for clothing in recent times was fueled by intense existing cultural anxiety about bad bodily characteristics being seen by others; the possibility of making one's body disappear from sight is welcome. Concern with alien commodities follows also from the way objects are focal media of social transformation and amelioration between Korowai themselves, across boundaries of nonbelonging. Possessing "demonic goods" is a way to relate to the new outsiders, because material exchange *makes* relations. One way in which the new foreigners are so culturally anomalous is that they violate the landownership system just by being present. The outsiders do not belong. Yet the possibility of eliciting goods from those outsiders is a familiar moral road to creating degrees of belonging, accommodation, and togetherness with them, despite the ownership difference. Korowai frequently report thinking or saying to tourists, traders, or government agents who are aggravating them, "This place is not your place!" as support for the sequitur that those foreign people should be forthcoming with material goods. By caring about acquisition and consumption of the new exogenous objects, Korowai pursue a familiar way to claim a position in a world that extends beyond their own sight and reach.

Writing about intercultural encounters in the nineteenth-century Pacific, Dening (1992) develops the figure of the "beach" to describe qualities of improvised, emergent social connection unfolding between newly involved people. The beach is a place "where everything is relativized a little, turned around, where tradition is as much invented as handed down, where otherness is both a new discovery and a reflection of something old" (p. 177). Korowai intercultural involvement of the recent era has very much had this quality. Yet what I have begun showing in this chapter, and will continue to show across this book, is that relations between Korowai and *other Korowai* also take place on "beaches" in Dening's sense. Korowai society is endogenously a "contact zone" (Pratt 1992: 4–7), a social environment of close interaction between people "previously separated by geographical and historical disjunctures," who hold different kinds of power over each other, and who are grappling with each other as cultural strangers. In the contemporary era, Korowai society is located *in* the very motion of people between forest and village and *in* the heterogeneity of evaluative and practical positions people take in relation to the contrast between forest and village space. So too in forest space alone, Korowai society is located in people's motions across a heterogeneous landscape and their disparities of position on that landscape.

CHAPTER 2

Pairing and Avoidance

An Otherness-Focused Approach to Social Ties

The Korowai understanding that social bonds are created around boundaries of otherness that are at once separative and connective is not limited to people's experience of space. This chapter looks at a widespread pattern in Korowai practices of categorizing entities as related generally: a pattern of otherness-focused pairing, in particular, pairing defined around avoidance. The pairs "owner" and "guest" and "human" and "demon" are examples of otherness-charged dyads that I have already touched on. Here I document the much wider prominence of pairs in Korowai categorizing practice by examining family resemblances across diverse areas of speech, interaction, and cosmology. Searching out pairs is only a first step toward addressing what *kind* of relation exists between paired elements. I argue that Korowai understand a pair to be less an assumed unit than a ratcheting into tensility of a problem of connection-and-disconnection. Pairs are means of asking what kind of relation can exist between paired elements. Much as Korowai geography is a landscape of relations across estrangement, so too a tendency of dyadic relations examined in this chapter is that they center on qualities of otherness between the paired elements. Often the relations are centrally defined by formal rules of avoidance. The linking of pairing and avoidance is a remarkably clear way in which Korowai make otherness the very basis of a relation.

This chapter also examines how pairs exist as practices of signification. Dyadic social relations are created through use or avoidance of words, through enactment or avoidance of modes of sensory contact, and through other expressive processes. I open a more explicitly semiotic side to the question of Korowai sensibilities about social relations by examining how people's distinctive approaches to social bonds are one and the same with their distinctive approaches to using signs.

PAIRING COMPOUNDS

One way in which two categories can be related is to be linked symmetrically and positively so as to create a more inclusive category. A site where such relations exist in Korowai life is a common pattern of compounding, in which speakers juxtapose two words to make a single word designating a larger entity the two paired constituents together make up or evoke. Examples are as follows:

bai-xajo	"bow and arrows"
gülun-walun	"night and day; ceaselessly, all the time"
gülap-sübab	"upstream and downstream; everywhere"
gol-lolol	"pork and shell or tooth valuables; payment media"
xul-melun	"guts and gall; thought"
lul-gelif	"eyes and nose; face"
menel-xamox	"maidens and widows; women of all ages"

Words of this type are rare in English. An example is *secretary-treasurer*. Linguists often call them "dvandva compounds," after their Sanskrit name, but I call them "pairing compounds," following Rumsey (2002: 278–80). They differ from other compounds in being based on coordination, not subordination. Rather than consist of a modifier and a head, a pairing compound consists of two symmetric complements. The compound's semantic and grammatical center is not in one element or the other but in the whole they add up to. The compounds are exocentric: their center is outside.

The two joined elements are often markedly different from each other. In *menel-xamox,* for example, young unmarried women and old widowed women stand together for women of all ages. The two categories have in common the prominent connotation "marriageable." Yet they also maximally contrast, in that they designate women at opposite extremes of adulthood. The elements' oppositeness and their complementarity as parts of a larger unit are two sides of a single relation.

Paradoxically, the compounds express a unitary category by building on a sharp contrast (cf. Munn 1986: 148).

Korowai use many pairing compounds referring to human social units. One pattern is to juxtapose clan names to form a larger grouping: Xaul and Nandup together are *xaul-nandup*, Dambol and Xawex together are *dambol-xawex*, and so on (van Enk and de Vries 1997: 19). The grouped clans are always neighbors who are conventionally recognized as unitary. They are sometimes spoken of as being the "same people" *(lelipanop)* and having the "same place." Paired clans might cooperate sometimes to sponsor feasts, site houses in the same clearing, or bail streams, but the pairings reflect only very indefinite trends of social association. Even single clans rarely act as a unitary group. The unity of paired clans is even more notional rather than practical. People emphasize this in underlining that pairings are a conventional *manner of speaking*: paired clans are routinely referred to using constructions of the form *xaul-nandup dəboxa* "Xaul-Nandup, as it has been said." Lumping is more common the farther people are from the land of the clans spoken about. On Dambol or Xawex land, for example, people rarely speak of these adjacent clans as a pair, but away from those lands speakers (including clanspeople themselves) commonly do so. Pairings are coarse-grained categories, appropriate when the needs to characterize people's identities are rough and long-distance. Clan pairing involves a principle of locating single entities by their position in two-part units. A single social element might be incomplete and unlocated until it is referred to as part of a pair.

Speakers also frequently juxtapose persons' names to make a compound designating the unit the persons together compose, such as *lefam-otifu* "Lefam and Otifu," or *xofim-yameap-manxa dayo* "the Dayo clan that has Xofim and Yameap." Usually it is spouses or same-sex siblings whose names are juxtaposed in this way. Here too speakers are more likely to construct these compounds when talking about persons geographically far from the conversation. They speak about paired persons as a way to call to view the broad social location of people and events they are referring to.

Speakers also commonly conjoin reciprocal kinship terms, to speak of the unit of two persons who stand in those relations. The most frequent compounds are

mom-sabül	"mother's brother and sister's son, uncle-nephew pair"
au-mopdol	"elder sister and younger sister, pair of sisters"

afe-mofexa	"elder brother and younger brother, pair of brothers"
yum-defol	"husband and wife, married couple"
lalum-bandaxol	"son-in-law and mother-in-law"

These words are used to refer to specific pairs of persons related in these ways, as well as to discuss the relation types in the abstract. The words are "dyadic kinship terms" in the sense of Merlan and Heath (1982: 107): "expression[s] of the type '(pair of) brothers' or 'father and child,' in which the kinship relationship is between the two referents internal to the kin expression."

Discussing similar terms used by Urapmin of Papua New Guinea, Robbins (2004: 300–303) argues that the terms' use exemplifies a relationalist understanding of personhood and social life. Urapmin take social relations between persons as basic and valuable, and they take individuals as derivative or less valuable. I follow Robbins, and the tradition of New Guinea ethnography shaped by Wagner (1974; 1981 [1975]) and Strathern (1988), in arguing that Korowai have strongly relationalist cultural sensibilities. Across a wide range of representations, Korowai portray persons as metonymic extrusions of social dyads. Dyadic ties are represented as basic, and persons are represented as pieces of dyads. The persons themselves are exocentric, or dyad-centered. Pairing compounds' popularity offers initial evidence of this tendency. In the formal structure of these compounds, each element's center lies outside itself in the overall dyadic unit, even as the dyadic unit is transparently composed of two distinct elements neither of which encompasses or subordinates the other.

Human social pairs are my main concern. Yet the grammatical continuity between pairing compounds signifying social relations and those signifying material, biological, spatial, or temporal entities underlines that people apply similar categorizing faculties to the world of human beings as they apply to the world of being generally. We can look to Korowai thought about nonhuman or quasi-human beings, as well as to practices of human pairing, for evidence of people's sensibilities about what it is to live socially.

DYAD-BASED PERSON REFERENCE

Compounds joining two kinship terms or two names refer to two persons. Ways Korowai refer to *single* persons also illustrate a tendency to understand persons as metonymic fragments of dyadic relations.

Although Korowai have proper names, speakers rarely call people by name in their presence. Even outside of people's earshot, referring to them by name is unusual. Speakers also dislike uttering their own names. Many persons' names are unknown to even their close relatives, due to lack of use. Name use portrays persons as being independent, valuable, and attention-worthy in themselves, a claim Korowai often shun. As one man put it, "People will mock us if we utter our names. They will hear the name and look at the person, wondering, 'Is that person good/beautiful?' and then they will see, no, the person is not good/beautiful *(manop)*. For that reason, we do not utter names." Instead, Korowai call each other by kinship terms and kinship-based expressions emphasizing people's location in social bonds. I turn properly to kin relations in the next chapter. At this point, I want to look at what can be called dyad-based forms of person reference, in which a kinship term is joined to a personal name. These expressions refer to one person via the detour of a kinship link with another person, whose name is used.

These dyad-based expressions are extremely common in Korowai discourse. The four most frequent patterns are to refer to a person through that person's relation with a child, wife, father, or mother. Referring to someone using his or her child's name is known in the anthropological literature as teknonymy. In Korowai speech, anyone who has a child can be referred to using the child's name, followed by kinship terms for "mother" or "father." For example, *wayap-ni* is "mother of Wayap," and *mbilam-ate* is "father of Mbilam." The other three Korowai patterns can be called uxorinyms, patronymics, and matronymics. Any married man can be referred to using the name of his wife, followed by the kinship term for "husband." For example, *mafem-um* is "husband of Mafem." People are also referred to using the name of their father, followed by kinship terms for "son" or "daughter": *wamil-abül* is "son of Wamil," and *xəle-lal* is "daughter of Xəle." Finally, anyone can be referred to by the name of his or her mother, followed by one of four terms meaning "first-born," "middle born," "last born," or "born of a remarriage, following childbearing and widowhood in a first marriage." If a woman named Abon marries a man and they have four children, the eldest is *abon-alop* "Abon's firstborn," the middle two are both *abon-alüpəxa* "Abon's middle born," and the youngest is *abon-xaja* "Abon's last born." If Abon's husband then dies and she marries some other man and has children with him, they are each called *abon-aibum* "Abon's widowhood-born." All these ways of designating persons are used in reference, in address, and vocatively. They can be used throughout the designated person's life and after death. The matronymic style is the most popular, followed by the teknonymic style. These dyadic person reference forms continue to make linguistic use of personal names, but not for signifying relationless individuals. Instead names themselves are made part of a relation.

Korowai use these expressions to refer to other persons, independently of a speaker's own kinship location and independently of whatever aspect of the referent's life is under discussion. The expressions are the basic, favored ways to designate persons as freestanding beings. Yet they do not describe persons as freestanding at all, but locate personal identity in dyadic kin ties. Speakers prefer to represent persons not as centers unto themselves but as metonymies of one another and as synecdoches of their dyadic relations, particularly their parental and spousal bonds.

Asked why they use dyad-based expressions, Korowai often say that calling someone by name is awkward (waxan "left"), whereas calling people by matronymics and the like is comfortable, elegant, or well matched (kül). People also say that through use, a matronymic expression "will become as though [the child's] own name." It is in fact common for a speaker to know someone's matronymic designation without knowing the person's name. The main reason people feel that this substitution of matronymic for personal name is good is that hearers will thereby know the person's maternity. As one woman put it, use of matronymics "is for saying, 'That is her son. That is her daughter.' Mentioning the child, [speakers] also say 'That is his/her mother. She is the one who bore him/her. That guy's mother is thus. That woman's son is thus.'" If persons are called by their own names, a hearer will be left wondering who their mothers are.

Matronymic expressions represent persons as based in dyads, but more precisely they represent persons as metonymic extensions of their relations with their birth mothers. The great popularity of matronymics is linked in speakers' explicit opinions to the special laboriousness and affective intensity of mothers' bonds with children, including the knowledge of what mothers endured gestating and birthing a child. One man, asked about the reason for using matronymics, linked their use to the anguish of birth events, through a contrast with the pathetic lack of suffering involved in men's contribution to a child's existence. "Men just play around, whereas women struggle enormously," he said. Here being born of a woman's body, and probably also raised by her, is highly valued as a bedrock of personhood.[1] The matronymics often draw attention to the identity of sibling sets and the fecundity of particular mothers, since the same woman's name is heard in the matronymic designations of multiple persons born of her body and since the matronymic expressions identify persons by their positions in a series of births. Geertz (1973), in a well-known account of teknonymic and birth order designations in Bali, interprets them as detemporalizing persons by inserting them in a closed, statically repeated set of positions. Korowai birth order matronymics in fact positively temporalize and historicize persons. The terms locate a person's identity in his or her ordinal position relative to other persons born earlier or later. People are who they are by virtue of their indexical, historical relation to a childbearing woman and their indexical, historical position in a sequence of siblings (though birth order itself does not have strong hierarchical associations). By calling a person by his or her mother's name and a birth order suffix, Korowai keep the identity of that person's mother constantly present to memory and discourse, even though the person's own body is separate from the mother's body and the birth event happened in a lost time, separate from the present. The popularity of matronymics is still more striking in view of the fact that people acquire clan membership patrilineally. The matronymics seem to be a way to emphasize strangeness in the constitution of persons: the designations say that people are not wholly what they are most taken to be in the clan system. It is common, in this vein, for people in conversation to identify themselves whimsically with a mother's clan rather than with what they and others know to be their actual group. For example, when some youths I was with once told a man jocularly that he was "a Nailop person," where Nailop is the name of the river where his clan place is located, the man denied this and said that he was actually an "Afium person," where Afium is the biggest stream in the vicinity of his mother's clan place. His playful denial was an oblique way to identify himself with his mother's clan rather than his own, even though the paternal territory is the one he actually owns and the paternal clan name is the one people normally link him to.

By using dyad-based expressions to say that personal identity lies foundationally in dyadic bonds, speakers also emphasize the value of kinship. In conversation Korowai tend to specify who persons are by describing their kin. In interviews and other contexts, my interlocutors routinely sought to locate a person by saying whom the person is married to, is a parent of, is a child of, and so forth. In a revealing idiom, speakers also routinely caution a relative against a stated intention to harm or seduce some other person by asserting tersely that the other person is "someone's child" (yaxo-mbam). The idiom states literally that the other person has parents but also, more generally, that the person is a vulnerable dependent, about whom other kin care very much. The idiom's force is to remind people that to impinge on another person's life is not something between oneself and that other person alone but also involves impinging on a whole nexus of social ties and investments centered on that person. A variation on this pattern came up tellingly in a brief interaction I had with a young boy in a house where I was living for a few days. I was moving to descend the house's unusually slender ladder pole, and the boy told me I was going to fall, as a way to urge me to be careful. In a would-be spirit of ironic fatalism, I replied, "Yes I'm going to fall, it's fine." In deep seriousness, the boy immediately countered, "You have your mother and father" *(gəniatemanxa)*. In other words, my well-being was not something I owed just to myself but also to my parents.

The constant, passing use of dyad-based person-referring forms does not carry a specific cautionary load, but people's use of these expressions does have the same more general effect of constantly underlining that every human is "someone's child." In these ways of speaking and thinking, persons are not free-floating. Before anything else, they are possessed, cared-for participants in close social relations.

JOKING AVOIDANCE PARTNERSHIPS

Another pattern through which Korowai represent individuals as pieces of dyads is the practice of two persons entering into a partnership of reciprocally calling each other by an idiosyncratic term that harks back to an event they experienced together.[2] For example, two youths call each other *nəwayo* "my Red-bellied Short-necked Turtle," commemorating when they shared a specimen of that small animal. Two women call each other *nəmbux* "my pitfall," based on having fallen together into a concealed hole. In each instance, the partners prefer the mildly humorous term of address and reference over kinship terms, teknonyms, and other usual ways of referring to people. Partners observe a formal rule against uttering each other's names. Avoidance stands out to Korowai as the crux of the special person reference pattern: They speak of the genre using the verb *laxa-* "avoid." To describe being involved in a person reference partnership with someone, a speaker says, "We are avoiding." Given the humorousness of the terms and the way they turn the serious subject of name avoidance into a joke, I refer to the relations as "joking avoidance partnerships," as well as just "avoidance partnerships," and I call words used in the partnerships "avoidance terms." A given person typically participates in between five and twenty partnerships, and most partnerships are lifelong. Speakers use these terms abundantly in routine conversation.

Avoidance terms are pragmatically hybrid between kinship terms and names. Speakers shape the genre as a kind of heteroglossic play on these other person reference forms. The main way in which avoidance terms resemble kinship terms is that use of an expression like "my Red-bellied Short-necked Turtle" to refer to someone involves another person as propositus, the perspectival subject who is the ground in relation to which a referent is specified. Danziger (2001: 29) sums up the propositus-dependent character of kinship terms with the statement that they "signify the relationship between a referent and a reciprocal, rather than simply specifying the referent itself" (see also Agha 2007: 346–47, 350–56). Korowai avoidance terms work the same way. Alongside the fact that people participate in partnerships in pairs, pairness is also obliquely signaled by the indexical organization of actual avoidance term use: the expression refers to one person, by way of who that referent is to someone else. Avoidance terms occur with possessive pronominal prefixes, parallel to the routine possessive prefixing of kinship terms. The terms are most frequently used with the first-person singular prefix ("my such and such"). Because of this, avoidance terms sound similar to kin terms, especially when they are used reciprocally in conversation by partners themselves. Korowai in some contexts quickly alternate between avoidance terms and kin terms, in ways that strongly construe the two as being the same.

The main way in which avoidance terms resemble names, meanwhile, is that the terms are specific to particular pairs of persons, as names are specific to individuals. Use of "my pitfall" and similar terms depends on knowing a conventional, idiosyncratic connection between a word and a pair. The word-to-person correspondence rests on a founding historical tie, similar to the kind of historical tie on which name use rests (Kripke 1980). Korowai are reflexively aware of this history-based aspect of names and avoidance terms. They seek to underscore the designations' historicity in their semantic content. Some personal names derive from events that occurred around the time the person was born. The boy Umon, or literally, "Uproar," is named after the controversy that arose when his older sister left her husband for another man around the time of the boy's birth. Many children are named after animals that their fathers were killing regularly at the time of the child's arrival. Like an avoidance term or kinship term, such names represent persons as metonymies of more basic dyadic social ties, and they represent name use as depending on little narratives of past events. Avoidance terms follow this pattern even more starkly. In them, the turning of events into identities is the entire logic of nomination. In normal naming, many people live their lives under the low-level pun of simultaneous conjunction and disjunction between a name's eponymous lexical meaning and the person to whom the names refers. (The artfulness of many nicknames cross-linguistically rests in this same ambiguity of being at once label and description.) Avoidance terms are even more elaborate pragmatic puns that hang on a threshold of taking the harking back relationship between term and past joint experience for a descriptive relationship between term and person (or term and relation). When Korowai call one another "my Red-bellied Short-necked Turtle," "my pitfall," and so on, they are speaking figuratively. The constant action of harking back draws the past event into the present, as memory and as a description of who the partner is. The little narrative of that event is the story of each partner's life and their social tie. Avoidance terms are thus a type of sign reflexively focused on the process of signification itself, including signification's conventions and possible confusions. The terms characterize persons and signification as centrally temporal and historical.

The popularity of avoidance partnerships again testifies to people's attraction to social pairs as units by which to understand the social world and everyone's positions in it. Part of the emphasis here, though, is that qualities of antipathy, avoidance, and transgression are central to paired persons' relation. Partnerships conjoin relatedness and estrangement by underlining that a bond is also a boundary. The range of terms by which partners call each other provides evidence of this otherness-focused quality of their bond.

Two-thirds of avoidance partnerships commemorate events of common ingestion. Usually, partners shared a single food body and now call each other by a noun denoting it: "my grub," "my kidney," "my banana," "my crayfish," and hundreds of other such terms, including many species of fish, frogs, lizards, birds, and so on. In each case the food body was broken in half, and each person ate a portion. Some moments later one person thought to utter an inaugural term usage, addressing the other as "my such and such." Another fraction of partnerships are based on deviant events of ingestion, such as "my turd water," from having drunk together from a contaminated pool; "my unripe," for having shared an unripe fruit; "my bile," for having eaten snake flesh contaminated with bile; and "my rotten," for having shared

rotten fish. Other partnerships recall other sorts of shared bodily transgressions or traumas, such as excretory mishaps, dirtiness, orificial
noises, skin punctures, lapses of locomotive control, and accidental
touches. Examples are "my cough," for coughing at the same time; "my
cassowary turds," for having stepped in this common hazard; "my hand
grabbing," for having gripped each other; "my falling," for having fallen
down together; "my forehead," for having banged heads; "my ash," for
having slept on a hearth together; "my outdoor sleeping," for having
slept outside together when shelters were too crowded; and "my ant,"
for having been bitten by ants together. Finally, a fraction of terms recall
shared stigmata, shared experiences of defamation, or other shared conditions of abasement. Examples are "my bald head" and "my person
without sago." Either the two persons spontaneously deprecated themselves while conversing together, or other people put them down. The
two then adopted the disparaging remarks as their common emblem.

Across all the variations, in each case the two persons went through
an event in which they were identified with each other. As one interviewee explained to me, "They think, 'We were together/identical *(lelip)*,
so let's call each other thusly.'" In identifying persons as parts of dyads,
the partnerships also identify persons with mildly transgressive and
grotesque intrusions or protuberances at bodily surfaces. Partners are
linked through images of spontaneity, contingency, penetration, ingestion, unboundedness, multiplicity, unintended closeness, loss of control,
and separation from collective ideals of propriety or beauty. Terms
based on transgressive bodily events such as "falling down" recall
impingements or irruptions at the borders of bodily being, when actors
experienced the uncertainty and hazards of their own margins. Their
sense of self-possession and self-determination was uncannily suspended or thrown into doubt by the bodily event and by the presence of
another person undergoing the same impingement at the same moment.
Even terms commemorating an event of food sharing are lightly
grotesque. They turn common ingestion of a single object into a figure
of the eaters' reciprocal identification, posing social interaction with
another person as like consuming food. Many founding events are accidents in time, emphasizing lack of control or rational foreknowledge.
The genre makes boundaries of bodily life into the content of who people are to each other. Avoidance terms are a playful and complexly
reflexive engagement with the idea of a bond between two people and
with the idea of signifying such a bond. Through lightly transgressive
use of language, persons are represented not only as parts of dyads but

also as effects and signs of past events. A person circulates as the detached part of a thing or event—as "turtle," as "falling," as "ash," and so on. Through these terms, speakers give attention to experiences of uncanny otherness within a bond of identity by commemorating having been beside themelves with clumsiness, ugliness, laughter, commensality, or some other small breach of boundaries.

Avoidance itself is another way in which partners mark their relational otherness. By avoiding each other's names, partners signal they are mutually separate and are not supposed to intrude on each other's being, particularly each other's possession of a name. They also signal that they are mutually connected *by* this obligation not to intrude, based on an underlying identification that creates the need for avoidance in the first place. The humorous genre conjoins contradictory relational qualities. Name avoidance is a way in which partners stay out of contact, making themselves reciprocally strange. Yet this avoidance commemorates and reproduces close mutual identification. The partnership genre highlights also that boundaries between persons and boundaries of sign use are in question together. Strange intimacy between two persons is signified by bending rules of more conventional language use, such as the use of names or kinship terms.

In many other areas of Korowai life, avoidance is a positive social practice, creating definite qualities and intensities of social connection. In the special partnerships discussed here, avoidance is parodic of more serious avoidance work. The overall similarities between joking avoidance terms and kinship terms suggest that Korowai see intimacies and identifications of kinship too as being transgressively strange, like the accidents and contingent historical events commemorated in avoidance partnerships. In their avoidance component, though, the joking partnerships are modeled after a more specific kin relation: links between affines, especially between mother-in-law and son-in-law. I turn now to that relation, to deepen the point that Korowai understand avoidance as creating bonds through marking two people as mutually separate and strange.

MOTHER-IN-LAW AND SON-IN-LAW

The relation designated by the compound *lalum-bandaxol* "son-in-law and mother-in-law" is an especially clear example of a bond built around estrangement. Korowai give this relation particular attention, amid the wider sweep of social life. People often draw figurative comparisons to the bond of mother-in-law and son-in-law when commenting on other relations. The bond exemplifies wider tendencies of Korowai thought about how persons can be mutually involved.

Interaction between all affinal relatives is typically edgy, but the tie between mother-in-law and son-in-law is the most marked. This markedness is registered in rules of sensory avoidance. Mother-in-law and son-in-law avoid catching sight of each other, speaking of each other in the singular, touching each other, sharing food, and uttering each other's names. Or rather, they *might* avoid these actions. Different pairs avoid each other with varying degrees of vigilance. Sight avoidance is more marked than other avoidances and is upheld by the fewest pairs. Korowai group the avoidance forms together as a relational practice under the verb *laxa-* "avoid," the same word used to speak of joking avoidance partnerships. The main word for "son-in-law" is *lal-um* (lit., "daughter's husband"), but women also frequently call their sons-in-law by the alternative term *nəlaxap* "my avoid." Avoidance practices are emblematic of the pair's overall relation.

Avoidance is hard work. Mothers-in-law and sons-in-law are typically in each other's presence a lot, because a married couple and the wife's parents visit each other regularly, if they do not live in the same house. Also, a married man usually has several mothers-in-law besides the woman who gave birth to his wife, because there are many women his wife categorizes as close mothers. For an avoiding pair to stay out of each other's sight requires a great deal of vigilance. A mother-in-law and son-in-law routinely call out warnings when they know they will be passing by each other, so that the other person will turn away or move behind a barrier. The middle wall that runs the length of most houses, helping pairs stay out of each other's vision, is the very image of the relation. Many times when I introduced the topic of mother-in-law bonds in interviews, my interlocutors would reach out to a physically present wall and say, "That is a matter of having a wall, like this." A man who for his whole married life has built middle walls in his houses might abruptly leave off the work and inconvenience of installing them in new houses after his mother-in-law's death.

Amid day-to-day food traffic, an avoiding pair and their coresidents carefully monitor who is eating what, so that the two do not eat from the same object. This practice of *not* sharing stands out against a strong Korowai understanding that people in each other's presence should share their food. To avoid bodily contact, a mother-in-law and son-in-law refrain from handing objects to one another or from touching each other's sleeping panels and wooden pillows. To avoid speaking of each other in the singular, avoiders call each other by plural pronouns and plural verb inflections, as well as the euphemistic plural expression "my people."[3] They also routinely refer to each other by adding a plural suffix to teknonyms and similar referring expressions. Since many people's names have independent meaning, avoiders often do elaborate work of circumlocution to keep from saying each other's names. For example, someone whose mother-in-law or son-in-law is named *dufol* "banana" might substitute the name of a differently named subtype of banana to speak of bananas in general, and a person whose in-law is named *manda* "no" might substitute *mafem* "none" in statements of denial.

Bundling these modes of avoidance together in the conduct of a single relation implies that Korowai understand looking at someone, referring to someone in the singular, touching someone, sharing food with someone, and saying someone's name as analogous and reciprocally linked. What the modes of interaction have in common is that they are understood as forms of touchlike contact, in which persons impinge intimately on each other. Sight, singular reference, touch, commensality, and name utterance stand as concrete images of a more abstract, crosscutting problematic of bodily and personal impingement. Support for this can be found in the sanction of the prohibition on name utterance. Korowai say that someone who utters an affine's name will have his or her feet sliced open by sharp sticks on forest paths, be bitten or stung by animals, be scratched by thorns, or be cut and bruised in falls. The skin-puncturing form of these punishments suggests that the crime of name utterance is understood as a matter of touching the affine too sharply. Korowai list the same misfortunes when saying the sanction against name utterance in joking avoidance partnerships (of the kind discussed in the previous section). In addition to acknowledging the identity of sanction across the two types of avoidance relations, some people say that joking avoidance partnerships "imitate" *(dadamo-)* or are "like" *(-ülop)* affinal avoidance: joking avoidance partnerships are recognized to be figurative of affinal kin relations. Both types of avoidance relation construe name use as invasive touch, akin to bodily injury.

Avoidance practices represent and create a quality of social relation. Through sensory avoidance, a pair make separateness into a positive social connection. In the bodily sensorium, mother-in-law and son-in-law are distant and out of touch. Each person's avoidance of singular number makes the other greater than one person, and less definite than a single object of perception. The avoidance practices define a pair as mutually strange. They are not "strange" in the sense of socially unacquainted or distant but rather in a sense closer to Freud's notion of the uncanny, an experience of visceral unfamiliarity in that which is nearby and familiar (1955 [1919]: 241, 245), or something closer still to the Daribi idea that "to look at one's mother-in-law is like looking at the sun" (Wagner 1967: 173). A common Korowai statement about why mothers-in-law and sons-in-law practice avoidance is that they are mutually "scared, panicked, uncomfortable" *(xonio, golo)*. Yet erasing an affinal counterpart as an object of perceptual contact does not erase that person as an interactant. Rather, avoidance is a form of intense reciprocal engagement. A pair's practices of separation brusquely intrude on everything else in a social scene. Other activities they undertake are dominated by their vigilance in staying out of each other's sight. The hard work of avoidance makes a bond "univocal," in the sense of Merlan (1997), who states of avoiding pairs in some Aboriginal Australian communities that "avoidance practices emphasize one aspect of their potentially multiple social relations as having overriding determination of their conduct towards each other" (106), such that "a man in his mother-in-law's presence finds it difficult to behave towards her in any way other than as her son-in-law" (108). Sensory interactions signal the depth and implacability of two people's relation as mother-in-law and son-in-law, across the layers of each person's bodily field from eyes to stomach. When they are in each other's vicinity, the affinal relation surrounds each of them as an intangible, invisible, and transcendent presence.

People's attention to upholding avoidance expresses the importance of mother-in-law relations. The opposite of "avoiding" *(laxa-)* is to be "indiscriminate, heedless" *(ndamblüm)*. Avoidance is a practice of discretion and carefulness toward a social situation. In each other's presence, two avoiders are defined by their dyadic bond and by absorption with their mutual strangeness. What Harrison (1993a: 148) says of a different scale of Melanesian social process (whole societies' concern with having architectural and religious styles that distinguish them from neighbors) also rings true of Korowai mother-in-law avoidance at the level of personal interaction: "in these processes of mutual differentiation, in the deliberate mutual heightening of each other's 'otherness,' there was the creation of a particular kind of value." Mother-in-law and son-in-law avoidance practices deepen people's mutual connections through intense attention to the separations between them.

The use of avoidance as a method of relation making runs through Korowai pairing forms more widely. For example, alongside the grouping of clans into positive pairs, there is a less prominent institution in which specific clans are paired negatively. These relations are described by the expression *ayulanop* "taboo people." Taboo people's lands always lie separately, and the clans do not have any other basis of connection that would single them out as mutually relevant. Members of clans who are reciprocally taboo people are supposed to avoid marrying each other, killing each other, killing each other's animals, entering each other's houses, sharing food with each other, coming into contact with each other's streams, eating fish from each other's streams, and entering each other's feast longhouses. Some taboo people feel they should sit back-to-back rather than face-to-face when in each other's presence, much as mother-in-law and son-in-law pairs do. When asked to explain these negative relations, Korowai assert that a demiurgic creator said that specific clans should be paired this way, or they say that if taboo people interact indiscriminately, then they will fall sick. This negative pairing of clans is typical of an overall tendency to conjoin pairing and avoidance at all different levels of social categorization.

Concerning the specific topic of mother-in-law avoidance, I have so far discussed pairs' interactional avoidance, without asking how interactional patterns articulate with the larger structural definition of the persons' relation. But in fact these practices of interactional avoidance have important political dimensions. A relation between mother-in-law and son-in-law is linked to other social bonds, including that between husband and wife. I address these aspects of mother-in-law avoidance in chapter 5. Suffice it to say now that qualities of standoffishness and mutual preoccupation created by interactional avoidance are closely tied to the wider, longer properties of the in-law tie. This is a bond defined by the mutual social otherness of two parties, by the woman's accommodation of the man's intrusion into her relation with her daughter, and by the man's obligation to acknowledge his mother-in-law's accommodation and the uncertainty of whether he will do so.

The qualities of connection created by mother-in-law avoidance in the space of bodily interaction resemble those created by place ownership in the space of the geographic landscape. Landownership supports a sensibility of geographic encounter, in which people seek relations with strangers but also question the certainty of those relations. So too affinal avoidance supports a sensibility of face-to-face encounter in which people experience themselves as bound to marked, fearful strangers. A striking aspect of mother-in-law avoidance is that it is explicitly contingent.

The avoidance imperatives are so difficult that it is impossible to carry them out perfectly. People have conventional understandings of what would happen if someone accidentally broke the avoidance rules, and they have ritual procedures for undoing the harm of a violation. Occasionally a mother-in-law breaks the rules intentionally, by looking at her son-in-law or saying his name, in order to express dissatisfaction with his actions. Often avoiders deliberately decide what degree of vigilance to apply to their relation, based on the perceived moral state of their relationship more generally. Avoidance imperatives are upheld more thoroughly when the relation is morally positive and less thoroughly when the relation is morally failing (Stasch 2003b: 330–33; chapter 5 below). Interactional avoidance, like landownership and travel across ownership margins, is organized as a questioning exploration of how people stand to each other.

THE UNDERLYING IDENTITIES OF THINGS

The practices of linguistic representation discussed so far begin to show how closely Korowai sensibilities about social relations are tied to sensibilities about signification. I can make this point still clearer by briefly describing a special register of speech known by the metalinguistic term *xoxulop* "transgressive substitute designation." In this register a substitutive term having independent semantic content is used to speak of an object in place of its normal designation. For example, the transgressive substitutive term for dogs is "death adder," and the substitute for pigs is "cassowary." There are several hundred additional conventional pairings in the register. Speakers often discuss the pairings using the frame, "X, its *xoxulop* is Y."

What is most important to Korowai about these lexical correspondences is that a substitute term bears a fundamental, obscure relation to the referent it can designate, such that it should not be uttered in that referent's presence, or the referent will be harmed. For example, a dog should not hear the word *lax* "death adder," or it will die. Some pairings are motivated by the notion that the referent originates from its *xoxulop*. People also often understand the substitutions to hark back to a time when a creator conferred *xoxulop* correspondences and avoidance imperatives or when a population of earlier people spoke of objects by the transgressive substitute terms but then decided those designations should be hidden. In these respects *xoxulop* correspondences resemble the European idea of Adamic language (Eco 1995), or the popular American ideology that etymological origins reveal demystifying truths behind the surfaces of contemporary semantics. The word *xoxulop* itself is usually felt by speakers not to have independent meaning, but people sometimes gloss it as "long ago name" (*mülxa yəfi;* Ind. nama lama). Paradoxically, transgressive substitute terms express a kind of deep cosmological truth that is not supposed to be expressed. The terms exist to be avoided, or to be used deliberately in acts of damaging transgression of the avoidance imperative.

There are strong figurative connections between transgressive substitute terms and their referents. Commonly, pairings are based on iconicities of shape, texture, appearance, feeling, sound, or other perceptual quality. Dogs and death adders are both fierce fanged killers. Pigs and cassowaries are together the largest and most anthropomorphized terrestrial animals in the environment. Other examples illustrate this emphasis on perceptual analogy.

Referent	Substitute Category *(xoxulop)*
yafin "notched ladder pole"	*anol lungul* "snake vertebrae"
ale p "canoe"	*semail* "crocodile"
fendon "barkcloth"	*yemül xal* "bat skin"
depon "tobacco"	*xofua* " bird species with bitter flesh"
waxi "bamboo"	*baliam* "sugarcane"
ati "bow"	*doxul* "freshwater longtom" (slender fish)
kembaxi "species of biting ant"	*melil üax* "ember"
melil "fire"	*bünxa* "blood"
lup "sun"	*waxol* "moon"
waxol "moon"	*bilal* "Nassa shells" (white and buttonlike)

Perceived likeness is probably present latently in nearly all correspondences. To Korowai, the iconicities are so basic to the pairings that speakers usually do not comment on them, except in asserting the substitutions as such. Interlocutors often agreed to my leading suggestions that a certain category is the substitute term for another "because they are similar [*kül*]." But it would be closer to people's understandings to put it the other way around: items are similar because of the *xoxulop* relation. The iconic commonalities are evidence and expression of underlying identity of being.

The substitutions explore iconicity as a relation cross-cutting the heterogeneity of phenomenal things and cross-cutting those things' normal mapping into different categories. Yet similarity here is tightly conjoined with disparity. Iconicity is a shock, running at right angles to paired terms' classificatory strangeness to each other, in normal taxonomic discourse and perception. Pairings are studies in uncanniness in the categorial ordering of people's life-world: they spotlight points of intersection where certain categories are at once mutually strange and mutually familiar. Classificatory uncanniness is most vividly underlined in correspondences that cross the boundary between animal and nonanimal, such as "crocodile" for canoe and numerous similar pairs describing vegetal objects in animal terms. The main point I draw from this pattern of conjoined iconicity and strangeness is that in positing *xoxulop* pairings, speakers do not merely take a more elaborate classificatory look at objects external to themselves. Through pairings, people problematize classification itself and express uncertainty about human classifiers' own categorial position and integrity.

That correspondences explore categorial uncanniness in which speaking subjects are themselves implicated is especially clear in pairings that are overtly grotesque. Alongside the focus on animality already touched on, common grotesque motifs in pairings are bodily wastes, separated body parts, sexuality and reproduction, painful impingements at the body's surface, decomposition, creeping or wiggling invertebrates, death, and death-causing agents. The substitute term for "rattan" is "human intestine," the substitute term for "steel ax" is "human shoulder blade," the substitute term for "dog canine necklace" is "maggots," and so forth. Grotesque pairings portray the close presence to bodily being of what is strange to it and what negates it. Besides highlighting that two items are at once mutually strange and similar, grotesque identification of the two items implicates human beings' categorial boundaries and dissolution. Many body-part *xoxulop* identities evoke the present immanence of past cosmogonic events. One set of correspondences, for example, involves parts of a beast named Faül, whose body a demiurge butchered to make the physical elements of the current creation. The substitute term for "earth" is "chest of Faül," the substitute term for "mud" is "fat of Faül," the substitute term for nylon rope is "intestine of Faül," and so on. Often the objects that attract *xoxulop* interpretations, or the underlying identities attributed to mundane objects, are ones that themselves stand out as uncanny in shape, coloration, repulsiveness, dangerousness, technological foreignness, or distance from human experience. The pairings are a meditation on many objects' and categories' refractoriness to simple, seamless cultural encompassment.

A focus on alterity in the relation between paired items is also clear in correspondences between mirror opposites. Most pairings are asymmetric: one category is the transgressive substitute for another, but not the reverse. In a few pairings, though, each category is the transgressive substitute for the other. Numerous fish species are paired reciprocally with counterpart species of birds, supported by perceived similarities of coloration, size, or overall morphological and behavioral impression. These correspondences emphasize that being changes with place. What something looks like depends on where it is, at the periphery of a human center. Humans in a central terrestrial habitat look downward and upward at two interchangeable extremes: an aquatic habitat and morphology and a treetop habitat and morphology.

Another set of three symmetric pairings does something similar at the level of regional geography. The following are each other's mutual transgressive substitutes: *nailop* "Ndeiram Kabur River" and *bafe* "Eilanden River"; *xofojap* "Xofojap people" and *aim* "Kombai people"; and *kolufo* "upstream people" and *banam* "Citak people" (map 2). Here the question of otherness-focused semiotic pairing intersects with the geography of perspective and otherness discussed in the previous chapter.

Pairing of the northern and southern main rivers as each other's *xoxulop* is symptomatic of these waterways' prominence in people's practices of orienting themselves in the world. The rivers are major thresholds of travel. Within wider Korowai patterns of constant stream-based spatial categorization, the transgressive substitute relation between the two largest rivers specifically emphasizes that they go together as a system. Even as the two waterways are opposites, they are also each other's covert identities. Some people think it is taboo for anyone to eat fish from both rivers or their tributaries on the same day, lest the eater's rectum "fall out." This restriction is taken as a sequitur of the rivers' transgressive identification: the human body should maintain the separateness of the streams. Even more strongly than the correspondence thematizes antipathy, though, it suggests that the two rivers and their locations are interchangeable with each other. The northern waterway is the southern one, and the southern is the northern. Even a physical body of water is not self-defining but relational. Each waterway is defined by its intimate alterity to a counterpart.

Ethnonymic substitutions do in categorization of humans what the river substitution does in categorization of streams: they reverse geo-

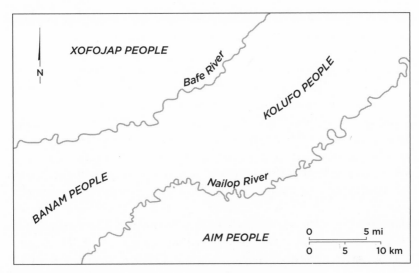

Map 2. The geography of rivers and ethnolinguistic groupings.

graphic poles. People of northern lands are the hidden identity of people of southern lands, and vice versa; people of downstream lands are the hidden identity of people of upstream lands, and vice versa. Korowai often mention the river pairing and the ethnonymic pairings in the same breath, as sequiturs to each other. Identification of northern Xofojap and southern Aim people as each other's underlying transgressive substitutes is closely allied to the substitutive relation between the Eilanden and Ndeiram Kabur Rivers, because the rivers are also roughly where Korowai landownership ends and those other ethnolinguistic groups' ownership begins. As a sequitur of the reciprocal transgressive identification of Kombai and Xofojap people, Korowai say it is taboo for those people to marry each other. Here too the link between paired items is a volatile identity-based antipathy, or antipathy-based identity. This relation in turn is based on paired items' respective positions of strangeness relative to speaking humans' central place of belonging. The margins' reciprocal iconicity lies in a shared quality of bounding otherness. They sit on the edges of the Korowai speech community's own position, strange to speakers but there as attention-holding presences. I take this focus on the interchangeability of surrounding margins as further support for my main argument about the *xoxulop* register in general. Substitutions dwell on unexpected similarities cross-cutting the normal categorial distinctness of parts of people's world. Specifically, they dwell on similarities that, in their uncanniness, draw categorizing subjects' own position into play, as part of what is in question in application of categories to objects. Through knowledge of transgressive substitutions that reverse geography or reverse animal habitat, speakers express a situation of being in relations of close strangeness with what is around them. Absorbed by the otherness of what is on their peripheries, humans do not know those peripheral presences as absolute and stable entities but rather as relative ones, the margins of humans' own perspectival location.

The uncanny content of many *xoxulop* pairings aligns with the sinister, damaging stakes of *xoxulop* utterance in a cultural valuing of experiences of shock. As I noted earlier, to Korówai, the most prominent fact about the register is that uttering *xoxulop* terms near their referents damages them. The moral imperative not to utter *xoxulop* words in the presence of their referents raises a constant twofold possibility of compliance or transgression. People sometimes define the register by saying that the substitute terms are "for wrecking" their objects (*lembutelonxalxe;* lit., "for making bad"). And, in fact, speakers regularly utter transgressive terms intentionally, to spite referents they are mad at. Someone might yell "death adder" at a dog that is getting in the way, or say the *xoxulop* of arrows when trying to heal a person with an arrowhead in his or her body.

Cautiously repressed or spitefully exclaimed, *xoxulop* relations rest on a notion that behind appearances and routine lexical semantics there is a more fundamental mode of nouns' direct impingement on the integrity and stability of worldly things. To utter an object's *xoxulop* in its presence is to present the object with a figurative truth more foundational than appearance, damaging its ability to remain what it seems. This is a more extreme version of the idea that language is a form of contact that has also been evident in mother-in-law avoidance practices and in joking avoidance partnerships. Like other pairing forms discussed in this chapter, the transgressive register describes a broadly exocentric model of being, according to which entities are not self-same but depend for their existence on their close, problematic relation to strange counterparts.

To people for whom it exists, a sign relation is itself a kind of pairing: one thing evokes something else. In many areas Korowai attend to the disparity between signifiers and what they signify as much as to their identity. This focus on otherness in signs intertwines with the focus on otherness in social bonds and personal being. The *xoxulop* register is a case in point. The densely metalinguistic register makes one semiotic code—normal vocabulary and its application—the subject of another semiotic comment: there is another code behind the apparent code, more truthful than it. It is *really* "crocodile," not "canoe," that means canoe. But the metalinguistic force here is also a bending of what a relation of "meaning" is to begin with. "Crocodile" *destroys* what it means; to represent is to damage. So too at the level of a speaker's overall actions of uttering words in context, someone who says "crocodile" around a canoe is commenting metasemiotically on his or her situation of semiotic action, expressing such understandings as "I can bend or break the rules," "I am discontent with language and apparent categories of perception," or "My cognitive and communicative situation is not seamlessly coherent but conflicted."

LIVING PERSONS AND DEAD PREDECESSORS

Individuals also have underlying *xoxulop* identities. This follows from a model of human genesis according to which a baby comes into existence as a reincarnation of a person who died before it was born. An infant's prior identity is determined by a spirit medium a month or so after birth. Children are sometimes identified with a deceased same-sex grandparent, but any same-sex person, whether a relative or not, can be recognized as an infant's predecessor. Throughout a person's life everyone else is supposed to avoid uttering the names of the predecessor in the person's presence, lest hearing the reincarnation identity shock, harm, or kill that person. Korowai call these avoided terms a person's *xoxulop*, as well as a person's "avoided" *(laxap)* or the person's "in his/her hearing" *(daibotop)*. These last two designations underline that the identities exist negatively, as sensitive orientations of surrounding speakers toward someone who is not supposed to hear the words. Even more commonly, Korowai speak of a reincarnation identity as a person's "hidden name" *(xondum fi)*.

The reincarnation model motivates a lot of locality-specific word avoidance. Whole households adjust their speech to protect certain persons. For example, one family I stayed with used *lul sa-* "throw eyes" in place of the normal verb *imo-* "see," because a man among them had *imon* "seeing" as his *xoxulop*.[4] Yet here too an avoidance rule raises the possibility of intentional transgression. Close kin sometimes maliciously call out each other's reincarnation identities while fighting. In a characteristic turn of expression, people told me that one mother-daughter pair "habitually say each other's *xoxulop*," as an elliptical way of saying they have a bad relationship.

People's notions of how identities pass from predecessor to successor are loose. In various other contexts Korowai speak of several components or phases of a person's existence, including a "soul, doppelgänger, image, shadow" *(map)*, a "body, corpse" *(loxul)*, an "after-death demon" *(laleo)*, and a "consciousness" (*lulxup;* syn. *yanop xajan* "true person"). When discussing reincarnation, though, people usually do not find it relevant to specify a component of personal identity that circulates. The most common way people discuss the model is by saying, of an earlier person, that he or she "grows" *(melu-)* in the belly of a pregnant woman, with the pronoun *yu* "he, she" serving as a sufficient description of whatever it is that passes from one person to the next. What Korowai care about is that the identity that circulates bears an ambivalent relation to the successor as a conscious, living actor. The circulating identity is foreign and dangerous to that person, such that the living person needs to remain ignorant of it. Besides name avoidance, a small indication of the reincarnation identity's foreignness is that close kin to the predecessor often avoid calling the successor by any kinship term at all in that successor's presence. Rather, they call the person *nəyaniyanop* "my stranger." In this usage, speakers respond to knowledge of a person's close identity with the speaker's own deceased intimate kin by adopting a strained artifice of portraying the person and the underlying identity as mutually alien.

The reincarnation model is perhaps the starkest instance of the overall pattern of dyad-centered personhood, because the model states that a person *is* his or her relation with another, the predecessor. Yet the reincarnation model also starkly underlines the otherness-focused character of dyadic bonds. The reincarnation model exists not primarily as a topic of theoretical discourse but as a spur to practical efforts to keep track of others' hidden names and carefully avoid them. The person whose identity a "hidden name" represents is also the person who is not supposed to know about it. Here as in the *xoxulop* register generally, a pair is a substitution and a negation. Paired terms are in a relation of simultaneous identity and antipathy. This blending of connection and repulsion is a common feature of Korowai dyadic relations. Reincarnation relationships, and *xoxulop* correspondences generally, suggest an understanding of being in which identity rests in structures of deferral and displacement. Beings and objects need to be separated from representations of their origins and their actual constitution, which lie somewhere else than their apparent character. A hidden name presents a subject with the trace of his or her own historical, social genesis, such that the play of identification and repression in people's practice of the hidden names model is also a play with an event-focused, historicizing definition of what people are. People exist as the effects of events they know only obliquely and partially.

A COSMOS OF VISIBLE SIDE AND INVISIBLE SIDE

The last pairing form I want to sketch in this chapter is the notion that the world of everyday perception exists adjacent to a counterpart world, inhabited by a population of invisible people. Korowai evoke the existence of the paired worlds in diverse contexts. For example, the model plays into another detail of the human reincarnation process, namely, that circulation of personal identities from predecessor to successor also involves passage between visible and invisible "sides" (-pe) or "territories" (bolüp). When a visible person dies, he or she is reborn as a baby on the invisible side. Later, after dying on that side, the person is reborn on the visible side as a successor to the earlier visible person.

Korowai emphasize the simultaneous closeness and antipathy between the two worlds. This emphasis can be appreciated from the terms by which invisible people are designated. One set of expressions for them all mean "fence people" (lenulanop, manianop, bajoanop), based on the notion that those people exist on the other side of a perceptual barrier from living humans. Another synonym is "wotop people," where wotop are the dangerous sites on clan land discussed in the previous chapter. Invisible people are thought to live at these taboo sites on the land. They are sometimes said to be survivors of an earlier world's apocalyptic destruction by the creator and to have fled into hiding in the taboo sites out of fear and shyness. The populations of visible and invisible people stand in a kind of avoidance relation. When landowners offer food sacrifices to wotop people or otherwise try to persuade them not to cause illness, a standard request they make is for the invisible people to "turn their backside" (banun lailo-) to the living, much as mothers-in-laws and sons-in-laws mutually turn their backs. A basic premise of the model is that Korowai would die if they caught sight of invisible people, and the world would end if the two populations were united.

Many times when I asked about the invisible "side," people invoked the image of one tree felled across the top of another, held out their arms one across the other, and described the two worlds as "reciprocally across each other's back" (xoloxolo daintax). These images emphasize that the two sides are close but askance. There is no transparent perceptual or social channel between them.[5] The two worlds are also separated by a barrier of epistemological oblivion: it is a feature of the reincarnation model that the identities who pass between worlds forget everything about their lives on the other side. Another term for invisible people is *xaüpanop* "underneath people," also based on the idea that the visible human world lies across the invisible one. There is a general figurative relation between the place of invisible people and Korowai experience of vertical space. People often say that the invisible people inhabit the treetops and streams of the perceptible world, and they sometimes identify invisible people with birds and fish. (This recalls the relation of transgressive identification between birds and fish, thematizing those animals' common position on the peripheries of human habitat.) Invisible people are also referred to as *xenanop* "angry people," further emphasizing their foreign, malign character. They are emotionally alien, in addition to being visually and socially separate. The great variety of epithets for invisible people itself reflects their foreignness. Their world is ripe for creative, oblique evocation because, by definition, it is not transparently knowable.

This idea of coexisting, analogous worlds separated by a boundary of perspectival inversion also informs some people's representations of the two populations of people as constantly undergoing parallel but opposite experiences. One correspondence is that when visible people experience drought, invisible people experience flood, and vice versa. Other correspondences focus on events of consumption and involve iconicity-based pairings of animals and vegetals, again reminiscent of *xoxulop* substitutions: when one population is perceiving or eating taro, the other side is perceiving or eating a crowned pigeon; when one side has possession of a sago ball, the other side has possession of a cuscus or other marsupial; and so on.

Korowai do not generally ask what invisible people and their world look like or how they live. To have such knowledge would be to court death. What people do emphasize is the perspectival relation between the two populations. To the invisible people, living Korowai and their side are invisible people, and the invisible people themselves are visible humans (cf. Schieffelin 1976; Viveiros de Castro 2001: 42 n. 23). People say this explicitly in using the sight-focused terms "visible" *(xəleptax)* and "invisible" *(xondum)* and in statements like "we are fence people to them." But the perspectivism is also signaled in the most common terms of all by which the two populations are referred to, which I have not yet mentioned. "Invisible people" are *xananop*, and "visible people" are *jananop*. The element *anop* here again means "people," but the elements *xan* and *jan* do not directly signify visibility. Rather, they are spatial shifters, like the categories "upstream" and "downstream." When I first learned these words, I thought one meant "inside" and the other meant "outside," because people used them to speak of objects being inside or outside a container. However, I was initially confused about which term had which meaning. It turned out that the words do not have fixed meanings on this dimension but rather are shifters. The word used to characterize an object as "inside" or "outside" of some containing boundary depends not only on where the object is but also on the location of the people talking. The category *xan* means "on the other side of a containing boundary from the talkers," and the category *jan* means "on this side of a containing boundary from the talkers." What is *xan* from one position is *jan* from the other, and vice versa. When talkers are sitting outside a house, they speak of an object outside the house (like them) as *jan*, not *xan*. Sitting inside a house, they speak of the same house-external object as *xan*, not *jan*.[6]

Korowai have a metalinguistic idiom by which they describe perspectival, shifting categorizations of this kind. The expression is *fɔxa di fɔxa di*, meaning "one says and another says," "it's said one way and it's said another way," or, loosely, "one speaks, acts, or experiences one way and a counterpart speaks, acts, or experiences a reverse way." The cosmological imagery of two coexisting, reciprocally invisible sides is typical of the Korowai emphasis on the perspective-based character of worldly existence generally and of the understanding that to live in a perspectival position is also to be surrounded and engaged by alien social others. Remarkably, the cosmological imagery of mutually exterior populations is vested in a pair of high-frequency spatial terms, *xan* and *jan*, that are themselves a phonological minimal pair. A small difference of sound form anchors a whole structure of opposed beings' reciprocal involvement as perspective and periphery: totally at odds with each other but also intimately close and similar.

OTHERNESS AS A RELATION

The pairing forms surveyed in this chapter are an eclectic mix. Yet I hope that juxtaposing them here has made apparent one main pattern of continuities across them, which I now sum up in closing.

Pairing is a vacuously universal form of categorization.[7] Therefore, beyond underlining that pairing is a characteristic Korowai mode of relation making, I have sought more specifically to make clear the *kinds* of relations, persons, and social worlds that are created through Korowai practices of pairing. The striking pattern in these materials amounts to an otherness-focused culture of personhood, social relations, and being. In practices of dyad-based person reference, mother-in-law avoidance, and the divining and avoidance of reincarnation identities, Korowai locate persons' foundations outside themselves, in their links to others. Use of pairing compounds, avoidance of *xoxulop* terms around their referents, and talk of the existence of "invisible people" apply the same pattern beyond humanity.

The emphasis on persons' ontological embeddedness in pairs does not portray pairs as self-standing atoms out of which larger relational complexes of the social world are built. For example, a mother-in-law and son-in-law's close involvement is part of a larger context of marriage and affinity. Rather than complete, stable totalities unto themselves, pairing forms are angles on wider processes of life. They are sharply drawn scenes where problems of "relation" are reflexively staged, commented on, and shaped.

Paired items' relations to each other are complex intermeshings of absence and presence. Matronymics locate the ground of a person's being outside his or her presence, in another person and the past event of being born from her body. Concerning poetic couplets in the ritual speech of Anakalang people of Sumba, Keane (1997: 128) argues that the pairing of lines is an icon of relations of deferral and displacement, such as the relation of a visible human world to a displaced other scene of ancestral power and authority. Part of the significance of a line is its incompleteness: the presence outside itself of a counterpart line and a unit made up by the two lines together. I have made similar points about the grammatical exocentrism of Korowai pairing compounds and about the other pairing forms discussed in this chapter. These pairings emphasize that a given entity is not a presence unto itself but a presence defined by links to something absent: a child or spouse, a human doppelgänger who fell down at the same time, a son-in-law, an underlying grotesque identity, a dead person, or a disparate world.

Avoidance illustrates the pattern best. There is a general affinity between pairing and avoidance in Korowai thought. Avoidance rules are an aspect of five kinds of pairings outlined in this chapter: joking avoidance partnerships, mother-in-law avoidance, the "hidden names" model of human reincarnation, *xoxulop* correspondences generally, and the model of two reciprocally invisible populations of people. We have glimpsed specific points of intersection between these different avoidance forms. The avoidance forms' reciprocal figurativeness suggests that avoidance is a focus of cultural awareness and iconicity. The way humorous name avoidance partnerships overtly parody mother-in-law avoidance, for example, is evidence that people reflexively see avoidance as a mode of relating and as a mode of problematizing what a relation is.

Avoidance practices embrace and create qualities of estrangement. In many pairing forms, active noncontact and the signaling of a negative presence are modes of relational unity. Here avoidance imperatives intertwine with additional modes of otherness between connected terms. Many pairings turn on imagery of deformity: skin punctures, the idea that uttering underlying identities "wrecks" their referents, the grotesqueness of transgressive underlying identities behind mundane objects, the bodily disfigurations and transgressions commemorated in joking avoidance terms, or the sense that a malign society of invisible people surrounds humans' visible environment. Pairing forms also turn on emotional or perceptual estrangement, such as people's amnesia about their prior lives, in-laws' fear of each other, human fear of the "invisible side" and its denizens, and the experiences of being outside oneself that are often recalled in joking nickname partnerships. Amid these other kinds of separations between paired elements, avoidance works as a highly effective technique for shaping otherness into close involvement.

The patterns of relating discussed here greatly resemble the geography-mediated relational practices discussed in the previous chapter. I argued there that through landownership Korowai shape their world as a space of mutual political estrangements, across which people are closely involved. Those patterns are to geographic or house space what patterns of formal avoidance are to language use and bodily actors' direct perceptual contact. A small but telling convergence in this respect is the continuity between use of the expression "angry people" as a name for the population of occult invisible beings who live askance to Korowai visible experience and the geographic cliché "Upstreamers are angry" (or other frequent but less formulaic uses of "angry people" as a description of geographic strangers). The relational quality of simultaneous unity and alterity between owners and guests is also closely comparable to the pattern of relation between other kinds of paired categories discussed here.

The attraction between pairing and avoidance described here, and the more general conjoining of unity and strangeness characteristic of

Korowai social categorization, bears similarities to many existing models of New Guinea social process, such as Bateson's (1958 [1936]) idea of "complementary schismogenesis" among Iatmul people, Schieffelin's (1976: 107–16) account of "opposition scenarios" as the dominant form of social event among Kaluli, Strathern's (1988: 14) account of a "dyad [that] is a unity only by virtue of its internal division," Merlan and Rumsey's (1991: 113–16, 198–210) account of "oppositional parity" and other types of social pairing among Ku Waru, and Rutherford's (2003) account of "fetishization of the foreign" by Biak people. These and other interpretive concepts that have emerged in New Guinea ethnographic work have in common that they describe strangeness as an integral basis and effect of the social relation between twinned actors. Strangeness is not peripheral to relatedness. In Bateson's model of schismogenesis, for example, it is two actors' close involvement as mutual counterparts that provokes them to ever-escalating acts of differentiation. The main point I wish to underscore is that we are seeing here not merely a pattern of how social relations work, but a sensibility *about* or *toward* social relations held reflexively by the people who create and experience those relations. Locating the pattern at the level of a reflexive sensibility about the practice of social relating is the only plausible way to account, in the Korowai case, for the similarities that are so evident across otherwise disparate areas of cultural process.

This pattern is also a culture of semiosis. Pairs are made and known through signification. Most pairing forms discussed in this chapter consist centrally of practices of language. All of them also prominently involve the use of signs complementary to language: images of crossed logs used to model the relation between visible and invisible sides, panel walls used to facilitate and portray mother-in-law relations, bodily events of birth taken as a basis for linguistic identification of persons, and so on. Further, to say that Korowai understand persons as metonymies of pairs is also to say that persons and pairs are signs of each other. A person stands for and calls to presence the two people's unity as a pair, just as a pair substitutes for and calls to presence a person.

The further question is, *what kind* of signification is at work? What views about signification, and what specific qualities of signifier-signified links or specific modes of sign use, do Korowai put forth as the shape of their social relations? The pairing forms considered here all centrally involve favoring some kinds of representations over others and creating some kinds of representations as commentaries on others.

A practice of avoiding a name or other word, for example, is a second-order act of signification. The act of avoidance itself signifies something, by building off of another sign, the word-to-referent relationship. One effect of avoidance is to emphasize that semiosis is a matter of activity, not a matter of codes existing autonomously of actors and actions. To avoid doing something significant reflexively construes signification itself as *doing*. Avoidance is a reflexive cultural practice of underlining that sign use, or people's practical set toward their codes and code-using acts, is the crucial issue.

In practices of pairing and avoidance, Korowai specifically focus on alterity as a core aspect of signifying acts. In avoiding utterance of a transgressive substitute designation or in signaling social involvement with a mother-in-law through noncontact, Korowai align sign relations with the otherness-based being of persons and objects. Relations between signifiers and signifieds, like relations between persons, are portrayed as an intermeshing of attractions and repulsions. A signified is both present and not present in its signifier; a signifier should be both present and not present to its signified.

Two facets of this cultural understanding of signification stand out in the pairing forms discussed in this chapter, and in the other subjects examined in this book: first, people's active interest in the possibility of transgressing semiotic rules; and second, their attention to historical, time-based dimensions of signifying. A focus on transgression as a positive possibility is apparent in speakers' deliberate utterance of *xoxulop* identities to damage objects or other people; in people's deliberate violations or adjustments of mother-in-law imperatives as ways to comment on the moral quality of a particular relation; in joking avoidance partners' positive, celebratory commemoration of transgressive acts and attributes; in the grotesque, transgressive character of *xoxulop* identities; and in the existence of conventional understandings of sanctions befalling persons who transgress avoidance imperatives. These active orientations toward transgression involve a view that any norm of meaning can itself become the basis of a further meaning-making act of departing from the convention. Transgression of signifying rules is a possibility present in those rules. Korowai are reflexively aware that signification makes relations and qualities of being. Sign users could signify other ways and could make people other than what they are.

This otherness-focused reflexive pragmatics of signification is remarkable also for the ways in which it portrays pairings as centrally temporal. Joking avoidance terms evoke the contingent history of a past event, and that event's transformation into a relational identity. Reincarnation pairings locate present persons in other times, as surface fragments atop deeper circuits of being. Dyad-based person reference forms, along with mother-in-law avoidance, signal people's histories of emerging from or being involved with others' bodies and bodily actions. Reincarnation identities and matronymics bear particularly striking comparison: both verge on saying that a person *is* the other whom the person has come from, but they locate those origins at different degrees of remove from persons' own conscious memory and experience. Matronymics, teknonyms, and similar terms, as well as joking avoidance terms and the local avoidance of reincarnation identities around a living successor, all also unfold through speakers' knowledge of people's kinship histories and locations. As such, the expressions constantly index the process of learning and knowing about other people. The diverse pairing practices portray signification as temporal. A present is not self-contained but consists of its relations to other moments outside itself.

CHAPTER 3

Strange Kin

Maternal Uncles and the Spectrum of Relatives

In 2001 I interviewed a woman named Ngengel who had borne six children in her life and had married a younger man after her first husband's death. An artful conversationalist, Ngengel, toward the end of our talk, summed up the social anthropology of her world in the following series of statements:

> A child will become a member of its father's clan. Another clan will become its uncles and mothers, and other clans will become its grandmothers and grandfathers. Daughters will be married by husbands, and sons will sit at their own places. As far as her own place, a daughter will only come and go [i.e., visit transiently]. She takes her grave at her husband's place.

In this chapter and the next two I examine central kinship processes of Korowai lives, including especially relations with the kin Ngengel mentions: uncles and mothers, grandmothers and grandfathers, daughters and sons, and husbands and wives. I show that across these diverse important areas of experience, Korowai understand their social relations to be centrally made out of mismatched, systematically conjoined qualities of closeness and strangeness. Korowai kinship is at all levels a system of otherness.[1]

Kin categories are Korowai people's most prominent reflexive terminology for making and knowing their society. Kinship is their way of talking about "relations" in general. For example, Korowai make heavy use of the word *lambil* "relative, kin" to discuss whether people are socially

Figure 9. Ngengel Nandup during an interview with the author, 2001. She wears wing bones of a flying fox as nose ornaments. Her looped earrings are quills from a cassowary's vestigial wings.

connected to each other at all and, if so, what quality of connection they have. Speakers use this word to do functional work similar to my own use of terms such as *link, relation,* and *belonging* throughout this book. Another indication of kinship's prominence for Korowai is that speakers address almost every other Korowai person they meet by kinship terms. Kin categories overlap with and are even more frequently used than the vocabulary of "together people" *(lelipanop)* and "strangers" *(yaniyanop)* that I earlier introduced as an important Korowai language of social relations. Social connections are kinship connections.

Yet the fact that Korowai practice what Barnard (1978) calls "universal kin categorization" does not mean all their social relations are intimate ones, or that Korowai are closer to one another than people elsewhere who do not apply kin categories so widely. As part of their universalization of kinship to almost all social relations, Korowai often use the term "relative" *(lambil)* to mean what English speakers would call a "friend" or an "acquaintance." Minimally, "relatives" are just people who are socially involved with each other in some way. So too kin categories more generally are media through which social questions unfold, not settled determinations of what people are to each other.

Otherness is integral to Korowai kinship in several ways that I explore here. One is that certain categories of kin relation are centrally defined as bonds of close strangeness. The main example I examine in this chapter is the tie between mother's brother and sister's child. To Korowai, the main fact about this bond is that the persons in it are both intimates *and* members of different clans, who own different places. Separation is part of what makes uncle relations poignant and valuable.

Another way in which otherness is integral to kinship is that people's overall field of relatives is what Lepri (2005: 710) calls a "spectrum of alterity." Some kin are closer than others, and taking the measure of distance is an integral part of being related. The "uncle" category is central to Korowai kinship's organization as a field of degrees of belonging and estrangement in this way. We will see that Korowai pervasively use the category "uncle," and related "grandparent" categories, to make degrees of generational difference figurative of social distance generally.

Because I specifically discuss patterns of kinship *terminology* in developing these points, it is worth emphasizing in advance that it is fundamental to my account that kin categorization is not a matter of linguistic terminology alone.[2] One trend of kinship studies in recent decades has been recognition that the emotional, moral, and philosophical dimensions of kin relations, and the quotidian practice of material kinship acts, are integral aspects of kinship qua categorial order.[3] In Korowai kinship, activities such as giving food, living together, visiting, and feeling love, longing, or desire are forms of categorization too. They interact with linguistic categorization in complex relations of cotextuality and mutual construal.

In the first half of this chapter, this point is exemplified by the way I describe "uncle" and "grandparent" categories as having direct geographic content and as being defined by practices of travel, social support, and social comfort. In the second half, I turn from specific kin categories to patterns of Korowai thought about relatives in general. Here the interplay of linguistic and extralinguistic categorization central to kinship is reflected in two linked patterns: a sense of "belonging" that people understand to be the characteristic moral, emotional, and political quality of kin bonds; and Korowai speakers' prominent sensibility to the effect that kin relations are made and unmade in action.[4]

People's understanding of kinship *as* intersubjective belonging and their close reflexive orientation to the making of kinship in practical acts are additional levels at which kinship is a system of otherness. Presence or attenuation of belonging is what makes people's kinship field a "spectrum of alterity" in the first place. People's attentiveness to the making of kin relations in action means that the alternative possibility of being strangers is a steady presence within the experience of being kin, while people vigilantly monitor material interactions for signs of others' care.

"THE PIG-CASSOWARY RELATION IS AN UNCLE-NEPHEW RELATION"

Ngengel's statement, quoted above, reflects a classic configuration of social norms from the perspective of past anthropological writings on social structure. When she said that "A child will become a member of its father's clan," and that "Daughters will be married by husbands, and sons will sit at their own places," she was describing the fact that Korowai are members of landowning patriclans, that these groups are exogamous, and that marriage is generally virilocal. I have already touched on these social norms in earlier chapters. But in Ngengel's statement, "Another clan will become its uncles and mothers, and other clans will become its grandmothers and grandfathers," she was talking about something new. She was describing the fact that Korowai make the relation between mother's brother and sister's child into a marked, emotionally important matrilateral alternative to life-defining paternal bonds. (Anthropologists sometimes refer to patterns of this kind as "the avunculate.") She was also alluding to the way that, aided by an Omaha-style kinship terminology, Korowai identify their mothers' whole clans with the "uncle" category, and they identify certain other clans with the category "grandmothers and grandfathers," one terminological generation beyond the "uncle" position.

My goal in this section and the next is to explain these ramifications of the "uncle" bond. Doing so involves bringing together the subjects of the two previous chapters: place geography and otherness-focused social pairing. In the relation between uncle and nephew pairs (as well as uncles and nieces), Korowai map ownership geography and kin class onto each other.

Not long after talking with Ngengel, I spoke with a man named Üa. I asked him about his marriages, his children, the politics of his son's recent marriage, and his clan's preparations for a feast. But the most interesting thing about our conversation was what Üa asked me: Did I

have any uncles? Were my uncles alive? When I said that I did have living uncles, Üa contrasted my situation with his own. He had no uncles,
and his closest one had recently died. Üa brought up the subject of
uncles several times, not because he had forgotten what we already said,
but because this was something he cared about. To Korowai, uncle relations are intensely valuable. For Üa to describe himself as having no
uncles was a profound self-accounting. Lack of uncles was a defining
condition of his life. So too when uncles are living, relations with them
stand out as emotionally absorbing bonds, against the wider run of
social links. Relations between spouses, siblings, or parents and children might involve more actual shared living and mutual emotional
engagement. Yet even by comparison to these relations, links of
nephews and nieces to their uncles stand out as poignant and attention
drawing. One man, after we talked about a gift of feast food he pre-
pared for his uncle, compared his uncle to his own heart and then said,
while squeezing his thigh, "I love my uncle. He's like the flesh of my leg"
(nəmom finoptelobo, nəxobülnop kül). Ideally, an uncle is a close part
of one's life, wherever one goes.

The special importance of uncles stems from the way relations with
them combine mismatched qualities of closeness and distance, in several
intertwined channels: linguistic terminology, clan membership, gender,
reproductive time, and, above all, geographic place. The term I translate
as "uncle" is *mom,* and it is used for mother's brothers but not for father's
brothers, who are called instead by the term for "father" (figure 10). Reciprocally, a man calls his children and his brother's children *lal* "daughter," or *abül* "son," but distinguishes sisters' children by the special terms
salal "niece" and *sabül* "nephew." The terms *mom* "mother's brother"
and *sabül* "sister's son," or *mom* "mother's brother" and *salal* "sister's
daughter," are the marked categories of adjacent-generation relations.
Lexically, they stand out against the background of less marked counterparts such as "father," "son," and "daughter."[5] This lexical pattern
(which can be schematized as "F = FB ≠ MB") is common in languages of
New Guinea and worldwide. In it, cross-sex siblinghood makes a lexical
difference, whereas same-sex siblinghood does not. The pattern applies to
parent-generation women as well as men. A mother's sister and a mother
are both called *ni* "mother," whereas a father's sister is called by the distinct term *mul* "aunt."[6]

Although uncles are as important in the lives of women as in the lives
of men, Korowai often talk about uncle relationships using the compound *mom-sabül* "uncle-nephew," referring to a pair of persons who

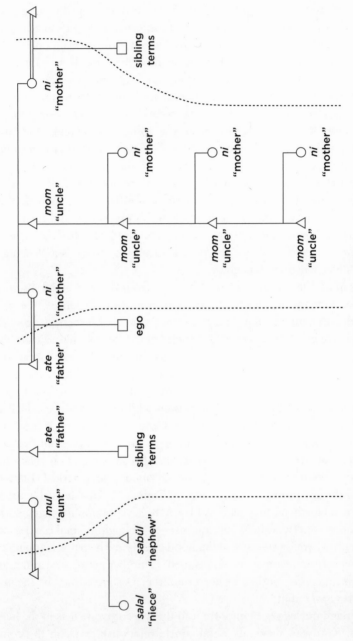

Figure 10. Uncles, mothers, fathers, and aunts. Dashed lines indicate difference of clan.

are respectively uncle and nephew to each other. By contrast, speakers have trouble saying "uncle-niece" as a single word.[7] Wide use of the pairing compound "uncle-nephew" is only one of many ways Korowai give this relation iconic, larger-than-life significance. Yet this is also a case of a pairing compound denoting a unity of antithetical counterparts.

There is a close fit between the terminological markedness of uncle relationships and the dominant practical side of uncles' strangeness to their sisters' children: their difference of clanship and place ownership. Since clanmates should not marry, a husband and wife are usually members of different clans, identified with different places. If the two have children, these children and their mother are also separated by a difference of clanship. Hence maternal uncles and their sister's children are also members of different clans, a difference indicated by a dashed line in figure 10. Yet people have close social bonds with their mothers and maternal uncles, despite the differences of clanship and geography.

In ways consistent with the strong spatialization of social relations discussed in Chapter 1, Korowai very directly spatialize the "uncle" category, identifying it with a place on the land and with a clan. Speakers routinely refer to their maternal clan territory as "my mother's place," or more often as "my uncles' place" *(nəmomel bolüp)*. They also routinely refer to whole clans as their "uncles" *(momel)*, such as in statements of the form "My uncles are Dambol." Sometimes people use the expression "uncles and mothers" *(mom-ni)* to speak of this clan, as in Ngengel's statement, "A child will become a member of its father's clan. Another clan will become its uncles and mothers."[8] More often, people use the masculine term "uncles" alone to refer to a mixed-gender set of kin, the whole maternal clan. If this is androcentrism, then it is a complex androcentrism in which women are included in the male kin type and in which the male kin type is itself understood as a feminine man. Speakers occasionally address a male uncle as "mother" *(ni)*, and even more often use "uncle-type of mother" *(mom-ni)* in place of "uncle" *(mom)* to refer to a single maternal uncle and his kinship role.[9] Here the same word *mom-ni* that can designate the plural entity "uncles and mothers" is used in a different kind of sense, to designate a singular referent, "uncle who is a kind of mother."

Ngengel's statement, "Another clan will become its uncles and mothers," is characteristic of people's teleological understanding of the uncle position. The category "uncles" is as taken for granted as "mother" or "father," as a basic aspect of personhood. "Uncle" sits alongside "mother" and "father" as a third type of parental kin. A particular set of people contingently emerge as fillers of that anticipated role, but the role itself is portrayed as a preexisting kind of desirable relative that a person needs to have.

Use of the plural kinship terms "uncles" or "uncles and mothers" to speak of a whole clan of maternal kin makes sense to Korowai because a given ego in fact calls virtually all individual members of ego's mother's clan "uncle" or "mother." This is in part because Korowai practice an Omaha pattern of kin categorization, in which relatives of different reproductive generations are categorized as being of the same terminological generation. All agnatic descendants of an uncle are themselves "uncle" or "mother." The son of an uncle is an uncle, the daughter of an uncle is a mother, the son of a son of an uncle is an uncle, the daughter of a son of an uncle is a mother, and so on (see figure 10). Thus even a wizened adult calls small children of his or her mother's clan "uncle" or "mother." The adult is called "nephew" or "niece" in turn by those young matrilateral male kin, or "son" and "daughter" by young matrilateral female kin.

In past anthropological work on Omaha kinship terminologies, one only partly successful line of inquiry about the linguistic pattern was to argue that the pattern correlates cross-culturally with patrilineal group membership and stresses the unity of those groups (see McKinley 1971). There is indeed an elegant fit between Korowai kin categorizations and clanship: to a given ego, the people of one clan are virtually all "uncle" or "mother." Actually, though, just *membership* in ego's mother's clan is reason enough to Korowai for that ego to call a person "uncle" or "mother," even without a genealogical tie being known. Term usage is often determined by clanship in the first place rather than being determined by genealogy (and then felicitously happening to match clan arrangements).[10] However, the interesting question about the categories "uncle" and "mother" and their reciprocals is not what other social institutions explain the terminology but how the terms and the uncle relation *work* for people to organize their experiences of clanship, geography, and history making. Through the terminological pattern, whole clans take the shape "uncle" and "mother." The landscape, or a place on it, also takes this shape. And a given ego's history of being born from another person's body, and cared for by her, also takes the shape of "uncles" and is retold in that shape over time, as one generation of uncles and mothers is succeeded by other generations who are called by the same words.

Uncles' practical importance often turns on their identification with a clan place separate from the nephew or niece's own. We have earlier seen how, through the landownership system, people belong in relation to one segment of land, their clan place. The rest of the landscape is strange to them. Maternity and resulting uncle bonds offer another kind of relational link to places on the land. A relation to a place of "uncles and mothers" is often the most important social connection that people have to any place other than their own clan territory (at least until marriage, when links to a spouse's place can become important). Usually uncles and their nephews or nieces are also separated by a difference of actual residence, parallel to their difference of landownership. Living "elsewhere" *(yani-bolüp)* is a basic feature of the Korowai concept "uncle." But when a woman moves to her husband's place and her children grow up there, those children and their mother's relatives ideally visit each other often. Uncles, nephews, and nieces are prototypical travelers. The stock phrase, "He/she took off to his/her uncle's place" *(yəmomel bolüp loxte)*, is common in everyday conversation and in myths. The phrase describes such a regular, stereotypical action that people even use the phrase in jest, to talk about inanimate objects that have mysteriously disappeared. Another idiom characteristic of the understanding of uncle-nephew bonds as paradigmatically relations of spatial displacement is the naming of the black band of mountains distantly visible to the north as *wola-sabül* or *lamol-sabül* "world's nephew." The odd, unknown margin between earth and sky is a nephew to the "world" proper, where Korowai themselves dwell. The mountain chain, like a nephew, is adjacent to the familiar world but markedly far from it. Avuncular relatives are the horizon.

It is prototypically at times of trouble, vulnerability, loss, and need that people take off to their uncles or look to avuncular relations for solace. When a man named People Are Scared returned from a trip away from the Korowai lands to find that a widow he hoped to marry had left with another man, his immediate response was to go to his uncle's place, where he stayed for a time venting his exasperation and weighing his options. In another typical turn, people of a certain clan wanted to exploit their mature sago holdings to put on a feast, but felt themselves too inexperienced and few in number to succeed in the project. They sought help from their nieces and nephews far downstream, descendants of their father's sister. "We are children," they said to the older relatives, in reference to their lack of skills, and the nephews and nieces came to their uncles' place for several months of work. Avuncular relatives also routinely help each other in smaller projects such as house building, garden clearing, or trap making. They visit to hear each

Figure 11. Yalun Xawex, 1997, napping in the house of his nephew Silom Dambol, where he lived following his wife's death. The author's field note-book is at right.

other's news, share food, and see each other. When people need to travel, or wish to bring about some social process across the landscape, avuncular kinship ties are major paths along which they move.

Meanwhile, "uncles and mothers" are off-limits as marriage partners. Marrying a maternal clansperson has strong connotations of parental incest, even if the spouses are not genealogically close. This rule indicates the strength with which Korowai feel all members of their maternal clan to be uncles and mothers. The prohibition is also an ele-ment of avoidance between intimately paired perspectives, comparable to the pairing-and-avoidance forms explored in the previous chapter.

What stands out about uncle relations is that they are valued *because* people involved in them are mutually strange. Uncles conjoin close social attachment with geographic separation and transient visiting. Part of the pleasure of avuncular ties is that they offer ways for people to go other places, have a sense of belonging there, and be linked to those places even when not present there. Uncles are strange in residence, landowner-ship, and clan membership, but intimate in emotional and moral orien-tation because they are close kin of an ego's own mother. (Stated from the other direction, nephews and nieces are strange in geography and clan, but emotionally intimate as children of ego's sister or other female clanmate.) These relations combine residential otherness with the close-ness of mother-child connection. Uncle relations are attractive not only because they contrast with sometimes more authority-laden relations of paternal kinship and patrimonial landownership (after Radcliffe-Brown 1952) but also because Korowai find aesthetic value in places, people, and experiences different from daily routine. Uncle relations thus have a quality similar to the contradictoriness of guests: the category "guest" describes people who are distant on the dimension of residence but close on the dimension of actual spatial presence in a host's house. Hospitality is motion across this mismatch of categorial statuses, in which strangers act as consociates. Uncle relations are this sort of hospitable interaction turned into an enduring category of bond.

Here uncle bonds encapsulate something important about kin rela-tions at large. As one man said, "An uncle's place is where a person goes when he thinks of not having any relatives, or thinks of all his relatives being far away." Korowai often associate kinship with lack, absence, and separation, as I sketch below. Attachment to uncles is felt most deeply as a matter of being separate from them and from other people generally. Bereavement following the death of an uncle is especially intense, as Üa's questions to me reflected. In mourning contexts, people assert directly that geographic separation gives the bond special importance.

The features of uncle relations discussed so far are all linked to the core fact that this relation depends on a history of marriage and mater-nity. A major dimension of this relation's quality of intimate otherness is the way the bond is figurative of the lives of women who were (or are) sisters, wives, and mothers to other people. Korowai are highly aware of the overlap between affinal and avuncular relations. People often take a future uncle relationship to be built into marriage from the outset. For example, at a time when one newlywed couple had no children and were not even openly acting as if married, I heard the groom hailed loudly by his brother-in-law as "father of my nephew" *(nə-sabül-ate)*. The boister-ous young speaker was implying that the couple *would* have children and that the addressee's future fathering of the speaker's nephew was the truth of the two men's relation. Transactions between sister's children and maternal clanspeople often merge with, and euphemistically substitute for, transactions between the linking woman's kin and her husband. But the most important pattern here is people's association of avuncular emotions with the life of the connecting woman. For example, one man described his "love, longing" *(finop)* for his matrilateral kin as a direct sequitur of his mother's geographic displacement at marriage: "My mother went far downstream [to the place of the speaker's own paternal clan], I love my uncles." Such statements are part of a larger pattern of Korowai narrating social history as consisting of events of women "going" or being "put" certain places away from their original homes, then "putting" sets of children there (i.e., bearing them). People often speak of their uncles' clan territory by the expression "the place my mother came from" *(nəni yələbotop),* or they elliptically refer to that place, their mother's land, as "my place of coming, my origin spot" *(nələbotop).*[11] Frequently people trace love between uncle and sister's child to the subjectivity of the linking woman herself. As one man said:

> If I get on my uncles' backs, then my mother will get on my back. "You shat and pissed on my thigh. You were sick and I held and watched you. You got well. You got big. Why are you getting on my elder brother's back? Why are you getting on my younger brother's back?" To the uncles, she will say, "You are my leftover blood, the blood left from my coming down. Those are your children. Why are you getting on your children's backs?"

Another woman put her statements to her siblings and children more succinctly: "When I die, don't get on each other's backs, just live well together."

Histories of a woman gestating and birthing a child loom large in people's sentiments about these bonds. Here is one person's account of the steadfastness of avuncular ties: "When a woman dies, the uncle and nephew don't give each other up. 'He whom our clanswoman bore,' they say." Just describing someone as born of a close female relative is itself an assertion and explanation of intense emotional attachment. Another man said of his nephews and nieces, "They whom my elder sister bore, it's as though I bore them myself." Likening a sister's child to one's own child is common in kinship talk. Men and women often speak of their siblings' children by prefixing "our" *(noxu)* to terms for "child," in statements such as, "Him? He's my younger sister [and me], our child." In these and other ways, "nephew" and "niece" do not so much contrast with "son" and "daughter" as overlap with them. The cross-children are special kinds of children. In these relations, closeness of parental identification is figured and mediated by a predicament of identification and separation between siblings. Sisters have separate bodies from their siblings, they marry other people, they often live elsewhere from their kin, and they predecease some of their kin. Similarly, from the point of view of nephews and nieces, matrilateral kin are figures of maternity and its contradictions: maternity is as close and as far as one's own body and its history of coming into existence. Uncles spatialize a history of maternal genesis into a location on the land, and they sociologize it into a clan of people. Through uncles the maternal past is a place a person can visit. These sensibilities color even the Omaha-style application of the "uncle" term itself. When I have asked people why the category applies to an uncle's sons, the sons of those sons, and so on, they have sometimes said, "Because they are not yet far." These relatives have a quality of being "close," despite disparities of geography and generational succession, because they are figures of maternity.

I have charted ways in which uncle relations are important and attractive precisely because they join together mismatched qualities of closeness and otherness. In the very act of denoting a type of relative, the Korowai kin category "uncle" is also figural of a whole relational problematic of combined intimacy and distance. The directness of people's association of the "uncle" category with a spatial quality of "elsewhere" (*yani-bolüp;* lit., "other/strange place") and other levels on which Korowai uncles are clearly figures of combined involvement and distance suggest that the anthropology of maternal uncle relationships crossculturally might be profitably reread as a literature on intimate alterity. Anthropologists have long approached avuncular relations as existing in a shadow dialogue with other relational categories dominant in the same cultural contexts. Korowai uncle relations' mismatch of close kinship with spatial and clan difference is coordinated with other mismatches, such as the figure of a male mother, the valuing of maternity amid a paternity-dominated system of group affiliation and landownership, and the valuing of combined qualities of intimacy and strangeness between cross-sex siblings or between mothers and children. Uncles stand as otherness-tinged, culture-internal alternatives to dominant cultural norms and categorial structures of paternal clan membership, paternal identification, and residence at one's own clan place.

All the preceding points can be usefully summed up with a look at the quality of close strangeness portrayed in a common Korowai aphorism about two animal species: "Pig and cassowary are nephew and uncle" (*gol-küal yexenep mom-sabül*). The animal pair "pig and cassowary" and the kinship pair "uncle and nephew" are here each signified by pairing compounds. The statement is a widely known bit of conventional wisdom, but in articulating it, people do not care about which animal is identified with which kin type. Rather, "pig-cassowary" as a relational unit is identified with "uncle-nephew" as a relational unit. The statement could thus be more faithfully translated, "The pig-cassowary relation is an uncle-nephew relation." But the aphorism says as much about uncle-nephew relations through an animal figure as it says about animals through a kinship figure. Part of what the statement says about the uncle-nephew relation is that this bond stands out markedly against the broader run of human relations, in the strange and valuable manner that pig and cassowary stand out against the broader run of animals. Korowai do not recognize pigs as belonging to the taxonomic class "mammal" *(nduo)*, and they do not consider cassowaries "birds" *(del)* (cf. Bulmer 1967; Majnep and Bulmer 1977: 148–57). The animals are too much bigger than other members of those classes and too morphologically and behaviorally different from them. They are each one of a kind. Instead, the two are paired together as "pig-cassowary," based on their common taxonomic oddity, their anthropomorphization, and their extraordinary value as game. The aphorism says in effect that uncle-nephew relations are the valuable categorial oddballs of kinship experience.

Yet though pig and cassowary are alike in being freaks of nature, they are also freaks to each other. They are both ground animals of the forest, but they keep apart, and they have little morphologically in common besides their meaty bulk. One way in which Korowai express an understanding that the two are mutually strange even while going together as a pair is through observing a taboo against eating the two animals' flesh on the same day. Mixing these meats inside one stomach causes the offender's rectum to "fall out" *(mongofeli-)*, an eversion of the body's insides matching the crime of internalizing wrongfully combined categories through the mouth. People attribute this taboo to the fact that the animals are uncle and nephew. The taboo seems figuratively parallel to the rule against marrying a maternal clansperson: mixing pig and cassowary meat in one stomach offends and unbalances the volatile bond of intimate antipathy between "uncle" and "nephew" animals, just as marriage to an uncle or mother is too great a suspension of the boundaries of close strangeness characteristic of avuncular relations among humans. With allegorical clarity, the minor statement about pig and cassowary underlines how Korowai dwell on intimate alterity as the very principle of uncle ties.

GRANDPARENT CLANS AND THE
FURTHER LANDSCAPE OF KIN

The pattern of matrilateral bonds sketched above shapes many areas of people's lives beyond uncle relationships alone. A good illustration of this is people's wide use of the phrase "same uncles" *(momel lelip)* as a reflexive principle of kin categorization. Any two people whose mothers were members of the same clan by definition share the "same uncles," and on this basis the two people categorize each other as siblings. The expression "same uncles" comes up a great deal in Korowai kinship talk as a compact explanation for why and how specific people are siblings to each other. Siblinghood based on having the same uncles is typically an important bond of mutual cooperation and trust, even though the relatives do not themselves belong to the same clans or live in the same places. Striking here is the way a relation of pronounced otherness, the bond with uncles, precedes and defines a relation of relative similitude, the bond between "siblings." Two people are categorized as mutually identical because of their common relation to a strange third. This is also typical of the notion that having an uncle defines who a person is.

A bigger ripple effect of uncle relationships is found across the whole wider structure of Korowai kin categorization, beyond the sibling and parental generations. If we posit terminological generation as a relevant dimension of Korowai kinship experience, then the categories of kin relations discussed so far are the zero and ±1 generations. Sibling categories are in the *same* generation as ego, and uncles, mothers, nephews, and nieces are *one* generation terminologically removed. I now turn to the grandparental or ±2 terminological generation of relatives. I can outline this level quickly, because it repeats and deepens patterns of the "uncle" level. The grandparent positions too are kin categories composed of simultaneous closeness and distance, and they are kin categories mapped onto clan geography. Grandparent and uncle relations together also make apparent the way in which kinship is centrally a degree phenomenon. The field of kin categories is structured as a spectrum.

While a given ego usually has maternal uncles who are socially and emotionally important relatives, so too that ego's own parents were each mothered by a particular woman, and had uncle bonds with that woman's brothers and other clanmates. Something of the importance of the parents' relations with their maternal uncles is usually preserved in the next generation: an ego forms important relations with his or her "grandparental" kin, the clanmates of that ego's paternal and maternal grandmothers. The +2 generation of Korowai kinship terms consists of only two categories, "grandma" *(max)* and "grandpa" *(andüop)*. The main principle of these terms' application is that any man whom ego's parent calls father or uncle is ego's grandpa, and any woman whom ego's parent calls mother or aunt is ego's grandma. All members of ego's mother's mother's and father's mother's respective clans are thus grandpas and grandmas (since ego's mother and father each call everyone in those respective maternal clans "uncle" or "mother"). Figure 12 outlines this pattern, in which all agnatic descendants of each parent's uncles are identified as grandpa and grandma, even if they are younger than ego in age and in reproductive generation.

Applying grandparental categories again does not depend on knowing genealogical ties. That someone is a member of the mother's mother's or father's mother's clan is itself sufficient basis to call that person a grandparent. Just as people speak of their mother's clan collectively as "my uncles," so too they call their father's mother's clan and their mother's mother's clan "my grandfathers" *(n-andüop-alin)* or "my grandmas and grandpas" *(ne-max-andüop-alin)*. To ask someone, "Who are your grandfathers?" is to ask not for names of persons but for names of ego's grandparental clans. Only a bit more weakly than possession of a clan of uncles, possession of two clans of grandparental relatives is a normal, defining aspect of Korowai personhood. Ngengel was expressing this teleological expectation that a person is a relational node who has whole groups of grandparental relatives when she said, of a generic child, "Other clans will become its grandmothers and grandfathers." One man put it this way: "As for my child, my uncles will become his grandfathers." The man chuckled slightly on stating aloud his and his son's differences of subjective position in relation to the same people. But the process of parents' own "uncle" clans becoming their children's "grandpa and grandma" clans is something Korowai are highly aware of, as a pattern of their world.

I was often impressed by the importance of knowing a Korowai person's "uncle" and "grandparent" clans, as an entrée to understanding the shape of that person's life activities and total social network. In a common structure, a person is a member of one clan but is importantly connected by maternal links to three others: a mother's clan, a father's mother's clan, and a mother's mother's clan. Figure 12 is a genealogical portrayal of this structure, with dashed lines again indicating differences of clan membership. Through diverse events, persons might end

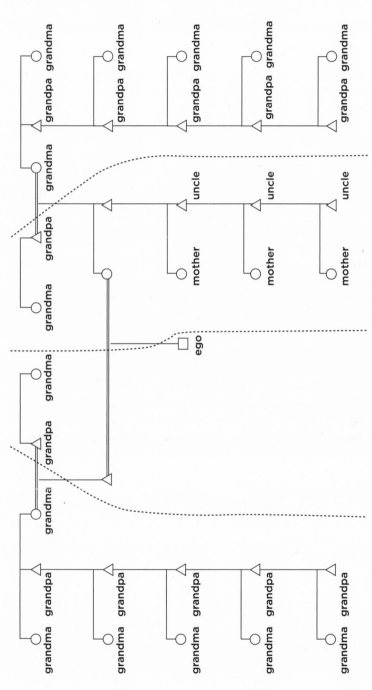

Figure 12. Grandfathers and grandmothers. Dashed lines indicate difference of clan.

up lacking active bonds with grandparental clans, and they might end up with intense social links to people of different clans altogether. But the tendency is strong for parents' uncles to be major social resources. Grandparental relatives are often regular visitors to each other's land and typically support each other in feuds, share food bounties with each other, or help each other with work projects. Like uncles, grandparents are people with whom a person has a caring, cooperative relation, despite alienness of place and clan.

The pattern of grandparent categorization means that here too Korowai experience kin relations geographically: grandparents are places as well as people. They are people *of* places. Conversely, the kinship structures further complicate the geography of ownership described in chapter 1. "Uncle" and "grandparent" categories temper the land-ownership system's effects of estrangement and autonomy, by providing additional ways of human relating, in which separateness and difference of land-focused identity are positive bases of connection. In grandparenthood, as in avuncular ties, the generational past is another country, a place to which one is socially connected, even though one does not own it.

Yet even as grandparental relatives are friends in a world of strangers, they embody attenuation of kinship bonds. People sometimes explicitly say that a grandparental relative is "a bit of a stranger, somewhat other" *(mamap yani)*, by comparison to a clanmate or a maternal clansperson. Another indication that Korowai associate distance of terminological generation with social distance is that, in contrast to "uncles and mothers," the members of a grandparental clan are marriageable, a point discussed in more detail in chapter 5. Another symptom of distance is people's pragmatic pattern of using grandparent terms self-reciprocally in address, even though the categories are not self-reciprocal in reference. The semantic reciprocals of "grandma" and "grandpa" are the terms *lalxafun* "child of daughter or niece" and *abülxafun* "child of son or nephew." However, speakers tend only to use these grandchild terms when describing relations to particular kin outside of those kin's presence. Conversing directly, a grandparent and grandchild (especially ones of the same gender) prefer to use *max* "grandma" or *andüop* "grandpa" symmetrically. By comparison to kin relations between adjacent terminological generations, kin categorization at two generational degrees of remove prompts neutralization of distinctions. No distinction is made between cross and parallel relatives, and in face-to-face interaction people neutralize the marking of asymmetric generational difference itself.

Remoteness goes with vagueness. "Grandpa" and "grandma" come to mean, in practice, a quality of middle-degree generic relatedness: the relatedness of people two terminological generations of distance from each other, divested of the idea that any one person is generationally prior to the other.

The strongest evidence that kin category use is in effect a continuous process of complimenting or insulting people's degrees of mutual close-ness lies at the third degree of generational remove. The category "great grand-relative" exists as a theoretical possibility in Korowai speech. At this level, neutralization of difference is total: a single category signifies male, female, ascending, and descending kin without distinction. There are many relatives in people's lives who could be called "great grand-relative" (e.g., anyone called grandpa or grandma by ego's parent, or the child of anyone ego calls grandchild). However, people almost never use this category in actual kin talk. Speakers occasionally call someone a "great grand-relative" outside of the person's presence, but the term is not used between face-to-face interlocutors. Korowai adhere to a "two degrees of separation" sociolinguistic constraint. For each person with whom a speaker ever comes into verbal interaction, that speaker is able to find some basis on which to categorize the person as a grandparent or nearer. (I touch on some of these bases in a moment.) To call some-one a "great grand-relative" would amount to saying the person is barely a relative at all. Continuing the logic by which avuncular relatives are a generationally adjacent, immediate degree of intimate separation and grandparental relatives are an intermediate degree of intimate separation, the "great grand-relative" category signifies dis-connection more intensely than relatedness, rather than a balance of qualities in which separation is itself a basis of relatedness. Denying relatedness runs against basic interactional imperatives of politeness and moral presence, so the category is shunned.

Although it exists as a theoretical possibility that is almost never applied in practice, the category "great grand-relative" offers significant insights into Korowai thought about kin relatedness. There are several synonymous words denoting this kinship position, but the main ones all mean "sago stolon" *(xogelif, xosilax, ndaügelif, ndaüsilax)*. A sago stolon is the underground stem that grows outward from the base of an established palm and sends up parthenogenetic suckers that are the palm species' most constant, visible mode of propagation (Flach 1997: 53). People speak of a main palm as "mother" and its suckers as "off-spring" *(maxayol;* also used for human children), and there are many

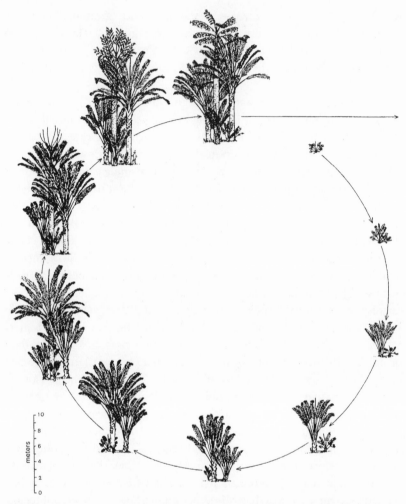

Figure 13. Growth cycle of a sago palm, showing some of the suckers that
would typically propagate over the life span of a single main trunk. Drawing
by Rik Schuiling, reprinted with permission from Schuiling and Flach 1985: 8.

areas of life where Korowai link sago palms to human growth or reproduction. What is emphasized by the image of a "sago stolon," in particular, is the combined discreteness and unity of generations. People
know a sago stolon's presence underground by the successively smaller
immature palms that stand at spatial intervals outward from a mature
parent (figure 13). By taking "sago stolon" as their kinship term for relatives of three generations' distance, Korowai seem to distill out, as the

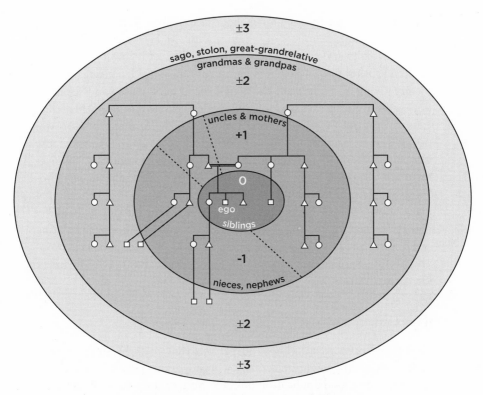

Figure 14. Terminological generations as a spectrum of otherness.

ultimate content of kinship, the growth of successive generations and the spatial visibility of temporal difference. Figure 14 uses a graphic convention of shading and concentric circles, in a manner loosely parallel to this image of sago generations, to sum up how Korowai kinship categories locate people's social relations across a layered spectrum of degrees of otherness, on the dimension of terminological generation.

The starkness with which Korowai spatialize "uncle" and "grandparent" categories, as described so far in this chapter, is again highly instructive for comparative anthropological thinking about kinship patterns: here, for the way this spatiality makes apparent Omaha kin categorization's force in shaping people's social world as a spectrum of alterity. A few authors have previously tried to explain this classificatory pattern as following from residential practices like the Korowai ones, according to which maternal relatives live in one location separately from their nieces and nephews (Titiev 1956; Hogbin and Wedgwood 1953: 248–49).

McKinley (1971: 239–40) argues that this explanation is falsified by the existence of large numbers of societies with similar residential patterns but no Omaha-style terminology. Yet the goal of trying to "explain" Omaha kinship terminologies is once again misplaced, considering that merely giving an account of the actual social experiences and sensibilities supported by Omaha terminologies—their effects rather than causes—has been ethnographically elusive. A major effect of Korowai people's own practices of this form of kin categorization is to transpose maternity-mediated difference of generation into a figure of involvement and separateness between coeval persons of all ages. The terminological pattern amplifies the social importance and clarity of maternal uncle relations, making maternal, generational time into a classificatory matrix for shaping the social world as a spectrum of otherness radiating out from the position of a speaking, living subject. Parallel effects probably occur in other linguistic communities practicing similar forms of kin categorization.

BASES OF TERM USE

How can Korowai call almost all persons they meet by sibling terms, parent- or child-generation terms, or grandparent terms? I have so far described the actual application of kin terms to a fraction of the relatives in people's lives: the genealogically immediate ones and the ones who belong to the same clan as ego's mother and ego's paternal and maternal grandmothers. But speakers' use of the kin categories to place persons in a spectrum of otherness reaches far beyond social others to whom ego is linked by well-known bodily histories of gestation and insemination.

One major additional basis of kin term use is foster-parentage. As I discuss in the next chapter, Korowai often lose a parent while still only children. When a surviving parent remarries, the new spouse is categorized as the child's foster parent. The two foster relatives address each other by parent-child terms, and the foster parent typically plays a large role in caring for the child. This relation in turn shapes a child's categorization of whole fields of people related to the foster parent: the foster parent's clanmates become the child's siblings and parents, the foster parent's uncles become the child's grandparents, and so on.

Marriage similarly creates categorizing options. Often a married person calls his or her spouse's relatives by the same terms the spouse does and is called by gender-appropriate reciprocals in return. Other sources of kinship options are pairing of geographically adjacent clans (touched on in chapter 2) and identification of geographically far-flung clans that have similar or identical names. For example, an ego might call "uncle" or "mother" all the members of a clan conventionally paired with ego's mother's clan.

The most consequential principle of kin term use is that two people needing categories for each other draw on other people's histories of categorization, especially their parents' histories. An ego knows how his or her parents each called dozens of other persons (or their parents) and can triangulate from a parental usage to arrive at a comfortable category. Frequently, two persons explicitly discuss their parents' categorizations in order to decide what they are to each other. Kinship is overtly historical and overtly a matter of speech use.[12] People are kin of specific categories based on other persons' ways of using words for one another, at prior times. Kin know the definitions of their present relations as an inheritance, pointing back to parents' relational practices. They know kin relations to be a moving structure of intertemporal connection, in which a relational present travels on tracks laid down by others just before (after Wagner 1981 [1975]: 41–42).

By these and other principles, many persons actually have *multiple* possible ways of categorizing each other in speech. In such situations speakers are often explicit that the figurative, connotational, and indexical value of term use in conversation is what is most basic and important in shaping categorization, not some decisive recipe for matching term choice to would-be literal facts preceding situated talk. In a typical turn here, for example, one man put to rest my efforts to sort out the logic of his use of multiple terms (including both *sabül* "nephew" and *sop* "aunt's husband") for another specific man by saying what all the terms basically signified: "We are just very close" *(mofu xalu-xalu)*.

At another kind of extreme, speakers who do not have a shared history (or who do not know of a parental history) can guess at an appropriate way to call one another, or agree on a designation on the spot, based on conversational comfort. Conversational context itself is a basis of kinship and a reason for it. Speakers who *do* have a history might, for whatever reason, recategorize their relation. One man, for example, described to me a decision he and his mother's brother's made, when they were already mature adults, to stop calling each other "uncle" and "nephew" and to switch instead to calling each other by sibling terms. The nephew requested the change because he felt "alone" in the world and because he felt the change was a good match with the uncle's shift to living at the nephew's clan land. This ad hoc change did not follow any wider pattern (such as a regular pattern of people regretting their lack of siblings and finding uncle relations less comfortable than sibling ones). But the change is typical of speakers' readiness to innovate in kinship life. The structures of kin categorization outlined so far in this chapter are guidelines, not constraints.

I have argued that important Korowai kinship categories, besides signifying kinds of relatives, signify relational otherness. A given category, besides denoting a person, is figural of a wider spectrum of kinship alterity and of a problematic of conjoined intimacy and distance. The further patterns of term application just outlined point to similar themes, now at the level of the *use* of kin categories rather than their taxonomic structure. A kin category is itself heterogeneous. While the kinship taxonomy comprises a spectrum of positions from familiarity to strangeness, there is also a spectrum from familiarity to strangeness in the pragmatic application of single categories. Some persons called "uncle" are more uncles than others. Certain uses of a kin category mark a relation of people in one situation of solidarities and alienations, and other uses mark a relation of people in a quite different situation. Korowai are very aware of these questions of alienness in the midst of using kin categories as a universal anthropology of their world. For example, when not in the presence of the persons they are talking about, speakers routinely draw contrasts between a "true" *(xajan)* or "proper" *(giom)* relative and a "just habitually so" relative *(mofu amomate;* lit., "they habitually do thus"). In one typical statement along these lines, a woman whom I asked about the basis on which she called a man "uncle" explained he is "just my uncle in the sense of habitually so" *(mofu amomatexaülop nəmom).* In routinely underlining a contrast between "own, proper" and "just habitually so" relatives, Korowai portray kinship as a field of differently close and distant relationships. Application of a kin category is not a seamless act but takes place on a basis of closeness or strangeness. Not only are there categories of attenuated kinship like "sago stolon," but there are attenuated ways to categorize someone as kin at all. The directness with which people know kin term application to be based on histories of use (such as parents' past speech practices) also involves an understanding of kin relations as conjoining intimacy and otherness. Here people recognize kin relations as being *made*, through humanly fashioned historical links across different persons' categorizing acts. These are speech practices of making intimates out of distant persons, distant times, and distant events.

In sketching a few patterns by which Korowai apply close kinship terms to most persons they meet, my focus has shifted from specific kin categories to patterns of talk about kin in general. In the remainder of this chapter, I look at some broad tendencies in Korowai discourse and thought about "relatives" at large in order to deepen the argument about otherness in kinship introduced so far.

KINSHIP AS INTERSUBJECTIVE BELONGING

People are conscious of kinship through their use of kin words, but they also know kinship as a matter of bodily genesis, sexual intimacy, feeding, care, emotion, location in each other's presence or on specific parts of the land, and histories of gift-giving and cooperative labor. Categories of kin relatedness exist as patterns of being and acting across a jumble of intersecting media. Some relations might exist mainly in one set of media; others might exist in a different set. Some relations experienced as kinship might be comparatively fleeting, weak, and idiosyncratic; others might be felt to be kinship of a more deeply person-defining sort. If almost all Korowai social interactions are kinship interactions, we should expect "kinship" to be many things.

Despite the variation in and complexity of what kin relations are, it is worth postulating an overall quality by which these relations are known and measured. I will call it a quality of "intersubjective belonging," echoing the similar quality of belonging between owners and land that I described in chapter 1. In my discussion of avuncular and grandparental relations, I noted that these categories of kin ties are defined in part by actions of mutual material care and geographic welcome that the kinspersons characteristically perform toward each other, as well as by their feelings of "love, longing" *(finop)*. These patterns of care and sentiment are part of what define persons' kinship field as a spectrum of otherness; the "spectrum" pattern is not defined by formal classificatory structure alone. The ideal of "belonging" that I suggest is typical of kin relations at large is a more generic version of these features we have already encountered in uncle and grandparent relations in particular.

One reason for speaking of "belonging" is that Korowai kin relations are dominated by imagery of possession and ownness. Virtually anytime Korowai use a basic kinship term to refer to someone, the term is possessively prefixed by a pronominal form such as "my" *(nə-)*, "your" *(gə-)*, or "their" *(yexene-)*. Strikingly, speakers sometimes represent their relation to a relative *purely* in terms of possession, without specifying the type of relative the other is. Speakers say idiomatically of someone else, "that's mine" *(afe nɔxa)*, as an expression of attachment and admiration. Often the idiom is used of toddlers or other small children for whom the speaker feels extreme affection. People use the bare expression "somebody's, that which belongs to somebody" *(yaxoxa)* with similar force. "That's somebody's" can be uttered to warn an interlocutor against trying to harm or marry a person being talked about, by recalling that the person has relatives invested in his or her well-being (paralleling the narrower expression "someone's child," mentioned in chapter 2). However, "somebody's" is also used in celebratory, praising talk, to mean "good." Saying "He's somebody's!" is a way to remark that someone is an ideal person. Possession-worthiness is a measure of human value.

Possession and senses of belonging are also prominent in kinship through the linguistic element *giom* "own, owning, proper." People sometimes speak of a person's parents, clanmates, or other close relatives as his or her "owners" *(giom-anop;* masculine *giom-abül* "owning man," feminine *giom-lal* "owning woman"). This is especially common when people are talking about a young woman's marriage possibilities, a child's need for protection and guidance, or needs of burial, protection, or retaliation surrounding a person who has died, been killed, or suffered an injury. Owners are the kin who are impinged on by threats or changes in the person's life; the person's whereabouts and well-being is their business. Even more frequently, "own, proper" *(giom)* is used in kinship talk as an adjective to emphasize that someone is an actual, close relative, as I touched on earlier when noting that Korowai readily distinguish between "proper" relatives and "just habitually so" relatives. For example, speakers often identify a man as their "proper uncle" *(mom giom)* or "truly own uncle" *(mom giom-xajan),* as a way to underline that the man is the actual sibling or clanmate of the speaker's mother, or otherwise make a claim about the closeness and uniqueness of the man's position as "uncle."

Possession's presence at the core of the idea of kinship is also apparent in the use of concrete imagery of clasping to express attachment. People speak of kin as "reciprocally holding" *(xolo-xolo ati-)* each other: they actively seize each other as valued others. Korowai also make statements like *bəmɔlemopɔleda* "I won't let go [of him or her]," to express similar intensity of feeling. A noun meaning "taking hold of" *(atibalef,* derived from the verb *ati-* "hold") is itself a quasi-kinship term. A speaker uses "my taking hold of" as a term of address and ref-

Figure 15. Ngengel Bolüop, 2002, happy after arriving at the house of her brother, where she can hold her brother's daughter, Soləni, who herself holds a puppy. The long string of dog canines on the girl's body materializes her parents' sense of her beauty and value. Ngengel celebrated seeing the girl by singing repeatedly, "My father, that which is his, my mother, that which is hers," as if the prelinguistic child were describing herself in song as her parents' prized belonging.

erence for someone the speaker embraces as a special friend or deliberately chosen kinsperson. In keeping with values of autonomy and separateness, Korowai adults are wary of casual touch or clasping. Thus the
idea of "holding" another person is all the more forceful as a willful
assertion of relatedness. In a frequent small ritual of kinship celebration, two relatives who live separately might shake each other's hands
when they meet after a period of separation, such as at a feast. They
lock gazes and enthusiastically repeat possessively prefixed kinship
terms for each other while pumping their forearms up and down, in a
harmonization of grasp and linguistically represented possession. The
entire act of symmetrical bodily, visual, and verbal contact is a stark
icon of their overall kin relation.[13]

Grammatical possession and acts of holding are quickenings of a well-
known property of kin categories in general, namely that they describe
forms of being-in-relation (Faubion 2001: 21): "The terms of kinship are
inherently linking terms; . . . they render the self in and through its relation to certain others (and vice versa)" (p. 3). As I have already touched
on, a kinship category applied to some person categorizes that person relative to another, the propositus. Categories like "mother," "uncle," and
"relative" involve almost seamless metonymic identification of persons
with relations and relations with persons. The categories say that a person *is* his or her relations with certain others: a person as a topic of discourse is surrounded by a periphery of relatives. Occasionally Korowai
figuratively identify themselves with a kinsperson's speaking perspective.
For example, a speaker sometimes uses the construction "he who killed
me" *(nülmoboxa)* to refer to a man who killed the speaker's close relative.
So too people's more routine possessive prefixation of straightforwardly
used kinship terms emphasizes that a kinship other is a predicate of oneself. A speaker recognizes the other as the speaker's own, and embraces
that other as an object proper to the speaker's own being.

In relations between kin even more strongly than in relations
between people and land, possession goes two ways. In my discussion
of the landscape of clan places in chapter 1, I indicated that in expressions such as "place owner" *(bolüp giom-anop)* or "my proper place"
(nə-bolüp-giom) Korowai often understand relations of possession
and ownness as being bidirectional rather than just a matter of unidirectional dominion over property. So too even more strongly with
possession of kin: a person is defined by and dedicated to that which is
his or her "own." The relation of possession describes the possessor's
subjectivity as being constituted and affected by the relation to the

other, not just the possessed other being defined by the possessor, and at the possessor's disposal. Categories such as "my relative," "my son," or "my younger sister" say as much about who the speaker is as they say about the referent. The categories describe not only relatives an ego has but also something of how two people feel about each other and how they act toward each other. This two-way quality is again why I consider "belonging" a relevant term of translation and interpretation. A statement of possession is a succinct, dense claim of intersubjective closeness: there is an emotional, moral dimension to these relations, according to which kin are people who think about each other, are attached to each other in love and affection, care about each other, and feel their life is incomplete without each other. Possessor and possessed belong together.

Reckoning with ways that emotion, value, and morality are integral to kin categorization, anthropologists have often previously linked kin relations to feelings of intersubjective mutuality of being, using such terms as "conviviality," "love," "care," "amity," and "enduring, diffuse solidarity" (Trawick 1990; Overing and Passes 2000; Overing 2003; Borneman 1997; Fortes 1969; Schneider 1980 [1968]). In a comparative vein, McKinley (2001) characterizes kinship as a "philosophy" that "many cultures hold about what completes a person socially, psychologically, and morally, and how that completeness comes about through a responsible sense of attachment and obligation to others" (p. 143). These vocabularies are all pertinent to understanding Korowai kin relatedness. Korowai themselves frequently describe specific kin relations in terms of a feeling of "love, longing, care" *(finop)* for a person, a mental activity of "caring for, loving" (*xul duo-;* lit., "thinking about") another person, or a moral condition of being "unitary, solidary, amicable" (*lelip;* lit., "together") with someone. Yet there are at least two ways in which this direction of anthropological thought needs to be qualified and elaborated, if it is to mesh with Korowai practice. One has to do with cultural models of consciousness. In typical New Guinean fashion, Korowai tend not to distinguish strongly between subjective feeling and material action, and they tend not to set much store by immaterial interior experience as a transcendental locus of truth. Thus intersubjective belonging, even in its moral and emotional dimensions, is a practice of concrete material actions, such as face-to-face presence or the giving of food. A second qualification is that kinship is not *Gemeinschaft*. Belonging, as an ideal of kin relatedness, travels with and by its resistances. Kin relations are experiences not only of mutuality of being but also of mutuality of being that is conditioned and supported by mutual strangeness. I close this chapter now by briefly exploring these qualifications together.

KIN AS STRANGERS

For Korowai, kinship belonging involves calling each other by kinship terms, being frequently in each other's presence, living together or near each other, giving each other food and other gifts, and interacting in a mode of unconditional sharing and generous mutual concern. Belonging is known by its objective correlatives: material actions are how people express and experience their emotional, moral involvement. This cultural emphasis on action as the proof of kinship is readily apparent in a lot of Korowai talk about being "relatives" *(lambil)*.[14] For example, people often directly link being relatives to travel into one another's spaces. One man volunteered this statement of principle after I had asked him about his specific kin relations to persons in a house he was visiting: "We are relatives, and so I just now came over here. Without there being any relatives [of mine], I would not have come." Another woman spoke generically of entry into people's houses as marking the difference between nominal kin and close kin: "Those who do not reciprocally enter each other's houses and shacks, they are tree and vine relatives [*du-nan lambil;* i.e., their relatedness is expansively vague and general, in the manner of forest vegetation]. The type who enter each other's houses and shacks, those are truly one's own [*giomǝxa xajan*]."

The type of material act that Korowai perhaps most vividly equate with kinship is giving. Often "relative" effectively means "person with whom one is in a giving relation." Once when I handed a man some tobacco and then told him to share it with bystanders, he retorted, only half in jest, that the other people were "not relatives." He was saying he had no obligation to share with them and would keep the tobacco himself. On another occasion, a youth whose mother was ill disparaged another man's expressions of distress about the woman's possible death by observing that the other man had not actually practiced his claimed relation with the woman. "It's not as though he has been coming around giving her food and calling her mother," the youth said. Korowai readily say that at feasts and on other occasions of encounter, relatives should spare no effort in eagerly giving each other food and other objects. Doing so means they *are* relatives; failing to do so makes their relation "just a matter of sight" *(luloptanux;* lit., "eyes alone"). People also identify cognitive categories such as "love" or "think about" with concrete giving. Once I asked a man whether it was a general quality of an uncle and nephew's relation that they "think about" each other. He answered, without missing a beat, that uncle and nephew give each other tobacco and small bits of food. What else could I have meant?

This intense focus on knowing kinship by concrete actions also means that Korowai expect states of kinship between persons to be demonstrated and reevaluated from one day to the next, or even from one practical event to the next. Many kin bonds rest in deeply sedimented habits and convictions of being, including people's taken-for-granted understandings of how their bodies have come to exist. Yet these same bonds are often characterized by back-and-forth influence between states of being and acts of doing. Kinship processes are an area of ambiguous meetings, gaps, and overlaps between what people take as givens of their relational being and what they take as changeable stakes of their actions.

A striking pattern here is the frequency with which Korowai describe someone they were not previously related to as having "become a relative" *(lambil-lelo),* through actions of reciprocal visiting, cooperation, and food giving. Stories of persons who were formerly strangers becoming kin in this way are common, and current changes are amplifying the pattern. Many people say that while "faraway people" within the Korowai-speaking population are by definition not relatives with each other, in recent times they are increasingly becoming kin. For example, in connection with tourism, with the late 1990s small boom in harvesting eaglewood (Ind. kayu gaharu), and with the founding of villages and increasing orientation toward village-mediated acquisition of imported store-bought commodities, Korowai men or couples travel more readily to distant lands than they used to. This often leads to residentially separate people describing themselves as having "become relatives."[15]

The Korowai understanding that kinship is determined by action is also vividly expressed, in an opposite way, by a recurrent type of myth episode in which protagonists deliberately *prevent* someone from becoming a relative, through an act of violence on that other character's dead body. Korowai myths *(waxatum)* are diverse in their plots, but a large fraction of them end in a single kind of coda. Through some sequence of events a morally corrupt male character gets his just desserts and dies. His corpse then turns into an animal body (if he had not already taken on animal form as part of his earlier mischief). In the stylized coda, the other surviving main characters in the narrative summon more people to the scene, to consume the dead animal body. The protagonists' and narrators' standard explanation for the act of consumption is, "Later children will become relatives" *(betopmbam lambiteloxai)*. This is an elliptical statement to the effect that if the myth characters did not eat the dead man's body, then the animal species into which he had transformed would be kin with humanity, making the animal inedible for all subsequent people, including present-day humans. Myth protagonists perform a pathos-laden duty of making the dead man unrelated. They actively deny their kinship with him, for the well-being of human successors and as a sequitur of the morally corrupt man's own previous relation-denying actions.

The idea that kin relations are made in action is well illustrated also by the joking avoidance partnerships I discussed in chapter 2. In that special person reference practice, two persons participate in a quasi-kinship relation that was created by their own highly specific shared history of a single event of interaction. Most often, as we saw, these were events of food sharing. The contrast with cannibalistic myth endings is instructive. In one case, destroying and incorporating a food object *together* makes persons related, and their relation is described by the very object they consumed; in the other, eating another person *as* food starkly asserts and confirms that the person is an unrelated stranger (see Valeri 2000: 204, 447–48 n. 57).[16]

In later chapters of this study I look more substantially at concrete actions through which kin bonds are made and known, including, above all, acts of giving food. Here I want to note the way in which this event-focused understanding of kin ties is another level at which Korowai kin relations are made of a systematic joining of intimacy and otherness, or belonging and estrangement. The focus on knowing kin relations through events means that these relations are highly subject to demonstration and skepticism. It is in the nature of kin bonds (as Korowai understand them) that the people involved in these bonds are very sensitive to the contingency of their kinship standing. Kinship belonging is an impossible standard: the ideal includes its own failure. People scan their actual practices of social relating against the standard for signs of relationships' confirmation or lapse. Kin are aware that a relation of belonging *could become* other than it is or seems, across time and events. They are also aware that relations of belonging have been *made* through past events, turning persons who were formerly strangers *(yaniyanop)* into relatives. In other words, people are aware of the past or potential stranger in the relative. The myth endings in which a transgressive character is deliberately prevented from becoming a relative of later humans can similarly be interpreted as crystallizing a sense that there is a systematic relation between some people in the world being strangers and some being close kin. In a world that is organized as a spectrum of alterity, certain persons have to be "food"; that is, one interacts with them without mutual care. I earlier quoted one person's definition of "uncles" as being relatives one thinks of and goes to be with, when one thinks about all people being strangers, not relatives; the man's statement was typical of how the sense of an overall field of people with whom one does not belong closely informs the experience of relations to people with whom one *does* belong.

This point is more straightforwardly apparent in the fact that saying someone is "not a relative" is a common Korowai turn of speech. This is like saying that the person is a "stranger" *(yaniyanop)*, or is "not together, not unitary" *(bəlelipda)* with oneself. All these are statements that people generally only make about someone else when out of the other person's earshot (notwithstanding the example above of the man to whom I gave tobacco). This type of relation-denying statement, together with people's pattern of calling each other by kinship terms almost universally in conversation, again highlights the systematic ambivalence of kinship as a mode of relating. Using kinship terms for people who in other contexts are described as "not a relative" is not a form of interactional bad faith, devoid of the forms of moral, emotional belonging associated with kin categories as such. On the contrary, people use kinship terms even with "strangers" because, according to Korowai social moralities, just acting in each other's conversational presence is itself a form of mutuality of being and calls for a degree of such mutuality. This calling is also in contradiction to the felt social strangeness of interlocutors to each other, on dimensions other than copresence in the same place at a certain moment.

Significantly, the term *lambil* "relative" itself has a two-edged quality. Like the German category *heimlich* in Freud's account, *lambil* is a word "the meaning of which develops in the direction of ambivalence, until it finally coincides with its opposite" (Freud 1955 [1919]: 226). In some contexts of speaking, people use the term mostly as an assertion of social closeness. They include as their "relatives" their closest family members, or any acquaintance with whom they regularly interact. At other times, though, people pose "relative" as *contrasting* with close kin positions such as parents or clanmates. In these uses, describing someone as merely a "relative" is socially pejorative rather than affirmative, analogous to the more focused force of saying that a person is only a "tree and vine relative," or "not a relative" at all. This versatility of "relative," as both a term of closeness and one of distance, is symptomatic of the ambivalence of many kinship positions in Korowai understanding.

A related common turn of discourse that is broadly characteristic of the alienations of kinship in Korowai experience is the frequency with which speakers describe relatives as something a specific person "has" or "lacks." Someone with a lot of relatives is "kin-having, with kin" *(lambil-manxa)*, while someone else is "kinless" *(lambil-alinxa)*. These are not idle observations but evaluative explanations and arguments. For someone to "have relatives" means having political supporters who will rise in anger when a person is wronged; it means being given food and other articles; it means being given bodily life; and it means having people to cooperate with in collective projects. Often people describe someone else as "having relatives" when contemplating conflict with that person. In a variant on the formula, for example, one young man told another why he was not trying to shoot the other for accidentally killing his pet cockatoo: "You've got your relatives' uproar" *(gəlambilaup-manxa; i.e., "your relatives would be furious")*. "Lacking relatives," meanwhile, is something speakers very often attribute to themselves. When talking about wealth or dearth of kin, speakers sometimes substitute the more general category "people" *(mayox)* for "relatives" *(lambil)*. For example, when I once asked a woman whether she was going to issue any formal invitations to her clan's upcoming feast, she replied, "It is not as though I have people. My people don't exist *[nəmayox manda]*." Being a relative is again most basically a matter of generic possession. A relative is "my person." That is already saying enough.

Having kin is valuable; lacking them is pitiable. This is an area where Korowai experience major social inequality. It is common for specific persons to see themselves as impoverished in wealth of people with whom they belong, or to represent themselves to others as piteously impoverished. Describing oneself as lacking relatives is saying one has no human home, in a world of belonging. Taking mutuality of being between kin as an ideal of life, Korowai also set up the terms in which persons articulate their separation from the structures of belonging by which others around them are living. These terms allow people to express belonging's alienness to their own lives. In keeping with the understanding that kinship is made through actions, when a speaker describes herself as kinless, this does not always mean that she is an orphan whose close kin have all died. Rather, it usually means that the person's hopes and desires for kinship are not well met by her actual interactions with the relatives she has. It is also telling in this respect that statements of kinlessness often arise as sequiturs to situations of *material* dearth. When I questioned people about whether they possessed specific objects or foods, often they immediately turned this into an issue of lacking relatives. Being kinless is the cause of material dearth, and it is the directly indexed obvious meaning of material dearth. "Who is going to give [that object] to me?" people would ask, in answer to my queries about whether they had tobacco, a string bag, bananas, or some other specific fixtures of life. Here again, kinship belonging rests in acts of people providing for each other's material survival and pleasure, but now negatively, as something that is regrettably absent from one's life.

In discussing patterns in how Korowai talk about relatives and main patterns in the shape of people's kin field, I have so far presented a lot of broad typifications, in order to build up an overview of Korowai kinship experience. But having outlined some main dimensions of otherness across the overall field of "relatives," I turn now to a more closely drawn account of the contingency of kinship belonging in a specific kind of bond, at the foundation of kinship processes in general.

CHAPTER 4

Children and the Contingency of Attachment

Korowai frequently describe their overall kinship lives as boiling down to the fact that people are certain to die and that there is an imperative that they be replaced by children. When one man and I were discussing the relation between the time of mythological narratives and the time of present human lives, he offered this description of human temporality generally: "A guy lives, has children, and dies. They stay, have children, and die. The children that initially grow and live, those people don't live, they die. The children have children and die, the children have children and die, the children have children and die out." Another woman explained people's thoughts about their existence more evocatively: "'We are like tree trunks, we will break and fall. Let's go down [from houses together] and make many children.'" Someone else responded to my question about the purpose of marriage with a similar narrative:

> [People] say, "Let's have children and go on eating and staying. Without children, we're going to die out, but with kids, we'll live, eat, and die, and the children will live on." They will eat, sit, and die and die. It goes like that and goes like that and the land becomes empty of people. Just trees and rattan, just smooth sago varieties, just thorned sago varieties. If there were no people, there would just be houses and shacks [standing empty]. So men and women, they do their business, and from that women become pregnant and children are born.

Children are at the center of this story that Korowai tell about the basic shape of their lives. From this, we might expect that a close look at Korowai understandings of children would offer important insights into core understandings of kinship generally. Parent-child relations are foundational to other bonds, children are the purpose of other bonds, and children are icons of a general existential dilemma of transience within which all human bonds unfold.

In this chapter I examine Korowai definitions of children for the access they offer to people's understandings of intersubjective belonging. Previously I suggested that for Korowai, kinship *is* belonging. This too is a reason to give a privileged place to child-focused relations in the analysis of kinship: Korowai experience links between parent and child as an extreme of what intersubjective belonging can be. Child-focused relations are probably the most emotionally intense social bonds of Korowai life. Parents and other adults take great pleasure in providing food for children and in having children's company in houses or on the land. They value the physical feel and sight of children's bodies and motions, and they value acts of mutual give-and-take with child partners. To keep in view this intensity of feeling typical of child relations, in my account of these relations I will use the term "attachment" interchangeably with "belonging," since "attachment" emphasizes not only a quality of homelike comfort between people but also people's desire for each other's presence and their sense that to be without each other is to be incomplete.

What is most striking about Korowai experience of children is that relations of child-focused attachment turn centrally on children's otherness. If Goldman (1998: 176) is right to claim that "anthropology in general continues to remain oblivious to the 'other' as child," the same cannot be said of Korowai people's own indigenous anthropology. The medium of otherness thematized most intensely by child relations is time. People's routine statements about human transience and generational succession, outlined above, are typical of the time-saturated character of child relations, but I want to look here at a broader range of ways that ties to children are made of temporal otherness. People's relations with children are defined by past, future, and hypothetical times alongside present moments. When they relate to children, people engage with the noncontemporaneity of actors who are in other ways mutually contemporary. In this way child relations foreground *intertemporality* as a cultural fact: difference of time and connection across separate times.

In Korowai social relations, a time is not a self-standing element that precedes its engagement with other times but is made out of its relations with times external to it. Different persons have disparate memories and futures, and this otherness of time is central to people's mutual attachments. We have already seen that Korowai focus on temporal otherness as a medium of social connection in such areas as relations to maternal kin that are colored by histories of a woman's interlocal marriage and bodily actions, person reference partnerships that locate relatedness in a shared past experience, models of human genesis that identify living people as reincarnations of dead predecessors, and models of place ownership that take belonging to flow from histories of action on the land. Yet it is arguable that relations with children dwell on otherness of time more intensely than all other bonds, such that children are taken up as major figures of social temporality at large.

A linked sense in which relations with children are vividly time-focused is the relations' rootedness in events, as well as in an indigenous semiotics of knowing relationships by actions. We will see that as *new persons*, children are the focus of social processes foregrounding vividly that attachment between people is *made* and that it is made in specific media of social relating. Attachment is not independent of time but has time as its content. It exists by virtue of interruptions, when something new happens, and it exists by virtue of two people sharing a sedimented history of other times when one person created and cared for the other. I refer to these patterns as an "indigenous semiotics" to underscore that kinship attachment is for Korowai a discipline of signification and sign-interpretation. I document the time-saturatedness of child relations in this chapter by surveying Korowai ideas about what a child signifies: the actions, persons, and times that define a child and that are made present through a child.

My discussion is organized around four kinds of intertemporal moments that are revelatory of a child's definitions. First, I look at a moment of futurity: experience of children as temporal successors to parents' lives. Second, I look at a moment of sexual history: the inferential links drawn between a woman's pregnant body and earlier bodily intimacy with a man. Third, I look at the moment of birth itself, including (in the past) people's occasional contemplation of infanticide, which underlined the possibility of no attachment at all between people. Fourth, I look at the time of child care and companionship in the present, and the creation of attachment through overtly contingent actions of one person making a difference for another.

CHILDREN AS FUTURITY: "REPLACEMENT"
AND THE ANTICIPATION OF DEATH

My mother, whom I loved and knew quite well, links
me to that foreignness, that other thing that was her
life and that I really don't know so much about and
never did. . . . Parents link us . . . to a thing we're not
but they are; a separateness, perhaps a mystery.

                    Richard Ford, "My Mother, in Memory"

Korowai take great interest in observing children's acquisition of
bodily and expressive abilities. Stages of childhood are measured not
in calendric units but in actions. Does an infant see other people and
smile in response? Does it climb up a house ladder pole, protected by
a parent climbing at the same time? Does a child walk about by itself?
Does a boy play with a toy bow and arrows, or a girl with a toy sago-
pounding hammer? Often myths include an episode in which a newly
married couple have a child and experience its stages of maturation.
A narrator lists in quick succession the different actions the child
becomes able to do. In daily life people note with pleasure the skills
and achievements of maturing children, such as a particular boy's or
girl's emerging abilities as a singer. Children are perceived as persons
undergoing a developmental process. They are on the way to becoming something other than what they are. Their significance is colored
by expectation. Children *are* their potential for future abilities and
actions.

This is very clear in statements about what children are for. In diverse
contexts people speak spontaneously of children's value. One main kind
of reason people cite in favor of having children is their expected bodily
acts on later maturation, in particular, acts of food procurement and
material provisioning. Often these are gender-specific. "Boys are for making houses, felling trees, and spearfishing. Girls are for pounding sago and
breaking firewood," one woman said. "Children's purpose is later on
they will provide food, make houses, and perform at feasts." A boy is
raised "so that he gets big, kills pigs, dams streams, digs pitfall traps, and
carves bows and arrows. [He's] for provisions *[folapun]*. . . . A daughter
is to cut firewood, pound sago, cook sago, and install clay in a hearth
[when a house has been newly constructed]." Through such statements
adults express an expectation of pleasurably consuming the bounty of a
grown child's work. Some people also emphasize companionship: "A

child is for going around together." "Children are for going around together in a big line [when traveling on forest paths]."

The focus on what a child will do in the future overlaps with the idea that children will outlive older people. As one man put it, "Children are peoples' replacements for when they die. People are pleased by this." I quoted similar broad statements about generational succession at the beginning of this chapter. Much of this discourse, though, focuses on children being the "replacements" *(lemoxop)* of their parents in particular. One idiom focuses specifically on relations of same-sex parent-child identification and succession (as in the relation between the father and son pictured in figure 16): an adult's "body reciprocation, body match" *(loxul-xolop)* is that adult's same-sex offspring. When a speaker uses this idiom to say whether someone has a "body match" or not, the usage implies that having a same-gender child who will live on after one's own death is a basic telos of personhood, and dying without having created a successor is regrettable.

The idea that children are replacements of their parents is again centered on concrete material actions, above all, those of exploiting an owned land base. As one woman put it, "Dying without children is not right [*bəkütenda;* lit., "not adequate"]. When there's a child, he or she will fell the sago groves. If there are no offspring, then strangers will fell the sago, or else the sago groves will be killed by the world. [Children are] also for felling trees and bailing streams." Statements in this vein join the issue of parent-child succession to the understanding that land exists to be exploited. As another person said, "Children are replacements of their parents. They cut trees and build houses where their parents did. They raise pigs and dogs, and eat pigs. Without children, upon dying, people will all be gone. A place without people is not good." Or alternately: "If people die without children, the land will disappear. Trees will grow and it will become primary forest." This sort of statement about children illustrates again how Korowai see as inherently good the actions of living on a place, modifying it, and eating food produced from it. Persons and land have these actions as their true fulfillment. As one woman succinctly put the principle, replying to a question about why people have children: "Who will go around on the place and eat?" Consistent with the patrimonial slant to clanship and landownership, people sometimes focus on replacement of male presences, as in one woman's statement: "When a father dies, his child enters and gets very big. He becomes big at his father's place, makes houses there, and lives. Kids are for replacing a father on his place, building houses, and having kids themselves."

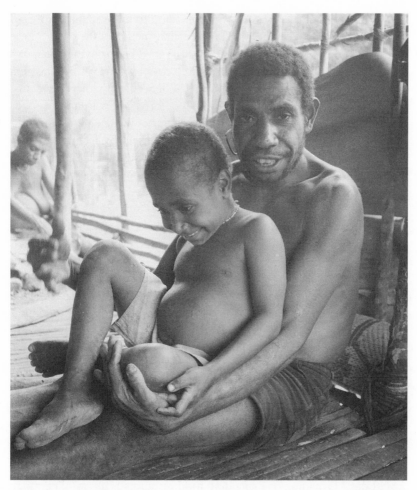

Figure 16. Yakop Dayo holding his son Musa, 2002. Musa's mother Ngain Xomai Xajaxatun is at left.

These convictions about children make visible the directness with which Korowai understand landownership as not only a geographic fact but also a temporal one. Korowai carry out cultural activities with a general understanding that they do what their predecessors did before them. When pressed to explain why they live as they do, people often make statements such as "Predecessors did thusly" *(mbolopmbolop amomate)*. The present is also colored by anticipation of current owners' own deaths, a hope that future successors will carry out similar activities on the land, and an anxiety that there will not be any successors to do so.

There are "extinction territories" *(bamol-bolüp)* all over the land: clan places empty of houses because all the clan members died off. These empty lands are sometimes eventually reclaimed by surviving, diasporically dispersed children, or they are taken over by relatives or strangers in other clans. Even for people of demographically thriving clans, human occupation of land at one time is colored by awareness of other times. The present is permeated by knowledge of living elders' and dead predecessors' earlier actions on the same land and by feelings of both identity and loss in relation to those predecessors. Ownership of land is an open activity, reaching to the activities and times of people who are beyond one's own moment, yet who have close ties to one's own life position.

Sago groves are central to the temporalities of ownership. These groves have a steady cyclicity. A new palm sucker takes roughly fifteen years to mature, loosely matching the tempo of children's maturation. Korowai are quick to compare sago propagation and human generational succession. They also often speak of groves as food resources of the distant future: it is current children who will be around later to exploit them. People's actions of planting, monitoring, and tending groves are actions of relating to their children as future adults. Sago starch is the staff of life, and through this food people relate to their children's futures—and parents' pasts—specifically in the registers of hunger and sustenance. One woman answered my question about why clan membership is inherited from fathers with the following sequiturs: "We [the people of a clan] all have a single common place. Children are so people do not die out. The children fell their parents' sago stands after the parents die. Otherwise, strangers fell the sago. We hold sago. Without sago we would die." Providing or expending food resources is a consoling mode of connection to other people across discontinuities of time and death.

Informing people's orientations to land exploitation as a point of contact with children's other times is a more general principle that persons are known by their signs, above all by the effects of their actions that remain even when the persons who acted are no longer there. People *are* the trees they fell, the sago they pound, the streams they bail, the fish they get from those streams, the holes they dig, and the paths they walk along. The presence of those activities' traces is the presence of people. We could call this a principle of footprints, since actual footprints are one common focus of talk about a person's past presence. Answering a question about why people have children, one person told me, "Children bury their parents and the children alone live. Our clan place will become devoid of people [if there are no children]. Parents' footprints disappear, and children replace them." Footprints' semiotic force lies in the way they signify so directly the person who made them *and also* the perceiver's separateness in time from the signified person's actual act of stepping in soft earth. A footprint is overtly a sign left behind, signifying historical disparity along with connection (cf. Inoue 2004: 39).

Children are also footprints in this sense. Another statement people frequently make about the purpose of raising children is that they exist to be demonstratively pointed out as the offspring of a dead person: they are so people can say, "His/her children are there" *(yəmbammbam xo bate)*. Children are "for saying that that is the son of the guy who died. The guy who died's son is there." This situation of pointing out a physically present child to someone, and identifying it as the offspring of some deceased man or woman, is a common one in day-to-day affairs. The concepts of a replacement or body match involve a combined idea that children are signs by which their parents' distinctive presence in the world will be known and prolonged over the disjunctions of time *and* that these children are signs of parents' transience.[1] Children are not just ways to know parents but also ways to mourn them, as one woman underlined when answering a question about her tie to her child: "I will die and that will be my replacement." Korowai anticipate their deaths as an integral part of their actions of having children and nurturing them toward adulthood.

In these ways children as social others are objects of a complex kind of intertemporal, intersubjective consciousness on parents' part. In a given present people think forward to a time of their own absence, when others will know of them nonetheless by signs that outlasted them.

CHILDREN'S ORIGINS

When Korowai look at a child, they see not only its parents' futures but also their pasts, including bodily actions that have made the child exist. People understand histories of fetal genesis, gestation, and childbirth as parts of a child's being. It is partly *as* an effect of parents' bodily actions that a child can stand as a parent's replacement. Concern with having a replacement is a movement forward from parents to child, whereas concern with bodily genesis is a movement backward from child to parents. These movements draw on each other. They converge in apprehending a child relationally as a sign of other persons and intertemporally as a sign of other times.

In the effort to "take kinship as an empirical question, not as a universal fact" (Schneider 1984: 200), anthropologists have sometimes taken culturally distinctive models of conception and pregnancy as keys to people's understandings of ties between relatives generally. Korowai do not talk elaborately about fetal genesis, in part because men and women alike think menses, parturitional fluids, and reproductive physiology are medically dangerous and repugnant to talk about. But they routinely express a couple of general views. First, though people hold varied, often quite vague notions about how bodily substances become a fetus, all adults consider semen a central component in a fetus's making, and they say that semen derives directly from the sago that people eat. Sago's presence in conception models is another indication of how fascinated Korowai are by their dependence on this food resource for bodily vitality. People also hold that breast milk derives directly from sago. In sago production edible starch is first separated from inedible fibers in suspended form, as a milky liquid. The experience of seeing sago in suspension is an important sensory basis for linking sago to semen and milk. Some people hold that mothers too have semen (dɔxɔte) that joins with fathers' semen to form a child's body. A few men and women hold that mothers are bodily vessels of fetal genesis but that their substances do not go into the child's body. (A small minority of persons even rationalize patrilineal inheritance of clan identity in these terms.) Most persons, though, hold that there is some unnamed, unspecified, but important maternal contribution to a fetus's body. The maternal physiology of fetal formation, including a fetus's relation to menstrual blood, is generally not something about which people are curious or talkative. Yet a sense that there are strong links of substance between mother and child surfaces obliquely, in such contexts as speakers' use of the expression "my leftover blood" to refer to a younger sibling. Overall, discourse on the substances that go into fetal formation links pregnancy to a vegetal substance and (indirectly) to bodily growth derived from eating. The discourse downplays blood and flesh.

A second, related view about fetal genesis focuses on events rather than substances. In a common New Guinean refrain, Korowai say that pregnancy results from a man and a woman having a lot of sex. It is through repeated sexual relations that reproductive substances build up in a woman's uterus to form a fetus. People often speak wryly of the actions that create a child as "big work" (lubutale), at which a husband and wife "struggle" (afu-). This theory of fetus formation makes a child's body a direct sign of a temporally repetitive, durative kind of intimacy and cooperation between its parents. A child is an effect of the parents' sustained actions. Also significant here is the overtness with which Korowai see a child as a prompt to inferential reasoning about unseen realities behind appearances. Another statement that Korowai routinely make about fetal genesis is that "a child doesn't grow by itself," or "a woman doesn't get pregnant herself." These statements assert that pregnancy, as an attribute of a woman's body, does not just happen but requires the agency of someone who is not present. That pregnancy doesn't just happen by itself might seem too obvious to be worth saying. But for Korowai, the statement resonates deeply with a general experience of the world as consisting of appearances that should be read for the hidden agents, actions, and relations behind them. Remarkably, the other event that Korowai regularly assert doesn't happen by itself is death. People assume that behind every death there must be the hidden agency of a male witch. Events of pregnancy and death are each in the first instance signs, provoking a mental search for the man who has had this effect. The conviction that pregnancy in particular doesn't happen by itself recalls the discourse of replacement, which relates parents and children as predecessors and successors on the land: a child, including an unborn one in a woman's uterus, is preeminently a sign of other people and their actions.

Models of how a fetus forms from bodily substances are elements in a wider field of ethnosemiotic, historicizing judgments Korowai avidly make about each other. Understanding who a child is and how that child is emotionally and socially attached to others involves knowledge of histories, such as who had sex with whom, who gestated and bore whom, or who owned what land and tended sago there. Relating to a child also involves knowing about other events of social contact, such as histories of care on a birth scene and histories or futures of food giving and companionship. Children are signs, at one time, of actions that have led to that time or that might follow after it.

AMBIVALENCE TOWARD NEWBORNS

The moments after an infant's birth are another time when reflexive views about child relations are highly visible. There are two simultaneous poles in Korowai relations to newborns: a pole of care, hope, and positive evaluation and a pole of indifference, fear, and dislike. I discuss these poles now in major part through a look at Korowai people's remembered but recently abandoned practice of infanticide. Over the past three decades Korowai became acutely aware that all new intruders into their lands disapprove of infanticide, and they stopped the practice. Prior to this shift, though, a significant fraction of newborn children were asphyxiated right after birth. Male and female newborns were killed in equal proportions. My fieldwork inquiries about infanticide in the 1990s and after were inquiries into "memory culture." I discuss here what Korowai told me about this practice, not so much for the interest of the practice itself as for the ways infanticide and controversies over it made visible complex sensibilities and assumptions that Korowai experience in relation to birth events generally. Infanticide was a consequential, important social practice, but my real concern lies in wider convictions about newborns and human relatedness that people articulate on the birth scene and that continue to stand out sharply in talk about infanticide as a past activity. In their thought about newborn infants, Korowai understand belonging as a contingent creation between humans, not a given. Events of confronting and overcoming absence of attachment by choosing to care for another person, and consciousness of the possibility that people could decide not to care for someone, are integral to the experience of care itself. My way to get at this model of human attachment here is to look at moral understandings that made infanticide thinkable, and complementary moral understandings people acted on in keeping newborns rather than killing them. The main motives for infanticide that I explore are judgments that birth processes and newborns' bodies are repulsive, classification of newborns as nonhuman, an explicit view that attachment to children arises only through social interaction, pessimism about the world into which children are born, and hostility to the hardships of caring for a child.

Men and women alike are intensely fearful of the medical dangerousness of birth fluids, birth odors, placentas, and newborns' bodies. They think that contact with these substances, like contact with menstrual blood, causes chronic and debilitating coughing, as well as male baldness. The perceived miasmatic danger prompts people to organize the physical events of birth around goals of physical separation. When a woman's labor begins, her husband digs a hole in the ground over which she will squat and lines it with palm fronds. This enables her to expel the infant and placenta into the ground, then lift and clean the infant while leaving the placenta and other wastes there untouched. Later the wastes are covered with dirt and heavy planks and fenced off, so pigs and dogs will not dig them up. A mother and her female attendant cannot help being in the birth area during the delivery, but other people stay away. Out of concern for a laboring woman's comfort and safety, a birth usually occurs in a clearing—but at some distance from the clearing's occupied houses, typically below a small shelter that has been built for the event or below an abandoned house that can be briefly used again. Out of fear of substances that flow or waft from a mother and child's bodies for some days after the birth, the two ideally live apart from their main household during this time, the woman sitting over a pollution-catching container fitted into the floor of her temporary shelter.

The physical layout of delivery meant that in the past when Korowai killed and buried a newborn rather than caring for it, they could do so without touching it. It was a mother herself, or sometimes her attendant, who carried out infanticide, by poking leaves into the newborn's throat with a stick while it still lay in the hole into which the mother had delivered it. The absence of bodily contact here seems to have stemmed from the central, creative power of direct touch in the making of kinship bonds: avoiding touch was part of a process of preventing even the most minimal social relations with the infant.

Korowai often disagreed over the fate of a particular newborn, as I discuss below, but they did not consider infanticide itself an immoral act. The basic reason for this was that newborns are categorized as inhuman.[2] Consistent with the perception that birth processes are repulsive and dangerous, Korowai say that a newborn is "demonic" *(laleo)* rather than "human" *(yanop)*. People explain this categorization by noting that a newborn's skin is uncannily pale, that newborns are torpid, and that their bodies are generally freakish. Babies are perceived to "become human," and acquire a "human body" *(yanop xatop)*, a month or two after birth, when their skin darkens, they begin reacting socially to others, and their proportions normalize.

As I outlined in earlier chapters and describe in more detail in chapter 6, the category "demon" refers mainly to the malignant, rotting, zombie-like walking corpses that humans become after death. Korowai also apply this category to an open-ended range of other anomalous, uncanny entities. Calling newborns demonic is one of these wider uses, and the use is typical of the "demon" category's status as an all-purpose term for anything experienced as strange and deformed relative to the perspective of a speaking human. Newborns' relation with monstrous after-death demons verges toward full identification. For example, it is a convention of dream interpretation that seeing a baby in a dream represents an encounter with an after-death demon. People occasionally express spontaneous fear that a recently born infant will "pluck the voice" of someone around it, ordering that person to die. This action of plucking the voice of a living person is normally associated with the walking-corpse type of monsters. The action is one of the monsters' characteristic attributes.

Categorizing newborns as deathly and alien supports parents' lack of felt attachment to children at the time of their birth. Humans feel no inherent moral obligations to the radically alien beings, and in the past this is what made suffocation of newborns possible to contemplate. As a number of women said when explaining how infanticide had been thinkable, "On the birth scene, there is no love" *(xondulbol finop manda)*. This lack of feeling for newborns is also expressed by the main verbs by which speakers narrate past infanticidal acts: *salmoxo* and *pümoxo*, both meaning "discard, throw away," with the implication that the discarded object was a little-regarded item of trash.

It is also relevant here that Korowai routinely say of an infant, "It has no relatives" *(yəlambil manda)*. A child acquires relatives only when it becomes an interactive person and enters circuits of mutual recognition and giving with specific others. This understanding is not something that people bring up in discussions of infanticide; a child's acquisition of relatives unfolds across a longer, slower temporal period than its quick passage from "demon" to "human" in the months right after birth. Yet this model of a child initially lacking relatives and then acquiring them through interaction is indicative of people's general standoffishness toward an infant around the time of its entrance into the world, such that infanticide was an imaginable possibility.

Because there is such a vacuum of felt belonging toward a newborn as a physical organism, acts of care that people do perform for it have extraordinary relational force. Spatial and categorial othering of newborns defines an arena of contingent relation-making action. The moments after a birth were times when people brought incompatible possibilities of infanticide and care into confrontation with each other, through verbal debate and physical actions.

Infanticide and care were separated by a literal knife's edge. By a tacit performative logic, when a mother or her attendant cut a newborn's umbilical cord and removed it from the hole into which it was born, the alternative of infanticide was negated. Infants were not suffocated once the cord had been cut. Cutting the cord and lifting the child are first events of humans acting on the alien being, making contact with it and incorporating it into their relations of care. The act of carrying a newborn into a dwelling has a similar ritual force of incorporating the child into relations of human moral attachment rather than leaving it in the domain of death. Following cord cutting and initial cleaning of the newborn's body, a mother or her attendant places the newborn into a segment of sago leaf midrib and carries this trough upward into a shelter. These bare actions of caring contact with a newborn's body are freighted with power. As one woman said in explaining a friend's lack of grief after a stillbirth, "It's not as though she carried [the infant] and entered [the house], and then gave the breast. No big deal." Mothers who have held and nursed an infant for some days or months explicitly describe their love for the child as following from this physical contact and from the child's increasing bodily responsiveness (cf. Conklin 2001: 128). The ritual force of cord cutting participates in this broader logic, according to which attachment to a child is made and expressed by *acting on* that child.

Cord cutting's force was explicit in the past when there were disagreements about a newborn's fate. I first became aware of such disagreements when studying joking avoidance partnerships. Acts of care on the birth scene are often commemorated in these partnerships. The single most common avoidance term is "my compassion" *(nainap)*. I learned of roughly one hundred fifty instances of two people calling each other by this term, out of a sample of two thousand joking avoidance partnerships. This term is always based on an event of a senior partner having expressed compassion for the junior immediately after birth, whether verbally or through a physical act. Usually the history commemorated by the term involves the senior partner having expressed care for the child when other persons were against keeping it. Two other common joking avoidance terms are "my umbilicous-cutting" *(nəmanüdun)* and "my carrying and climbing" *(nəbandolun),* also always based on the senior partner having performed the named act on the junior partner just after birth.

Parents never formed "cord cutting," "carrying up," or "compassion" relations with their children, even though parents and children do form joking avoidance partnerships commemorating other kinds of events, such as shared snacks. A "compassion" relation is between a child and a nonparental relative. Often the senior "compassion" partner acted *against* the wishes of a parent in expressing care for the child. (For the parents' parts, mothers and fathers spoke out against keeping a newborn with equal frequency, sometimes disagreeing and other times converging in their views. There was no tendency for the wishes of mothers to count more strongly than the wishes of fathers, or vice versa.) In about one-third of "compassion" partnerships, a senior partner prevented an infant's suffocation not just verbally or hypothetically, but by physically cutting the newborn's umbilical cord against a parent's wishes or even by removing leaves from the infant's throat. It was only women who intervened physically in this way, because men were too fearful to approach the birth site, but men could influence a newborn's fate by calling out or by sending messages. The tenor of discussion and action around a birth was highly characteristic of Korowai egalitarian decision making. Persons might speak up in conflict or agreement, but no single person or deliberative process was recognized as an ultimate authority. A newborn's fate was often the emergent result of unpredictable, impetuous acts.

The verbal arguments for or against keeping an infant that adults articulated on a birth scene offer further insight into Korowai understandings of children and human attachment. Speaking in favor of keeping a newborn, relatives expressed their compassion in terms of diminutive acts of service and companionship the child would later perform: "That's the one who's going to go around with me"; "That's the one who's going to hand me my tobacco pipe"; "That's my grandfather, he will toss fishing line and catch little fish"; or, as one person said after the birth of a female infant to a woman with several sons, "Who will pound sago for the brothers?" Consistent with categorization of newborns as monstrous, people put their feelings of compassion in terms of what the infant would become, not what it already was. The child's future actions and skills were the reasons to care for it. Further, these statements located human value and attachment in small, iconic acts of giving and helping. A child will perform little acts of care toward the same adults who have cared for it (cf. Rosaldo 1982: 204). These experiences of reciprocal care, and shared small bounties of a child's productive action, are the signs in which an interpersonal bond is pleasurably known. One youth I met regularly gives fish and other small gifts to his "compassion," a senior woman who saved his life at birth. This giving is unusual, in that "compassion" relations (like other joking avoidance partnerships) do not conventionally involve formal practices of giving or assistance. Yet the youth's case illustrates well the affection usually felt in compassion relations. The relations link birth events intertemporally to later experiences of shared pleasure, and they link experiences of shared pleasure to an earlier time of dramatic actions on a birth scene.

Parents who spoke in favor of infanticide at the time of a child's birth later often express disbelief at what they wanted. By the same logic of companionship that people spell out when they talk about a child's future acts of giving, a parent begins feeling intense affective attachment to a child after experiencing the child's responses to parental acts of care, in the form of pleasure, recognition, and return acts of care.

At the time of a child's birth, though, if a parent or other relative advocated discarding a newborn, he or she often gave explicit reasons. While the "demonic" status of newborns fosters indifference to them, there were generally more specific motives for infanticide atop this one (cf. McDowell 1988: 18). One way in which a parent or other person argued in favor of infanticide was to express pessimism about the world. Some persons cited perceived or expected apocalyptic events such as environmental degradation or the presence of foreigners in the land. Parents frequently argued for infanticide by maligning the meagerness of their sago holdings, their poor skills as hunters and gardeners, or their land's lack of food. A newborn was a cipher around which persons articulated harsh critiques of the quality of their lives. Food-focused critiques are notable for having located children's significance in the same place as positive discourses of attachment. The question of the child is the question of caring for another through the provisioning of food, and being cared for by those others or by the overall environment. More generally, a child's status as a sign of the present moment and its futures cut both ways: a view that the world is turning "bad" *(lembul)* could be expressed by denying the desirability of raising a child at all.

Protesting against more immediate social circumstances, a parent or other relative sometimes argued for infanticide by citing bad paternity. The mother's relatives often supported infanticide on the grounds that the father had not given appropriate bridewealth. It was also common for someone to support infanticide on the grounds that the newborn was a "stealth baby" *(nanem-mbam)*, born of adultery. Posthumous babies, and sometimes the first baby born to a remarried widow, could be discarded on the grounds that the newborn was associated with the malign demon of the mother's deceased earlier husband. Paternity-focused ambivalences are again evidence of the directness with which Korowai see a baby's body as a sign of a man and his intimacy with its mother. Paternity-focused arguments also underline how an infant's birth was broadly answerable to wider moral logics of marriage and death: there are standards of payment, of collective sanctioning of a couple's intimacy, and of a man's ongoing survival that some people felt should be met if they were to be comfortably disposed to a child's existence.

Other arguments for infanticide objected to the moral bargain of child-raising, especially its self-sacrificial aspect. The elliptical expression "shit and piss" *(ol-dul)* was a conventional argument against keeping a newborn, focused on the visceral unpleasantness of early child care. An unwilling parent often also described raising a child as a "big bother" *(lubutale)*, or mentioned specific hardships such as sore shoulders or reduced food portions. Mothers who had already mourned many children's deaths, after growing attached to them, sometimes advocated discarding a newborn, because it was going to die later anyway. (Conversely, parents also cited past children's deaths as a reason to *keep* a newborn.) These statements all underscored that a mother and father are closer than other persons to the wearying, painful, repulsive, and demoralizing sides of bearing children and caring for them. Parents are particularly aware of these sides at the time of an infant's birth. Korowai at large routinely say that the physical deterioration of adults' bodies is caused and accelerated by having children (cf. Biersack 1987; Clark and Hughes 1995: 323). A hostile, Laius-like perception that children are their parents' deaths lurks in the background of the past practice of infanticide and of the ongoing categorization of newborns as death-associated and death-causing demons.

What is striking about parents' rationales for infanticide is how close all the various types of antichild protests are to even stronger discourses of parental *celebration* of child relationships. The idea that children "replace" their parents is one of the most important, valuable features of children in Korowai eyes. Here too there is an intrinsic connection between children and their parents' deaths, but it is a connection that makes the idea of death bearable rather than leading people to feel hostile to children. When parents contemplating responsibility for a new child maligned their land and its resources, they put into words the same link of children and human activity on land that in other contexts is expressed as hope that future persons will exist to exploit a place's bounty. Parents assert these positive values of children ("replacement," being a sign of a father, exploiting land after elders have died) even more intensely than other relatives. Positive and negative poles of people's regard for newborns are in close proximity.

Having dwelt on infanticide, I should make clear that even at the time of birth most parents welcomed the prospect of a child. At other times virtually all parents are deeply attached to their children. A small illustration of the value placed on children is women's routine use of the expression "my child's father" *(nǝ-mbam-ate)* to address or refer to their husbands. Another indication of children's value is parents' severe bereavement on a child's death, sometimes provoking extraordinary expressions of abjectness such as going about without genital coverings, sleeping atop ashes, wearing a dead daughter's skirt around the neck, or living in the same house with a child's corpse. In all sorts of mundane contexts, even processes of gestation and birth are posed as grounds of extraordinary attachment and relational value, despite people's squeamishness about these bodily processes when in direct contact with them. Everyone dislikes talking about pregnancy, and people's overt statements about actual events of delivery are generally ones of anxiety, pain, and repugnance. Yet in talk at a remove from the birth scene, birth is a figure of intense identification. Explaining love for their mothers, speakers often cite the pain women endured giving birth to them and mothers' work of dealing with the speakers' bodily wastes throughout infancy. These sacrificial maternal labors of engagement with the repulsive, painful inhumanity of newborns become the basis of intense connection. The oft-used expression "my mother, she who bore me" (*nəni nəfubolxa;* lit., "my mother the one who put me") conveys exceptionally poignant attachment and indebtedness. These recollections are more acute variants in a general pattern of attachment that could be paraphrased as, "I was dependent, and you gave to me." The child, now grown, would not exist at all but for the other's sacrifices, underpinning the child's sense of depthless attachment to that other.

These patterns of thought about children make clear that the difference between care and its absence is a sharply felt duality. Involvement in a relation of belonging is informed by feelings about what it would be to have no relation at all. This duality can be lived and remembered as a transformation in time. A child changes from a source of fear, disgust, pain, death, and hardship to a partner in mutual recognition and love. The relation's negative early state makes the change all the more dramatic, and the contingency of early acts of care remains a standard by which parents and children know their later relation. Once I heard a boy scream out, amid a fight with his mother over whether he would travel elsewhere with a party of men, "Mother, if you are going to be this way, why did you cut my umbilical cord?" People take special pleasure in children's companionship, in part because children embody acquisition of attachment as an interpersonal possibility. Children are others who are learning, or will learn, the very possibility of performing acts of care, such as fetching a household object, catching little fish and sharing them, or pounding sago. When interacting with a child, an adult encounters the outlines of any human bond. But even if attachment is something people create by actions of care, the volatile duality of care and its absence remains an ever-present boundary, as the son's shouted question illustrates. He implied that his mother's present treatment of him showed as little belonging and care as would have been shown to a newborn whose cord was not cut. So too when an adult and child feel amicable attachment toward each other, they know this as something lived *against* other possibilities.

This systematic conjoining of attachment and nonattachment as relational possibilities itself overlaps intensely with the duality of life and death. Burial in the earth in a bed of palm fronds is the paradigmatic way Korowai dispose of corpses, so it is striking that children are born into a kind of small tomb from which they may be lifted into life. Whether people's fears of birth fluids and newborns' bodies reflect unease about life-and-death aspects of pregnancy that humans hardly control, or are a rationalization of lack of attachment to newborns stemming from the postnatal demands of child-raising, the monstrous otherness of newborns and the monstrous otherness of the dead are much the same in Korowai eyes. So too talk of "replacement" and other positive statements about children's value squarely locate human attachment as a matter of life in the midst of death and death in the midst of life. I examine these connections at more length in chapter 6.

LIVING WITH CHILDREN: SIGNS OF CARE

I have looked at three temporal layers of a child's meaning: the time of a future when a child will be its parent's replacement, the time of past actions leading to a child's existence, and the time of a child's birth. The time of *living with* children is part of these other times, and they are part of it. I turn now to parent-child copresence itself.

A child's parents are the persons who care for that child most constantly, if they are alive and married. The main verb used to speak of rearing a child, *manopo-*, says a lot about parent-child relations: the word means "cause to be good, improve, make well." This lightly implies that children are "bad" prior to adults' care for them, consistent with negative evaluations of newborns and with people's frequent description of even adolescent children as "inept, deranged, heedless" *(afitun):* they are incapable of certain tasks, they are socially unreliable, or they need protection from hazards. Relations with children are sites of cultural contact. Deliberately showing them how to do things is a major part of raising them, alongside looking after their bodily well-being. For example, parents and other close family members routinely instruct small children who their kin are and what to call them, such as when the children newly encounter those kin during visits. The parents say they do this so that children will know the visitors as relatives rather than strangers.

Yet the verb *cause to be good* also construes children as that which is valuable in life. At each moment of surviving, becoming a little stronger, and becoming a little more skilled, a child is a paragon of the "good." Korowai often drape large necklaces of dog canines or cowries on small children's bodies. I once suggested to a woman that people do this because they think that children are "a bit like the valuables," and she responded with a litany of statements about what a child and valuables have in common: they are both "our that-which-is-good, our that-for-which-we-yearn, our that-which-we-are-holding-hard." One way in which the goodness of children is experienced and expressed is in feelings of great love for them. Parents commonly describe such love directly in statements such as "My feelings for my child are unbelievable" (nəmbamlxe bamondinda; lit., "for my child, it's impossible"). Much more often than they narrate sentiment abstractly, though, caregivers express attachment to children by narrating bodily interactions, bodily sensations, and material transactions. My purpose in sketching now some objects and actions prominent in talk about children is to show more deeply how parent-child bonds are relations of intense belonging, and to clarify further the culturally distinctive shape of bonds of belonging as Korowai experience them.

Parents often express care and longing for their children by speaking of a child's body as a close counterpart to the parent's own in daily life, or by speaking of heat and weight. The woman Ya described her son Nakup as "what I put at my heart, what I put on my chest, what I put on my thigh." Another man spoke of his small daughter as his "leg hair," a metaphor of extreme proximity. People often describe their children as "those who are at [their] shins": children are beings who hold onto parents' legs at shin level, while parents go about their day. Women often speak of a child with whom they sleep as "the warmth at my chest." Parents describe their bond to a child by speaking of sore shoulders, or the child's weight on the parent's body. Often parents thematize weight when they are dealing with loss. For example, a woman might describe her feeling of the missing weight of her child as a way to express her intense grief over its death. One woman, after describing to me a bodily sensation of lightness in the wake of her young daughter's death, went on to explain that she was now comforting herself by carrying her older son to feel his weight, even though he was too big to be carried. She was also now sleeping with the surviving boy at her chest. After his wife's death, a man is similarly likely to speak of the heaviness of the child he carries everywhere, as a way to express his grief and his loss-imbued intensified attachment to the child.

Another representation of children as teleological complements to parents' bodies is the idiom "Just her body exists" *(yəloxütanux bau)*, which is how speakers say a woman is childless. For a woman to be "just her body" is a marked state of lack, by contrast with the better state of being complemented by a child's body the woman has created. This expression parallels the earlier-discussed idiom of a "body match," which construes a child as a replacement whose ongoing life will provide a consoling countermovement to the parent's death. The childlessness idiom, though, is concerned with a time before death, and portrays motherhood as a state of being not "just [one's] own body," but a body with an outside counterpart.

Korowai thus experience a social relation between parent and child as a corporeal condition. Being linked in care to a child is felt in the body. This is true not just of bodies alone, but of bodies as media through which people act in their surrounding world. For example, Korowai associate children's weight with the slowing of travel. A life stage of taking care of children is known as a time of immobility. In addition to curtailing their travel because of the physical difficulties of walking with children, couples divide their daily activities: a mother stays home with small children while their father goes about for food, out of fear that the children would be injured by animals or witches if they too went out. Parents experience relations with children and their concern for children's well-being as a whole adjustment of how they organize their lives and their movements on the land.

Korowai say that a house is "warm" or "heavy" when there are children living in it. Here too people speak of children by describing their effects on the feel of a living situation. These statements are strongly evaluative. To use the idioms is to say that a warm or heavy house is better than a cold or light one. A house with children is better, because children's boisterousness is pleasant and because a bustling, raucous household repels prowling monsters. This contrasts strikingly with the notion that witches are *drawn* to birth smells and to the bodies and voices of newborns—another reason for people's unease on the scene of birth events. Children pass from being demons and witch bait to being shields against these deadly monsters. (The antipathy between boisterous children and monsters clarifies a bit the monsters' own meaning:

they are figures of silence, solitariness, and demographic extinction.) Through idioms of weight or warmth, adults describe themselves as feeling settled, stable, and secure when children are present in their lives and unsettled when they are not. The dominant semiotic pattern is to know attachment to children metonymically, through attachment's material media and effects. Children are the sensation of a heavy, warm, boisterous body in the vicinity of one's own body. They are the changes to life rounds that people make, when they cannot travel far and need to provide for others. Children are the swaying, yelling tumult of a tall house that repels furtive monsters, who otherwise want to approach quiet, unguarded people.

An even stronger metonymic pattern is to know attachment through food objects and the economy of desire and care these objects support. A focus on food as a medium of attachment to children surfaces in many different contexts. We have seen nonparental adults on a birth scene expressing compassion for a newborn by talking about small foods the child will later provide. A similar pattern runs through mothers' expressions of grief at being separated from a child by death. For example, a woman killed in an interlocal feud long before my research used her dying breaths to speak to her younger co-wife about her infant son. With her intestines protruding from her body, she said, "I'm not going to live, I've let go of him, I'm going to die. You will raise my son, you eat the fish he spears." Those fish were what she was losing, in the traumatic interruption of her relation with her son. The fish were the crucial sign for describing the moral shift that was unfolding as she died and her co-wife became the boy's only female caregiver. Mothers bereaved by a young child's death often wail lyrics consisting of names of foods the dead child would have procured and given had it grown to maturity. A woman whose infant son was dying of illness in a house where I once stayed, for example, sporadically broke into sobbed litanies of sung fish species, prefixing them with the possessive pronoun *my*, or putting them in negative sentences describing acts of food giving that would never take place: the dying infant would not give his mother fish.

In a similar vein, parents frequently describe their children as lacking specific foods, and the parents regret their inability to give the foods to them. These patterns stood out to me in part because exotic products now available for purchase in villages are favored foods that parents discuss in these terms. My presence thematized people's desires and prospects in relation to such foods. For example, when I once paid a woman some cash for a globe of sago starch, she spontaneously mentioned she was going to use the money to buy rice and ramen for her young son, who "knows nothing of those sorts of foods." When I spoke with one man whose wife had recently died, he returned again and again to the fact that his young daughter did not have rice or noodles to eat, and that he could not give them to her. This was a tacit appeal to me in particular, but it was also a form in which the widower was regularly experiencing his bereavement. His wife's absence was figured by the pathos of his living daughter, for whom he could not adequately provide. Another man, who is heavily involved in the cash economy, once explained to me that a husband and wife alone would be able to save money, because they could resist the requests of nonhousemates, but that it is impossible to refuse foods or other purchasable objects to one's own children.

In many Western cultural contexts, identifying love between persons with material objects arouses moral anxiety and suspicion. This pattern has no parallel for Korowai. Noodles, fish, and other food objects in stories of parent-child relations are to Korowai potent icons of experiences of mutual attachment. Foster kin bonds emphasize this same principle. Korowai mortality is so high that, as I noted in passing in the previous chapter, it is common for a child to lose at least one parent in early life and be fostered by a substitute parent. The main pattern is for a child's surviving parent to remarry, which makes the child's parent's new spouse its foster mother or foster father. These are what are normally called *stepchild* relations in English, but *foster* is a more apt translation because it echoes the Korowai emphasis on "making good" as the essence of parenting, and also because of the etymological link of *foster* to food. Strikingly, all Korowai linguistic terms for foster kin relations are formed by prefixing words for "pandanus" to more basic kinship terms. A foster father is a "pandanus father," a foster daughter is a "pandanus daughter," and so on for foster mothers and foster sons. To speak of a whole network of foster kin, such as a foster parent's clanmates, a speaker adds a plural suffix to "pandanus": foster relatives are a person's "pandanuses."

Pandanus is a large coblike fruit that can be split, roasted, and kneaded to produce a deep red, edible oily sauce (figure 17). When Korowai use words for "pandanus" to speak of foster relatives, they are highly aware of the food-designating meaning of the terms.[3] Asked to explain why foster kinship is spoken of as "pandanus" kinship, Korowai say that acts of preparing pandanus for a child are characteristic of the fosterage relation and of parenting generally. People also use

Figure 17. Xalxü Malonxatun squeezing red pandanus sauce onto cooked sago, 2007.

the verb phrase "prepare pandanus" idiomatically to say that an adult is foster parenting a child. Foster children commonly recall particular adults' actual actions of preparing pandanus as a way to evoke their filial relations with those adults. Often when explaining the pandanus series of kinship terms, speakers also list other food-providing actions that foster parents perform. Speakers take cooking pandanus and squeezing its sauce as a synecdoche of the overall bundle of ways that parents give sustenance to children.

To provide a vulnerably dependent child with food is to be that child's parent. In joking avoidance partnerships, when people become quasi-kin by sharing a small snack and then calling each other by that snack's name, the kinship is playful. Pandanus kinship involves the same principle that giving food makes kinship relations, but the relations here are not just lighthearted. Calling someone a pandanus relative does not imply unfavorable comparison to birth-based parentage. Rather, there is a special force to pandanus relations. An adult's acts of regularly preparing pandanus sauce for a child are more powerful *because* the adult did not make that child's body in the first place but has come into the child's life later, crossing the boundary into care through food giving itself. In most cases the pandanus parent is caring not just for any child, but specifically for a child whose mother or father has died. This child is dependent and vulnerable in ways all children are, but embodies the additional pathos of having lost a parent who would normally attend to its well-being. Korowai speak of pandanus parentage as an especially poignant form of attachment, by virtue of the way in which the pandanus parent steps into a breach opened by parental death.

Some foster parents rarely prepare pandanus for their foster children because the fruit is not plentiful on their lands. The fruit is not usually a dominant part of a household's diet. Why then do speakers single out pandanus over other foods as an icon of parental care? When asked, Korowai do not offer rationales for the choice, other than to say that the usage is conventional. Yet in other contexts people identify pandanus (which, again, is brilliantly red in color) with blood, with such explicitness that it seems worth speculating a bit about possible blood-related motivations for the place of pandanus in foster kinship.

Korowai think pandanus becomes blood when eaten. According to this humoral model, eating pandanus increases the volume of a person's blood. Meanwhile, words for "blood" are transgressive *xoxulop* designations for pandanus. Speakers are not supposed to say these words in the presence of pandanus, lest this cause persons eating the sauce to vomit uncontrollably. Korowai also hold that pandanus is taboo for menstruating or pregnant women to eat, lest they suffer profuse bleeding. (Three subvarieties of pandanus that are yellow, rather than red, are not taboo in this way.) From even these schematic facts, it is apparent that pandanus is a volatile and ambivalent sign, paralleling the volatile ambivalence of blood itself. When blood is something inside people's bodies that makes them strong, pandanus's resemblance to blood means the sauce is a sign of vitality. When people think of blood as something coming out of a woman's body in association with reproductive physiology, pandanus's resemblance to blood makes it a threatening sign of human vulnerability and fleshly mortality in processes of birth. Meat of wild game animals is also taboo to menstruating or pregnant women, sanctioned by threat of severe bleeding or uterine prolapse. These taboos also imply a problem of dangerous similarity between menstruation or pregnancy and bloody animal death (cf. Valeri 1990; Stasch 1996). I suggest that people perceive pandanus as an apt metonymy of foster parentage for the same reasons that pandanus is dangerous to menstruation and parturition. In a double movement, pandanus as linguistic sign makes fosterage bloody but vegetalizes bodily blood. In the context of parenting, this red sauce can support the perception that feeding and resultant growth *make* the very substance of a child's living body. Foster relations are implicitly figured as blood relations and drawn into the ambit of a child's life-and-death dependence on the bodily generosity of another person. Yet pandanus is also attractive because of its difference from blood. It takes fleshly, life-or-death aspects of parent-child ties in a vegetal direction. Pandanus is too much like animal death to be compatible with menstruation and parturition, but in the safer contexts of day-to-day care for a developing child, this vegetal food's semiotic connection to life and death is a virtue: the red sauce becomes a good name for parenting itself.

One reason that such interpretations are worth developing, though Korowai do not overtly describe pandanus's similarity to blood as bearing on pandanus's salience in fosterage, is that the interpretations show relation-defining parental feeding of children to be in direct dialogue with the mortality-imbued repulsion to birth physiology so apparent in people's attitudes toward newborns. Categorizing newborn babies as inhuman and contemptible is closely related to men's and women's similar feelings of repulsion toward menses and other aspects of female reproductive physiology. Adults' giving of pandanus to their children, or the total practice of food giving that pandanus synecdochically embodies, is not an isolated practice but joins with a child's miasmatic bodily history and turns that history in a direction of human mutual attachment. To give pandanus is to "make good." Adults push off from a child's bodily status as "bad" *(lembul)* with gestures of food-based care that humanize the child and draw it away from death.

Another vegetal mediation of bonds with children lends support to these interpretations: women's use of sago palm parts in several perinatal acts of care that initially draw a newborn into human relations. First, the most common instrument that women use to cut a newborn's umbilical cord is the stripped midrib of a sago leaflet. Second, newborns are carried up into domestic space in a segment of a sago leaf base. Third, when a child is kept, a woman eats a palm heart from a sago tree soon after she gives birth. The meal, called "pregnancy palm heart" *(xondul-aun;* lit., "belly palm heart"), is the first food a mother eats after labor. Fourth, once a newborn's residual piece of umbilical cord dries and detaches, the mother inserts this bit of cord amid the leaf bases of a sago plant in its immature rosette stage, when the palm is a trunkless clump of fronds. Often the midrib, palm heart, and leaf base used for the first three acts just listed are collected from a single palm. To Korowai, the main interest of the various sago-connected rites is that they create a lifelong avoidance relation between child and palm. A person would go "crazy, oblivious" *(enonon)* on ever eating food produced from a sago plant that was the source of objects used at his or her birth, or that was the palm into which the child's umbilical cord had been placed. As with the notion that children are reincarnations of dead predecessors whose identity they must not know, so too in connection with these small perinatal rites Korowai define a child by relations of intense identity and antipathy between it and a certain external object. Often the avoided palm (and its later offshoots) stands on the child's clan land, and the child passes by it regularly in later life. The plant spatializes the event of birth and signifies the person's intimate links to place. But this is an ambivalent intimacy. Aspects of a person's identity are by definition alien to that person's own consciousness.

The small rites also involve the notion that sago-derived objects support an infant's health and growth. Some of the rites appear to use sago's vegetal goodness as an antidote to the bloody, deathly badness of a newborn's body. We have seen that in infanticide no differentiation was introduced between the infant and birth substances. The newborn was left entirely in the category of inhuman and polluting. Sago parts are media for introducing difference here. Sago is generally an icon of value, nurture, and healthy growth. People say matter-of-factly that sago is what makes them strong. The word for all thornless sago varieties together (the varieties that people actively plant and that they use to make starch) is "good, valuable" *(manop)*. People routinely link sago growth to human growth. They use sago biology to quantify age, by describing a person's maturity in terms of how many generations of offspring have propagated from palms that were full grown when the person was born. People also commonly express how old a child is by pointing out a palm and describing how small it was at the time the child was born. In a typical turn of explanation, one mother answered my question about the purpose of putting umbilical cords in young sago palms with the assertion, "The child and sago together will mutually become elders." Here a sago palm not only is a *measure* of growth but also is loosely thought to *cause* a child's growth and health, even to be foundational to a child's sanity and rationality. People likewise say that the reason a mother eats a palm heart soon after giving birth is that this makes the child strong, healthy, and fast growing. The point of using a sago leaf base, which is shaped like a trough, to carry an infant up into a house is that it is an ideal container for keeping the bearer from having to touch the newborn's cough-inducing flesh and fluids. These several rites of putting a newborn in contact with sago substances, as the first human acts toward it, move maternity and human embodiment away from fleshly, bloody birth toward the bloodless processes of palm growth and sustenance by sago eating.

While the prominence of pandanus in Korowai thought about children stems from its redness, not primarily from dietary importance, sago starch is so much people's prototypical food that it is identified with eating itself. "Hunger" is simply "pain for sago" *(xo-lep)*. To eat sago is to be human and social. Soon after the initial acts of perinatal care, an infant enters the economy of sago-based sustenance in a deeper, more repetitive way. We have glimpsed that a mother's action of breast-feeding her infant is explicitly recognized to generate desire and love between the two, and that breast milk is held to derive from sago that the mother eats. Speakers allude to this, for example, when they refer whimsically to breasts as an infant's "sago bag."[4] Breast-feeding is a prime locus of the defining moral pattern of parent-child bonds, a pattern of care.

The Korowai concerns with pandanus, sago, fish, noodles, and other foodstuffs obviously reflect broad convictions that to rear a child is above all to feed it and that social attachment is known through objects and bodily sensations. Much of the evidence for this emerges from situations of lack: a mother speaks of fish when her infant son dies, a child speaks of a "pandanus" parent following loss of a birth mother or father, a father speaks of the foods his child is not able to eat, and so on. For Korowai, children epitomize lack and desire. Terms such as "Famine," "Hungry," or "Wanting Sago" are popular children's names. (Other names, such as Himself Alone or Houseless focus on lack of kin.) A child is a person in a state of pronounced want, dependent on others for well-being. Parental bonds with children are forged in circuits of perceiving a child's desires, acting to meet them, and seeing the effects of those actions in the child's pleasure and actions. A parent desires the child's desires, in the sense of acting to meet those desires. Consumable objects are so prominent in Korowai experience of child relations, it seems, because foodstuffs are the media of people's caring contact with each other's desires. Thinking of others' hunger, and giving them food or other lack-ameliorating objects, is what a social bond is. To speak of foods is to touch the core of a history and future of interpersonal care. Children embody this understanding with particular poignancy, by virtue of their extreme dependency on others. Children also embody the emergence of *reciprocities* of giving and caring. People especially value children's responsiveness to caretakers' actions, such as a maturing child's early acts of providing food and small favors to surrounding persons. Adults' care to meet a child's desires returns as a child's care for adults, confirming tangibly the mutuality of care about each other's desires and dependencies that is the full promise of social bonds.

Another side of parents' experience of children as external presences is children's increasing independence, self-determination, and lack of regard for what parents want. We have glimpsed this in my mention of one boy's fight with his mother over his desire to travel away from home. A child enters the world in a state of ontological otherness, as "demon." Once humanized, though, the child takes on qualities of political otherness, as an autonomous actor.[5] It is common for a mother angry with a young son to call him a "little witch" *(xaxualena)*. This is an extreme expression of ill regard, given how deadly serious is Korowai people's loathing of male witches. Yet acts of care, and the objects used in them, are what most dominate people's portrayals of social bonds between parent and child. My abstract language of care and desire in this chapter, however approximate its relation to Korowai experience, has tried to make explicit the outlines of a reflexive sensibility about human attachment immanent in the striking ways Korowai speak of children and act toward them. A bond of belonging lies in histories of caring acts. But the "little witches" epithet points to the broader sense in which we might see children as the witches, demons, or, simply, radical *strangers* of Korowai kinship. Children are irreducible others, not just when feared as monsters, but also when most loved as objects of attachment.

SIGNIFYING CARE FOR OTHERS IN TIME

There have been four main threads in this chapter's discussion of Korowai thought about children and parent-child attachment. First, attachment is temporal. Second, attachment is not given but is created in histories of caring action. Third, bonds of attachment are built from conditions of otherness and coexist with the possibility of repulsion. And fourth, attachment is overtly understood as a matter of signification. I close now by recapping these threads and underlining how they run together as alternate aspects of a single cultural sensibility.

People feel attachment through consciousness of other times and consciousness of relational transitions. Attachment comes into existence over time. I have shown that people are highly aware of events of sex, gestation, birth, and caring that have created children and people's bonds with them. People are aware that children were formerly repulsive nonpersons who have become valued companions. In a "compassion" relation, for example, a senior and junior partner commemorate a past event of foiled infanticide that has created present social conditions as against other possibilities. Conversely, Korowai are aware that attachment to children is attachment to a future, involving hopefulness about future times. People value infants for what they will become as they mature. They also value children as longer-term answers to adults' own deaths. Across these patterns, different times are held together in the link between two persons, and two persons are held together in the link between different times. When relating to children at a present moment, Korowai transact with temporal peripheries. They relate to states of affairs different from present circumstances, out of reach of their experience or control, yet of great concern and value. A bond with a child does not exist at a self-identical moment but instead in persons' consciousness of who they have been in various pasts and who they will be in possible futures.

The second thread, that attachment rests in histories of caring interaction, is the most elaborated aspect of people's experience of attachment as temporal. Infanticide illustrates the principle that attachment is created rather than given: parents might feel no attachment toward an infant on its birth, but then explicitly feel great love for it as the parent and child build up a history of caring bodily interaction. Variations on the idea that parent-child attachment is created through care for a dependent other, and through a dependent child's responses of gratitude or return care, are of course culturally and historically widespread. A variant on the theme is well known in Melanesian ethnography through Strathern's (1988) model of New Guinea sociality, according to which a person is directly seen as what other people did: a person is the living, acting embodiment of others' actions, such as their actions of care. But the principle that relations of attachment are contingently made *in* acts of care has been worth spelling out nonetheless, because of the unusual clarity and depth Korowai give to it. The principle is a reflexive sensibility about social relations that Korowai themselves prominently dwell on. We have seen this in the way adults' actions of perinatal care become the very names of their relations with specific children, in the way children are taken as signs of parents' actions of "making good," in descriptions of parenting as a matter of giving food, and in how children are defined by what they lack and thus the care they need. One corollary of the focus on attachment's creation in action is that people are highly conscious of attachment's contingency. A relative might never have intervened to cut a newborn's umbilical cord. One person might not have given another food. So too a relation of attachment is a question of degree. What kinds of events of care or neglect have taken place between persons, and what events will take place later? Persons' attachment is not a single state but hangs between different possibilities. Mutual attachment is shown again and again by actions, and it is known by memory of actions. But actions are measured against other relational hopes and doubts. Events provoke questions of relatedness as much as settle them.

The third thread of my account, that attachment is built out of otherness, is illustrated most starkly by people's revulsion toward newborns. Characteristic of Korowai understandings of social life as intimacy with strangers, the relation of greatest attachment people ever experience—that between parent and child—is built atop a relation of extreme antipathy. Perhaps the strangeness and precultural formlessness of newborns contribute to the pleasure of later bonds with them: attachment is even more vivid by virtue of how contemptible the child was on first arrival. Yet Korowai also understand children as figures of otherness at additional levels of the temporality of parent-child attachment. Otherness can be a quality that coexists with belonging across the life of a relation. For example, parents care for a child *because* the child is a creature of a separate future the parents will not live to see. The poignant bond of a "compassion" partnership thickens along a boundary of otherness. An adult creates the kinship relation across a generational divide, across a divide of kinship distance (by comparison to the comparative immediacy of parenthood), across an imaginative gulf between the present situation and the child's possible future maturity, and across the divide of newborns' stigmatization as monstrous.

The fourth major thread has been how Korowai overtly understand relations with children as questions of signification. I suggested at the outset that parent-child relations consist of an indigenous semiotics of knowing relationships by events of making, giving, or caring. Korowai take adult-child attachment to be lived through signs in such practices as knowing a child by the fish it will catch or the sago it will pound, knowing a child by its weight on a parent's body, knowing a parent by pandanus or breast milk, knowing parent-child succession by sago groves, and knowing two persons' relation by an event of one having saved the other's life. The principle that attachment is created in histories of care is a facet of this indigenous semiotics. A relation is defined and represented by specific material events. So too signification is at the center of the overlapping principle that attachment is temporal: a child is a sign of time and in time, standing for pasts and futures different from the present. People can look to the child's body to know that its parents existed and that the parents related to each other and to the child in certain ways.

The principle that attachment is a semiotics here also overlaps with the principle that attachment coexists with and builds from alterity. Sign relations are not relations of pure identity. Parents' attachment to children is partly attachment to what is strange to them. A child's weight, heat, diminutive movements, and companionship are presences outside a parent's own body. The adult's body is unsettled on its own and needs something outside itself in order to be settled. A child's significance as a substitute for its parent even more strongly involves alterity as well as identification. The child who survives its parent is a displacement of that parent and a poignant sign of that parent's passing, as well as an ongoing effect of the parent's former worldly presence. Attachment between parent and child is a link between different times, but this intertemporality of relations is also an encounter with limits of the present, as well as limits to what a person can experience. Relating to parents or children, Korowai relate also to what is alien to them, from within horizons of their life and eventual death.

One way to sum up the Korowai sensibility about social attachment—including its principles that attachment is temporal, is created in caring acts, is built around alterity, and is expressed and lived through signification—is to describe this sensibility as a reflexive *pragmatics*. It is a set toward categories of relatedness and toward the ways those categories of relatedness may exist between persons, in the processes of time and through the use of media such as words, foods, bodies, and memories. Given that children undergo not only the acquisition of specific social relations but also the developmental acquisition of social relating in general and given that other kinship relations are transitively formed and affected by parent-child bonds, it is likely that the broad patterns of Korowai parent-child attachment are representative of people's approaches to social attachment at large. One relational process of Korowai life that is comparable to child raising in cultural prominence—and closely intertwined with child raising in practical conduct—is marriage. I turn to the subject of marriage now, to deepen my inquiry into Korowai people's distinctive pragmatics of social attachment.

CHAPTER 5

Marriage as Disruption and Creation of Belonging

In anthropology it is a truism that marriages are close relations between people who are socially other and hence that bonds by marriage are specially charged. Korowai too understand marriages as marked, attention-drawing bonds. Marriages are the most frequent subjects of political controversy in Korowai collective experience. Often a specific existing or potential marriage is the single overriding issue a given person is engrossed with at a particular time of life, whether the person is distressed or delighted by the marriage and whether it is the person's own marriage or the marriage of someone else that is such a consuming focus of attention.

Marriages are such attention-drawing concerns in part because they are highly consequential bonds that are made through contingent events. Korowai often state axiomatically that it is "strangers" who marry, not "together people" or "true relatives" *(lambilxajan)*. Marriage systematically disrupts what I described as a normative alignment of kin category, emotion, geography of ownership, geography of residence, and mode of interaction (see chapter 3). According to this principle of kinship belonging, close kin live together, they feel intense mutual attachment, and they interact in moral styles of sharing and unconditional generosity. In introducing this principle in the first place, I underscored that kin relations do not purely conform to it but are also known by their divergences from it. Marriage turns on direct violation of the norm. It brings into close contact spouses who do not belong together, it disrupts relations of belonging between spouses and their other relatives, and it puts each spouse into close contact with in-laws who are not close relatives. Creating such consequential and disruptive bonds of social involvement is no smooth matter when egalitarian separateness and strangeness are basic to social life.

The axiom that marriage takes place between strangers is part of a broader range of ways in which Korowai understand marriage as a science of otherness. In my examination of otherness-focused relations so far, I have argued that for Korowai the crux of a social bond lies in its conjoining of mismatched relational qualities, such as belonging on some dimensions and strangeness on others. I continue this line of analysis here by showing how the conjoining of mismatched qualities of closeness and otherness is central to Korowai understandings of marriage. The subject of marriage provides an opportunity, though, to clarify the tie between otherness-focused social relating and a second major theme of this study: the pattern that bonds are made in actions. The link between otherness-focused social relating and the notion that bonds are made in actions becomes clear if the idea of conjoined relational qualities is restated using event-oriented terms such as "disruption," "impingement," and "violation" as additional names for the zone of mismatch constitutive of a social bond. To say that Korowai understand relations as closeness with strangers is to say that bonds disrupt relatively established states of belonging or nonbelonging and that they disrupt egalitarian separateness. Korowai often most vividly know social bonds in events of disrupting separateness with closeness, or disrupting close belonging with acts of estrangement.

The sensibility about social relations that is my subject in this book is thus also a sensibility about qualities of action and their relation-defining effects. In addition to showing that marriage relations are defined by conjoined closeness and strangeness, this chapter seeks to understand *how* people live bonds centered on gaps between their mutual strangeness and closeness. The answer I develop is that such relations are possible through a distinctive stance toward relational processes on the part of people involved in them, according to which actions that disrupt belonging may be not only traumatic but also pleasant, ameliorative, and closeness making.[1] Korowai approach contact between people who do not belong together as a substantial mode of social connection in its own right, even a mode of intimacy. This approach to social relating is contradictory and not easy to live by. It does not lessen the crises of social connection people experience, but it orients people's understanding of crises and successes alike.

Like so many Korowai social practices discussed in this book, marriage turns centrally on spatial belonging, spatial presence, and spatial separation. Often marriage's disruptions are specifically displacements. Within the general axiomatic understanding that it is "strangers" who marry, a narrower well-known marital rule is that clanmates are not supposed to marry. This means that marriage is by definition a relation of interlocality. As noted in chapters 1 and 3, marriage often involves a woman moving from her own natal clan lands to another place. Marital mismatches of closeness and strangeness are concretely lived as spatial contradictions, such as the contradiction of a woman and her husband living separately from her parents in space but being attached to them in memory, emotion, and morality. This chapter continues my inquiry into geographic mediation of social relations by documenting how marriage is understood as a matter of spatial displacement and how spatial distance is understood as a matter of marriage.

Once again, though, spatial issues intertwine with temporal ones. To say that Korowai people's emphasis on otherness in social bonds and their emphasis on events are the same thing is to say that Korowai see temporality and change as constitutive of social ties. My term "disruption" underscores the temporal character of marital relatedness. Other past or alternative states are part of a marriage's present. Mismatches of conjoined belonging and strangeness unfold in time as a dialectics of disruption and creative recognition of relational belonging. In exploring this dialectics here, I also explore people's understandings of the nature of events and temporal succession: how events occur, what they follow from, and what they produce.

The most prominent face of marriages' disruptiveness is spousal intimacy's offense to a bride's relations with her existing kin. Several practices discussed here are classic subjects in the anthropology of affinal relations. Yet I analyze marriage as disruptive closeness with strangers across more levels than are usually considered this way. I begin by examining how Korowai centrally define marriage as a practice of a husband and wife sharing life activities. I then look at some actions by which marriages are first created. Next I discuss a pattern in choice of marriage partners, namely, a preference for union with grandparental kin. Finally, I turn to bridewealth and other affinal institutions that express and ameliorate a marriage's disruption of the bride's relations with her own kin.

THE INNER MARRIAGE: CLOSENESS BY
SHARED LIVING, CLOSENESS BY DISRUPTION

Korowai marriages vary immensely in their characteristics. Yet in people's use of marriage-related words, and in their other categorizing practices, the category "marriage" is a fairly unitary umbrella. Some evidence for the category's existence is linguistic. The terminology of marriage-related states and events includes "husband" *(yum)*, "wife" *(defol)*, and "married couple" *(yum-defol)*. The terminology also includes the verb *gadi-* "mix, accompany, guide, carry off, marry," and more prominently the verb *fo-* "take," which means "marry" when used with a person as direct object ("he took her," "she took him," "they took each other"). This latter verb's image of seizing an object and removing it from its prior place is symptomatic of marriage's character as disruption.

The core of marriage in Korowai discourse and practice, though, is closeness between a husband and a wife, across several areas of bodily living. I refer to the bond between spouses as the "inner marriage," by contrast to the spousal bond's circulation in the thought and action of other people. This is not meant to suggest that the two sides of marriage are independent, or that one of them is primary. A married couple lives under the influence of other people's stakes in their relation, and they live in terms of a notion "marriage" that is itself a category of collective recognition and circulation. Yet it is worth drawing attention to the inner marriage as a level of activity, because of anthropology's limited record of attention to bonds between spouses. Major accounts of spousal relations are surprisingly rare, considering how much anthropologists have said about marriage generally (see Trawick 1990 for one exception). Korowai themselves discuss spousal relations a great deal and put spousal sharing at the center of the definition of marriage. It would be foolish to assimilate Korowai thinking to Western ideologies, which identify marriage with spouses' intersubjective companionship, intimacy, and desire. Yet ignoring the companionate emphasis of Korowai marriage would also be a mistake. The idea of "companions" relevant to the Korowai context is the etymological sense of "those who eat together." It is possible to acknowledge an emphasis on companionship in this sense of the sharing of concrete activities without assuming also the dominant Western models locating companionate bonds in partners' subjective interiority of emotional and sexual fulfillment (Hirsch 2003).

Korowai consistently define what a spousal relation is by referring to four interlinked areas of sharing. They mention these prototypical activities in all sorts of expressive contexts, such as when describing specific marriages, explaining why people want to get married, answering questions about whether certain persons are married, or answering generic questions about the nature of spousal bonds. First, marital unity is embodied in the total activity of living together in the same house. Shared residence so epitomizes the relation that people routinely use "live together" *(lelip babo-)* as a euphemistic, nonerotic way to say that a man and a woman are married. For example, my female interviewees often described themselves as living together with specific men, as an indirect way of telling me the identity of their husbands. Yet in another sense such statements are not at all indirect. Korowai do not have formal wedding rituals. Rather, a transition to living together is itself tantamount to marriage coming into existence. For a couple to cohabit means they are married.

Second, Korowai narrate bonds of spousal unity by describing a couple as "descending and going about together" *(lelip aixai-)* and procuring food and other provisions in common. Giving and sharing of food is a major focus of spousal bonds in daily practice, in talk about marriages, and in myths. When newlyweds are mutually "fearful" and embarrassed about their marriage, elders tell them to go around together fishing, gardening, and carrying out other quotidian acts, so that they will grow comfortable. One woman, in a typical idiom, told me that couples pass from shyness to comfort and familiarity thanks to the fact that "[she] eats and stays together [with him], [he] eats and stays together [with her]" *(lelip lebau, lelip lebau)*. Most couples clear, plant, and harvest gardens cooperatively. Spouses usually own separate plants within a garden, but they coordinate their labor and share their produce. Cooperative processing of sago palms is another prototypical spousal activity. Spouses also casually share snacks and meals each prepares. Women are attracted to specific men because of their ability as game providers, and they disparage husbands who are inept or stingy. Men similarly evaluate possible wives by their work skills. A spouse is a person who produces and gives food. The spouse is appreciated for this, as a partner in sensuous pleasure and relief.

Third, a marriage is understood as a sanctioned relation of recurrent sexual intimacy. The element of collective acknowledgment is clear from the fact that any nonmarital sex is by definition "illicit stealthy action" *(nanem).*[2] Korowai are reluctant to draw attention to their own sexual encounters, and spouses usually refrain from bodily contact around other people because of embarrassment about the erotic implications.

Yet sexuality is often present in silences and substitutions. For example, spouses typically avoid addressing or referring to each other as "husband" and "wife," because these words connote sexuality. Instead, couples call each other by consanguineal kinship terms, teknonyms, expressions like "the man I live with," and other nonerotic alternatives. Most sex occurs in the forest, during couples' daytime activities of traveling around together. Housemates can be very aware of what else a couple is doing when they "descend and go about." People are explicit about the sexual aspect of spousal relations in moments of heated argument or ribald joking, in same-sex discussions of marital politics, and in talk about other people's marriages. Korowai often infer that a particular person's main motive for marrying someone was sexual lust (*lil-lep* "desire for a vagina"; *dul-lep* "desire for a penis").

The fourth major shared activity characteristic of spousal relations is the creation and raising of children. Spouses are unified through their joint relation to a diminutive third. This area of reasoning about spouses' marital unity overlaps with the future-oriented meaning of children discussed in the previous chapter. One person responded to a general question about why people marry as follows: "It's so they will have children, who will point out [various land features] as 'Our mother and father's memorial objects.'"

What is interesting about the portrayal of marriage as a bond of shared living across multiple levels of activity is the directness of metonymic transfer that Korowai perceive between category of action and category of relation. I have described shared actions of cohabitation, consumption, sex, and child rearing as being prototypical of marriage, but we could say more specifically that Korowai take these activities as *indexical icons* of spousal bonds. The activities are indexes in the sense that they are causes, consequences, and parts of the spousal relation. They are icons in the sense that they are pictures or emblems of that relation: the relation seems to be described by the activities themselves. Spousal closeness involves multiple mediations that poetically complement and amplify each other. In routinely talking about marriage by talking about residence, eating, sex, and babies, Korowai define the relation as a total practice of sharing a life, in which each of the different activities is suggestive of the others and the overall bond. Korowai discuss and perceive marriages above all in terms of what spouses *do*. Events create and confirm categories of relation and vice versa. This sensibility is overtly historicizing and practice focused. It locates a spousal bond as something that happens in time and over time, in histories of acts.

On the whole marriage is culturally assumed to be a normal aspect of adult personhood. Practices of shared residence, shared child-raising, shared domestic economy, and shared sex are central to why Korowai think marriage is desirable. These practices are concrete forms of inter-subjective closeness. When narrating the practices, Korowai portray spousal relations as an extreme of what social belonging can be.

Yet these same norms of close spousal sharing organize experiences of intense estrangement. In an essay on conflict, Simmel (1955 [1908]: 45–48) argues that it is when people try to be close across the full range of their being that their experiences of disparity run the deepest. Korowai marriages confirm this insight. Alongside imagery of close sharing, a common stereotype about spouses is that they are people who fight a lot. Korowai now often compare themselves unfavorably to missionaries and tourists in this regard. People assert that husbands and wives among these ethnic foreigners harmoniously heed each other's instructions, in ways Korowai couples do not. Such judgments reflect unease in Korowai experience of their own marriages, perhaps more than close knowledge of foreigners' actual bonds. In any event, ideals of close spousal sharing shape experiences of marital distance and dissatisfaction, whether these take the form of physical attacks, fleeting judgments of stinginess, or something in between.

The idea of two adults thoroughly sharing lives is a contradiction in terms, given the high premium Korowai place on autonomy and their strongly held notion that persons are irreducibly separate in their thoughts and desires. Even in peaceable marriages, sharing is a matter of degree. Different marriages vary in what couples actually share, and any one couple's practices of sharing ebb and flow. The event-focused sensibility cuts both ways. It locates a husband-wife bond in acts like giving a crayfish or an armload of firewood to a spouse one day but also in negative acts of *not* giving such objects another day, and in thinking forward or back to other times of withholding. Married persons frequently represent themselves as mutually distant, and food (like the other media of sharing) is as frequently a measure of estrangement as a measure of closeness. Often a woman tells others about her husband's failures to give her game or other food. One very expressive woman, for example, listed to me diverse foods and durable objects that her husband does not give to her and that she has to provide for herself or do without. This was her way to describe the quality of their relationship. Even when spouses feel steady affection, their attachment coexists with gender boundaries that mark the two as mutually uncanny, such as the division of house interiors into men's and women's sides. Whatever a marriage's balances of sharing and estrangement, few marriages are dissolved other than by death, though the experience of being left a widow or widower is extremely widespread.

Another aspect of people's historicizing conception of spousal bonds is their awareness of past times when the persons now together were not close. This is prominent in a well-known typical cycle of spousal emotions. Husband and wife are "scared" or "shy" of each other early in their marriage, and they grow "at home with" *(kome)* each other over time, through shared actions. Newlyweds feel fear toward each other, and long-married persons keep finding each other alien, in part because spouses are socially unfamiliar in the first place. Lévi-Strauss (1969 [1949]) described restrictions on marriage to close relatives as a commitment to social involvement between people who are other. He was only interested in the affinal relations between men via women, but the point applies to the inner marriage too. For Korowai, a spousal relation is a narrative of disruptive, creative contact between strangers. The couple's bond rests in knowing and narrating events of transition from strangeness to familiar companionship.[3]

Marriages are also narrated as processes of disruption in the register of geography. Frequently a woman says her husband's clan territory "has become as though my own place" *(nəbolüpxaxolelo)*. By this, she describes herself as having grown into familiarity with her husband's clan land, its resources, and its people. About natal clan land, a married women sometimes says, "My place has become as if I am a guest" *(nəpa nəbolüp xuol xaxolelo)*, or that the place feels "awkward" *(waxan)*, even though she is inalienably an owner of that place. Because of the life-defining importance of geographic belonging and estrangement, narratives of refashioned belonging are among people's most powerful images of what marriage is. Ruptures of place-relatedness engendered by marriage are major forces in the overall land-organized social world.

In sum, Korowai understand marriage as a relation of intimate closeness between spouses, and they understand this closeness as historical, not self-explanatory or self-consistent. Closeness occurs temporally, in events of people crossing a boundary from strangeness to sharing. Closeness also occurs negatively, as a standard of relatedness that is present in *not* being achieved. These various points about intimacy and historicity are interestingly encapsulated in a widely known, infrequently discussed item of esoteric knowledge. I described in chapter 2 how Korowai posit that persons come into existence after being born, living, and dying in an invisible counterpart world. Another detail of this model is that the circulation involves an alternation between spousal relations and sibling ones. Married couples on the visible side were brother and sister on the invisible side. Brother-sister pairs were invisible-side husbands and wives.

This too reflects the understanding that spousal relations are bonds of closeness. Cross-sex sibling ties are bonds of intense identification. Maternal uncle relationships are one place this can be seen. For a man, a *sister's child* is a focus of intense care, as a way for him to know and understand his relation to the sister. People also construe siblingship as a relation of unity in marriage-related contexts. Often a woman addresses her brother's wife as "my old wife" *(nəyain)* and is addressed by her as "my husband" *(nəyum)*. This identifies cross-sex siblings with each other, as far as the brother's marriage goes.[4] In the reincarnation model, marriage is portrayed as a form of closeness via the detour of siblingship. If cross-sex strangers can be so close as to live as husband and wife, it is because they were already close as siblings. Conversely, cross-sex siblings' closeness is defined and understood through comparison to spousal closeness. While the cross-sex closeness of brother-sister pairs and of husband-wife pairs are extreme opposites in normal understandings of kinship and marriage, the two bonds are covertly identical.

Yet this densely figurative cultural proposition also states that however close spouses might seem, their relation is built on obliviousness to the nature of that closeness. It is integral to the model that pairs forget their previous relation on passing between worlds. Closeness is couched in terms of death, amnesia, and avoidance. Spouses are strangers to the basis of their own intimacy. What seems to be a new relation between coevals is actually an intergenerational history. The bond rests in a history of transformation that exceeds its present appearance. The identity of sibling and spousal relations is something people mention only rarely, in a mode of acknowledging a truth better left unsaid and unrecalled. When the proposition does cross people's minds, they are supposed to refrain from marital sex until they have forgotten it again, lest one of the spouses die. People concurred with my own view that the proposition made all marriages transgressive and fearful. In marriage people are involved closely and guardedly not just with strangers but also with gaps in their own rational consciousness.

GETTING MARRIED: THE REGULARITY OF VIOLATION

Given that Korowai represent marriage as closeness between spouses forged in shared actions overwriting their past strangeness, we might expect marriage's distinctive moral terms to be especially visible in initial events by which people cross from married to unmarried. These are times of greatest mismatch between actors' closeness and their otherness. To look at marriage-making acts is also to begin locating spousal closeness within the field of other people who have stakes in the spouses' lives.

I survey here three kinds of marriage-making events: communication between prospective spouses, actions of brinkmanship, and betrothal. I have singled out these events because of their frequency in marriage stories and because they exemplify marriage's shape as a dialectics of disruption and ameliorative creation of relational belonging.

About half of marriages come about through a pair privately communicating romantic interest. Men and women who are not close kin tend to avoid casual interaction, precisely because Korowai are so sensitive to erotic subtexts of cross-sex interactions. Within this environment, many spouses' marital histories turn on a furtive event of one of them signaling attraction. A standard way to proposition someone in a houseful of other people is to take hold of the love interest's hand at night, through a fissure in the house's middle wall. Another is to throw a wood chip. People also signal marital interest by a stealthy brush of fingers or squeeze of flesh, such as when handing food to a guest, or accepting food from a host. Women initiate furtive communications as often as men.

These acts point forward to fuller possible forms of bodily contact, sharing, and possession. Furtive overtures often turn out to be welcomed. When they occur, though, they are startling violations of a major rule of life. As I noted in chapter 3, in most contexts Korowai adults carefully avoid clasps or touches of the hand and other forms of bodily contact. Their concern is to keep from intruding on others' self-determination and to avoid seeming to be making sexual advances. Even accidental same-sex touches are embarrassing. Often a person who has touched someone else dispels the shock with the laughing remark, "It's not as though we are a man and a woman," such that seduction could have been intended.[5] Cross-sex touches, meanwhile, are scandalous. In one house where I stayed in 2002, a woman had recently taken hold of a young man's arm during a scuffle in which household members stopped him from assaulting a kinsman. The young man's wife grew angry at this touch and for months kept voicing her concern that her husband and the other woman were mutually interested. "Women shouldn't grab men, the men have wives," was the moral people kept repeating about this controversy.

Touch avoidance is most visible in the care people take to transfer food or other objects without making bodily contact. The main technique is for a giver to roll an open offering hand over and away from a gift while the recipient rolls a hand underneath from the opposite side. Yet a transferred object is itself a medium of contact. The everyday scene of persons handing each other food while carefully avoiding touch signals involvement and separation at the same time, and the act is highly typical of the entire wider Korowai pattern of otherness-focused social relating. That a man or a woman can prefigure a whole marital future with a brush of fingers while feigning only a transfer of food is a measure of how intently people monitor their closeness and separateness in these channels. Violation of this interactional rule is startling to the person touched, but people anticipate such violation and know how to interpret it.

The furtiveness of erotic advances is typical of a general climate of conflict between an inner marriage and other people's relations to the couple. Touching silently, a couple breaks norms of interaction between themselves, without the knowledge of surrounding people who also have stakes in their staying apart. Brinkmanship and betrothal, by contrast, are marriage-making acts of publicity, not stealth. They illustrate how the history of relational transformation between spouses is also a history of disruption, separation, and closeness in wider social fields around them. To Korowai, a married couple and surrounding affinal relations are directly at stake in each other. The unfolding of these stakes is also central to understandings of what marriage is.

"Brinkmanship" is my term for some men's actions of confrontationally asserting their own wills, despite knowing that if they get what they want it would violate what other people consider right. A prototypical act of brinkmanship is to shoot at someone. A partial cognate of my category "brinkmanship" is the Korowai word *xen* "anger, violence, violating," which I introduced in chapter 1 as a prominent term in Korowai accounts of social distance. "Anger" is an all-purpose idiom for describing others as negatively or neutrally related to oneself, and speakers routinely describe others' specific actions as "angry, violating." Another action exemplary of brinkmanship is bare utterance of

the first-person pronoun *nup* "Me" (or *nup-ε* "Hey, me") as an assertion of desire for something and a request to be given it. Men and
women alike make this statement concerning movable objects, and men
make it concerning brides. Typically the statement is a non sequitur to
prior interaction: the possibility of the object being given to the utterer
was not previously under consideration. Bare assertion of one's presence and desire has a transgressive interactional quality, even when
uttered only softly or semiseriously. The assertion goes against strongly
felt egalitarian norms of being interactionally unobtrusive and deferring
to other people and their property rights.

My discussion of brinkmanship here is partly an effort to reckon with
one of Korowai society's most prominent characteristics: the high frequency of physical violence. The discussion is also an effort to complicate the idea of relational personhood in Melanesianist anthropology, on
which this book's idea of otherness-focused social relating builds. On
first consideration, it might seem that a self-assertive utterance such as
"Me!" should not occur in a "relationist" society. Yet brinkmanship is a
style of action cross-cutting all areas of Korowai political life. Its role in
the creation of marriages is particularly great. Marriage patterns offer
insight into broader cultural conditions under which brinkmanship
makes sense to people, even when it deeply upsets them.

The overall pattern of brinkmanship is exemplified by a turn of conversation that occurred when I was once trying to understand leviratic
marriage and asked a man named Sixwoli the question, "Why does a
man marry his brother's wife when his brother dies?" I thought I was
asking why the woman did not just marry someone else altogether, but
Sixwoli's quick answer was, "Because if he married her when his
brother was alive, his brother would shoot him." The first thing Sixwoli
thought of in response to my question was not "Why does a brother
marry his sister-in-law *at all*?" but instead "Why does he wait to do
so?" Sixwoli's lack of intended irony in this response underscores the
distinctiveness of his expectations about where marriage's interesting
questions lie. When can a man's aggressive pursuit of a desired match be
successful? What are the limits of male appropriation? Where does violent appropriation lead?

Events of brinkmanship are frequent means by which marriages are
made. In one episode, a man agreed to another's request to marry his
foster daughter, because he had grown weary of so many men asking for
her and because the latest suitor said he would "break apart [the foster
father's] house" if he was refused. Besides intimidating women and their

relatives verbally, men occasionally seize girls or women and run off with them, even killing other people to do so. It is very common for men and women to elope by mutual agreement, with the brides' kin nonetheless seeing this as a heinous violation. Brinkmanship is not only characteristic of suitors' actions. A woman's relatives often respond to even peaceable marital inquiries with expressions of murderous anger, as if the asking itself is an offense. Any match, however achieved, usually elicits outraged responses from people who had other ideas. Beyond their importance in bringing about marriages, brinkmanship and anger are also ordinary qualities of affinal relations and ordinary qualities of political relations between separate people generally.

The gender dynamics of brinkmanship are complex (cf. Schieffelin 1990: 202–38). "Anger" as a quality of action, including physical blows, is far from exclusive to men, but it is associated more with masculinity than femininity. Men are the main persons who create marriages by force or intimidation. In extreme instances, men's brinkmanship presses out all space of women's initial marital self-determination. This contradicts strong Korowai regard for personal autonomy in most other life contexts. In the gender-divided economy of staple sago starch production, for example, women exercise great determination over their labor. They readily decide not to work if they do not feel like it, whatever other people's desires and hunger. Men's brinkmanship in marriage making is part of what Korowai recognize as an overall patriarchal logic to the marriage institution (as against the somewhat more egalitarian cast of gender relations in many other areas of life activity).

Yet women also pursue marriages in a preemptive manner. As one woman said about another's boldness, "Women are like that and thus she did it. They see a man and want him, they marry him." One common way in which a woman forces a marriage is to enter alone the house of people who are not her kin. Even in the absence of the woman explaining herself verbally, her presence in the house amounts to pressing for immediate marriage to the desired man there. The pattern says a great deal about normal restraints on women's movement: lone women do not enter other people's houses under normal circumstances. The pattern of bringing about marriage by simply entering a man's house also says a great deal about how mere copresence in house space is a day-to-day sign of two people being married. Women can also be willfully assertive in refusing a marriage their relatives have arranged or insisting on a match their relatives refuse. For example, in 1997 a woman named Saxip rebuffed her visiting parents' and other intermediaries' attempts to bring her home from the place of a man with whom she had eloped by yelling, "Am I your wife? Is this the woman you are fucking?" She thus shamed the visitors, by pointing out that they were not married to her and not having sex with her: her marriage to her new husband was an accomplished fact, and they had no business asserting rights of control over her marital closeness to a chosen man.

A typically complex relation between femininity and brinkmanship was enacted by one young woman I met who twice ran away from her husband in pursuit of some downstream youths. The first time she came to the youths they had affairs with her, and the husband afterward raged at them. When she came to them a second time, the youths rebuffed her advances and said they would chaperone her back to her husband's place. In response, she bashed her steel ax against a stone and yelled, "Is it that I am a man and you are women, such that I am the one who came to you, and you are taking me back upstream? If you were men you would keep me here." Here she articulated a stereotype that it is men who come to women to join maritally with them and that this is an appropriate process. Yet she invoked this stereotype as part of her argument that *she* was the person showing boldness of action and that the youths should cooperate with what she was trying to accomplish. Many different people act with this kind of boldness, in their particular ways.

Brinkmanship's importance is also complicated by people's tendency to downplay their own agency when narrating marriage histories. Often spouses each deny having taken any initiative and fatalistically describe the other as the insistent one. People actively enter marriages for those relations' pleasures, but they avoid representing themselves as persons who would desire intimacy with another and brashly make contact.[6]

Under these contradictory conditions of people valuing separateness but also desiring intimacy, interactional and even physical violence are regular occurrences. Shootings, abductions, and less drastic brash acts are all-consuming traumas for people whose lives are disrupted by them. Yet the same people routinely treat brinkmanship as a call to connection. They expect violation to have a relational future, and they seek dialogic responses to it. The response might be a matching riposte, reception of a violator's will as bearing the force of inevitability, or a campaign for redress leading even to an amicable tie. Receptiveness to brinkmanship as a mode of contact is receptiveness to a stranger who is overbearingly immoral and intrusive, from the point of view of one's prior peaceful existence. On an aggressor's side, brinkmanship is often a volatile insistence on contact, despite the way other people exist autonomously from oneself.

It is integral to the egalitarianism of Korowai political life that people not only avoid others but also aggressively project themselves against others in reaction to their presence. Often willful acts are responses to violations men claim to have suffered themselves, and some of these violations are quite telling. For example, not only do men get upset when women betrothed to them marry other men; they also sometimes request compensation for marriages of women to whom they were never engaged but for whom they had feelings. They also occasionally request payment following marriages of women for whom they never had feelings but to whom other people had linked them. Occasionally a man who has no intentions toward a woman but has been gossiped about accusatorily by her kin acts on the gossip by marrying the woman after all. Relatives of a marriageable woman often speculate together about possible intentions of outsider men toward her. To Korowai, it makes sense that a man who hears about this would not only be exasperated by the false talk, but might press to marry the woman as a sequitur to it, making the woman's relatives seem the initiators of the union and himself only a reluctant and mistreated party.

These specific patterns of masculine political assertion are minor and slightly ridiculous in the wider sweep of marriage processes. Yet the examples help locate brinkmanship in its context, a world in which desire for closeness is in contradiction with people's concerns with separateness and self-determination. In the strange examples, rash demands continue a logic set in motion by male marital desire itself being experienced as a violation of separateness (whether the man experienced the desire or had it attributed to him by others). When separateness is a foundational premise of people's lives, any overture of relation making, or any inkling of the possibility of an intimate bond, is already a bit of an offense.

Polygynous marriage is a structural pattern also reflecting the overall climate of male brinkmanship. About one in seven married men is married to two women at once, and a few men are married to three women. By contrast, no women are married to two men simultaneously. "The husbands would shoot each other!" exclaimed one woman when I raised the idea. Polygynous marriages cause a demographic imbalance between unmarried young women and unmarried young men, prompting many men to pursue betrothals with immature girls. This in turn leads to many women outliving their older first husbands and then as middle-aged widows marrying younger second husbands (cf. Keen 2004: 178–79). Often these remarriages to much younger men occur at the widows' initiative.

A variety of cultural forces underpin polygyny. The main rationale people mention is that if a man's sole wife dies, then he will be left single and without further marital prospects, whereas a polygynous man whose wife dies will still have a wife living. Women and their relatives usually object to matches with a widower, because people fear that a woman who marries a widower will herself die. By contrast, when a woman's husband dies many men desire to marry her. That men seek polygynous unions as insurance against being left an unmarried widower testifies to the close links people see between mortality and gendered spousal intimacy. It also testifies to how aware people are of the likelihood of their spouses' early deaths. Further, it testifies to how much men value being married rather than living without marital companionship.

Another way in which people answer questions about the reason for polygynous marriages is to spell out the same intimacies that people focus on when describing marriage itself. As far as men's interests are concerned, polygyny is good for the same reasons marriage is good: men get more children, more domestic bounty, and more sex. For example, one woman explained that men marry polygynously "for going around for provisions. [He] descends and goes about with the one, and descends and goes about with the other."

Polygyny's bearing on the topic of brinkmanship is that plural marriages often occur through husbands insistently pressing their wills over the desires of their wives. Women sometimes support polygyny or grow well disposed toward it over time, valuing the added companionship and the security from monsters it brings. The kinship expression for "my co-wife" is "my other-side-of-the-hearth" *(nəsinanbolmen)*, an image connoting that the two women polygynously married to the same man are mutually close. Occasionally a first wife facilitates her own sister's marriage to her husband, as a way for the sisters to benefit from each other's company while otherwise living among strangers. However, most women oppose polygyny or accept it only grudgingly. A woman and her husband often quarrel violently when he initially tries to bring a second wife into the marriage. Co-wives also frequently fight. About half of homicides committed by women involve one co-wife killing another, or a woman killing her husband because of polygyny. When divorce does occasionally occur, it is often because a woman is unwilling to live with a co-wife. Men's overbearing assertion of their own interests is sometimes the crucial element enabling husbands to bring about polygynous unions. Polygyny's existence as a conventional cultural practice is a collective normalization of male brinkmanship.

Brinkmanship's role in Korowai marriage making is similar to that of "willfulness" in the communal political processes of Urapmin people of Papua New Guinea. In Robbins's account (2004: 182–214; 2007; see also Burridge 1975), Urapmin moral processes turn on a tension between lawfulness and willfulness. Community leaders act willfully, which is an immoral, unlawful mode of action, but also a necessary and productive one that creates social contexts in which community members at large can act lawfully. Leaders' willful actions are thus foci of intense moral ambivalence. Male brinkmanship among Korowai similarly tends to be experienced by others as an immoral violation of their self-determination and their existing social bonds of belonging. Yet it is by some sort of brinkmanship that most marriages are made. People sometimes expect, understand, and accept brinkmanship as a routine, socially productive way to achieve relations that persons on all sides might eventually come to value. Korowai are so committed to kinship belonging that it takes an act of disruptive violation, of greater or lesser degree, to effect a marriage at all, separating persons from their existing relations and joining them together in new intimate bonds with strangers.

Under these conditions, people are highly aware that getting married is a practical process and that the outcome of any attempt to create a marriage is uncertain. Characteristic here was one young woman's rebuke to me when I asked her whether she thought a marital overture she was asking me to deliver to someone else would lead to an actual match: "Right now it's just talk. It's not as though we are of the same place [such that I would know how he feels or what he will do]. It's just for the seeing of thoughts." To her way of thinking, processes of bold inquiry across boundaries of separation are explicitly open-ended and exploratory.

The third method of marriage making that I want to examine briefly is betrothal, an institution again illustrating marriage processes' organization as a dialectics of disruption and ameliorative creation of relational belonging. About half of young women's marriages involve betrothal. Sometimes a woman's parents take the initiative in engaging her to a man, because they approve of him as a prospective spouse and son-in-law. The groom himself might be initially quite fearful of the whole prospect. More often it is a man who seeks others' agreement. Usually a man initiates talks with a woman's parents indirectly, by sending an intermediary who is related to them, because the candidate himself is fearful of the people and their likely response. Some betrothals jibe well with a bride's desires, follow from pressures she has exerted, or fall apart due to her objections. On balance, though, betrothal works as a site of collective domination of women in marriage making. Brides are more subject than grooms to other people's influence over their marital fates. Mothers and sisters are as prominent as male relatives among those who try to exercise authority over a bride. It is symptomatic of patterns of power asymmetry in marriage that people often use the verbs "give" and "put" to describe what a young woman's parents do with her: they "give" her to a man, or they "put her in a husband's house." Men are generally not spoken of in these ways. Within this environment of inequality, betrothal often specifically piggybacks gender asymmetries on stabler power asymmetries of age. Parents of a young woman frequently preempt her possibility of forming independent marital desires, by agreeing early to a future marriage.

A pattern in women's experience of a special subset of betrothals clearly illustrates the way marriages involve systematic violation and remaking of specifically *emotional* belonging. These are betrothals in which a girl is not only promised to an older youth or man, but is taken to live with him while she is still young, whether because the girl's parents have died or because the parents especially trust the man as their child's caretaker. The girl is raised to maturity by her husband, prior to erotic involvement. Most women who have experienced this describe themselves as having been impossibly frightened of the man and then having grown comfortable with him and unregretful. In a standard turn of phrase, these women say the man "became like my father." The category "father" here signifies a nonsexual, nonauthoritarian unconditional benefactor (in contrast to incest-focused associations that the comparison of husband and father carries in the post-Freudian West). Adults generally praise this pattern of husbands raising their wives. They say it fosters unusually strong spousal harmony, by contrast to marriages in which a bride joins her husband at a less impressionable age and experiences him as permanently alien. Child brides' experiential pattern is the most extreme variant of the fear-to-comfort cycle typical of marriage at large. Marriage is a disruption of kinship belonging that creates in a new location the same kind of belonging, here quasi-paternity.

As for betrothals in general, even more than they are a way to control brides, they are a mode of damage-control toward men and brinkmanship. Parents commonly feel pressure to betroth a daughter in the first place as a way to preempt the possibility of her later being carried off by a stranger, or becoming the focus of a dangerous political uproar. Betrothal makes disruption of kinship belonging a negotiated accommodation, in which the bride's relatives have some directing role. In cases in which a bride's relatives actively seek out a betrothal, they even see their closeness to the prospective son-in-law as a goal of their daughter's marriage. The child bride phenomenon illustrates how betrothal can foreground a care dimension of social relations that is the opposite of the anger dimension foregrounded in brinkmanship. The idea of creating a relation of belonging with a son-in-law is sometimes present from the outset, not just something that emerges long after an initial period of disruptive impingement. Yet betrothal itself puts a groom into an edgy, marked relation with a bride and her relatives. People speak of betrothal by the verb "designate, mark" *(dali-)*. Betrothal attaches to a woman a linguistic mark of who her husband will be: news of the pair's designation as future spouses is collectively circulated, and the future affines themselves enter into a kind of "marked" social status toward each other. Even after accepting a proposal, a woman's kin often maintain a demeanor of anger, oscillate erratically in their expressed feelings about the union, or express lingering opposition through extreme bridewealth demands. While betrothal arrangements are an attempt to channel and disambiguate the future shape of social relations, even a well-established betrothal is often surrounded by uncertainty and dissatisfaction. For a betrothal's duration, the groom and his fiancée's kin observe formal avoidances indexing a fraught affinal relation, the same avoidances they will practice after the couple is married. Besides the circumstance that the suitor is impinging on his in-laws by marrying their person, everybody is in a state of suspense. Will the marriage actually come into existence? If so, when, and under what relational terms? Betrothal is a category of reflexive alertness to the temporal unfolding of an uncertain bond of intrusive contact between people normally separate.

I have sketched patterns of betrothal, brinkmanship, and furtive courtship because they deepen the finding that marriage relations are made of mismatches of closeness and strangeness. These three kinds of processes are elements in a much wider range of events by which marriages come to exist, and even between the three, there are major differences. Brides are central agents of marriage-making actions in some acts of courtship, brides' parents are central agents in some acts of betrothal, and grooms are central in some acts of brinkmanship. Direct courtship has a moral quality of furtive transgressiveness, brinkmanship has a moral quality of belligerent expropriation, and betrothal can have a moral quality of solicitous cooperation. Despite these and other differences, there is an important family resemblance across the marriage-making forms sketched here. All involve people breaching boundaries of each other's existing lives, creating close social contact that awkwardly does not match the persons' background of separateness and lack of relation. This mismatch of close contact and nonbelonging might involve one person transgressively clasping another's body in a hopeful gesture of seduction, a woman transgressively entering alone the house of a man in whose space she does not belong, or other boundary-crossing acts of requesting, demanding, promising, gossiping, persuading, shooting, or threatening. There is a regularity to violation, across these different interactions. Korowai tend to recognize the mismatch-creating acts as not only troubling social impingements but also relation-producing ones. They approach marriage politics with a reflexive understanding that normative ruptures might be livable, even desirable forms of contact. Strange intrusion is how closeness occurs.

WHO MARRIES WHOM? CLOSENESS AND STRANGENESS OF KIN CATEGORY

Reflexive concern with how to have relations of closeness with strangers can also be seen at the level of who marries whom. In this section I look at Korowai views about the marriageability of people standing in a specific kinship relation, the relation of grandparenthood. Notions of the special marriageability of specific kin were once a classic subject of anthropological inquiry. This interest was shaped by Lévi-Strauss (1969 [1949]), who posited that prohibitions and prescriptions of marriage to specific kin amount to a whole organization of social dependence between people who are mutually other. Lévi-Strauss understood a marriage rule to be teleologically constitutive of a larger regime of reciprocity: a specific pattern of marital alliance with system-level powers and shortcomings, as far as its task of orchestrating relations between different elements of society. In approaching marriage in these terms, he tended to take a marriage rule as a self-evident fact rather than a representation with a wider pragmatic context of being experienced and enunciated. This approach assumes what social otherness is, as a universal problem. By contrast, I seek here to read a Korowai idea about marrying kin as itself a reflexive investigation of otherness, and a reflexive investigation of how social involvement between others is possible. Patterns of who marries whom are refractions of a larger question of marriage's very nature: a question of people's reflexive pragmatics of marriage, their sensibilities regarding *how* to engage in being socially connected to others. Approached from this perspective, any pattern in who marries whom has no privileged status as the foundational marriage fact but stands in relations of reciprocal influence and interpretation with other social forms, such as spouses' practice of closeness by sharing or the actions by which people first bring marriages into existence.

One aspect of Korowai thought about who marries whom is the axiom that it is "strangers" who marry, not close relatives. Korowai state this axiom many different ways, all expressing a basic association between marriageability and social otherness. "True relatives aren't married," one person said. Another, telling the scandalous story of a Kombai man who married his foster daughter after his wife's death, noted, "It's strangers who are married" *(yaniyanopto fomate)*. Someone else quoted a demiurge's instructions: "House people are taboo. Marry people from elsewhere" *(xosüxaanop;* lit., "over-there people"). Another person said, "Own people are distasteful" *(giomanop bəsixda)*. One woman quoted the mockery heaped on persons who marry clanmates: "People will say, 'They are people who married their own'" *(xaifo fo-;* lit., "married themselves"). Korowai often experience the imperative to marry strangers as an unquestionable, taken-for-granted truth. They feel visceral "fear" *(golo)* and "embarrassment" *(xatax)* at the prospect of close marriages; they describe the rule as a creator-determined law outside what humans need to discuss and justify; or they say that violating the rule would automatically cause catastrophes like death of the married persons, collective demographic decline, or the "flipping over" of the earth. Categorial alignment of marriageability with otherness is of the same order as the world's spatial stability, such as the alignment of up with up and down with down.

The rule against marrying close kin coexists, though, with a desire for marriage with people who are at least a little bit socially familiar and reliable. Korowai are often ambivalent about entering marriage relations at all, as spouses or as affines, and these misgivings are linked to the fact that marriage is by definition close contact with undependable strangers. Many myths include episodes in which a virtuous man or woman lives a cloistered life in a hidden chamber within a house, to preclude marriage and other social contacts. When these attractive characters do first encounter a possible love interest, they often spontaneously describe themselves to that other person as a loner who is not supposed to mix with others. So too actual humans often disavow any marital desires and refuse all possible matches for long periods, or are dissuaded from matches by relatives. However, it is rare for anyone to reach middle adulthood without marrying at least once. Marriage's attractions override hostility to it. A more common strategy than avoiding marriage altogether is to mix commitment to marrying strangers with an opposed principle of favoring marriages between people who are not absolutely strange but rather are already "a little" close. This is a strategy for making marriage livable and harmonious, in a world of angry nonrelatives and unpleasant events of brinkmanship, elopement, and spousal or affinal fighting.

There are many different ways people end up marrying someone who is a bit related, but the paradigmatic one is marriage to a grandparent. "Grandparent" here means any member of the patriclan of a given ego's maternal or paternal grandmother. As outlined in chapter 3, a major feature of many people's early lives is that while they are members of one patriclan and are at home on that clan's land, they also stand in relations of kinship belonging with members of three other localized clans: their maternal clanspeople or "uncles and mothers" and their two sets of "grandmas and grandpas," the clanspeople of their two lineal grandmothers. These three other patriclans are often islands of welcome in a sea of places one does not belong. People in the clan of "uncles and mothers" are unmarriageable, but " grandparents" (the "uncles" of a person's mother or father) are preferred spouses. About one in seven marriages are between grandparents of this kind. When persons related in this way do marry, the spouses find it very comfortable to call each other "grandpa" and "grandma," as they did prior to marriage.[7]

Korowai say they favor grandparent marriage because the spouses are not "far" or "strange" and so will not be mutually scared, shy, or quick to anger.[8] Their statements illustrate the broader pattern that marriage is understood as a problem of relating across boundaries of nonbelonging. As one man put it, "If I marry a stranger, then later [my wife's relatives] will be angry and shoot me. Whereas if I marry a grandma, then we are alike. It's pleasant, it's good." By comparison with closer relatives and with the wider run of persons who can be disparaged as "not a relative," a grandparent occupies an intermediate position of both stranger and intimate. This kinship position has elective affinities with marriage's definition as close engagement with a person who is strange but in whom one yet seeks belonging and cooperation. A typical way in which the association between grandparent relations and the idea of marital closeness comes up in daily life is that an unmarried man and one of his grandfathers or grandmothers will occasionally address each other in jest by affinal terms for "daughter's husband" and "wife's father" or "wife's mother." Though no actual marriage has been discussed, the kin portray their relation as one of caring for each other so much that they could be in-laws. Similarly, sometimes a bachelor will tell a same-age grandson that he plans to get married, raise a daughter, and marry her to the grandson. (The girl would be a grandmother to the other man.) This idle speculation is a way the youth expresses his affection for his friend, matching the grandparental kin relation between them.

Korowai also emphasize closeness in a cliché likening grandparent marriage to a yam vine circling back to an old tuberous root and fusing to itself there, putting down a new root. The cliché's most common form is *lajopülop gelif fomate* "Like the *lajop* yam they take [marry] the rhizome." Speakers immediately recognize this as a statement about grandparent marriage, even when uttered out of context. The image portrays grandparent marriage as a person rejoining with his or her own body and origins. People often stress that grandparental spouses are connected by relations of parentage, especially maternity and maternal geographic movement. As one person put it, "They marry back to their own offspring. From that, they won't be quick to anger." Grandparent marriage is also frequently rationalized by general spatial images of reconnection and impulses of appropriating one's people to oneself rather than letting them stray out to interlopers: "Lest they go, return right back"; "Don't bother with strangers"; "She's going to go far away there, [lest that happen] I myself [will marry] my little grandpa."

Grandparent marriages are sometimes easier to create in the first place because kinship closeness lessens the separateness to be crossed by marriage-making acts. Grandparents might already want to aid each other, or a grandparent and grandchild pair might have grown up already friendly rather than fearful. In grandparent marriages, marriage and affinity are less of an anger-provoking violation than they otherwise would be, because spousal and affinal closeness is precedented by an existing link of care and cooperation. These marriages also make grandparental relations a fuller version of themselves, by adding the benevolence of marital closeness and affinal giving. Here impingement is not an outrage, but matches an existing situation of kinship involvement.

These sides of grandparent marriage recall the idea, discussed earlier, that all married couples were cross-sex siblings in past lives.

Grandparent marriage's significance may lie less in its actual frequency than in the allegoric clarity with which it too expresses the core organization of marriage processes. Many grandparental relatives are completely estranged, extinct, or mutually unattracted, such that possible marriage between them is not considered. The great majority of marriages are not between near grandparents but go all different directions, and are contracted between persons having all manner of pragmatic bases of mutual kin categorization beyond parentage and clanship. Yet it can be said that there is a grandparent quality in all marriages. This is in part a quality of closeness, whether figured through a fantastic image of sibling marriage or just a desire to live with someone of compatible temperament. But the grandparent quality is also a quality of mismatched joining of strangeness and closeness. A grandparent is a figure of *qualified* belonging, who is marriageable because he or she stands at a position of attenuation and remove in the kinship spectrum.

In marriage contexts, the strangeness in grandparental kinship is most visible in statements connecting a present-day marriage to the life of the linking grandmother who married a man two generations earlier. Korowai are not alliance theorists when it comes to relating marriages across different generations: people are usually indifferent to the gender-directionality of the present marriage in relation to the past one. For a man to marry his maternal or paternal grandma (i.e., a woman in his maternal or paternal grandmother's clan) or for a woman to marry her maternal or paternal grandpa are all common. "This is marriage, not murder," one woman said when I asked about whether people disliked asymmetric marriage sequences. A history of repeated murders between kin networks would cause enduring anger, at least if it were asymmetric. By contrast, an intergenerational history of two marriages between kin networks connotes mutual support and life-affirmation, not life-taking, even if the history is unidirectional. Even so, the fact that the woman thought to contrast marriage with murder is symptomatic of people's understanding of marriage as an act of kinship-violating appropriation (and murder as an act of involvement). Marriage and murder are conceptually in the same family.

Yet matchmakers do sometimes draw *qualitative* intergenerational links between present and past marriages. One pattern is for a parent to betroth a daughter to the parent's own uncle, the bride's grandfather. Because of the close love felt between parent and uncle, the parent favors the uncle as a place to which to entrust a daughter. Here again, people voice stereotypes of marriage as frightening contact with unreliable strangers. As one woman said about having strangers as son-in-laws, "They would kill me. They're not relatives, so that is what would happen. [Instead, girls] are given to one's own uncles." Another man spoke in the same way: "My niece told her daughter to live with me. The niece gave her daughter to her uncle. Land of strangers, no, not that, they would get on her back. Rather, an uncle's place."[9] More specifically, matchmakers are often motivated by death and maternal absence. One woman narrated her daughter's engagement in these terms: "I gave my child to my uncle. [I said,] 'You live together.' [Brides] are given, and people become elderly. It is for the fact that they are all going to die out. My daughter went to my mother's place." Another woman said about betrothing her daughter to a man of her uncle's clan, "My mother's footprints disappear, it is a replacement for that." A father reported thinking, "I am going to give [her] to my uncle's child at my uncle's place. My mother's path will be overgrown with trees, so I'm going to place my child over that way." Many of these statements focus on metonymic signs of a woman's past life and her absence in the present: disappearing footprints, the forest growing where she once walked back and forth between her natal land and her husband and children's place, or the old mother's bed where now nobody sleeps. These signs underscore that love for an uncle is rooted in separation and loss. It is based on a mother's travel to a strange place and her mortality, typically including a history of dying separate from her natal kin and being buried on her husband's land. In grandparent marriage, the self-identity an ego doubles back to and rejoins is not a seamless unity with that ego. Omaha-style application of grandparent categories to relatives of one's own age and reproductive generation allows a socially thick connection to the past. There are grandparents who are contemporary in time and reachable in space. Yet this proximity is also a reminder of present people's separation from predecessors no longer on the land. Replacement in kinship is colored by the loss of what is replaced. Differences of time, genesis, and mortality, figured as a disparity of terminological generations, condition grandparents' closeness and make marriage an event of mourning as well as reconnection.

The grandparental element in all marriages is a situation of dual impulses. On the one hand, it is "other people," not relatives, who marry. On the other hand, marrying strangers is bad. A grandparent, as a kin category defined by a mix of belonging and otherness, exemplifies a general duality in any social bond. A relation is a disruptive engagement between people who do not belong together, but a relation is also the confirming or creating of belonging between separate persons, even extreme strangers.

Another, even more common way in which people ameliorate disruptive effects of marriage to strangers is to favor unions between people whose places are geographically close. About one-fourth of marriages are between spouses whose clan lands are adjacent or are separated by just one or two intervening territories. The geographic pattern overlaps with mixing of closeness and distance of kin category. Kinship is so much a matter of geography that people routinely express the principle of marrying strangers (and specifically, the rule of clan exogamy) as an imperative to marry "elsewhere people" or "people of another place" *(yani-bolüp-anop),* not people of one's own land. Yet owners of adjacent places, if they have histories of cooperation, often describe themselves as sharing a "unitary place" *(bolüp-lelip)* and as being "together people" or "unitary people" *(lelip-anop).* This general claim of collective kinship is often supported by more specific kin relations between persons in the two clans. Like grandparent marriage, marriage between geographically adjacent people is two-faced: it is a bond between people who are at once "different" and "unitary."

When arguing against long-distance matches, prospective spouses and affines often cite the bad characteristics of faraway people (such as their anger, witchcraft, and poor food resources), but speakers fix in particular on the loss of interactional contact that a long-distance match would cause. A woman's relatives often argue that if she marries a faraway man, then she and they will not hear each other's news of time-sensitive events (such as illness or the butchering of a big game kill) quickly enough to make themselves present, and they will seldom visit each other. For example, the father of the eloped woman Saxip (whose insistence on staying with her husband I sketched earlier) objected to her marriage at first by saying that the husband's place is far away upstream where he does not go and that if Saxip died, then he would not hear about it. Rather, the father said, he wanted Saxip to live nearby, where he would see her body and then bury her. As I discuss in the next chapter, concern with death and mourning pervades Korowai thought about social relations. This particular man's focus on death was a way to bring into view the extremeness of the social loss he was experiencing in contemplating his daughter's marriage to a man from a distant place. But people also have more mundane concerns about social access in mind when they weigh the geography of particular marital unions. Marriage between neighbors enables the couple and their respective relatives to enter each other's houses frequently and give each other a lot of food. Sometimes a couple can even live at both places simultaneously.

The interest of geographically close marriages is again how these marriages throw into relief a deeper duality. Marriages of whatever proximity or distance pose the question: In what ways is this interlocal relation one of impingement, severance, and disruption, and in what ways is it also a relation of amelioration and connection? In weighing the disruptiveness and desirability of a marriage, people take into account many attributes besides geographic and kinship distance. These include current marital status, demeanor and other personal qualities, and histories of prior interaction. Who marries whom could only be adequately described by a long series of marriage stories, illustrating the complex particularity and open-endedness of social processes. My account here has sought to show only that issues of who marries whom unfold, on the plane of residential geography and kin categorization, along much the same lines as actually getting married unfolds on the plane of interactional contact, personal autonomy, and interpersonal belonging, and also along much the same lines as spousal intimacy unfolds on the plane of shared living. Conjoined closeness and strangeness—and simultaneous disruption and creative recognition of relational belonging—are at work here too.

AFFINAL ACTIONS

I turn, finally, to certain actions central to the politics of affinal relations, including mother-in-law avoidance, bridewealth payment, and direct marital reciprocation. These processes too are organized by a problematic of closeness and strangeness. I document here the coexistence of two forms of articulation between spousal closeness and the couple's relation to the woman's kin. First, people experience this articulation as a tradeoff: the husband and wife's closeness comes as a hostile disruption of the wife's relations with her kin. Second, the husband (or the couple) can be closely *involved* with the wife's relatives, in parallel to a husband and wife's closeness. The parallelistic articulation emerges through actions that partly ameliorate the disruptiveness of a husband's impingement in other people's lives. But the dominant pattern is a paradoxical, unstable one of impingement and separateness working as forms of intimacy.

Mother-in-law avoidance offers the clearest instance of this pattern. In chapter 2 I argued that interactional avoidance practices (avoidance of sight, touch, commensality, name use, and singular number) make two persons closely connected by their practices of careful separation. These sensory practices link up to their social context, the existence of a marriage, in ways I did not earlier address. Korowai explicitly tie mother-in-law avoidance to spouses' intimacy. Their most vivid statements arise when an avoiding pair accidentally see each other. A woman whose son-in-law catches sight of her thinks or says, "You married my daughter, so why are you looking at me? Aren't you having sex with my daughter?" By the same token, a wife who learns that her husband has glimpsed her mother might say to him, "Since you've just been looking at my mother, why are you wanting to have sex? Don't have sex with me, it's my mother you should have sex with." Such angry outbursts posit a direct tradeoff between the sexual intimacy of a married couple and the husband's visual separation from his wife's mother. The quality of each relation is a sign of the other relation. Although women's focus in these statements is on sex, erotic intimacy is a flash point in a wider spectrum of ways people can be in mutual contact. Mother-in-law avoidance is embedded in the broader moral structure of affinity as a qualitatively distinctive type of sociopolitical relation. I noted before that people expect someone who says an affine's name to suffer skin-puncturing injuries. The bodily impingement and contact emphasized in this sanction and in actual practices of mother-in-law avoidance are iconic of a more general politics of social impingement. A son-in-law intrudes presumptuously in his mother-in-law's world. He demands or accepts her accommodation of his presence, an accommodation out of proportion to any moral commitment they would have were it not for his marital intrusion. The intimacy of husband and wife is dependent on the wife's relatives' toleration, recognition, or even encouragement of the husband's impingement on the space of their own intimate social bonds with their daughter, sister, and niece. As I emphasized in chapter 2, an avoiding pair's practices of segregation constantly index their in-law relationship, whatever else they are doing in each other's presence. The two enact a paradoxical quality of closely engaged separateness, iconic of their moral situation of being closely linked by the man's presumptuous impingement. Avoidance practices, in registering a pair's quality of mutual involvement, are acts of recognizing the mother-in-law's accommodation.

Mother-in-law avoidance perhaps ameliorates the immoral disruptiveness of marriage, by *expressing* it. The avoidance practices signify affines' relation of wary impingement, and they signify a general moral position of "abiding obligation" (Merlan 1997) that the son-in-law occupies with respect to his wife's mother. A mother-in-law's possible outbursts about the married couple's sexual intimacy, quoted above, reflect this sense that avoidance expresses the son-in-law's abiding state of owing something to his mother-in-law because of his closeness to her daughter. The link between avoidance and obligation also surfaces when women stop observing avoidances due to their son-in-law's failings. For example, one woman told me she no longer practiced sight avoidance with a son-in-law because he had not built her a fire when she arrived at his house sick. The most common reason women suspend sight avoidance is to express dissatisfaction with a son-in-law for not providing adequate bridewealth gifts: no meeting of affinal obligation, no avoidance. Sometimes a mother-in-law's deliberate breaking of an avoidance norm leads a shocked son-in-law to step up his bridewealth giving right away, reestablishing the pair's recognized bond of accommodation and obligation.

Bridewealth, even more than avoidance, is explicitly motivated by an idea that spousal closeness comes through other people's loss. A bride's relatives generally expect her husband to give them valued articles and work, called *lal-xalüx* "girl/daughter requital." Bridewealth demands vary greatly, and so does the scale and timing of actual payments. Prototypical gifts are pork or other meats, necklaces of dog canines or cowries, Indonesian paper money, and expensive imported goods such as axes, machetes, and air rifles. To support their bridewealth requests, a woman's relatives talk about the same spousal practices of shared residence, domestic provisioning, sexual intimacy, and child making that are emphasized when describing the nature of the spousal bond alone. In-laws often note that a husband's benefit is their loss. One woman, for example, described herself as continuously wishing that her daughter were living with her instead of the husband, to bring her water and firewood and keep her company when she dies. Demanders narrate past actions of caring for a woman from childhood as the ground of intimacy that has been offended by a husband's intrusion. People also rationalize bridewealth by evoking an overall situation of lost access. "Our niece, our daughter, our sister," they say, the bare assertions of kin category standing as claims for restitution. People also commonly associate affines' experience with death. "[Bridewealth] is reciprocation for the fact their girl is going to die," said one woman. Speakers often express the meaning of a woman's postmarital residential change by saying she will "take her grave" at her husband's land, so thorough is her departure from an earlier place of belonging. Marriage resembles death, in its harsh disruption of people's practices of growing older in each other's presence, across histories of shared food and recognition.

While the main rationale for bridewealth is that spousal closeness disrupts others' links to the bride, bridewealth's effect is to counteract the loss. As one person put it:

> Like having an object stored away, the anger in itself keeps existing on and on. But then articles are paid, and [the husband and his in-laws] go about without fear and anger. They can go about before each other's eyes. Without paying, they are jittery. If they go about before each other's eyes, the parents-in-law will shoot him, or they will pull back the girl, and that will become a huge uproar.

Or as another woman said of her son-in-law, "If they give, I will let go. Without that, I will keep being wracked by anger." In a characteristic image of separation, people say of a conclusively adequate payment that it is "like a wall" *(damonülop)* or that it "walls off" *(damo-)* the man and his wife's kin from each other. A husband's "taking" of their daughter puts him in contact with them, out of proportion to their prior lack of relatedness. His intrusion creates a situation of closeness without belonging. Bridewealth redresses the violation, creating a livable distance. Yet rarely does bridewealth payment bring an end to actual socializing. It just creates a wall against further demands, as the image of people's closeness. Bridewealth materially signifies the son-in-law's recognition of his wife's relatives as having been impinged on by his presence more than it balances out or undoes their loss.

In an occasionally achieved ideal, a bride's kin match their son-in-law's food giving with gifts to him. These gifts of groomwealth (*wafil-xalüx* "guy requital") are smaller than gifts given by the husband. The wealth is paid directly by the wife's relatives, not by the wife herself, and it is paid to the husband, not to the husband's relatives. Groomwealth is thus a transaction atop bridewealth rather than an independent groom-focused inversion of the bridewealth pattern. Groomwealth is typically given only when affinal relationships have matured and stabilized, following a period of initial volatility. Reciprocal giving, in the medium of food, becomes an end in its own right. This construes the affinal relation as one of cooperation and closeness, displacing its definition as hostile impingement (cf. Valeri 1994).

Bridewealth is one element in a wider family of affinal actions of marking and ameliorating marriage's disruptiveness. Betrothal, mother-in-law avoidance, and many of the other social forms discussed in this chapter are additional elements in this family. Grandparent marriage, for example, is a strategy for arriving at the same kind of détente to which bridewealth can lead, but via the shortcut of marriage between kin who are already in relations of giving and cooperative regard. (Affines sometimes lessen their bridewealth demands in grandparent marriages, or lessen the stringency of avoidance practice, in consideration of the existing bond.) Through these ameliorations, affinal links might become bonds of valued closeness, in parallel to the spousal relation.

Mainly, though, bridewealth is a focus of discontent. Valuables paid as bridewealth are scarce, and husbands have difficulty accumulating them. Unmet expectations and jittery discomfort are normal. The bridewealth institution works as a medium by which people know and express their feelings of violated belonging. Dissatisfaction and delay in bridewealth processes are themselves ways in which a relational quality exists, the quality of two sides being connected by an awkward link of impingement and distress. There can be movement from early constant anger through payment to mutual giving and goodwill. Different affinal relations settle out at different points in this range. But it is usual for contradictory relational qualities such as estrangement, indifference, or warm companionship to be present together in bridewealth affairs all the time, sometimes as felt realities and always as hopes or fears.

Linking of two women's marriages together as "reciprocations" *(xolop)* is another pattern by which affines reshape relations of disruptive impingement into ones of closeness. Although people widely acknowledge that marriages should be reciprocated, only about one-fourth of unions actually follow this norm. Sometimes a bride's relatives make her marriage conditional on a female relative of the groom being married or betrothed to some man among them; and sometimes the case for reciprocation is pressed only after an initial marriage has occurred. Anthropologists usually call this marriage pattern "sister exchange" (e.g., Århem 1981a; Busse 1987; Gell 1992), but in Korowai practice it is not only a groom's sister who might be categorized as reciprocation for that groom's own wife: a groom's daughter, foster daughter, niece, or classificatory female relative of any kind might be so categorized (cf. McDowell 1978). I thus refer to the pattern as "direct marital reciprocation." People's attention to issues of *coeval* reciprocation contrasts with their lack of concern with intergenerational reciprocation, noted above in connection with grandparent marriage.

Direct marital reciprocation is another affinal action meant to ameliorate a bride's relatives' social loss. People often say that if a marriage situation is "one-sided" *(xolodoptanux),* then relatives of the bride will be permanently angry about the husband's residential, commensal, sexual, and reproductive closeness to her. As one person put it, "They will say, 'There should be a reciprocation for our little sister,' and they will struggle and fight." The ideal of reciprocation again mainly exists as a touchstone against which people form judgments of dissatisfaction. Reciprocation occurs or falls through as an outcome of uncertain processes of persuasion, brinkmanship, and demography. The norm of reciprocation is part of marriages' larger pragmatics of suspense, as people attempt to make intrusive connections across boundaries of separateness.

The ideal of direct marital reciprocation is supported not only negatively, by threat of affinal anger, but also positively, by imagery of valued closeness. Speakers routinely say that people related by two reciprocal marriages are "like sago leaf bases" *(xobaniülop).* From the top of a sago palm's trunk, fronds arc upward on troughlike stems, and where the bases of these stems attach to the trunk, the troughs tightly imbricate around the trunk's circumference. Korowai explain the image as referring to dense links of visiting, hospitality, food sharing, giving, and kinship that reciprocal marriages create. The image is one of contact: people are pressed together tightly along multiple surfaces of relatedness. Speakers also routinely say of people who live near each other and have histories of intermarriage that they "reciprocally hold each other," emphasizing their active seizing of mutual relatedness. These positive images again underline that direct reciprocation is a way to turn disruptive impingement into valued contact and belonging, by making intrusion and accommodations mutual rather than one-way.

Another area where affinal relations characteristically conjoin hostility and amity is a bride's relatives' stances toward spouses' raising of children. As children are born and mature, a man's affines frequently describe themselves as "giving up" their anger over unpaid bridewealth and other offenses. Siblings of a woman with children say that when they think of her husband, they think also of the couple's children, the nephews and nieces who are objects of unconditional love. One woman told me a sister's husband "becomes a relative" *(lambil-lelo)* when children are born of the marriage. Yet it is also an item of conventional wisdom that a woman's relatives grow angrier at her husband when children are born. They can curse those children to grow skinny and die, out of spite for the man's failings. They do this using a power of death-causing speech that is unique to in-laws and after-death demons, a grouping that says a great deal about the ambivalence of affinal ties.[10]

Contradictory stances of care and anger toward a marriage's fertility can coexist in the same relation.

Affinal institutions such as betrothal, bridewealth, and direct reciprocal marriage are all important enough, but the real litmus test of affinal bonds is spatial copresence and the crossing of spatial distance. The landscape consists largely of marriage-focused ruptures and connections. On the one hand, a woman's relatives experience the interlocal geography of marriage as a deathlike loss and a focus of anger. Spatial distance is a medium of otherness. This distance both incites and facilitates people's unkind actions toward each other, such as elopement, refusals of marriage, or refusals to give bridewealth. Marriage conflicts are the most common reason that people categorize particular parts of the social landscape as off-limits to them. Yet on the other hand, residential separateness of a bride from her relatives creates possibilities of visiting and hospitality between people of different places. A prototypical act of a married woman is to "come see her mother and set off." Korowai sometimes figuratively liken a married woman to a bridge across a stream, connecting places that are separate. Often people also talk about marriages, and the geographic patterns of travel and social connection they foster, by referring to the literal paths between clan territories of the married persons. A woman might describe herself as "standing at the halfway point" between her own clan place and that of her husband as a figurative way to say that she and her husband live at both places. There is much variation in how often a couple visit the woman's home place or are visited by her relatives, and there is much variation in the terms of these visits (such as who advocates them and whether persons feel rewarded or slighted by the encounters). People value the possibilities of pleasurable interlocal travel and cooperation that marriages create, even as they are sensitive to disappointments, insults, and inadequacies in these spatial actions.

The geographic dynamics of marriage thus qualify and elaborate landownership's effects of organizing people's lives around belonging to place and around acts of crossing spatial margins to engage with owners of strange places. In marriage-related movements across the land, structures of belonging and nonbelonging are disrupted and refashioned by forms of social engagement with unfamiliar people. Marriage's similarities to host-guest interactions are particularly striking. In chapter 1 I described the physical presence of guests in a house as a mismatch between categories of persons and categories of space: persons who do not belong are in a space of belonging. Marriage is also composed of edgy interactions of conjoined strangeness and closeness, or change and adjustment to change. Often affinal interactions *are* host-guest interactions. But where host-guest encounters are tied to a transient moment and a specific house, people related by marriage are stuck with each other in longer, broader ways. They are in close contact not just in the space of a house, but in the total space of spousal closeness and its effects on surrounding people's lives.

BELONGING AND EVENTS

I have argued that relational qualities of closeness and strangeness are conjoined across many different levels of the total relational field of Korowai marriage. I now close by deepening a claim outlined at the beginning of this chapter: people conduct these bonds of close strangeness through a reflexive morality and pragmatics of social relating, according to which disruption and recognition of belonging are not mutually exclusive.

I can clarify this point by comparing it to Sahlins's (1972 [1965]) well-known model of a correlation between social distance and exchange morality. In that model "generalized reciprocity," or unconditional sharing and giving without keeping of accounts, occurs between close relatives. "Balanced reciprocity," in which accounts are kept, occurs between persons of more tenuous relatedness. Theft and other forms of "negative reciprocity" occur between persons who are least related, such as geographic strangers. I have suggested in this chapter that there is a correlation between a category of social relation and morality of interaction. However, Sahlins's model posits that social proximity (or "kinship residential sector") is unidimensional. Different relations are defined by where they are on a one-dimensional spectrum. By contrast, I have documented qualities of closeness and strangeness unfolding on multiple dimensions that are often out of joint with each other. People can be residentially close while having no major relation of kinship belonging or history of shared actions. A mother-in-law and a son-in-law can be a few feet apart, engaged in intent conversation and linked closely by the man's marriage to the woman's daughter, while also remaining markedly separate in sight and other sensory channels. A same-age "grandparent" can be close in kinship but also distant in group membership and terminological generation. Spouses can be close, as reincarnated siblings, but also strangers to the knowledge of that closeness. Courting lovers can touch each other physically while being mutually distant in public definitions of them as separate and unrelated.

Corresponding to this complexity in how people can be mutually close, there is a similar complexity in the moral quality of people's interactions. In Sahlins's typification, people share, or they give, or they barter and steal. Korowai, in their marriage relations, by contrast, often hold multiple moral understandings of the same relations and actions. A hand clasp, a betrothal, or an observance of avoidance rules is at once a morally negative violation of other persons *and* an act of recognition that creates relations of closeness with them. This is the distinctive morality and pragmatics of interaction that correlates with marriage as a type of social bond. It is a mixed morality, in which the same actions are often relation violating and relation making. Spousal acts of shared eating or other life intimacies, and affinal acts of giving bridewealth, negotiating a reciprocal marriage, or causing and witnessing the growth of children, are measures at once of stingy, self-serving expropriation *and* relation-oriented generosity and mutuality. In this moral sensibility, disruption and creative recognition of relational belonging overlap. Disruption and belonging contradict each other, yet the zone of their contradiction is where people live.

A linked quality of this morality is that people involved in it are intently aware of the temporal constitution of their actions and relations. A relational quality of conjoined closeness and otherness involves a stance toward events as a relation's sign. People read events for categories of relation, and they read categories of relational belonging and estrangement for demonstrative events. A relation of conjoined belonging and strangeness is not only an exploration of the otherness of other persons but also a hermeneutics of change. A temporal horizon of change and adjustment to change is integral to people's relations of belonging.

Courtship, histories of shared living, histories of affinal conciliation, and other marital processes are often dominantly processes of the formation of belonging. We have seen ways in which relation breaking is an integral element of these processes, but attachment is the main chord. A contrastive area of life experience, dominated by the temporal experience of relational loss, is death. I turn to it now.

CHAPTER 6

Dialectics of Contact
and Separation in Mourning

When I once gave some money to a widow named Yalun, she entrusted it to her young son, Ngop, to buy her some ramen noodles in a village to which he was making an overnight trip. While still in the village Ngop became hungry and ate the noodles he had bought. Entrusting cash to travelers for purchases is a common Korowai practice, and in such situations everyone is scrupulously careful to see that the entruster's rights of ownership are upheld. When Ngop returned home his mother was furious at him. She quickly gave up her anger, though, saying, "It's fine, my child, your father is dead, who will give such food to you?"

Dying is a subject of seemingly constant attention in Korowai people's thought about their day-to-day activities. The vast majority of persons die young or in middle age rather than as elders. "We are mortal humanity," people say. They frequently insert the elliptical formula "mortal humanity" (xomibənengaanop, xomunanop) in their speech, as a passing reminder that death is humanity's main attribute. Specific persons also often speak spontaneously of themselves as being in the process of dying. Aged men, if they are awake before dawn, often sing softly about their upcoming deaths. When I gave a mirror to Gia, a middle-aged woman, her immediate way to express how much the object pleased her was to say that she would be buried with it on her chest. Another man, coaxed by his friends into sitting with me for an interview, began our conversation with an unprompted disclaimer: "They told me to talk. I said, 'I have no people. I'm just myself alone. They all died.' But they said for me to talk." The man felt his life was defined by the dying out of his kin, and there was nothing for him to say, at least to a foreigner known for asking about people's relatives. A married couple I encountered on a forest path in 2001, whom I had known individually five years earlier, cycled rapidly through several death-focused subjects with me, in a mode of cheerful melancholy. Had I died, they asked? I said I had not, and asked the same of them. Then they recollected specific persons who had died since my last visit. Finally they speculated that they would both be dead when I next came to the Korowai place, or that my return would be so belated that all Korowai would be dead. To this pair, my death, their deaths, other persons' deaths, and Korowai people's collective extinction were measures by which to define the time and space of our encounter on that path, including our mutual care, our pleasure at seeing each other, the hiatus between this encounter and our previous times of mutual presence, and the new hiatus we entered by walking away from each other again.

This chapter puts Korowai experience of deaths into interpretive dialogue with the approach to relations of kinship and belonging set forth thus far. There are at least two reasons for making death my culminating ethnographic subject. One is the special cultural weight that death has in Korowai life experience. Death events have great importance as variously a horizon, an underside, and an explicit focus of kinship processes. I have discussed the fact that Korowai are intently conscious of mortality as their basic reason for having children and that death is a main ingredient of the poignancy of parent-child bonds. The more specific ethnographic subjects that I discuss here similarly reflect the sheer prominence of certain death-related practices in people's daily lives. My first main subjects are two death-related monsters, the "witches" *(xaxua)* thought to cause all deaths and the "demons" *(laleo)* that humans are thought to become after death. Korowai speak ubiquitously about these monsters and orient to them as social others in everyday conduct. Another, equally important level of death's consequentiality is people's orientations to the dead as memories: as social interactants who are located in the past and who figure in the present negatively, as absences. The dominant way the dead are present as memories is in people's grief over particular deaths and in their practices of expressing and transforming grief. One such practice I examine in detail in this chapter is commemorative food renunciation. I also go on to examine closely the practice of a dead person's housemates paying valuables to the deceased's spatially separate relatives. In this prominent institution, Korowai make some person's deaths the measure of survivors' ongoing relations.

The second reason for giving special prominence to death is that the approach to kinship developed in the previous chapters offers an excellent foundation on which to understand mourning, and mourning practices offer exceptional further access to the Korowai sensibilities about social relations I have so far sought to document. Mourning is an area of life in which Korowai reflexively analyze the nature of social relations with special urgency. If Korowai organize their social relations as processes of relating across divides of otherness, then mourning is a particularly intense variation on this pattern.

Whether the dead are coeval monsters, memories, or ongoing subjects of contention between the living, to relate to these dead is to struggle reflexively with challenges of social involvement across margins of separation and strangeness. Death's cultural prominence is itself characteristic of Korowai people's otherness-centered relational sensibility, according to which social bonds consist of dialectical conjunctions of closeness and separation. Relations with the dead, I argue, throw into relief how the copresence of living persons is not self-evident and seamless but is composed of concrete semiotic media of contact. The media death foregrounds include bodily presence experienced through specific sensory channels, such as sight of a face; expressive gestures, such as laughter and linguistic address; a body's flesh and materiality; commensality, food producing, and food giving; gifts and possessions, such as Gia's mirror; the space of a house interior; the distance between houses; the time that people are together; the connections of memory or habit uniting different times people are together; and the connections between times when people are together and times when they are not. People's loss of copresence due to death events underlines for them the more general fact that media of human presence move out of joint with each other and themselves. Different strands of people's connections pull apart. Specific strands turn out to work as channels of both separation and connection. Korowai death concerns are a reflexive anthropology, laying bare media through which people live social ties and laying bare people's concern with the conventions and pragmatics of concrete media *as* media—as the signs in which relations exist.

The most scrutinized medium is time. Expressions such as *waluxtelo* "languished" or *ütelo* "gone, disappeared, absent" are routine ways in which Korowai say someone is dead. Copresence with the dead—being "together" *(lelip)* with them—is no longer possible. When the dead are conceived still to act in the present, they are not the normal persons they once were, who could be met in routine interaction. Yet even if dead peo-

Figure 18. Betüdal Dayo reaches into a plastic bag to unpack a harmonica, cotton blouse, lock of hair, and nose ornament that belonged to her deceased parents and sister, 1996. She stores the "commemorative articles" *(lanül mis-afi)* over her sleeping place in the dark string bag hanging at right in this photo, above the striped piglet. Durable objects that are intimately metonymic of a dead person's body are very powerful mementos: they vividly signify both the dead person's presence and that person's separateness.

ple are absent as living visages, they can be intense presences in people's minds. As a focus of emotion, they sometimes seem more alive than ever. A mourner feels strong emotional and intellectual closeness to a person who is not there, such that there is a painful disparity between the present as a world of living perception and interaction and the present as a world of memory. The emotion of "longing, sadness" *(finop)* is a form of this pain. As a woman named Betüdal said, regarding her collection of body ornaments and other metonymic mementos of her deceased parents and sister, "When I look at these, I'm so sad I almost die" (figure 18). The difference between what is seen and what is remembered or felt is unbearable. All practices discussed in this chapter express mourning's character as a present at odds with itself, and some of the practices work to ameliorate the present's contradictoriness. Here again a social bond is most known through processes of interruption that put people in situations of mismatched involvement and strangeness. Where marriage is disruptive *creation* of attachment, mourning is disruptive undoing of attachment, a kind of reverse courtship.

Mourning makes apparent that moments of social copresence are not identical with themselves but contain signs of other times, when a relation was or will be different from what it currently is. Alongside people's orientations to the already dead, another level of death's weight in Korowai social relations is people's awareness of their own deaths. As Gibson (2004: 291) puts it, "To exist in relation to death is to be a transitional subject and object in relation to both self and others." We will see many examples of people prefiguring future deaths as part of present relations. This is one way in which the problematic of separateness and togetherness thematized in mourning is an aspect of social relations generally.

Intertwined with time, another basic medium of social contact that is strongly thematized in mourning is the human body. Many death-focused representations that I discuss in this chapter take as a main focus of attention and trauma the disparity between rotting corpses and living bodies. A minor example of the pattern is speakers' routine use of words meaning "rotten" *(nentelo)* and "foul" *(extelo)* to say someone is "dead." Corpse-focused representations are reflections on the living human body's qualities as an expressive and figurative medium through which social relations occur. A cold, motionless corpse evokes a dead person's distinctive human presence as an interactant *and* the absoluteness of the person's departure. This contradictory sign is a site of the larger contradictory situation of mourning as time out of joint. The corpse's disappearance is a central focus too of people's experience of how it is possible for social connections actually to change.

This chapter follows Korowai people's own reflections, in mourning practices, on the media through which social relations exist. I aim to read mourning actions not only to gain better insight into Korowai understandings of temporality and living bodies but also to spell out a little more fully what Korowai understand residential separateness and closeness to be, and what they think of meals, sight, gifts, and other major channels of signification in which social contact is lived.

DEATH-CAUSING WITCHES

The single most dramatic way Korowai are preoccupied with death in their lives is their concern with male witches *(xaxua)* within the Korowai population who are considered the agents behind all human

deaths. Witches are believed to cause deaths by compulsively and invisibly eating the bodies of other humans. A victim is unaware this has
happened, but soon after the attack the victim suffers a fatal illness, falls
out of a tree, drowns, is gored by a pig, or undergoes some other lethal
event. People know that a witch attack has taken place from the fact of
the death itself—and sometimes from a dying person's identification of
a particular man as the witch he or she infers has caused the crisis.
Korowai feel intense anger and revulsion toward the witches responsible for loved ones' deaths. Witchcraft imagery portrays the witches as
sociopaths who are literally no longer human *(yanop)*. Historically, as
well as sporadically in recent times, Korowai upset about deaths sometimes conspired to kill an alleged witch. Execution for witchcraft was a
very common fate of male Korowai through the 1980s.[1] Also until the
recent past, a man arrested as a witch was in many cases sent away
across the landscape to unrelated people, who butchered and consumed
his body as part of the overall process of angry reaction to the existence
of death-causing witchcraft.

This historical Korowai practice of "cannibalism" has been a focus
of intense, lurid interest on the part of Western television and magazine
professionals representing Korowai people to international audiences in
the past fifteen years. It is in part because of the prominence of cannibalism in currently existing representations of Korowai culture that I
give the subject of witchcraft only brief and schematic treatment here.
This book's pages are better spent bringing to view the proportional
importance of other death-related concerns of Korowai life. Moreover,
any detailed account of the witchcraft institution would have to be built
on the foundations of a careful description and interpretation of these
other death-related concerns. (I hope to present such an account elsewhere, but see also Stasch 2001a: 433–85; 2001b.) Even so, I want to
outline here at least a few broad interpretive points about the witchcraft
complex, to give a sense of how the complex sits in relation to the total
network of subjects discussed in this book and how much mortality
weighs on Korowai social consciousness.

Korowai are deeply wrenched by the existence of witches in their
world and by the tragic histories of witch execution that have touched
all persons' lives. One link between witchcraft and this book's overall
argument is that the figure of the witch *(xaxua)* is heavily marked by
qualities of otherness to humans *(yanop)*, even as the figure is intimately
close to humans. For example, the witch takes commensality, which
Korowai understand as a paramount act of otherness-engaged social

unification, and draws out the horrifying, corrupt potential in it: destruction of people rather than unity with them. If *sharing* food is "the most primordial act of social constitution [because] in it, the table companions recognize one another as persons by denying that the living being they treat as food is a person" (Valeri 2000: 204), witches by contrast take the other humans in their presence *as* food, in an ultimate repudiation of mutuality of being and mutuality of care. Here and elsewhere, the witch underlines points of vulnerability and ambivalence internal to major Korowai cultural concerns. However, a witch is not just an intimate counterpart of humanity at an abstract conceptual level. Witches are also close to humans at the level of kinship and daily living. When a dying person sometimes quietly tells select housemates the identity of another man who is the witch who has attacked that dying person, the accuser and the accused are often close relatives. To Korowai, the problem with witches is that they are *not* strangers, in terms of their proximity to daily life. They live on the same land and in the same houses as other people. Korowai live in steady fear of witch attacks. People's daily actions of being together with other people, or staying separate from others, are deeply structured by this fear. For example, people work to avoid being alone (and thus vulnerable to a witch attack) in making decisions about what to do in the course of a day and where to sleep.[2] So too fear of witches is a standard reason that people limit their travel to unfamiliar houses and clan places.

The fear and anger Korowai express toward witches is typical of the wider emotional troublesomeness of death events. Witches are death's otherness personified, but this personification is only the most extreme of a range of ways that we will see that deaths are sites where Korowai grapple with otherness as a property of social relations. Witch beliefs are also typical of a pervasive Korowai expectation that deaths are socially actionable. An injurious event of death "doesn't just happen by itself," as people say in asserting that a witch attack must have taken place (even though humans have no direct perceptual knowledge of it): a death is obviously a violation that some *agent* has caused, and so it is possible to ameliorate traumas of death through social processes, such as (in the past) violence against a death-causing man. Relatedly, witch-focused beliefs and practices are typical of the volatility of Korowai social bonds, the close link between egalitarianism and violation, and people's expectations that transgression will be a regular, generative aspect of social relatedness. I have earlier described egalitarian autonomy as a dominant but contradictory Korowai value, one that creates social problems as much as solves them. In this same vein (thematized by Munn 1986: 232), a witch's furtive crime is an image of unbridled autonomy (he acts free of others' determination) but also of radical violation of egalitarian autonomy (he takes a life without that person's knowledge or agreement). The real, visible violence that Korowai committed against accused witches was obviously also highly inegalitarian: people coercively took charge of an alleged witch's life and death.

The main way in which I have sought to theorize Korowai egalitarianism as generating its opposite is by showing that in the Korowai sensibility of otherness-focused social relating, interaction routinely centers on the violation of boundaries of separation and autonomy between people. There is an affinity between Korowai expectations of transgressive disruption as a normal aspect of social life (in marriage processes, travel to other people's places, forms of touch, joking avoidance partnerships, etc.) and their openness to the possibility that a mundane appearance of bodily health and human conviviality could be the deceptive mask over an underlying reality of furtive, destructive witchcraft. Another level at which transgression and relatedness mingled in the witchcraft institution in the past was the interlocal organization of many witch killings. The tenor of interactions between people from different places on the landscape was often a volatile combination of hostility and cooperation. For example, in the aftermath of a killing, relatives and killers of a supposed witch stood to each other as formal "enemies" (*xololanop;* lit., "bone people"), which required them to observe certain rules of segregation, such as avoidance of commensality. Yet this enmity and associated feelings of anger often led over time to interlocal marriages, or at least to rituals of commensal and social unification. Korowai approached witch-focused violence as in part a call to social connection, not merely the absence of social community.

Having outlined some main aspects of Korowai people's involvement with the disturbing figure of the death-causing witch and ways in which the witchcraft complex fits in broader patterns of Korowai social experience, I turn now to a more detailed examination of another death-related figure Korowai care about immensely, the "demons" that humans become after death

"HUMAN AND DEMON TOGETHER IS TABOO"

Korowai mainly describe the demons that humans become after death as horrible monsters, but people's relations with these monsters once again combine separation with closeness, and even desire. Demons are close to humans on three overlapping levels. First, the intensity of people's concern with demons *as* objects of revulsion makes humans and demons intimately involved. Second, the demon category is a close deformation of humanity's characteristics. Third, in some contexts people subtly express overt emotional attraction to the demonic dead and seek social involvement with them.

Korowai use the term *laleo* "demon" very prolifically in speech. While the monster signified by this term is held to be a real presence in the world, humans cannot meet a demon and live to describe the experience. If demon and human meet face-to-face, the demon thinks, "Become like me!" and the human instantly dies. To be social with the demonic dead is to join them in death. This lethal malevolence is one reason I find the word "demon" the best English label for the monsters.[3] Korowai describe demons with vivid horror and worry daily about danger from them. They frequently urge relatives not to stray away from companions or travel to dangerous places, using the compact exhortation: "Beware demons!" or "Demons will get you!" *(laleomaman).* Korowai talk about demons far more than they talk about any other component of personhood thought to continue existing after death. The Korowai category "ancestors" *(mbolopmbolop),* for example, only designates people who existed in the past but do not exist anywhere in the present. The figure of the torpid, barely sentient demon dominates people's orientations to the dead as still-existing beings.

Demons are like walking corpses. Korowai often understand the monsters to be distinct from a dead person's actual corpse, which rots away in its grave. Yet even when this distinction is made, demon imagery clearly makes them phantasms of the dead human body. They move around corporeally like people, but (in the standard imagery) their eyes are turned up blindly in their heads, their hair is unkempt or absent, their rotting skin and flesh slide from their bones, they stink, their fingers are cramped with rigor mortis, and their rib cages are exposed to air and stuffed with leafy vegetation (as if this could repair the emptiness of their insides). These signs of deadness are repulsive in their own right, but Korowai also immediately associate the bodily disfigurements with demons' intrinsic malevolence toward humans. When a demon orders a person, "Become like me," it is the demon's rotten body that defines who the demon is.

Demons are creatures of what Taylor (1993: 655) calls "the hiatus between the cessation of life in a physical person and the continuity of that person's life as a mental object." The emphasis on rotting bodies dramatizes an end to the possibility of normal face-to-face interaction with someone who has died. Bodily copresence is now a nightmare. The corpse, at once the same as the living person's body and radically different from it, is a focus of people's efforts to bring about separation from someone with whom they are mentally and morally involved. Usually corpses are buried near an occupied house. Close mourners often remain in that house to "accompany" *(xəndemo-)* the grave, but their attachment to the site quickly turns to fear. At night they hear the dead person's demon whistling at them provocatively and breaking sticks with its clumsy footsteps. These perceptions build to an unbearable pitch, and after a night or two the survivors flee elsewhere, even when the house was one they initially hoped to keep using despite the death. People then avoid traveling near a grave site for many years. This spatialization of death contributes substantially to the rapid pace at which people build new houses and abandon old ones across their lives. There is a special term, "mortuary house" *(lux-xaim)*, for a house where a human died and was buried. When narrating histories of residence in different houses, people immediately identify a particular house as a "mortuary house" when they come to it in the sequences. A death stands out as the defining attribute of a dwelling and people's period of coresidence there.

Human and demon, like human and witch, are joined closely in a relation of pairing and otherness. Descriptions of demons focus on their deformation of human characteristics. Many deformities are specifically *inversions*. Demons are said to perceive night as day and day as night, which is why it is during the human night that demons most often come to harass people. Similarly, demons perceive earthworms as sago grubs, whereas humans think earthworms are revolting and sago grubs are delicious. On these and other counts, demons and humans are separated by a perspectival boundary that is also a boundary of unity. Demons live in a coherent world that humans can imagine occupying.[4] That world is structurally analogous to the human world, and physically overlaps with it, but the demon world is upside-down.

In speech the words *laleo* "demon" and *yanop* "human" are paradigmatically contrastive. Statements such as "He is demon, not human" or the reverse are common. The tense unity of the pair is also apparent in the common statement, "Human and demon together is taboo" *(yanopfəxo laleofəxo lelip ayul)*, which people raise as a self-evident cosmological truth. The presence of the category "together" *(lelip)* in this statement is an indication of the close link between monstrosity and understandings of social togetherness. A monstrous figure is a query into the possibility and conditions of persons being socially unified. In a well-known myth the rule that humans and demons must live separately is attributed to a living woman's unwillingness to touch her husband's rotting corpse while it is being carried in a string bag by a dancing old demonic woman at a feast. The living and dead could have stayed together, were it not for human revulsion at decomposing bodies. Here rottenness is again a sensuous sign evoking the whole tragic structure of humans' and demons' social incompatibility. Yet the principle that humans and demons are supposed to stay separate is two-faced. Just because some event is "taboo, ontologically dangerous" *(ayul)* does not mean the universe conforms to the appropriate order. People are regularly anxious about specific dead persons thought to be lurking around their relatives' living places. They also talk about demons as a collective, anonymous ethnic population that does not keep to its proper "demon territory" like it should. The statement, "Human and demon together is taboo," expresses fear of encounters with single demons, but also fear of the world-ending advent of the whole population of monstrous dead among the living. It is in the nature of this anxious statement of cosmological principle that it expresses what is in danger of occurring. The more people emphasize separation and revulsion in their relations with demons, the more thoroughly humans entangle themselves with their imagined demon counterparts.

This is most clearly illustrated by the main psychological property Korowai attribute to demons, namely, that demons experience "longing" *(finop)* for their living kin and want to be reunited with them. Misfortunes in the wake of death are often said to be caused by demons who lovingly desire their relatives to die. For example, when a young boy was killed by a fall only two days after his mother died, everyone affirmed that the old woman's demon had knocked her son out of their house. "Human and demon together" might be taboo, but the dead do not easily accept this separation.

Demons do their worst indirectly, through the medium of food. The most charged point of deformity and inversion in the demon model is that demons try to make living relatives die by leaving them gifts of food. These gifts are fatal to anyone who consumes them, by the logic that eating food gifts from the demonic dead is tantamount to sharing with them. The food objects are "remainders, leftovers" *(luntefu, luntaifun)* of demon meals. A human who shares food with a demon joins the community of the dead (cf. Carneiro da Cunha 1981: 166), based on an implicit principle that to share food is to become part of the same society and same category of being. The whole model is summed up in the existence of a special word, *lumbel,* that means "lethal food gift from a demon." People are daily wary of encountering *lumbel* objects. Any foods of unexplained origin, such as animals found dead or fruits or nuts unaccountably discovered in houses or along paths, are suspected of being demonic gifts, and people avoid eating them.[5] The fact that any food of unknown origin is a marked, uncanny object indicates how powerfully food objects are normally imbued with histories of who has provided them. Any foodstuff without a personal identity attached to it is a death-imbued anomaly.

Like their other monstrous characteristics, demons' practice of leaving food gifts for their kin is fascinating and attractive in its horribleness. The representation is so imaginatively compelling because the action is at once deeply moral and deeply immoral, by living people's own standards. It is normal that a person would long intensely for a relative from whom the person has been separated by death. It is also normal and admirable to give a relative food, as an act of care and unification. Demons' psychological state of "longing, love" for their relatives means that humans and demons share core moral attributes. But demons twist normal desires of being unified with another person in a perverse and deceptive direction. They perform good human actions, to lethal ends. They kill for love and companionship.

The forms of intimacy between humans and demons that I have discussed so far are indirect: the intimacy involved in humans' intense preoccupation with staying clear of demonic danger and the intimacy involved in demons' deformation of core human attributes. A more straightforward form of closeness between humans and demons lies in people's portrayals of interaction with demons as something that is overtly desirable. In many myths, for example, a living human ends up living cooperatively with an opposite-sex demon, often the human's recently murdered spouse. Here is the "eel-tailed catfish story" *(abun waxatum),* narrated by a man named Dəxil:

> Mister Right [*Xuf-abül* "Right Guy"] hunts birds from a blind. He unwittingly shoots his own pregnant wife Beautiful Woman in the ankle when she appears before him in the form of a pinon imperial pigeon. She returns to the house they share with Mister Right's elder brothers, and she dies. She is buried, and the elder brothers leave out of fear of her demon and disgust at their brother's act. The younger brother follows them, but when he tries to cross the Eilanden River a huge eel-tailed catfish bites off his foot at the ankle.

The fish is the murdered woman's mother in a demonic form. Mister Right crawls back to the house. That night, Beautiful Woman's demon brings her newborn boy to Mister Right for him to raise. She lives hidden behind a wall in one end of the house, and goes out at night to get sago and other foods for the husband and son, as well as demon foods for herself. She is always careful to keep herself concealed. She never gives the man and boy cooked sago and never shares with them the ends of bits of food she has eaten. The boy grows up quickly and becomes a great provider. During a drought, he kills the big fish in the Eilanden, gets his father's foot from its stomach, and reattaches it to his father's leg while he is sleeping. Father and son go out hunting, and day after day each kills a cassowary or pig. One day the son comes home first, carrying a cassowary. Tired and hungry, he asks his mother to give him cooked sago, but she tells him this is taboo. He insists stubbornly, and looks at her through the dividing wall. Seeing her for the first time, he is shocked by her putrescence. She leaves in anger, saying she will come back shortly to kill them. The father and son flee, as *ngenan* birds. The mother comes back with a large troupe of other demons, who begin climbing the tree where the man and child have alighted. The two fly elsewhere, and the tree breaks, crushing most of the demons. The surviving demons eat the demon woman who summoned them, in anger for getting their friends crushed.

Episodes of human-demon cohabitation never last long, and they end badly, almost always due to the human character's breach of rules of segregation. (These are rules that it is easy for myth audiences to envision, since people concretely observe the same segregations in their day-to-day practice of mother-in-law relationships.) Yet myth narrators and listeners find these episodes poignant and remark sympathetically on the ill-fated desire of human and demon to be with each other. The stories describe household activities emblematic of spousal love: providing game, pounding sago, sleeping in the same house, and experiencing together a child's growth. Through these narratives, people perhaps acknowledge that reunion with a demon could be a latent desire of their own.

In myths humans can eat food given by coresident demons, as long as the human does the cooking and the two beings do not share the food. In life, by contrast, all food from demons is generally feared as lethal. Yet there are certain contexts in which people take a more positive view of the possibility of food transactions with the dead. Hunters sometimes say that wild pigs they kill are raised and placed before them by deceased intimates and that such gifts of living game are not lethal *lumbel*. The idea that demons' domestic pigs are experienced by humans as wild is typical of the play of analogy and inversion in human-demon relations, and typical also of demons' association with what is alien to humanity. One youth told me that after his mother died he caught wild pigs every time he tied a cage trap, because she was raising pigs and putting them in the traps for him to eat. The pigs embodied his mother's continued caring presence in her son's life even when she could not be mother to him in person. By the time I met him, the youth had given up building traps, after several unrewarded efforts. He interpreted his change of fortune to mean that his mother's demon had abandoned him and gone elsewhere, which he regretted.

Another positive interaction involves humans giving food to demons rather than the reverse. On occasion a person wraps up a skinny packet of sago grubs, hangs it from the end of a house roof, and tells a dead parent to eat the gift. Making this offering, the giver also exhorts the parental demon to stay separate from affairs of the living, using the expression "turn your backside," an action that many sons-in-law and mothers-in-law perform toward each other and that people also describe as the appropriate posture of "invisible people" (discussed in chapter 2) toward living humans. The sago grub offerings are thought to keep the demonic dead from sowing sickness among the living.

Where the idea of "lethal food gifts from a demon" *(lumbel)* describes a fantasy of reunion that Korowai attribute to demons alone, these other pig and grub transactions are welcomed by humans. In positive interactions with the demonic dead, people relate not to generic monsters but to demonic parents, spouses, or other specific deceased relatives. Here an ongoing relation of interaction with specific dead persons is thinkable if it occurs through the indirect medium of food gifts rather than through food sharing or face-to-face encounter (see also figure 19).

A similar pattern is apparent in uses of the term "demon" *(laleo)* beyond its core reference to after-death monsters. I noted in chapter 1 that Korowai call whites, Indonesians, and non-local Papuans ethnically by the category "demon." This usage dominantly connotes distance and revulsion, but the term can also be made to express affirmation and desire. For example, in narratives of politically controversial involvement with whites or other foreigners, it is common for one faction of people endorsing involvement to say things like "That's our demon!" *(afe noxulaleo)*. Here "our demon" (parallel to forms like "our person" and "our uncle") is an assertion that speakers desire involvement with the other, not despite, but *because* of that other's deformity. A pattern of deformity being attractive and valuable, as well as repulsive, is also apparent across the overall pragmatic life of the "demon" category. "Demon" is a paradoxical sign for categorizing what is refractory to categorization. It is in the nature of the demonic that humans *expect* it

Figure 19. Gifts set atop logs over the grave of a young girl, 2007. The water, firewood, sago starch in a leaf wrapper, and miniature sago hammer were left for the dead person's demon so that she will know her living relatives care about her.

to take protean and unintelligible forms rather than conform to a type. Thus the term is readily applied to referents beyond its core designation of the monstrous dead. Characteristically, "Demons!" and "Demons would be good!" *(laleo-xup)* are also common interjectional swearwords, expressing a speaker's exasperation with a surrounding object or circumstance. In these uses the monster's embodiment of contradictory social impulses of separation and union works as a figure of combined contact and otherness in the quality of humans' expressive, categorizing relation to the world around them. A human speaker's own categorial position and integrity is intimately in question, with the categorization of something else as demonic.

As for the canonical figure of the after-death monster, the contradictory impulses of separateness and closeness dominating people's understanding of their relation to this monster are also assertions of contradictory qualities of discontinuity and continuity in the time of social bonds. Orientations of extreme aversion to demons are a way people try to extricate themselves from involvement with the dead. Yet activities of avoiding dangerous encounters with these monsters—such as living in houses high above ground, watching out vigilantly for foods that appear out of nowhere, or urging each other not to wander off alone—all put lost relations with the dead squarely in the middle of people's daily routines. The demon figure illustrates how people's consciousness of death centers on a problem of being connected by a history of close consociation to someone now deeply strange, such that basic media of human relating such as bodily presence or food giving are now filled with distress.

"WE SHOULD EAT IT TOGETHER": MOURNING BY RENUNCIATION

King Phillip: You are as fond of grief as of your child.
Constance: Grief fills the room up of my absent child,
Lies in his bed, walks up and down with me,
Puts on his pretty looks, repeats his words,
Remembers me of all his gracious parts,
Stuffs out his vacant garments with his form;
Then, have I reason to be fond of grief?

King John III.iv

An even weightier presence than the monstrous dead is the dead as they are remembered to have been in life. Like demons, though, the dead as subjects of memory and desire are somewhat indefinite entities. They are known through media other than the person as a living presence. One activity by which Korowai mourners relate to a dead person's painful absence is renunciation of foods. These renunciations too amount to an analysis of media by which humans are ever in mutual contact. The renunciations portray rotting, avoidance, and commensality as social signifiers that go in multiple meaningful directions at once. In mournful food renunciations as in preoccupation with monstrous demons, social otherness and the ambivalent otherness of signs are intertwined.

Food renunciations are carried out by relatives who stood in the most intimate kinds of relations with a dead person, such marriage, parenthood, or siblingship. The main types of renunciations are as follows. First, a hunter might for months or years after a death angrily abandon pigs and cassowaries that he has killed, instead of bringing the carcasses home to share with others. Men often do this specifically out of grief over the death of a parent. Second, a mourner might refuse to eat meat from a pig that a dead person had been raising, or that was raised in the dead person's presence. When others eventually kill and consume the pig, the mourner just stands by. Third, soon after a death a close relative might angrily fell the dead person's cultivated plants and trees, leaving the food to rot. When one old woman died, for example, her daughter cut down two pandanus trees and dozens of mature banana trees of the dead woman's, and she uprooted the dead woman's taro. Survivors might also simply let a dead person's plants rot on the vine. Fourth, a mourner often gives up eating a particular food species associated with the deceased, such as a species the person ate on his or her last day or a species the deceased and the mourner shared on that day. For example, following the death of a young son with whom he shared many sago grubs, one man refused to eat grubs for the rest of his life, even spurning them when he himself sponsored a sago grub feast. Renunciation of all game meats is a common response to the death of a spouse. One woman gave up eating pig, cassowary, mammals, and snakes on her husband's death, recalling that he used to bring these animals home for them to share. A man I knew very well gave up eating game for a long period after his wife's death, because he remembered meat provisioning as central to their relation.[6]

Mourners practicing these various forms of food renunciation describe what they do using the verb "renounce, give up" (yaxtimoxo-). There is also a single turn of phrase that people use to explain why they have given up the foods. What a mourner usually says about any specific renunciation is, "We should eat it together" *(noxu lelip lemalɛxüp* and variants). By this compact subjunctive statement, the mourner says that if she cannot eat the food together with the dead person, then she does not want to eat the food at all. As one man elaborated concerning his dead relative, "He should have remained alive such that we could eat together. As for me eating alone, I refuse."

In people's experience of relatives' deaths, interruption of commensality and food giving is a basic site of trauma. Yalun's statement of forgiveness toward her son when he ate her instant noodles reflects this primacy of food in experiences of loss. So does the model of lethal food gifts from demons. Another vivid instantiation of the pattern, touched on in an earlier chapter, is mothers' wailing of food terms in grief over the illness or death of a young child. The prominence of commensality as a figure of loss underscores commensality's status as a prime medium of social presence and social connection in life. Renouncing a formerly shared food species after a relative's death is something like the inverse of taking up a food species as a term of reciprocal person reference in joking avoidance partnerships and of other representations in which people take events of food giving as forms of elemental social contact.[7]

Mourners who refuse to eat plants or pigs raised by a dead person often emphasize that the deceased worked hard to produce the food, in anticipation of eating it. The food exists at all as a sign of that person's desire for it. Since that desire will now be unfulfilled, nobody else should get to eat it. As one woman recalled her thoughts when chopping down a relative's garden crops, "Our dead person's plants, those people [unspecified interlopers] will eat. Let's fell all of that, then they will eat their own plants." When a mourner refuses to partake of a pig that a dead person merely *saw* on a day-to-day basis, the understanding is that seeing a valued food itself amounts to anticipating its consumption. These patterns indicate that Korowai experience of the social truth in food giving and food sharing resembles the pattern explored by Munn (1986) in another New Guinea context. By witnessing or making possible another person's ingestion of food, a food giver or food sharer is in a deep social relation with that person, because the giver or sharer sacrificially orients his or her own desires to recognizing the other's desire to eat and pleasure in eating. Sharing food is when Korowai most powerfully know they are "together" at all. Other people most feel a dead person's absence through objects the person desired, because it is through these objects that others were most in contact with the person as a face-to-face presence.

Renunciations involve a chain of contacts. A dead person was in visual contact with a pig but never ate it. Now a mourner's contact with that same pig puts that mourner in contact with the dead relative's desires and the fact that they will never be fulfilled. A mapping between desire for food and the social desire that is the content of human relationships carries over into the time and position of the mourner. Survivors move quickly in speech between their own lack of desire for eating a food and their desire and pain of longing for a dead person. The pleasure that would be involved in eating a food is incompatible with the pain a mourner feels about his or her relative's absence. People say that they decide to resume eating a renounced food when their pain and desire of longing is gone. Destroyed or abandoned foods, such as big game carcasses, are major items of value. Even just abstaining from food that other people eat can be a major social and physical hardship. But these losses match the mourner's state of living in a lacerated present. As Battaglia (1990: 198) writes of personal mourning renunciations in another Melanesian society, "Observances like these keep fresh the sense of emptiness as an inner reality. . . . They break up the course of life like invisible 'no trespassing' signs, silent interdictions that keep the dialogue going between the dead and the living as inner voices." Renouncing a food object divides a person's senses from each other in the present, as a figure of discontinuity between the present and other times. A mourner sees a foodstuff or a growing plant and touches it destructively but does not taste or swallow it. This splitting in the sensorium is a splitting of the here-now, between a present of memory and desire and a present of separation.

Korowai often talk about a death by speaking of items on the landscape that are traces of the dead person's work and by remarking that the longed-for person will not be making the objects again. One man narrated the pattern in the following terms:

> When people see places where a deceased person made gardens, planted sago, or killed animals, when they see bones, stumps, houses, shields, or bows, then forgetting [the dead person] is impossible. They will see those objects and think that when that person went away for a long time, such as guesting, or to a big village, or to a feast, then when the person came back and saw the house getting bad, he repaired it ["made it good"]. But now this is the final house, the final clearing. The person won't make another one. He won't kill another pig or cassowary. The character of his designs [carved] on arrows, pipes, or shields are different from other people's. We won't see [him and them] again.

The man describes mourning as a matter of a survivor dwelling on memories of the distinctiveness of the dead person, the ways the person's singular effects in the world contact the experiencer, and the knowledge that the future holds no more such contact. Here once more we see Korowai locating persons in their actions, the things they *do*, including those actions' perceptual effects on other people who see, eat, and touch what the persons have made. In a specific example of the pattern, another man I met described himself as often looking at a string bag his mother made and used before she died. While looking, he would think sadly of the fact that the bag was going to break up and disappear and that his mother would not make another one. Often people speak of dead people's practices of "improving, caring for, making good" *(manopo-)* objects and spaces as the crucial thing that has been interrupted. The word for "cultigen" is literally "hand's goodness" *(melmanop)*, reflecting the same understanding of livelihood-producing labor as a matter of personal acts of making something good. Food-bearing trees and plants tended by their owner embody the intentionality of care understood by Korowai to be a core mode of human presence. In another variation on the general pattern that people are known obliquely by means of their signs, a sago palm or domestic pig is a posthumous sign of the person who made it good. But the object also intensely signifies the person's permanent absence. The sign is a substitute that stands for that person but is not that person. The posthumous object signifies in both directions.

A mourner's own separation from an object, in an act of not eating it, travels a similarly paradoxical path of making concrete an experience of absence. Like avoidance rules (such as in mother-in-law relations or relations between the human population and the coexisting population of "invisible people"), renunciations turn marking of separation into a definite way of life. A mourner does not just defer eating food in order to give it to a social other, as in relations among the living. Rather, a mourner defers eating indefinitely. The act is answered only by the lack of an answer, the social other's inability to eat and enjoy.

Evidence of the place of semiotic ambivalence in renunciations can be seen in people's focus on rotting and destruction, alongside their main focus on not eating. Although renunciations focus on a mourner's relation to the dead person as a memory, these renunciations signify that relation partly through the dead person's current material state. When a bereaved hunter abandons a large animal in the forest, he calls the carcass a "body match" or "body rejoinder" *(loxül-xolop)* of the dead person. The animal's wasteful death and decomposition reprise and respond to the decomposition of the dead person's corpse. The identification of animal body with human body is probably why only the largest, most anthropomorphized species of game animals, pigs and cassowaries, are left to rot by mourning hunters. Yet the identification is marked by disparity, and the disparity is what stirs up a hunter's grief. As one youth quoted his rhetorical questioning of the relation between a slain pig's presence and his father's absence, "Is this my father's rotten body? Let this itself rot."

In big game kills, as in renunciation of cultivated plants, rotting foodstuffs are figures of the deterioration of a dead person's body and the disappearance of the deceased as a face-to-face interactant and food sharer. This is part of how food renunciations can facilitate mourners' gradual giving up of the dead person as a remembered presence and a focus of longing. Renunciation separates a mourner from other people in the present, who go on eating, or who wish a mourning hunter would bring game home rather than leave it to rot. But mournful renunciations also point forward to a process of letting go of the dead person as a painful memory. They do this by signifying a person's absence and by dwelling on an object that is different from that person. Making dead people present in the form of a food object can be a step toward making them go away. A normal aspect of species renunciations or the abandonment of big game animals is for the mourner to resume eating the renounced food again, after a long period has passed. This marks an end to intense longing. A mournful present is systematically two-sided, as a time of disruptive change *and* ameliorative adjustment to change. Renounced foods are markers in this transitional zone of divided time.

Destructive acts of killing an animal or cutting down plants also involve an agentive, sacrificial dimension. By lashing out at a living object, a mourner takes on a role of willful transformation toward the world and toward the dead person, responding to and slightly erasing the damage the world and the dead person have done to the mourner. The animal's or plant's killing is not only explicitly compared to a relative's transition from living to dead, but is probably also implicitly experienced as a sign of the mourner's possible transition to having destroyed a memory, and being no longer in grief. Even so, letting felled food rot is also an act of recalling that the mourner cannot touch the dead relative. Separation from a food object is an act of forgetting, as well as remembrance.

This point about the concomitance of remembrance and forgetting is commonly made in studies of mourning (e.g., Battaglia 1992; Ash 1996: 221; Conklin 2001: 100–102, 171–76; Gibson 2004: 288). The philosopher Dastur expresses the idea in the following terms:

> In the experience of the death of the other I have at one and the same time the experience of the current absence or of the fact of the deceased who no longer responds, and the experience of his copresence with me in the 'spiritual incorporation' that mourning assumes. It is very significant that Freud spoke in this context of the 'work' of mourning, stressing thereby the latter's profoundly 'dialectical' character, consisting both of keeping the departed alive by incorporating him into our interiority and of what amounts to putting him to death by agreeing to be his survivor. (1996: 47–48)

I have sought here to document how this kind of double movement is central to Korowai food renouncers' mourning processes, and I have argued in particular that mourning's ambivalent doubleness is closely linked to the semiotic nature of mourning work. In renunciations, food objects stand for persons and their bonds. This relation of substitution *is* the relation of mourning. Memory, desire, sign relation, and social relation converge in a single cultural form. While mournful renunciations thematize that it is through semiotic media of contact that a relation is known, part of what stands out about these media of contact is that they are also channels of separation and that they mediate a bond's end, not just its continuity. Food objects and events of not eating them are complex and contradictory signs, like the contradictoriness of memory itself as the presence of something separate from the present. Food objects signify the person and relation that is being mourned, thereby making that person present again in a substitute medium. A plant, pig, or intended meal is a trace of a past person. Yet part of these objects' poignancy is that they are *only* metonymies, not the actual deceased. Processes of simultaneous involvement and separation in relation to a dead person—and processes of moving from involvement to separation over time—play out figurally for Korowai in this way that food objects simultaneously signify a dead person's positive presence and the gulf between the current time and that actual person.

"MORTUARY SAGO" AND "EXTINCTION FEASTS"

Food renunciations are part of a more varied field of mourning practices that follow the same broad logic of ambivalent signification. To make that logic stand out a little more, I wish to glance briefly at two other eating-focused rites. The first is a special meal eaten soon after disposal of a corpse. Following about half of deaths, close survivors decide to fell several sago palms. They extract the tender edible palm hearts, and they also produce a small quantity of sago starch from one trunk. Back at their house, they completely consume the sago products. The meals are called "mortuary sago starch" *(lux-xo)* and "mortuary palm hearts" *(lux-aun)*. About a month later the mourners break open the same sago trunks to collect beetle larvae from them, which they consume as a meal of "mortuary grubs" *(lux-non)*.

One aim of the meal of starch and palm hearts is to provide nourishment at a time of exhaustion. Yet the rite's main rationale centers on decomposition rather than eating. People say they fell the palms "so the human body and grub body decompose together." Here, "grub body" *(non-loxül)* is a normal expression for a whole sago trunk in which grubs develop. As one woman explained, "That [sago] body and that [other sago] body decompose and the human body also decomposes. From there longing will lessen, longing will become unknown. Without doing so, longing will increase." Another person similarly explained that the rite is carried out "for decomposing together. The person alone dying is sorrowful." Dissipating palm trunks are physical icons, in a process of adjusting to a dead person's disappearance. Like the demonic dead or renounced foods, the trunks are paradoxical media of commemorative forgetting. They make a dead person present, in order to make him or her absent.

The sago-felling ritual is in this way composed of both a gesture of contact and eating oriented to the vital bodies of surviving humans and a gesture of separation, sight, and rotting oriented to the disappearing and dead corpse. That the meal is centrally organized on a logic of ambivalence is further indicated by ways in which the appropriative side of the ritual is surrounded by rules of restraint. People's positive acts are accompanied by vigilant concern with what they do *not* do. Main restraints include that survivors must not cut down an excessive number of palms, that they must not process a normal large quantity of starch, that they must complete the food production early in a single day, that they must not let the food remain around their house uneaten, that they must not let the grubs develop to maturity before extracting them, and that they must not put their ears to the felled trunks to estimate the grubs' developmental progress. People observe these restraints out of fear that otherwise "another person will die." Yet mourners perform the meals in the first place also out of fear that if they do not do so then "someone else will die." Survivors feel themselves between equally dangerous alternatives of action and inaction.

The root ambivalence expressed here seems to be a dilemma of relating too little or too much to a dead person. A survivor experiences mourning as a dual process of simultaneous connectedness and separateness in relation to the deceased. This is suggested by people's further understandings of the motives for and dangers of funeral meals. People's statements here are diverse, but one typical notion is that if mourners return late from sago production, then the dead person's demon will be sitting in their house when they get there. Another idea is that if mourners leave funeral foods lying around, these will become lethal *lumbel* gifts from the dead person. Some persons say that in producing and consuming small funeral meals while letting the bulk of the sago trunks rot, mourners think about the fact that the dead person saw, owned, or tended the sago in life but now will not eat it. Another common idea is that a dead person will be angry at survivors' neglect if they do not cut funeral sago but that when the mourners do fell sago, the dead person thinks about the terrible difficulty of dying that he or she has endured and feels that under those circumstances the survivors have no place looking out for themselves by eating well. The mourners' place is to eat as a way to mark something that has happened to the dead person, so they should eat quickly and in moderation.[8] Mortuary foods tend toward being meals with the dead, in support of the dead, or given and allowed by the dead—if not perhaps meals *of* the dead, in the form of a substitute vegetal body. The nightmare of lethal *lumbel* gifts and the heartache of voluntary food renunciations emphasize the end of commensality between mourners and their dead relatives. Mortuary sago meals instead enact an ambiguous dream of ongoing intimate transaction and psychological negotiation with those dead. Here too, though, signs of involvement with the dead are also signs of separation, restraint, and forgetting.

Funeral meals also thematize a dilemma of tempo. Survivors should neither be too fast nor too slow in forgetting their dead. Mortuary meals are reflexive about time as a social medium in which contradictions of social contact and separation exist and a medium through which those contradictions are sometimes ameliorated. The euphemistically vegetal object has a certain therapeutic power, as people imply in the statement, "So the human body and grub body decompose together." A felled sago log makes materially present an idea of something disappearing across time, much as we have earlier seen living sago palms signify human temporalities of growth and reproduction. Making this material object a sign of a human body is a way to imagine time-based extrication from subjective involvement with the whole human presence associated with the body. Yet the idea that "another person will die" shadows this use of palm trunks. Deaths are meta-events, felt to lurk in the wings behind mundane moments of living.

A second rite of mourning worth briefly setting alongside food renunciations is the practice of the relatives of an extinct clan holding a sago grub feast on the dead people's land, long after the landowners have disappeared. Feasts are a major Korowai institution. In a normal feast, living owners of a clan place decimate their sago holdings in order to host troupes of visitors from across the land (Stasch 2001a: 487–653; 2003a). The events are performances of encounter between owners and their geographic others, across divides of spatial belonging. Feasts dramatize the whole geographic organization of social life as a dialectics of separation and involvement. When close relatives initiate feast preparations on land of an extinct clan on a substitute basis, this is special genre of feast, called an "extinction feast" *(bamol-gil)*. Feast workers explain their actions with statements such as, "That's not strangers' place, that's the place of our people"; "Lest the sago flower and die [without being felled and exploited]"; or "Who is going to do it?" (i.e., Who else is going to carry out the land's telos of feast production?). Much as normal feasts are performances in time of owners' existence as the people identified with a given segment of land, so too an extinction feast is a marking of this identity's combined existence *and passing*. The feast asserts connection to the owners but also relegates them to the past. Now it is all right to alter their land and benefit from its resources. Some disgruntled relatives of dead owners typically threaten to sabotage the feast, in anger over the exploitation. But bringing off a feast of this kind generally involves landscape-wide reconciliation with owners' passing and a transition to forgetting them. Contact with the owners' land and with food produced from it follows and facilitates detachment from pained consciousness of their absence. Surviving relatives often emphasize that they are exploiting sago groves that were habitual "destinations" of specific dead persons, where those people repetitively traveled to produce their staple food. The term *destination (xauntop;* lit., "going place") connotes a lifetime of intentional activity toward a vicinity on the land. Yet bodily travel, work of stewarding plants, and intention to consume them do not translate automatically into actual enjoyment. Sago groves, as destinations now exploited by survivors, signify simultaneous contact and disparity between body and landscape, just like single cultigens of a dead person that a mourner renounces or destroys. The *lack* of contact and identity between a dead person's body and the food he or she grew but never ate is here part of how survivors make real the person's absence.

"Extinction feasts" and "mortuary sago" help situate the personal food renunciations discussed earlier within a problematic of simultaneous restraint and appropriation, separateness and contact, that is typical of the memory processes of mourning work generally. Food renunciations pursue a path of separation, where mortuary sago meals combine restraint and ongoing contact in the same practice. Renunciations portray heightened contact with the fact that a dead person is gone, not lingering involvement with that person as a positive presence. Only after a long period of ongoing representation of loss is there a return to appropriative contact with objects, marking an end to severe bereavement. "Extinction feasts," meanwhile, differ from renunciations in being possible only at a late mourning stage, when acts of contact and appropriation toward a whole group of dead people's food resources are not felt to violate memory and loss but are instead positive ways to relate to memory and resolve emotional distress. But an obvious common element across all these practices—and across people's concerns with monstrous "witches" and "demons" as well—is that eating works in them as a charged act of contact. Appropriation and restraint are alternative, coexisting options that carry volatile figurative force, under mourning's contradictory conditions of mental involvement with a social other who no longer bodily exists. A mourner's relation to food materializes the dilemma of trying to live in simultaneous intense contact with a dead person and total separation from that person.

"PAY ME FOR HIS FACE"

I have suggested that in dealing with deaths, Korowai orient reflexively to the media of their social contact. They examine how a social relation exists through its signs and how a relation's signifying media pull apart from each other and from themselves. Mourning practices examined so far dwell on such media of relatedness as commensality, food provisioning, face-to-face copresence in living bodies, memory of a person, and passage of time. I turn now to another mourning institution, the payment of death indemnities, that focuses above all on the social medium of residential dispersion across the landscape. In this institution, noncoresident relatives of a dead person demand payments of pork, shell or tooth currencies, paper cash, or steel tools from that dead person's coresidents. If the housemates give, then the demanders' grief abates. If the demanders are not paid anything, then these relatives go on feeling angry and sorrowful about their loss.

Death indemnities are big politics. In the wake of a death, the deceased's housemates are often subject to an overwhelming flood of indemnity requests, and they stop traveling in order to avoid encountering angry unpaid demanders. Specific persons' descriptions of where they stand in the world are almost always heavily colored by histories of indemnities paid to them in the past, unpaid indemnities others want from them, and indemnities they think they are owed. Indemnity histories strongly condition people's understandings of whether they are "unified" or "not unified" with one another.[9]

Why do spatially separate people demand and coresidents pay? In many Western social settings, people assume that residential intimates of a recently deceased person should *receive* material and emotional support from other people, so it is striking that Korowai expect the opposite. I first address only why residentially separate people desire payments, leaving for later the issue of why coresidents are answerable to these desires.

Demanders express indemnity requests using idioms such as "Pay me for his face" or "Give to me for her head." As one man reported his request, "The person's head, for my having seen her face, give to me for her face." Or as another man put it, "Our having seen him, the dying of our uncle, for that we must eat [pork], that's it." When asked to explain the meaning of "face" or "head" in payment requests, or when trying to bolster the persuasiveness of a request, demanders talk about their histories of interaction, conviviality, and cooperation with the deceased. They speak of the dead person's jokes and laughter, the dead person's gifts of food to them when they visited, or the ways the dead person and the survivors cooperated during some past social struggle. For example, one man rationalized his request by noting that his relative had repeatedly picked him up and carried him as a child when his own parents tired of carrying him. When people first hear that a relative has fallen seriously ill or died, they express their anguish by reciting histories of interaction with the afflicted or dead person and by describing the payments they will need to receive because of such histories.

In the expression "Pay me for his face," the category "face" (*lulgelip;* lit., "eyes and nose") refers to the remembered person's whole interactional presence. What mourners ask to be paid for is their loss of contact with that person. Demanders often spell out that their problem is that they will not see the dead person again. The deceased's head or body has disappeared, and that is why they need to be given valuables.[10]

Indemnities represent and reshape the field of relatives a person had in life. The death of someone with "many relatives" provokes a large number of indemnity demands, whereas there might be no demands following the death of a small child or the death "of an elder who has withdrawn from wide social circulation." Indemnities are another context in which Korowai explicitly equate kinship with histories of shared activity. Here too a "relative" is anyone who claims a sense of relatedness to someone else, based on histories of interaction.

Korowai view seeking payment for a social relationship as a moral compliment to that relationship, not an insult to it (cf. Ramos 1995: 9). In contemporary Western capitalist societies, love and money are often deeply but contradictorily interdependent. Kinship relations are often described as the opposite of payment-based, commodified social relations, and much cultural work is devoted to managing the interdependence of payment and kinship, hiding that interdependence, and worrying over improprieties of that interdependence. Paying for people and engaging in commodity transactions to express, create, or end kinship attachment are morally problematic. Korowai see things differently. They understand indemnity requests as powerful, truthful ways to express how much a social relation means to them.

Once an interviewee and I stopped talking so that she could speak with a party of travelers passing through our clearing (figure 20), including a woman of her mother's clan who was suffering from a terrible hernia. The afflicted woman told my interviewee that she was dying, and she narrated the taboo violation she thought had caused her problem. My interviewee kept saying back to the woman, in intonations of sympathy and distress, "my mother, my pig head" *(nəni nəgolxabian)*. She was saying she needed a pig head because the other woman, her mother, was dying. This was a way to tell the woman how much she cared about her and would be affected by her death.

The indemnity institution reflects a general principle that relations with geographically separate people are exceptionally valuable. In 1996 a youth named Auson, exasperated at being accused of food theft by one of his clanmates, stayed for several months at the place of a distant acquaintance. His host at one point killed a wild pig. When Auson protested about being given an inequitably large cut, the older man pressed the meat on him with the statement, "It's not as though you're

Figure 20. Travelers stand for several minutes to exchange news with a clearing's occupants, 2001. One of the travelers was gravely ill. A relative of hers, seated behind a house wall through which the photograph is being taken, requested a pig head from her, as a way to express concern and sorrow about the sick woman's condition.

a person who lives together [with me]. You yourself are an upstream person." The man represented his relation to his long-term guest as a bond of special status. Such bonds are both difficult and desirable. They require different work than do bonds of coresidence. The fact that residentially separated people mourn each other in a special way, by demanding indemnities, points to a Korowai understanding that those people had a different kind of copresence than is shared by coresident people. Non-coresident people have a social relation distinguished by its temporal quality of *intermittent* copresence. Their moments of being together are informed by other times when they are normally apart.

In light of uncle relations' particular character as bonds built around a mismatch of care and separateness (see chapter 3), it makes sense that half of indemnity payments are made in recognition of uncle ties. Either a mother's sibling dies and a niece or nephew is paid, or a niece or nephew dies and a mother's sibling is paid. Another fraction of indemnities recognize relations based transitively on an uncle link, such as a relation of "same uncles" siblinghood or a relation of grandparenthood. About one-eighth of indemnities are paid by a dead woman's husband or son to her natal relatives back home, such as parents or siblings. Payments are also sometimes made to an outmarried woman by her natal relatives, for the death of someone among them. Indemnities can also be paid for in-law relations. For example, a man might be paid for his parent-in-law's death. The vast majority of interlocal relations recognized in an indemnity payment, including uncle ones, are thus based ultimately on an interlocal marriage. Also recognized through indemnities are relations between persons who call each other siblings because they are members of geographically and politically separate segments of the same clan. Across the entire open-ended variety of relations recognized by payment, the strength of claims depends on histories of interaction.[11]

Strikingly, the same category of relative can be on one side of an indemnity transaction in one case and another side in another case. A woman's parents and siblings are subject to indemnity demands if she dies while living with them. Yet parents and siblings of some other woman might be among those who demand and receive indemnities, if the woman resided separately from them, at her husband's and children's place. Living together or living apart is the basic issue under scrutiny. Thus beyond that indemnities are paid in recognition of loss and that they mark the value of interlocal relations, the central logic of indemnity payments is that certain mourners' problems of relating to a dead person are refracted across a difference between two spatially defined categories of living people. To understand what death and residential separateness are made to say about each other here, I need to address not just why "elsewhere people" receive payments but also why it is coresident people who *give*.

WHY HOUSEMATES PAY

The indemnity institution focuses on experience of relatives from else-where. People talk a great deal about why these relatives should receive payments, but they do not say much about why coresidents should pay. There is no clear notion that housemates caused the death. Belea-guered coresidents sometimes point this out, in asides such as "It's not as though I killed him/her myself!" Overall, though, people take for granted that coresidents of a dead person are answerable to others' demands. Coresidents are themselves usually deeply distraught by an intimate housemate's death, but they are told to take care of other peo-ple's grief too.

Even so, a few statements about the accountability of coresidents do occur, and there is other oblique evidence about people's reasoning here. One issue that demanders draw attention to is the "provisioning" or "productive bounty" *(folapel)* of the dead person: the food he or she daily provided to other people. In contrast to demanders' histories of receiving food from the dead person *occasionally*, the coresidents bene-fited from the bounty produced by the dead person day after day. A related statement demanders make is that they must be paid because oth-ers around the dead person's residence are going to eat the deceased's sago stands, bail the person's clan streams, and so on. Demanders think coresidents resume eating too easily, which is an offense against the deceased's absence and the demanders' loss. If no indemnity is paid, aggrieved outsiders often then instruct local survivors of a death not to exploit sago stands, under threat of violence. Like other mourning practices, indemnification focuses on the ambivalent semiotic status of a person's material traces. Mourners take these traces as untouchable embodiments of the deceased's absence and mourners' own traumatic condition. Demanders also sometimes say straightforwardly that the housemates lived with the dead person and they themselves did not, as a self-evident rationale of payment.

Indemnities underscore that Korowai view human interactional con-tact and enduring intersubjective copresence as what is valuable in life. Specifically, Korowai value copresence with other persons who are gen-erously and pleasurably life-supporting toward those around them. When seeking to understand and respond to the trauma of a death, rel-atives turn to lamenting their residential separation from the deceased when he or she was alive. This is symptomatic of how geography is a resource of first resort in Korowai thinking about life problems. Being separated residentially from a relative is compared to separation by death.[12] Earlier residential separation now appears as a moral injury, echoed and amplified by the more absolute separation of death.

The turn to residential geography makes death socially actionable. In the terms of the indemnity institution, not only is copresence valuable; it is zero-sum. Housemates' gain was other people's loss. The logic of indemnities thus resembles that of bridewealth. Both institutions are exchange-based attempts to define the meaning of people sharing their lives and to ameliorate experiences of relations of closeness being wrongfully disrupted. The two institutions also use the same payment media to express and transact the value of interpersonal copresence. Further, bridewealth and indemnification affect each other directly in diverse ways. If a married woman dies at her husband's place and the husband has never given bridewealth, her relatives make heavy indemnity demands, whereas they might demand little if he has earlier paid valuables. Where bridewealth is paid for women and is linked to their transition from sharing lives with one set of people to sharing lives with a different person, indemnities are a generalized bridewealth that people feel they are owed for having lived separately from *any* relative to whom they felt attached. The payment is for a history of separate living as such, now made hurtful by the relative's passage to death.

The reasonableness of demanding valuables from coresidents is also supported by a cultural association between death and houses. A man who travels to a death scene and demands an indemnity might shoot arrows at the house, in rage. This is an act of hostility to people inside the house and a way to communicate distress. But attack on the physical house itself is also consistent with wider patterns. Several taboos construe houses as potentially death-ridden and death causing. Wall panels consisting of flattened sago leaf bases are the most durable part of houses and are recycled from one house to the next, but panels from a house in which a death has occurred cannot be used again, lest another death occur among the new house's occupants. Similarly, a new house must be completely abandoned if the builders see a shooting star during the house's construction. Shooting stars prefigure death, and to occupy a house built under the sign of a meteor's streak would bring death to that household. In the days after news of a death has been heard, house construction, tree felling, or planting of sago and banana sprigs or other cultigens are all prohibited. These are paradigmatic labors of creating and occupying a clearing, with its nested spaces of domestication and nourishment. To carry out such work while a corpse is on the landscape would, again, bring death to the household. All these restrictions assert an imperative to segregate domestic space and death, in ways that presuppose death and houses are linked in the first place. Death *could* inhabit the walls, or the physical dwelling at large.

Covert association of houses with death is most succinctly expressed by the fact that the underlying identity *(xoxulop)* of houses is "death platform." Occasionally Korowai leave a corpse exposed in a house, because the dying person expressed special fear of burial. "Death platform" *(lux-lail)* normally designates an abandoned house containing a corpse. A typical use of the expression as a transgressive substitute designation for houses occurred once when I clumsily knocked against a house's protruding sticks, and a youth nearby swore "death platform" at the building, in sympathy with me. This convention of swearing characterizes every house as a tomb. The corpse-bearing death platform is the figurative, hidden truth of a house and people's day-to-day copresence inside it.

Death is a transition in time that Korowai pervasively apprehend in spatial ways. We have already seen that Korowai classify any house where a death occurred by the special category *lux-xaim* "mortuary house," that moving away from sites of death and burial is a regular part of people's mourning processes, and that the demonic dead are a territorial population with their own "place." People relate to the dying out of whole clans not only through "extinction feasts" but also through poignant emotional concern for the dead relatives' empty "extinction place" *(bamol-bolüp)*. Another face of people's tendency to see mortality as a matter of geography is present-day trouble with village living. Death is one reason villages are often empty (beyond the other reasons already outlined in chapter 1). People fear the sheer accumulation of graves near a village and the demons linked to those graves. Settling permanently in one central place undermines the possibility of dealing with traumatic ruptures in time through moves in space. Living together in one place with a lot of other people also means living with death-causing witches.

The diverse Korowai practices of spatializing death are part of the context of housemates' answerability to indemnity payment demands. The place where a person lived and died *is* the death event. Houses are answerable to mourners' trauma of bereavement, on a general logic of the lethalness of people's living places.

An important aspect of the divide between coresidents and relatives from elsewhere in indemnity politics, though, is that the housemates are not only negative figures to the demanders. The indemnity institution differentiates people according to type of past relation to a dead person, but this act of division also sets up one party as able to heal the other. Residential separation is enough like death to be injurious after a death has occurred, but "elsewhere people" feel these injuries, and seek redress, due to their sense of attachment to the deceased. They shared with that person and benefited from the person's generosity. The people in the world who can understand, recognize, and signify that such a relation ever existed are the coresidents, who now embody the idea of closeness with the dead person. Non-coresident relatives' ambivalence to housemates in indemnity politics is analogous to many mourners' conflicting impulses toward a dead person's plants. Housemates are objects of both anger and desire, much as exploiting sago stands or other foods of dead people is both an offense against bereavement and a redemptive means to lessen that bereavement. In both cases the melancholy object of attention is *charged,* as at once a sign of contact and loss. Coresidents' ambivalent status as both damaging and validating to non-coresident mourners helps explain the frequent volatility of indemnity transactions. From releasing arrows and shouting angry words, demanders can quickly turn to cooperating supportively with the coresidents. Interlocal relations are particularly valuable, but their value is insecure. All sides may *want* to be close despite separation, even as they have other reasons to feel and express hostility.

Coresidents often respond to relatives' demands by saying they should just come to the coresidents' places, enter, and be together with them. Demanders might join amicably with the coresidents only after an indemnity is received, they might do so without receiving a payment, or they might never reunite with coresident survivors at all. One of the most common reasons people break painfully with their maternal uncles is failure of a junior generation of these uncles to provide indemnities when senior uncles die. Earlier in this book, I cited as an illustration of Korowai egalitarianism the fact that house owners do not exercise control over guests' presence in their houses. The few extreme cases I have encountered of house owners breaching this egalitarian logic involved a guest arriving at a house whose owners felt the guest owed them an indemnity. Enough time had passed since the death that the guest thought it would be all right to visit. But the owners were still too aggrieved by the earlier death and lack of payment to tolerate the guest's presence, and told the guest to leave their space. The definition of what copresence is and the question of whether survivors of a death can be close to each other are in the balance in indemnity controversies.

"OUR BROTHER'S WIFE SHOULD JUST STAY BY HERSELF"

The idea that coresidents signify closeness to the dead person, and this is what makes coresidents answerable to demands, is supported by the special status of spouses in indemnity politics. Who is an indemnity-paying coresident of a dead person varies with the life stage of the deceased and with other contingencies of the deceased's history, but if the deceased was married, then his or her spouse is sure to be the main person to whom indemnity demands are expressed, even if other supporters help the spouse deal with demands. Spouses' closeness with the deceased makes them a focus of others' grief. People understand death to be located not only in residential space but also in spousal intimacy. Relatives of a dead person are particularly strident in demands if they know the spouses have fought a lot, perhaps because such fighting is an insult to a mourner's longed for ideal of contact. Even when there is no history of fighting, widows in particular are often subject to overwhelming anger on the part of their husbands' relatives. When a man falls sick, his wife is likely to exhort him not to be ill on the grounds that if he dies his relatives' demands will be impossible. Widows commonly perceive that their husbands' relatives "almost killed" them when their husbands died (though I have not heard of actual bodily injuries to widows). Two specific young widows I met call each other by the joking avoidance term "my demon" *(nɔlaleo),* on the basis of their shared experiences of almost having been killed by indemnity demanders when their respective husbands died.

Even starker is widows' standing as objects of positive concern. When a woman is widowed before old age, many men usually want to marry her. Yet her remarriage is offensive to all grieving relatives of her late husband, who feel she should go on living alone, as a kind of museum of the dead man and other people's separation from him (akin, it would seem, to mourners' feelings that land and foodstuffs intimately associated with a dead person should be left untouched). Mourners commonly make statements such as "Our brother's wife should just stay by herself." Widows themselves might quickly desire marriage, or they might share the ideal of staying isolated. One typical turn is for a widow to spurn a prospective husband on the grounds that he is no substitute for her dead husband: she, like other mourners, says the suitor is "not like" or "not adequate to" *(kül)* the husband.

When a widow does remarry, this usually provokes renewed indemnity demands from people who have not previously received payments. Now demands are directed not at coresidents of the dead man but at the new husband, whose offense is described as "crushing" or "falling atop" *(boxe-)* the head of the dead man. Following widow remarriage, even the dead man's coresidents demand indemnities for their relative's face. In other words, there is nothing essential about the divide between coresidents and non-coresidents in mourning. With a widow's remarriage, the salient divide shifts to the spousal pair versus everyone else. The widow, wherever she is residentially, stands for the idea of closeness with the mourned man. Her intimacy with the dead man and her separation from him, as well as her separation from men in general, are a focus of other people's contradictory situations of connection with and separation from the deceased. What is constant is that a relation of closeness is brought into contrast with a relation of attachment across distance. The distant person is deeply invested in that other relation of closeness, as an ambivalent icon in the process of coming to terms with mortal separation. Spousal relations, taken as prototypical of what social closeness can be, flash up as especially relevant to people's struggle to understand social closeness in the face of closeness's extreme opposite, separation by death.

A widow is also maritally attractive precisely because of her link to a mourned man. She substitutes for, displaces, and preserves a lost relation. A man who marries a widow of his male relative experiences this as a resolution of bereavement, even as the marriage aggravates other people's grief. Close or distant brothers of a dead man in particular see widow marriage as a way to resolve grief. A collective norm of leviratic marriage is so strong that the kinship term for "brother's wife" *(xamox)* is also the word for "widow." For a man to call a woman "brother's wife" strongly and embarrassingly connotes future marriage to her. A relation to a sister-in-law, and the possibility of marriage with her, is already figurative of a brother's death and the mourning of it, even before the death occurs. Clanmates of a dead man, including his sisters or other female patrikin, are often themselves supportive of leviratic remarriage, because it spatially preserves their socially close relation with the widow and with any young children she has.

The special status of widows illustrates with particular clarity the basic finding of this chapter, namely, that Korowai contemplate closeness and death in relation to each other. Here a widow's relation of closeness is the sign through which other people seek to come to terms with their own closeness and strangeness to a deceased man. Widows' status again exemplifies a wider tendency to see death as an ever-present underside of people being together and a wider expectation that closeness and separateness are conjoined relational qualities in central processes of life.

Affinity between spousal closeness and death is also apparent in the status of widowers. Men whose wives die are intense focuses of other people's grief but in a mode of anger rather than desire. Widowers too are usually targets of strident indemnity demands after a spouse's death. But far from being attractive as potential marriage partners, widowers are usually reviled (as noted in chapter 5). A prospective bride and her relatives often oppose a match with a widower on the grounds that the new wife will die like the old one did. The space of spousal intimacy is particularly accountable for a woman's death, whether by means of an unstated inference of male witchcraft or some more general notion that the man's copresence was the ultimate locus of the wife's death and other people's loss. Husbands tend to be associated with irremediable lethalness, by comparison to wives who are associated with the poignancy of loss and the redemptive hope of connection to what is lost, or substitution for it. These gender differences aside, widows and widowers alike are *loaded* figures. Disruption of social bonds makes visible once again marriage's core definition as a paradigmatic extreme of human closeness.

THE TRANSFORMATIVE EFFICACY OF PAYMENTS

The question of why housemates pay indemnities to nonhousemates is not only a matter of judgments of loss and injury. It can also be addressed from the other direction, as a matter of what indemnity payments do, how payments have these effects, and how the payments are achieved.

The main media of indemnification are pork, paper money, steel axes and machetes, headbands of Nassa shells, and necklaces of cowry shells, dog canines, or pig incisors. All these media are valued for their usefulness in a wider economy of transacting human life (e.g., paying bridewealth, paying for murder, or paying compensation for physical or moral injury). Shell and tooth currencies are valued particularly for their permanence. In contrast to other objects, these currencies "will be destroyed with the end of the world," not sooner. The shell and tooth currencies are also valued as heavy, bright, attention-drawing adornments that people wear against their bodies. Human bodies are probably a major focus of all valuables' significance, albeit often contrastively and negatively. Articles like teeth or pork are points of contact with the end of a body as a living transient material presence. They are media of severance.

Korowai discourse about these objects as payment media emphasizes the valuables' psychological effectiveness. People say that on receiving an appropriate indemnity, their feelings of anger or sorrow "disappear," and they stop remembering their dead relative. When narrating an indemnity transaction and its effects, recipients often vest particular significance in the blood of butchery, as well as the transport of a pig carcass or set of butchered cuts away from the dead person's house to their own residence for division and cooking. "My thoughts were cleared when there was pig blood on my hands and feet," one man said. There is a sacrificial dimension to the killing of a domestic pig (often a pig owned by the deceased or by the deceased's spouse) and to the transfer of the animal's vitality outward from coresidential space to non-coresident relatives' places and bodies. This sacrificial element can be seen in the fact that live pigs are never given as indemnities. When no adult pig is available, housemates of a dead person sometimes earmark a piglet for a particular demander, and raise it to maturity over a long period before finally making the promised payment. As far as pigs go, indemnification always involves slaughter. An indemnity recipient exercises displaced life-and-death control over the deceased person, over coresidents, and over remembered or desired social relations (see also figure 4 for the anthropomorphism of pig carcasses).

The sought substitution between indemnity valuable and human presence is a relation of effacement, not equivalence and commemoration. People's emphasis is on relief of bereavement "at once, suddenly" *(mün-diop)*. In a typical sequence, for example, when a man named Fedauman died, his mother's sister's son came to the house where other mourners were collected around the corpse and shot three arrows while shouting that he should be given a machete. The dead man's wife threw down a machete belonging to herself and the dead man, and after Fedauman picked it up he entered the house calmly to help with the corpse, no longer angry. The logic here is in many ways opposite that of personal food renunciations performed by a dead person's closest kin, usually coresidents. An intimate can only give objects up, watching them slowly dissipate. The coresident is imbued with death and the dead person's absence, a relation for which there is no replacement. Only a discrepancy of time overcomes this spatial closeness. In indemnity transactions, by contrast, a momentary transaction is used to overcome spatial discrepancy, which is now a focus of the pain of loss. Residentially distant persons end up with positive objects on or in their bodies. These persons seek instant forgetting of their interactional relation with the deceased.

In people's narratives, what an indemnity object seems to signify more directly than the mourned person is the transactional relation between survivors. The most prominent feature of indemnity transactions is that they are hard to accomplish. They unfold across the distances between social places, seize those distances as their problem and subject, and define the quality of those distances. Indemnity objects bear on the demander's remembered relation with the dead person, through those objects' signification of the difficult, valued accomplishment of the contemporary transaction. The relation between demander and coresident recapitulates practical qualities of the earlier relation between demander and dead person when that person was alive. I discussed earlier some logical bases of the idea that coresidents should pay demanders, but that idea itself has a practical life. Pragmatic dimensions of how the idea is formed, transmitted, and fulfilled are a major reflexive concern of indemnity conduct.

The biggest practical fact is that only a small fraction of indemnity requests are ever met, due largely to scarcity of payment media. Many persons do not own a single steel tool, or a single shell or tooth necklace. Few households have more than one adult pig, and existing pigs are often already accounted for (as gifts or payments promised to specific persons) long before they are mature enough to kill. Deaths provoke longing across huge networks of people who interacted with the dead person, exceeding housemates' ability to pay, even when they feel committed to doing so. Housemates of a dead person might also snub an indemnity request simply because they do not recognize the demander as having had a significant relation with the deceased, because they do not themselves care about the demander, or because they want to keep articles for themselves. As part of the overall system of people living far apart and autonomously, coresidents to whom demands are expressed do not assume that they have to do what other people want.

People on all sides of an indemnity process are very aware of the emergent character of their interactions. They know that demands change or subside over time, that some demands are taken seriously and some not, and that the moment at which a demand is first expressed is not necessarily when the truth of a relation is ultimately defined. One reflection of the difficulty of interlocal persuasion is the prominence of anger in indemnity transactions. Anger is part of mourners' emotional response to deaths generally, but angry brinkmanship is also a special quality of indemnity requests. One typical act of brinkmanship is for a man whose demand has been spurned to kill and furtively consume a

domestic pig belonging to coresidents of the deceased. This usually provokes an angry confrontation, in which the man is forced to replace the
killed animal. Yet the fact of having forced recognition of his claim by
killing the people's pig often affords a man (and the other interested
parties who shared the pork with him) satisfaction in its own right,
whatever the ultimate balance sheets. If a large number of relatives
travel together to communicate a demand, they sometimes do so in a
stylized genre of martial procession *(xasam)* connoting life-and-death
confrontation between places. Brinkmanship was similarly in evidence
in a typical small event I witnessed after a woman died of sudden illness
in 1997. Following her burial, her husband removed a long string of
dog incisors from his neck and passed it to be given to the dead
woman's mother, sitting elsewhere in the house, with instructions that
she cut the necklace and share it with the deceased's various same-clan
relatives. The recipient's husband (the dead woman's foster father)
angrily interjected, telling his wife not to cut the necklace. The two of
them would keep the entire string, and the widower would have to pay
other valuables to the dead woman's clanmates.

Anger follows from people's separateness and their possible recalci-
trance to each other's hopes, but it also signifies investment in the possibility of a relation. The uncertainty and difficulty of indemnity transactions
is part of what makes them so valuable, when accomplished (Keane
1997). Indemnity claimants are well aware of the immediately sociological character of anger, and they are well aware that their demands are
unlikely to be fulfilled, such that anger will become an enduring condition
of the relationship. Distant persons occasionally even decide deliberately
not to demand for a death, because they know the demand would not be
fulfilled and do not want their children to be separate from their relatives
in later days. Persons who are avoiding each other due to unmet indemnity demands are similarly deliberate and reflective about their anger.
When one man died, his mother's brother's son unsuccessfully leveraged
demands on the coresidents. When I knew him, this man was avoiding all
travel upstream to the general region where those people lived, because he
knew that if he encountered the dead man's coresidents he would get
angry and shoot an arrow, and he wanted to avoid this violence.

A major point of transfer between the relation of indemnity demander with dead person and the relation of indemnity demander with the
dead person's housemates is the issue of sensory contact with the death
event. In deciding whether to request indemnities and how much to
request, non-coresident survivors give particular significance to whether

they saw their relative while ill or injured but before death, whether they saw the corpse before burial, or whether the deceased's housemates brought news of the death to them in person. A residentially distant relative faces a trauma of transition. Korowai feel that seeing a dying person, seeing a lifeless body, or just being told of the death in person by the housemates lessens the severity of their distress, whereas being denied sensory contact with the death transition makes their distress worse (cf. Conklin 2001: 71–74). As one woman described her own experience of her mother's death, for example, "I was only by talk." She had not seen her mother's burial, and this pained her.

It is basic to interlocal social relations that people's knowledge of each other's lives is opaque. To coordinate activities requires deliberate work of travel, sending messages, and listening for gossip. The most urgent focus of this difficulty is knowledge of illness and death. People often spontaneously wonder if a certain relative might be ill or dying. I once overheard Yalun ask a visiting man if her sister had died. The sister was elderly but not known to be in danger of death. The visitor replied matter-of-factly that if the sister had died, then they would have come and told Yalun so. In practice, though, coresidents of a dead person often do not have the ability to inform all relevant people that a death has occurred. Sensitivity to seeing or hearing the facts of a death again foregrounds contact as what is at stake in indemnities. A death throws into question the sense of presence with a relative, as well as the sense of being a part of that person's life. Enactment of contact around the death event itself becomes a reflexive measure of the distant person's importance to the deceased and his or her coresidents. To inform a distant person of a death is to draw that person toward the space of copresence and coresidence, such that the disparity between coresidents and distant people does not flash up so acutely as a problem needing resolution.

Indemnity demanders often immediately drop their requests on traveling to the place of death and spelling out what they want. This too is typical of people's awareness of the pragmatic contingency of indemnity transactions and their awareness that transactions have as their subject the very disparities of social space across which they unfold. One demanding man, on being told that there were no articles available, said, "It doesn't matter. [My coming] is just for me to say words and you to listen." There can be social and emotional efficacy to merely traveling, speaking, and being heard. These forms of contact and recognition are consolation enough to help mourners unite amicably with coresidents and get on in life without the dead person. Coresidents, for their part, often strike an interactional pose of attentively acknowledging an indemnity request as a worthy communicative act in its own right, without saying whether they will actually pay valuables.

Residential space is the most prominent social medium reflexively at stake in indemnification, but of course issues of *temporal* connection and severance are also at stake. Here, as in other death-related practices, people address a problem of the relation between times that are painfully different. We have seen some ways in which people explicitly dwell on the temporal organization of indemnities, such as their awareness that good payments instantly erase grief, that unmet demands generate permanent social rifts, or that an act of expressing a demand might be followed by unpredictable changes of mind. There are two additional major forms of temporal connection making that I want to mention in closing, because they underscore the indemnity institution's conversion of death into a basis of active social involvement.

The first is a norm of reciprocation. When the recipient of an indemnity payment dies, people who paid the original indemnity should themselves receive a comparable indemnity back. Often indemnity payers, at the time of giving a payment, state their intention to request a matching return *(xolop)* when the person they are addressing dies. This is an assertion that the indemnity has a future. In other cases, the atmosphere of an indemnity demand is so fractious that no future return is ever mentioned. Even when indemnity payers do later request a return, those requests are not automatically heeded. However, the occasional persuasiveness of the norm of reciprocation is characteristic of a constructive relation-making sensibility that some participants bring to indemnity transactions. To request or pay indemnities is to seek connections. Indemnities themselves create social relations, on the basis of which further requests or payments may be made. In this way indemnity payments become interconnected signposts, joining past, present, or future events of people's lives into larger narratives of relatedness.

The second form of temporal connection making is the common occurrence of premortem indemnity payments, in which the very person who is going to be mourned gives pork to his or her relative. Sometimes the giver is not even ill or old. For example, a pair of unmarried young men related as uncle and nephew once raised two pigs, killed them on the same day, and gave them to each other as indemnities for each other's deaths. Most premortem indemnities, though, are asymmetric rather than balanced. Usually the participants say they want to carry out the transaction because they know that when the older, beloved person does actually die, coresidents will not pay and the surviving relative will be permanently bereaved. When an indemnity transaction *is* carried out in advance of death, the recipient later is indeed not so grief-stricken as he or she would be had the indemnity gift not already occurred. These premortem indemnities are further characteristic of people's reflexive focus on the pragmatics of indemnity norms, such as the difficulty of actually getting surviving coresidents to make a payment. Death-anticipating transactions are also typical of the power that separation by death has, as a measure of attachment in life. Korowai fashion their mutual attachments in part by thinking about how intensely they will mourn each other's future deaths and by acting materially on that thought.

MEDIA OF BEING TOGETHER

I have approached mourning practices in this chapter as contexts in which Korowai analyze what it is to be socially "together" *(lelip)* with other people. To close, I want to highlight some main patterns I have traced across different areas of mourning and some main ways in which these patterns bolster this study's argument about Korowai people's distinctive sensibilities about social relations. My interpretations of different death-related representations have converged on a main theme: Korowai reflexivity about the media of their mutual social involvement, in particular reflexivity about these media's simultaneous effects of relational contact and severance.

Korowai preoccupations with relations to the dead parallel the pattern of otherness-focused social relating documented throughout this book, in which social bonds are lived centrally as mismatches of close involvement and strange separation. Demons' simultaneous intimacy and monstrosity in relation to humans is typical of patterns of pairing and avoidance across other areas of life. The sense that social contact between demons and humans is at once desirable and undesirable, normal and against people's natures, is characteristic of Korowai understandings of being "together" more generally. Food renunciations and indemnity payments similarly support the finding that figures of alterity are central to Korowai social experience. Food renunciations use material signs to dwell on the condition of being separate in time from an intimate relative and estranged from the present. Renunciations and indemnities make otherness-focused relations with the dead into the crux of relations between living people. The living are mutually separated and related by their states of mourning in relation to the dead. It is also typical of Korowai relation-focused personhood that mourning is expected to have a *social* solution. Given that persons themselves exist as embodiments of relations, if a mourner stands in an unbearable relation of separateness from a lost other, somebody else should be able to answer for the troubles.

Another level of this chapter's findings has been that Korowai mourners dwell on ways that a social relation is not a unitary condition but is composed of different media in which people affect one another. Mourning practices decompose bonds into constituent paths of signification, drawing attention to those paths in their own rights: what properties they have, how the media are alternately relation-breaking barriers and relation-making channels of contact, and how different media work out of joint. Persons are one thing to each other in some strands of their involvement and something else in other strands. This turn toward media is implied in the idea of otherness-focused social relating itself. A relation of mismatched intimacy and estrangement is, by definition, a relation having different aspects. Otherness-focused social relating implies problematization of *how* people are connected to each other.

Different mourning practices thematize some media more strongly than others. Demons are monstrous in how they separate corporeal animacy from being alive in a healthy, unitary body: they are moving, acting, bodily beings who are dead and rotting. Other mourning representations also dwell on human bodies as social channels, in trying to understand separation from those who have died. We have encountered less terrified engagements with corpses and bodily deterioration in people's concern to see the lifeless body of a relative before burial, in their linking of felled sago trunks to a deteriorating body, and in hunters' similar linking of pig and cassowary bodies to a parent's corpse.

Demons also pull apart gift giving and life giving, and they separate gift giving from bodily copresence. In leaving gifts for their relatives, demons turn the normal human activity of caring for each other through food gifts into a practice of life-taking aggression. Demon imagery here explores the idea of indirect, object-mediated interaction as a fallback possibility, when face-to-face encounter is not possible and the interactants do not even share a common category of being. Food renunciations and indemnity demands similarly scrutinize commensality and food giving (in the form of the foods a dead person desired to eat, or gave generously to visitors) as sites where a relation existed and its interruption is known. These practices also single out for attention the sight, sound, and feel of a dead person's former actions in life, such as actions of laughing, smiling, tending plants, and making string bags or arrows.

In indemnification, the medium of social relating under closest analysis is geography. The indemnity institution underlines once again how intently Korowai understand who persons are and what they are to each other as questions of spatial practice. The institution makes visible how dispersion across the land is central to people's organization of their lives as a matter of otherness-crossing social engagement. Here again space is not a transparent channel of contact. People's copresence is not self-evident and selfsame. Indemnities say that living far apart but being related is a special situation, and a delicate source of pleasure and anxiety. It is a *problem* that some people lived close to a person and others lived far away. When "elsewhere people" are in each other's presence, their encounter is saturated with the other times and spaces of their separate living. Indemnities also say that copresence of people who enduringly dwell in the same space is shadowed by another time, when a once-copresent person is later permanently absent from the world.

In mournful analysis of human copresence into concrete media through which connection and separation are lived, emphasis on social otherness once again overlaps with emphasis on the otherness of signs through which social relations exist. In a study of material signs in European death processes, Hallam and Hockey make the following point:

> The dead body, as represented in European memorial and memento mori imagery, became temporally distant and "other" by virtue of its material disintegration. But the visibility of this "otherness," its recovery within the present, was a significant feature of memory objects in medieval and early modern systems of memory making, which were also used to offer moralizing commentaries upon the transience of the material domain. Situating the "otherness" of the dead body in relation to the living body of the self, memory objects were used to sustain connections between life and death. (2001: 47)

The Korowai mourning representations discussed in this chapter also dwell on the otherness of semiotic media in which social life is lived: not only the otherness of a dead body, but also the otherness of living bodies, faces, food objects, events of eating together, gifts, cultivated trees, spaces of productive action on the land, spaces in which people dwell together, and spaces of dwelling apart. Death-focused representations reflect on (or "recover within the present") ways in which these media are strange to the persons and relations they signify. A body signifies and *is* a person, or a body signifies and *is* social relations with that person. But as a demonic monster, that body does not measure up to what it signifies. While a food gift left by a demon is a substitute for bodily presence with a dead person, it is a deceptive and fearful substitute. So too a remembered act of sharing food in the past, or a renounced act of eating in the present, is a sign of "together" that also acutely signifies "apart." The human face and faculties of sight that are the main media of copresence also signify, after a death, that copresence is far from unmediated. Korowai know their togetherness with people by other times when they are not together with them, by the geographic distance that separates people's main places of living, and by third parties who were socially close to a mourned person but who now stand mainly for the mourned person's absence from the world. Breaking down social relations into media of contact, Korowai also undertake processes of reflexive estrangement from the signs of their lives. They dwell on signs' character *as* signs: not a person, not a social relation, not any route to direct presence, but a mediation. The same signs by which Korowai are copresent to each other are also limits to copresence.

In showing that mourners understand media of social relating as channels of separation as well as contact, I have also suggested that Korowai take media of social relating to be ambivalent at any given moment and relationally transformative over time. In other words, Korowai have a reflexive pragmatics of the coming into and out of existence of social bonds. Signs such as a sago palm, a cassowary carcass, a house, a coresident of a dead person, or a payment of money are points of enduring contact with the dead and also ways to get rid of those dead. The ambivalence of relational media is time-implying and time-enacted. Korowai are consistently sensitive to ways in which becoming related, and becoming unrelated, are what is at issue in media of people's bonds. We have seen this, for example, in the conjoining of attraction and repulsion in humans' relations to demons; in the ambiguities and time-based therapeutic effects of renounced food objects, as vessels of involvement and severance; and in the two-sided threshold between memory and forgetting presented by an indemnity demander's claim of intense involvement with a deceased person and desire for release from grief. In this paradoxical understanding of social bonds, a relation exists most starkly in moments of creation, change, and violation. Being "together" is known through its accompanying resistances. This understanding is already familiar from my account of marriage and from other evidence I have given of a Korowai principle that actions make states of relational being. The reflexive understanding can be described as a "pragmatics," because it focuses centrally on the idea of subjects *using* media of social connection, at times and places of unfolding relatedness. A major quality of Korowai people's reflexivity toward social practice is their sensitivity to creative acts of asserting relational connection through a concrete medium, their sensitivity to creative acts of asserting separateness, and their sensitivity to creative acts of doing both of these at once.

The arguments of the previous paragraph can also be put in an idiom of time *as* a relational medium, intertwined with the other media that signify relatedness and that are reflexively problematized in mourning's overall problematization of people being "together." Copresence is not only made out of people's facial and linguistic expressions and their bodily proximity in the same space, but also their proximity in the same time. Temporality as a medium of involvement is separative as well as connective. The time of people being together is not selfsame but is intertemporal and intersemiotic with other times. Hallam and Hockey's point about the "recovery within the present" of a dead body's otherness is one illustration of this issue of the internal alterity of a given social moment. This chapter has examined diverse practices in which Korowai mournfully portray present moments' noncontemporaneity with themselves. Such practices include feelings of longing and love toward a dead person, assertions that a dead person should be alive to share food, memories of a dead person's generous acts of hospitality, and memories of living together with a dead person over time. In mourning, these intertemporal links across disparities of time are the vivid sign of the quality of a social bond. Yet the problematic of separateness and articulation between different times that is so wrenchingly brought into focus in mourning contexts is not specific to those contexts alone. Rather, as outlined in earlier chapters, this problematic is an internal property of Korowai social bonds generally.

Conclusion

The idea that social bonds are most naturally based on pure identification might have enduring appeal, but I hope the preceding chapters
have made this idea harder to believe in as a human reality. Korowai
practices of social relating follow an opposite pattern, according to
which otherness is foundational to persons' mutual ties. This pattern is
even more remarkable given the great hold of identification-dominated
stereotypes in urban dwellers' images of demographically and geographically small-scale societies. Korowai social life, far from being
organized by a logic of "tribal" homogeneity of sentiment and consciousness, is organized as an intricate system of strangeness.

There are several finer-grained interpretive themes that I have developed across the chapters of this book, to make sense of this overall
appearance of an otherness-dominated social world. In this conclusion I
sum up a few of these themes to make them stand out more clearly for
possible adaptation to work elsewhere. I begin with the recurrent *spatial*
emphasis in Korowai people's definitions of social relations. I then consider the more general pattern that a Korowai actor's world has the overall shape of a field of otherness, stratified on multiple dimensions into
relations of closeness and distance. I next consider the main method this
book has pursued for understanding Korowai people's otherness-
focused sensibility about social relations: analysis of specific relations as
contradictory unities of close intimacy and distant otherness. I elaborate
on this point about mismatched closeness and distance by revisiting how

Korowai understand loss as integral to relatedness and other ways in which Korowai social relations unify closeness and distance in the medium of time. Finally, I describe Korowai people's own sensibilities about their lives as a "pragmatics," based on the way their otherness-focused approach to social relations involves a strong reflexive orientation to *events* and *media* of social contact as the truth of relations.

GEOGRAPHY AS SOCIETY

Korowai talk pervasively about social relations by talking about space. They know the particular characteristics of a social bond by its spatial properties, and certain spatial institutions massively influence the overall shape of people's world. Following Korowai people's lead, this book has sought to contribute to the anthropology of space, by giving an account of a social environment in which practices of space play very immediate roles in defining persons and their relations. In doing this, I have tried to craft interpretations that do not separate the categorial principles of actors' social relations from the phenomenological form of their spatial experience.

Division of the physical landscape into owned "places" *(bolüp)* is one major force by which Korowai make their social lives thoroughly geographic. When I introduced the landownership system (and Korowai people's geocentric vision of society) in chapter 1 I noted the strong ties between place ownership and another major feature of Korowai life, residential dispersion. A specific contribution I have sought to make to the anthropology of space is to try to grasp the cultural principles that are materially enacted and experienced in dispersion as a physical practice. It is in this spirit that I interpreted landownership and residential dispersion together as materializing social values of autonomy and egalitarianism and as physically grounding an overall experience of the world as saturated by qualities of belonging and otherness.

A side of this last point that bears special notice is the way that Korowai use of the category "place" embodies an apparent cultural principle that geographic belonging, or having a place, is a basic attribute of all acting beings. This premise is prominent in people's second-nature understanding that humans are members of clans and that membership in one of these human "species" or "types" *(gun)* means owning a specific place *(bolüp)*, just as owning a place means being a member of a clan. But the premise about being and territorial belonging is even more strikingly evident across another range of "place" usages touched on in this study: the idea that the monstrous dead have their own "demon place" far downstream from the Korowai lands; the categorization of different halves of houses as "men's place" and "women's place"; and the routine designation of the Korowai region at large as "the Korowai place" *(kolufo-bolüp)* or (synonymously) "the human place" *(yanop-bolüp)*. These last usages coexist with parallel designations for territorial lands of other ethnic groups, such as the "Kombai place," the "Citak place," and other broad ethnic territories abutting the Korowai lands, as well as the "Javanese place," the "American place," and other ethnic territories known to exist at greater spatial remove (Stasch 2007: 102–5). "Places" are how Korowai imagine the world and the categories of actors in it, whether these are gender categories, clan categories, categories of ethnic population, or categories of ontological being (e.g., human vs. monster). In my fieldwork inquiries, interlocutors and I often used the expression "Korowai place" to anchor reflexive discussions of Korowai cultural practice in general, by implicit or explicit contrast with social practices in other "places." Talking about an ethnic *land* is the obvious way to talk about an ethnic population and its norms, in Korowai understanding. The idea of a place, and the category "the Korowai place" in particular, can be taken as an apt synecdoche of geocentrism in Korowai thought about humanity at large: the whole Korowai pattern of living out social relations as being preeminently defined by space and by questions of spatial belonging.

An additional pattern in Korowai thought about persons and their places that should be singled out as a contribution to the comparative anthropology of space is the way that Korowai understand geographic belonging to be known through actors' practices of exploiting the land and leaving on it the traces of their presence. Actors themselves are in turn defined by their perceptible, knowable geographic traces: a human's existence is most forcefully confirmed by actions on the land. One of the most remarkable examples of this pattern is the land-focused teleology of child rearing. By this I mean that people's stated reason for having children is so that the land will continue to be exploited. The parents' sites of dwelling, walking, and laboring will continue to be scenes of human presence rather than become cold and overgrown. Even human procreation across time has a geocentric rationale. Belonging is something occupants actively impose and renew in relation to land, as well as something given to them by landedness as a premise of personhood.

Place ownership's contribution to motivating child rearing is an instance of another facet of the Korowai geocentric social imagination: in addition to knowing persons by their places, actors know relations and relational life-course events by their spatial characteristics. The parent-child tie is a relation of sons and daughters replacing their mothers and fathers as specifically exploiters and owners of certain bodies of land. Other relations that are centrally defined by spatial correlatives include avuncular and grandparental bonds and spousal and affinal ones. "Uncles" are a place "elsewhere" *(yani-bolüp)* on the land. Marital relations are similarly mapped onto landscape through the principles that a spouse is by definition a person of elsewhere, that spousal unity rests in shared dwelling, and that the central character of spousal and affinal relations rests in the related people's histories of traumatic residential change and new interlocal travel.

These specific kin relations bring to view a few more patterns in how place defines relations, beyond the pattern of certain relations being known by land-focused succession (illustrated by parent-child ties). One principle here is that relations are known by people living physically "together" in the same locations. A person's particular network of kin is created above all through histories of living at specific locations and in specific houses, to such an extent that an actor's relational life can largely be narrated as a sequence of dwellings. Another mode of defining relations by spatial properties, though, is that some relations are most known by people being separate. It is separateness in geography, combined with felt emotional belonging, that centrally defines an uncle relation, or a relation to an outmarried daughter or sister. The indemnity institution at large is an elaborate practice of mourners concentrating on spatial separateness as the defining fact of the former bond with the deceased, and struggling to come to terms with the disparity between that bond of separateness and other people's past bonds of more immediate spatial unity with the same person.

More could be said about specific ways in which Korowai apprehend social relations and relational events in spatial terms, but having already summed up a few of the most important patterns, I want instead to raise the general question of *why* Korowai society might be so intricately space mediated. I offer three broad and speculative answers to this question, each suggestive of different avenues of comparative investigation.

The first answer is that there might be nothing remarkably unique about Korowai space-centrism. The particulars of Korowai space-based definition of social bonds are only reminders that social relations are spatial everywhere and that tracing the spatiality of those relations always needs to be an integral part of describing and theorizing social relations as such. Korowai patterns only throw the universal point into useful relief.

The second line of thought, though, allows that there is something culturally unusual in the particular degrees or modes in which Korowai spatialize their lives. One answer in this vein to the question of "Why space?" tries to link the pattern to culturally distinctive theories of mind and knowledge. As I indicated at certain points, Korowai do not elaborately theorize subjective interiority as a knowable, trustworthy, and consequential realm of thought, separate from perceptible material action (see also Robbins and Rumsey 2008 and references there on the wider New Guinea–focused literature on this pattern). As with persons, so too with relations: in this cultural vision the mental, emotional component of relations is indissolubly material rather than ultimately immaterial. As is well known, the Maussian literature on elaborate, consequential society-making exchange practices found throughout the New Guinea region can be read in this light. People define their social relations through forms of giving, because gifts are thoughts and feelings in material, knowable form. Perhaps the Korowai focus on space, and on the immovable landscape across which people themselves move, has a relation-making efficacy parallel to this anthropologically better-understood power of movable, tangible gifts. Where people are and what land they own are facts with a certain physical concreteness. People can see, touch, and feel the ideas of their relatedness, when this relatedness takes geographic forms.

The third and final linked speculative answer to "Why space?" is that the focus on land is underpinned by egalitarianism. Not only are Korowai averse to the idea of knowing other people's minds, except through materially perceptible signs; they are also averse to telling other people what to think and who to be (Stasch 2008a). Within this indigenous political framework, social relations are easier not just when they are enacted across a buffer of spatial separation and independent landholding but also when the relations between people are enacted through the detour of a relatively impersonal material medium rather than through direct claims of interpersonal authority. The specific kind of geocentrism described in this study seems to be deeply entwined with a specific mode of political culture.

SOCIETY AS A FIELD OF OTHERNESS:
CLOSENESS AND DISTANCE IN PLURAL MEDIA

Geography is a relatively concrete topic. A more abstract theme that has
also been important across this book is that of the many ways in which
Korowai experience their social environments as stratified along lines of
familiarity versus otherness.

I first set forth the image of Korowai actors' social environment as a
"field of otherness" in chapter 1 through an account of the interlinked
subjects of landownership, residential dispersion, and political egalitarianism. As a summary characterization of the overall world this book
has described, this image of a "field" is aptly suited to the fact that the
types of others in Korowai people's lives are *numerous*. From early in
my research, I was impressed by the number and variety of otherness-
marked personae, relationships, and relational situations in people's
lives. Mothers-in-law, joking avoidance partners, witches, demons,
uncles, grandparents, children, guests, dead reincarnation predecessors,
and the diverse further figures mentioned in this book are only a small
sample of the overall variety but enough to establish the general point
that Korowai lives are full of otherness-focused relations. However, an
advantage of starting with spatial position and landownership (as
dimensions on which people's worlds are differentiated into the familiar
and the strange) is that these geographic materials foreground another
aspect of the "field" image. The world is not simply a jumble of types of
others; it is a gradient. Korowai are steadily evaluating different others
as being relatively near or relatively distant.

This stratification of people's worlds along lines of otherness is not
exclusively geographic. In addition to routinely representing their world
as a gradient of otherness by using space-based polarities such as
"close" *(xalu)* versus "distant" *(ləxinga)*, or "owner" *(giomanop)* versus "not an owner" *(bəgiomanopda;* also *xuolanop* "guest"), Korowai
even more ubiquitously characterize their relations with specific persons
using the categories "unitary, together" *(lelip)* versus "other" *(yani)*.
Routine use of kinship terms, I have argued, also implies a stratified
field, albeit one that is not exclusively spatial. We saw that kin categorization uses terminological generations to place persons in a spectrum
of relatives and that kin term use is itself differentiated into application
of a category to relatively "true, proper" kin and application of a category on the basis of it being "just done thusly." In deference to the
importance of space in Korowai thought about social ties and the

metaphoric power of spatial categories as terms of interpretation, I have used the language of "close" and "distant" to talk about relations of otherness that are not only spatial. A main proposal this book has contributed to ethnographic work in societies that are organized as elaborate systems of otherness is that we make the *stratification* of people's social environment along lines of familiarity and otherness a central focus of analysis and that we do so in part by applying an analytics of "close" and "distant" to the whole sweep of people's social lives.

One precedent for the image of society as a stratified field of others can be found in the writings of Alfred Schutz, such as in his well-known typification of a lifeworld as comprising four "regions" or "spheres," populated by four different kinds of social others (see, e.g., Schutz 1967 [1932]): those others from whom an actor is separated in time, termed "predecessors" and "successors"; those others from whom an actor is separated in space but not time, termed "contemporaries"; and those others with whom a person interacts directly in the same spaces and times, termed "consociates." Significantly, Schutz examines ways in which his named types are not absolutely contrastive but are "poles between which stretches a continuous series of experiences" (1967 [1932]: 177; see also pp. 178–79). He also explores ways in which each "region" is itself internally differentiable into further more fine-grained modes in which actors can be spatiotemporally close or distant (e.g., pp. 168, 180–81). Schutz's model helpfully schematizes the same basic idea I am advocating here: actors experience their world as pervasively differentiated into figures or situations of relative familiarity and figures or situations of relative alienness.

We have further seen, though, that a major feature of Korowai people's lifeworlds is that they are differentiated by forms of distance and closeness in multiple social media at once. An actor's field of social counterparts is not a single spectrum of otherness but a shifting tangle of intersecting ones. Closeness and distance in landownership is different from closeness and distance in actual bodily position on the land. Each of these is different in turn from closeness and distance in food sharing, or in bodily genesis. Separateness in time from a predecessor in a reincarnation cycle is different from separateness in time from a deceased but remembered parent or spouse, and both of these differ from temporal separateness from a deceased relative who was residentially distant in life, or temporal separateness from myth characters. Schutz's typology helpfully foregrounds time and space as main dimensions on which people are in contact or separate. Yet there are multiple ways people can be mutually present in the same times and spaces and multiple ways they can be spatiotemporally involved with each other beyond limits of direct bodily perception. Nor are time and space the exclusive media through which social relations exist.

At the same time, the different relations, relational events, and relational media discussed in this book are interimplicated in substantial ways. For example, marital relations, parental relations, avuncular relations, and grandparental relations all reciprocally mediate each other. People generally marry before having and raising children, even as the goal of having children precedes and motivates marrying. Uncle and grandparent relations follow from marriages and parenting but are also goals of marriage and parenting, and they precede marriages as part of their context (as when, for example, grandparents marry). These several interlinked types of kin bonds, discussed in the middle chapters, are all intricately entwined in turn with mourning, the subject of chapter 6. Initial making and raising of children usually precedes parents' deaths, and people's births precede their deaths, but mourning also precedes and conditions births, in numerous ways. People orient to children as replacements prefiguring and ameliorating the parents' deaths. Infants are understood to be reincarnations of deceased predecessors. Newborns are categorized as demonic death-imbued monsters *(laleo)*. And the possibility of children's own deaths is strongly present in people's ways of relating to them. In these and many other ways, the different life-crisis events and relational processes discussed in this study are "in" each other.[1]

One interpretive category that might be taken as a centripetal element in the field of otherness, uniting disparate relationships and relational issues into a single plane, is what I have called "belonging." I have used this interpretive term to draw together Korowai categories like "together, unitary" *(lelip)*, "own, proper" *(giom)*, and "love, longing, affection" *(finop)*, as well as a wider range of ways in which Korowai express unity or comfort with people, places, and situations. This has also partly meant using the term as a close obverse of the category "otherness" itself. Qualities of relational belonging are central questions of Korowai social experience and are central to people's experience of their world as stratified into zones of proximity and distance. A social world shaped as a "field of otherness" is also a "field of belonging."

Yet it has been important to my account that *not* all forms of closeness are forms of belonging. For example, interpersonal belonging, as a quality of moral and emotional feeling in relation to someone, is not the same thing as closeness in space and time to that person. Guests are people present in space who do not *belong*, spatially and socially; dead relatives are objects of intense feelings of belonging, who are distant in space and time; and so forth—in more nuanced ways I have sought to spell out in each relational instance. In other words, even a dimension of people's lifeworld as general as "belonging" exists distinctly from other dimensions on which the world is also stratified.

The main way I have sought to understand Korowai people's social world, as a field of otherness, is to identify specific media of social involvement out of which different relations are most centrally composed and to trace the ways people are close or distant in those media. Yet as the examples of guests or the absent dead (both of which embody a mismatch between state of belonging and state of spatiotemporal presence) make very apparent, to recognize Korowai people's world as being stratified on plural dimensions of otherness leads very directly to a more basic subject: the way that *single* relations are themselves internally plural. Relations join together disparate modes and qualities of contact between the same persons.

SINGLE SOCIAL RELATIONS AS COMPOSITES OF CLOSENESS AND DISTANCE

This book's main argument has been that Korowai practice a reflexive sensibility of social relations, according to which otherness as a relational quality is itself a basis of people's bonds. Actors are in close contact through and around their otherness. What this means empirically is that a social relation, examined closely, turns out to consist of multiple strands, some involving relational qualities of closeness, and some involving qualities of distance and otherness. A social bond not only lies on continua of familiarity and otherness in a wider stratified social world but also contains these poles as its own internal qualities. My overall approach to Korowai persons' lives has been to trace the mismatched joining together of close intimacy and distant otherness in specific social relations, on the understanding that the crux of the relation lies in that joining.

Without revisiting all relations I have described in these terms, I want to at least gesture here at a sample of them, to keep the model concrete. As mentioned a moment ago, for example, the relation between hosts and guests unites closeness in the medium of face-to-face spatiotemporal presence with otherness in media of place ownership, residence, and mutual spatial belonging. Yet we saw early in this study that the relation of belonging between owners and their own land also combines intimacy and estrangement. Owners and land are identified, but the land is separate from owners, it registers their absences, and its occult denizens are antagonistic to owners' acts of appropriation. So too, at a quite different interactional scale, people's daily acts of handing each other food join separateness in the medium of bodily touch with intimate, caring contact in the medium of food and food-focused desire. Conjoining of closeness and disparity is also the central theme of my account of pairing relations and kin bonds. For example, joking avoidance partnerships and transgressive lexical substitutions each combine close identification and elements of avoidance and grotesque strangeness. Matronymic designations, like feelings of attachment to mothers generally, pose birth events and maternal presences as both near and distant to personhood. Uncle relations extend this pattern geographically and sociologically, by mapping maternal intimacy onto separateness of place and clan. Newborns are repulsively alien in the time of current presence but attractive and valuable in the time of anticipated future provisioning and attachment. Spousal relations turn on mismatches between close sharing in present times and histories of formerly being strangers. In mourning practices, signs such as a human corpse, food objects, and coresident intimates of a dead person vividly represent both the presence of the deceased and that person's permanent separateness from bereaved survivors.

To understand social bonds as made of the conjoining of disparate relational qualities, a first step is to decompose the relations into distinct strands. The significance of this step can be more fully appreciated by noting how another author has put the same idea. In a brief passage on the problem of different kinds of relations of otherness in *The Conquest of America* (1984: 185–86), Todorov proposes that such relations have three distinguishable axes. First, there is an axis of evaluation, involving issues of whether an other is experienced as good or bad; as a focus of love, hate, or some other affect; or as a superior, an equal, or an inferior. Second, there is an axis of knowledge, involving issues of how much or little a self actually knows about its other (cf. Schutz 1944: 500). Third, there is an axis of practice, involving issues of actual closeness or distance; identification or disidentification; and self-submission, self-imposition, or indifference toward an other. Todorov's main concern in differentiating these axes is to assert that these aspects of a relation can vary independently:

> There exist, of course, relations and affinities between these three levels,
> but no rigorous *implication;* hence, we cannot reduce them to one another,
> nor anticipate one starting from the other. . . . Knowledge does not imply
> love, nor the converse; and neither of the two implies, nor is implied by,
> identification with the other. (p. 185; original emphasis)

My interpretations of Korowai social bonds align well with Todorov's
call to recognize relations of otherness as having multiple dimensions
that do not operate in lockstep congruity. The specific axes Todorov
proposes are also broadly relevant to Korowai patterns. For example,
distinguishing relative value of self and other from issues of practical
assimilation or identification is a good match with the Korowai phenomenon of egalitarianism that keeps people apart. This same delink-
ing of evaluation and assimilation is also relevant to the related
Korowai pattern of closeness by enmity: morally negative evaluations
of another's actions often become the basis of intense practical preoccupation with that person and can lead to further close amicable
involvement. Also in this vicinity is the Korowai pattern of love without
assimilation: actors often evaluate very positively certain others (such as
uncles) despite—or due to—their unassimilable difference (see also
Rutherford 2003).

Overall, though, I have described Korowai social relations as much
more multiple in internal composition than Todorov's proposals allow.
His axes are too general. We have seen, for example, that Korowai practical involvement is not one single pursuit but involves a range of coexisting ways that people affect each other. Land, time, bodily touch,
bodily genesis, food, gifts, sight, and modes of person reference are a
few of the media of involvement in which people relate to each other
practically all at once, and when these media are themselves examined
closely they turn out to be internally differentiated into even more particular strands.

In addition to differentiating media of social involvement more
finely, though, my account of Korowai social relations has diverged
from Todorov's proposals in that I have shown that different strands of
Korowai social bonds are *systematically* disparate and contradictory. It
is not just that the different strands work independently of each other
but that the joining of closeness and distance in different aspects of single relations is at the core of what the relations *are* to Korowai.

An idea of systematic contradictoriness is important in another existing contribution to theorizing social relations of otherness, the model of

Amazonian kinship offered by Viveiros de Castro (2001) that I referred to in my introduction. Viveiros de Castro proposes that in Amazonian kinship processes (by contrast to "Western kinship ideologies"), otherness is the given, unmarked quality of social relations. He posits that close identification is also an irreducible element of social bonds, albeit a marked quality that people create against the background of generalized otherness. Viveiros de Castro describes Amazonian social worlds as consisting of a large assortment of otherness-dominated social relations, nested within each other. For example, one of his diagrams (p. 32) portrays a society's kinship field as composed of people who are residentially distant versus close, with the residentially close people in turn divided into cross-kin and parallel kin, and the parallel kin in turn divided into cross-sex versus same-sex relatives. The same-sex kin are further divided into siblings and a self, and a self is further divided into a placenta and a body. Viveiros de Castro is especially interested in the "perpetual disequilibrium" or "irresolvable internal tension" (p. 29) between otherness and identity in these and other Amazonian social relations. Otherness and identification stand in a relation of mutual implication, mutual antipathy, and mutual irreducibility.

Viveiros de Castro's model is abstract, and I have made it more schematic here. I sketch it, though, because it has some features in common with my own argument and can thus help clarify the nature of my claims. One of these features is that his model starkly conveys an idea of cultural variability in what people understand otherness to be and in what role they give it in their social lives. The model sets forth in sharp outlines an idea of fundamental cultural difference in the very definition of a social relation, which I have also tried to do in this study. Further, the specific claims Viveiros de Castro makes about Amazonian sociability are parallel to my generalizations about Korowai relational sensibilities. We both describe systems in which otherness is basic to relations and in which relations consist centrally of contradictory composites of distance and closeness. Significantly, Viveiros de Castro's model posits a very direct relation between people's sensibility about single social relations and the shape of their overall otherness-saturated social world. He holds that the contradictory makeup of single social relations, premised as they are on a "disjunctive synthesis" of identification and otherness, is what generates the overall shape of Amazonian societies as a "motley crowd of Others" (p. 23). Society here does not take the form of discrete positions of alterity-free identity and identity-free alterity. Rather, the contradictoriness of single relations fuels a proliferation of ever more particular relations of otherness with close intimates and ever more general relations of distance-spanning intimacy with radical others (pp. 28–29). Concerning the Korowai materials I have discussed, we might suggest more moderately that the overall stratified field of others in which actors live is the shaping context, as well as shaped product, of people's otherness-focused sensibility about single relations.

My argument that social bonds are centrally composed of systematic mismatches of relational intimacy and otherness cannot be set forth very elaborately, even in the abstract, without discussing specific media of people's social involvement. I turn now to important patterns of conjoined intimacy and otherness in one prominent Korowai medium of social relating, that of time.

LOSS AND BELONGING: THE TEMPORALITY OF RELATIONS

I began this conclusion by drawing renewed attention to the strongly spatial bent in Korowai understandings of social relatedness and to this book's effort to contribute to the anthropology of spatial forms by following closely how Korowai define their relations in directly spatial ways. Equally and correlatively, I have sought to understand how Korowai make temporality a direct constituent of social bonds. At this point I want to underline and synthesize some of the largest time-focused patterns in Korowai social relating and suggest that links between temporality and relatedness are one and the same with the problematic of otherness-based relating that has been my overall subject.

An important link between temporality and relatedness is Korowai actors' consistent construal of relations as being made by actions.[2] We have seen Korowai posit direct back-and-forth influence between categories of relational being and acts of doing in the way people talk about spouses' bonds mainly by talking about activities a couple does together, or in the way indemnity demanders support their requests by appealing to histories of giving, laughter, or cooperation. The pattern can be seen too in the way demons, as a type of being, are defined by their paradigmatic *action* of giving malignant food gifts. Most vividly, the sensibility that doing is the truth of being is apparent in the way parental bonds are defined by food gifts, bodily sensation, and contingent acts of care. The sensibility is also evident in the more general notion that people become relatives through contingent histories of interaction and that people who already are relatives remain so only if they practice ongoing acts of giving and cooperation. Assignment of particular relations to values of "close" or "distant" is not given but is actively created, through people's acts of leaving each other, coming into each other's presence, giving food to each other, and so on. Structures of lifeworld stratification are enacted, inferred, and abandoned through interpersonal actions, in addition to preceding and determining those actions.

This orientation to relations as created and defined by acts shades into a wider pattern of intense cultural attentiveness to *events,* in particular events that seem new, unexpected, unwished for, revelatory, confirmatory, or mysterious. Events stand out as "where the action is" in life and as where the meaning is. This cultural thematization of events is apparent, for example, in joking avoidance partnerships, which make a single fleeting event into the name of a relation. It is also clear in people's active concern with possibilities of transgressing norms, in mother-in-law avoidance, avoidance of "hidden names" *(xoxulop),* and many other areas of life. The pattern is attested too in what I have described as the "regularity of violation" in marriage and feuding: the ways in which people approach disruption of moral expectations as sometimes a productive basis for close belonging.

These temporal themes can be summed up by saying that Korowai understand becoming related as central to the experience of relatedness as such. This could be described as the "courtship" side of all bonds, and the side of bonds that finds belonging to inhere in temporalities of repetitively experienced mutual presence. But there is also a "mourning" side to Korowai understandings of social connection: actors consistently portray belonging not just as an accomplishment, but as an accomplishment that is transient and tinged with loss.

An understanding that belonging itself has transience as a defining characteristic is present in the way that love between parents and children is made contingently by concrete actions of material care. Here the relation of belonging itself amounts to a premonition of loss, in the form of the parent's own death. This relation of belonging is also defined more generally around the temporal disparity between two persons' lives, including the child's pathos as a figure of lack, the poignant moral asymmetry between a vulnerable child and a capable adult, and the pleasures of the child's growth into skills of provisioning and self-care or care for others. Although a vulnerable child has not been literally dispossessed of something it once had, there is still loss in the broader sense that the child stands in a condition of deprivation relative to the security of self-provisioning it would have if it were an adult. Parents are intensely aware too that a child's vulnerability can lead to actual loss of life.

In a similar way uncle relations center on a dominant experience of being lamentably separate from the loved other. The relations are also imbued with mothers' loss of belonging in relation to their own natal lands and the transience of children's time of closeness to mothers. The relations are marked too by fragility of ongoing amicable status. Not only do uncles or nephews and nieces die; the intense desire for interaction with these faraway relatives is often matched by disappointments of achieved involvement. For example, people fail to visit or fail to give, they see in each other's actions a relation-breaking slight, or they fall out over indemnity grievances. As I have outlined, ties to relatives at large are strongly colored by similar fragility. Actors know themselves as having become relatives with certain persons only within recent memory, and they skeptically monitor their concrete interactions for knowledge of what their mutual standing actually is. People often veer in the direction of describing life in a world of kinship as a life of lack. Actors see themselves as being deprived of kin. The alienness of outer regions of a social field, or the potential alienness of any interactant, has the character of a kind of loss, when measured against ideals of belonging.

My account of marriage processes as systematically joining creation and violation of belonging can similarly be understood as an account of close links between relatedness and loss. A woman and her relatives lose their presence to each other, and spouses lose whatever overall equilibrium of relational lives they had been living out with other people prior to marriage, in favor of the awkward process of acclimating to one another through shared activity. Even inalienable ownership of land is strongly temporal. Land is a figure of lost human presence when it stands empty of owners and unmodified by them. Living owners' routine occupation of land is structured by strong orientations to dead predecessors who are no longer there on the place and to the transience of their own presence.

Sensitivity to the transience of relations of belonging, as something made and lost in events, is another facet of overall Korowai sensitivity to otherness as an irreducible basis of social connections. Looking to events for the truth of relations is a way to query a present of action, such as a time and space of two people being "together" *(lelip)*. This sensitivity queries a social here and now as being different from, and relational to, other times, places, and possibilities. Numerous subjects discussed in this book consist centrally of people linking a present social state to other spaces and times. They understand the present of interaction as connected to and disparate from those other scenes, and they understand this complex blend of spatiotemporal linkage and disparity to be the very problem and definition of the present. For Korowai, a face-to-face social relation is not a bond of pure spatial and temporal copresence but exists as a conjunction of multiple, conflicting temporalities.

Mourning is the area where it is easiest to see social relations as being temporal composites in this way. (The specific pattern of *loss* and belonging being integrally entwined is also most visible in mourning, and in people's appeals to death as a reference point in daily life, such as when they make prospective mourning a measure of relatedness between people who are not even ill or old.) In a mourning practice such as food renunciation, intimate survivors of a dead person dwell on a present social moment's difference from past times when the deceased person was living. In indemnity transactions, people put that same temporal disparity between a "now" of absence and an earlier "then" when the deceased person was alive into dialogue with disparities between an intimate household space and other parts of the landscape. Here mourning is a relation to the consociate in the predecessor or the predecessor in the consociate, so to speak. The remembered relation of past consociation stands in contradiction to one person being a survivor and another being dead. So too in demon imagery, people relate the idea of the imaginable current presence of a living body to its other imaginable current presence as a rotting corpse. They align this relation of body-focused similarity and disparity with a similar close contrast between the caring, moral actions of food giving and love, and shockingly destructive, immoral actions of giving poison gifts (the *lumbel* foodstuffs that demons are thought to leave mischievously around). In these and other death-focused representational practices, Korowai dwell on human presence as being full of other times. Moments of mutual presence are saturated by connections to other times when the same people are separated by death, just as times when people are separated by death are saturated by links to other moments when people are mutually present.

But if the portrayal of a social relation as being by definition an intertemporal condition of change and adjustment-to-change is particularly sharp in mourning, social relations across countless other areas of activity are also defined around thresholds of double consciousness of different conditions of time. Spouses know their present relation by how they were formerly not close but have come to be close through relation-creating gifts and cooperative actions. A married woman's relatives are concerned with the space elsewhere of spouses' closeness and with how that closeness affects their own present place, disrupting a past time of sharing with the woman. Affines know their relation to a son-in-law or brother-in-law by histories and futures of interaction with him: his intrusions, betrayals, ameliorations, attentiveness, or growing familiarity. Uncle relationships make events of past women's lives part of the relational present between other people but a part of the relational present often known by the women's absences. Place ownership involves projects of linking a present of human action on the land to pasts of predecessors' similar actions and to hoped futures of other related people being there too. Travel and hospitality unfold as departures from other times, when people normally lived separately on their own places of established belonging. These events of travel are later avidly remembered aloud for their difference from where the participants are at the later time of narration. In bonds with children, a present relational state is experienced in various ways as resting in ties to pasts and futures different from that present. These include times when the child did not exist, times when the child will be grown, times when the parent will not exist, and times when parent or child has cared for the other. Person reference practices such as the use of joking avoidance terms, teknonyms, and other dyad-based forms link a present person to a social relation, and to that relation's other times, places, and bodies, as a foundation of identity lying both beyond and within the referred-to person. Intertemporality is also prominent, for example, in the mix of historical identifications and disavowals making up the reincarnation model, according to which present persons are reborn predecessors but must not be told their predecessor's identity.

Korowai people's relational practices are of interest in part because of the directness with which these practices construe even the time and space of face-to-face copresence as questions rather than self-evident givens. Copresence is composed out of culturally distinctive definitions of being "together," definitions that conjoin people's mutual perceptual presence with specific aspects of their mutual disparity. The indemnity institution, for example, makes visible Korowai people's frequent orientation to the contradictoriness of face-to-face copresence in its spatial aspects. Between some persons, being together in space is informed also by awareness of usually living in separate places. Copresence between coresidents is a different quality of relation from copresence between people who live apart. Host-guest interaction, landownership, and many other institutions involve distinguishing consociates with whom face-to-face interaction is a marked form of boundary-crossing from consociates with whom this interaction is an expected daily event.

There are numerous ways a particular time can be defined as connected to and separate from other times, and I have sought to chart a few concrete ones. My purpose now has only been to draw attention to the general way that many Korowai relational situations are centrally composed of a mismatch between different, coexisting temporalities of the social bond. The disparate times coexisting in a single relation are one side of a larger pattern of the systematic internal heterogeneity of single social ties. Actors' own concerns with the divided temporalities of a social relation are a mode of their artfulness in building relations out of mutual otherness. Korowai attraction to events as the truth of bonds can be understood as an aspect of this concern with temporal heterogeneity of relations. Whether an event disruptively contradicts an assumed earlier state of relatedness or confirms and revitalizes an already felt understanding, the event maps between disparate scales of people's presence to each other. Like other channels of contact, time works as a boundary medium, indexing qualities of simultaneous belonging and alienness between the people who seek to know their relations through it.

The simplest and most important lesson that I want to draw from the themes of temporality recapped here, though, concerns the overall shape of Korowai people's social world, which I have characterized broadly as a field of otherness. What becomes obvious from Korowai emphasis on relation making and relational loss, as constant concerns of life, is that people's world of social others is by nature a field in motion. People's lives are a whirl of the making, measuring, and loss of attachment. Actors come into pleasurable relations of belonging with one another, escape or violate established attachments, and mournfully adjust to bonds of belonging that have been ruptured by death or other traumatic separations: this is what relations are. Relation making and relation loss are central to Korowai experience of relatedness as such. This centrality flies in the face of any notion that social relations in spatially and demographically small-scale, kinship-based communities are predominantly relations of stable mutual identification.

THE ORIENTATION TOWARD EVENTS AND
MEDIA AS AN INDIGENOUS PRAGMATICS

The final point I wish to summarize briefly is that this book's subject has been a cultural pragmatics of social relating. Here I do not mean that

Korowai approach social relations calculatedly and nontheoretically, with a view to obvious economic or political gains the relations can provide them (as in the dominant sense of "pragmatic" in English speech). Rather, I take "pragmatics" in the special technical sense associated with the disciplines of semiotics and linguistic anthropology. These disciplines understand social life to be foundationally built out of processes of signification, which have their own orderliness and systematicity. The pragmatics of signification are those aspects of systematicity of signification that specifically have to do with *use* of signs, such as relations between signs and the actors who use them, the time and place of use, the other signs contextually present in the same field of action, the possibilities that signs will not work right or will not work in one way only, and so forth. The notion of "a pragmatics" is a notion to the effect that sign-using action is itself systematic and is central, rather than peripheral, to the nature of sign systems generally. Cultural order lies in people's culturally distinctive patterns and models of sign use. This tradition of scholarly thought thus takes the existence of semiotic structure as its central subject, but understands the idea of semiotic structure removed from action and existing independently of action to be a chimera; semiotic structures are structures of action, in the double sense of being "about" action and "made out of" action.

What all this has to do with Korowai practices of social relating is that Korowai themselves consistently take an action-centered approach to understanding social bonds. The question "What is a social relation?" itself (both as I have asked it and as Korowai ask it) is a question of signification. Korowai define what they are to each other by signifying it, through all the specific kinds of media of contact I have touched on: pandanus, pigs, kinship terms, word avoidance, forms of person reference, architectural forms, ownership of land, material gifts, acts of touch, facial expressions, laughter, and much more. This study has documented several overlapping tendencies in Korowai semiotic approaches to defining and knowing social bonds that align with the idea of "a pragmatics" invoked in the previous paragraph. One of these tendencies is, again, people's strong orientation toward events as the truth of relations, along with the broader range of ways Korowai take temporality as an integral feature of their relations. In my account of parent-child relations, for example, I described difference of relatedness across time as being both *how* interpersonal attachment is known and *what* is known. The temporality of parents' and children's relations, as bonds that are created and lost, is what signifies their relation and is the meaning of this relation.

This is a signature feature of pragmatic dimensions of sign systems generally and pragmatics-oriented studies of those systems: the event of signification at a particular "now" and the particular construal of this event's relations to other times is a central focus of the system of signs that is in play.

An even broader tendency that makes Korowai sensibilities about social relations a pragmatics is people's reflexive scrutiny of the media of their social contact. I have argued that mourning practices, for example, are organized as forms of reflexive analysis of the channels of contact by which people are related to each other, dwelling on how these media are variously points of close intersubjective connection and points of separation between related people. The whole problematic of closeness and distance that Korowai bring to social relations (not just in connection with death but also in the many other areas discussed in this book) involves spotlighting concrete media of social involvement as themselves having specific characteristics through which people are intimate or alien. This focus on media of signification—such as their own proper characteristics and what these characteristics bring to or take away from the creation of meaning—is also why it makes sense to describe Korowai people's sensibility about social relations as a pragmatics.

Linked to reflexivity about time and other media in which relations are wrought, another feature of Korowai social relating that aligns with the idea of a pragmatics is the way a general problematic of otherness-focused social relating very much envisions *acting subjects* as integral to the systematicity of semiotic processes. Documenting the Korowai sensibility of otherness-centered relations has involved writing an ethnography of acting subjects who look and speak outward from their particular bodies, possessions, and places toward a surrounding field of other actors, places, and times.

There are other topics in this book that are matters of pragmatics in narrower and more specific ways. For example, Korowai descriptions of some uses of kinship terms as "just done thusly" are a clear case of reflexive construal of signification as a matter of "doing." People's attention to transgression of rules as an active, consequential, and potentially constructive social possibility is likewise a mode of reflexivity about conventions of action as something actors live not only within but also alongside. Contingency is an integral, productive part of actors' experience of rules. Specific genres of social involvement I have discussed seem also to stand in relations of intertextuality with each other, in ways that involve Korowai practicing a reflexive pragmatics of defining their acts of doing by figurative relation to other acts of doing. Joking avoidance is a figurative elaboration on kin term usage and name usage, in their pragmatic organization (as in the joking avoidance terms' mimicry of a kinship term's dependence on a propositus for its reference, or mimicry of a name's dependence on a social history of name conferral). Avoidance practices at large are reflexive about what it is to "do" an action: these practices make an act out of not acting. Bridewealth is often covertly or overtly intertextual with indemnity payment, as when Korowai liken women's residential displacements following marriage to death. These modes of modeling one *kind of acting* on another involve cultural reflexivity about forms of action as such.

But I have had my chance to make those connections in earlier chapters. At this closing stage, I am interested in a simpler, broader point: Korowai people's otherness-focused culture of social relations is a *culture of action,* and can be described in that way.

Notes

INTRODUCTION

1. The articles about Korowai or their culturally similar Kombai neighbors that have appeared in high-circulation English-language magazines include "No Cannibal Jokes, Please: Upriver into the Swamps of Irian Jaya, and Back in Time," *Outside* (October 1992); "Irian Jaya's People of the Trees," *National Geographic* (February 1996); "The People That Time Forgot," *Reader's Digest* (August 1996); "Strangers in the Forest: A Guided Tour to an Isolated Tribe," *New Yorker* (18 April 2005); and "Sleeping with Cannibals," *Smithsonian* (September 2006). The television broadcasts (again listing only English-language productions) include "Treehouse People, Cannibal Justice," *Arts & Entertainment Network* (July 1994; European release: "Lords of the Garden"); "Warrior Tribes: Korowai," *Discovery Channel* (1996); "Tribe, Series 1, Episode 3, Kombai," *BBC Two* (January 2005; broadcast in the United States as "Going Tribal," *Discovery Channel*); "Last Cannibals," Australia's *Channel 9* (*60 Minutes* episode of May 21, 2006); "Living with the Kombai Tribe: The Adventures of Mark and Olly," *Travel Channel* (January 2007, 6 episodes); and "Tribal Odyssey: The Gentle Cannibals: The Stone Korowai, Western Papua," *Discovery Channel* in the United States (2004) and distributed internationally by *National Geographic Television*. In the wake of the Australian *60 Minutes* segment, the competing *Channel 7* show "Today Tonight" unsuccessfully tried to send a crew to the Korowai area in September 2006, at which point the two TV channels' efforts to exploit the story of an orphaned boy named Wawa in their ratings war became the subject of a weeklong front-page Australian media firestorm. At that time the entire Australian media-consuming public received basic imagery of Korowai as primitive, tribal people.

2. Durkheim favorably reviewed Tönnies's *Gemeinschaft und Gesellschaft* in 1889, three years prior to publication of his theory of mechanical and organic solidarity in *De la division du travail social*. See Cahnmann (1973: 240–47) for one of several available translations of Durkheim's review and Tönnies's 1896 counterpart review of Durkheim. While accepting the main lines of Tönnies's typology, Durkheim rejected Tönnies's evaluation of *Gemeinschaft* as a utopian social condition more integratively viable than urban industrial living. Tönnies, for his part, maintained that Durkheim lost sight of the typology's focus on whether or not persons perceive the collectivity to be a goal or merely a means, and he described Durkheim as a Spencerian apologist for increased occupational differentiaton. For one broader sketch of precursors and heirs to Tönnies's formulation, see, for example, Stråth 2001.

3. Fabian (2006) has more recently advocated involvement with others' disparities of memory. However, he does not address the important problem of distinguishing the forms of temporal othering he criticizes from those he supports.

4. Strathern's influential model of Melanesian social life can also be read in these terms, notwithstanding the possible *Gemeinschaft* flavor to her perception of the identity of persons with relations (with debts to Leenhardt and perhaps Fortes) and to her denial of "alienation" as a major quality of Melanesian person-product relations. For the emphasis on separation and disjuncture as the crux of relations, see, for example, Strathern 1987; 1988: 191–224), and citations and clarifications in Viveiros de Castro forthcoming.

5. The approach I am outlining can only *loosely* be referred to as the "Orientalism consensus" because turns of analysis in this vein are not limited to work influenced by Said's well-known *Orientalism* argument. For example, studies drawing on Kristeva's concept of abjection, as well as earlier Durkheim-shaped sociological work on the functionality of deviance, are also part of the broad constellation of thought to which I refer. In addition, the consensus is not limited to analysis of representations of society-external others promulgated by intellectuals (which was the subject of Said's study).

6. Compare, among other statements of this kind, Ricoeur's (1992: 356) defense of "dispersion" or "polysemy" in his typology of kinds of otherness: "Only a discourse other than itself . . . is suited to the metacategory of otherness, under penalty of otherness suppressing itself in becoming the same as itself." See also Kearney (2003: 65–82), for criticism of monadic, all-conflating accounts of otherness in works on social treatment of strangers by Derrida, Kristeva, and Girard. Fabian himself refers skeptically to "the floating and inflationary use of other, otherness, othering, and, not to forget, the umbrella term alterity, in the social sciences and humanities" (2006: 141).

7. OED Online, "*other, a., pron., n.,* and *adv.,*" March 2005. http://dictionary .oed.com/cgi/entry/00334840. Accessed January 15, 2007.

8. In discussing the idea of social otherness here, I do not mean to exclude the overlapping question of otherness to oneself. The idea of intersubjectivity is generally taken to involve an observation that self-consciousness is equiprimordial with intersubjective consciousness, such that one's relation to oneself is socially mediated and might even reasonably be understood *as* a social relation. For reasons of space and simplicity, in this book I center my discussions on oth-

erness between persons, but I try to do so in ways that are suggestive of points about otherness "internal" to persons as well (see also Stasch 2008a).

9. These orientations are not exclusive to semiotic and linguistic anthropology but are found in the writings of all anthropologists of a symbolic, culturalist bent centering their work on the categories "action" or "practice." There are many precedents in these wider literatures for the notion of a reflexive sensibility about social relations summed up in my expression "indigenous pragmatics," but a particularly close precedent is the concept of metapragmatics, which has been important in linguistic anthropology specifically. Highlighting how reflexive sensibilities about signification often pivotally focus on pragmatics, or sign use, Silverstein (e.g., 1976, 1993) has influentially advanced *metapragmatic* as a term designating processes of reflexive signification of the pragmatic conditions of signification. Further, he has sometimes advanced the term *ethnometapragmatic* to name the fact that people in different sociocultural contexts of semiosis hold to qualitatively distinctive reflexive ideas about the pragmatics of signification, with major consequences for the actual organization of semiotic actions. The burgeoning literature on linguistic ideologies, or semiotic ideologies generally, is also directly concerned with the shaping of language structure and linguistic practice by sign users' models of what they are doing in signifying.

10. On Korowai involvement with Indonesian police, see Stasch 2001b. On attitudes toward the Indonesian language and increasing bilingualism in Indonesian, see Stasch 2007. I hope also to publish studies of village formation and tourism, respectively.

CHAPTER 1. A DISPERSED SOCIETY

1. These points about Korowai mobility echo Lowe (2003), who shows how Togean Islanders' intimate attachment to and knowledge of places is produced out of mobility, including being not present at places, or being surprised by what is found on coming to a place. Cresswell (1997) offers a useful call for studies that actually describe practices of mobility as having locations, situations, and contexts. Practices of mobility are cultural. They are historically specific, efficacious ways of world-making; they are not the opposite of culture, or place. See also Reed 2003: 79–82 for an apt reflection on contemporary anthropological thinking on residence and mobility generally and on the need to relate these dialectically in ethnographic work rather than naturalize residence.

2. Sahlins's (1972 [1965]) account of negative reciprocity as a mode of interaction between socially distant people does not explicitly address negative reciprocity's character, in some societies, as a form of active social involvement with a history and a future but leaves the label "negative reciprocity" itself to do the needed theoretical work. See Harrison 1993b for the best development of the point that violence in some New Guinean cultural contexts is a mode of substantial relational connection, including apt comments on the Sahlins model (pp. 15–21).

3. Korowai egalitarianism is fundamentally different from doctrines of egalitarianism in Western societies (see Robbins 1994). Korowai care about the equality of the actual personal conditions of people who are relating to each

other, whereas Westerners dominantly care about ontological equality (e.g., equality of democratic citizenship) and occasionally equality of opportunity but not equality of outcome. Also, Korowai care about direct interpersonal equality, whereas Westerners primarily care about interpersonal equality via the mediating step of persons' relations with a state.

4. Under many circumstances, a speaker's owned place does actually shift with the context of speaking. It can shift within single conversations; it can shift with changes in conversational location, conversational participants, and conversational subject; and it can shift with long-term changes in a person's social situation and biographical identity. But I am concerned here with an even more fundamental level of ownership's perspectival character.

5. Significantly, in first introducing *shifter* as a term of linguistic analysis, Jespersen (1922: 123) offered as canonical examples not only personal pronouns and spatiotemporal deictics but also "father" and "home."

6. Numerous authors besides Simmel have sought to theorize boundaries as relations. Works in this broad vein include Barth 1969; Lévi-Strauss 1976 [1971]; Wagner 1974: 110; Tsing 1993; Abbott 1995; Bashkow 2004; and Merlan 2005.

7. In an influential passage in the same work, Certeau (1984: 117–18) spuriously distinguishes two kinds of spatiality. In "place" *(lieu)* elements are stable and where they belong, whereas in "space" *(espace)* elements are spatially ambiguous, mobile, and interlinked. My account of Korowai spatial life, by contrast, is concerned with interdependencies of spatial belonging and spatial otherness. One of these qualities does not exist without being informed by the other. The Korowai landscape, even at its most local, is a landscape of disarticulations, uncertainties, and estrangement. Korowai places are made out of other places distinct from themselves and made out of the strangeness between home places and other places.

8. Between the two poles of "owner" and "guest," an intermediate category is *laboxdun-anop* "accompanying people, joiners," mentioned earlier.

9. Shryock (2004: 36) similarly examines how "hospitality creates a momentary overlap between inner and outer dimensions of a 'house.'" Other studies of hospitality that address issues treated here include Pitt-Rivers 1977 and Munn 1986. Keane (1997) usefully thematizes "encounters" more generally.

10. This approach is again symptomatic of Korowai sensitivity about personal autonomy: one does not presume to order someone else how to be or act. Rather, one expresses one's own worry, in the hope that this expression of being affected by another will be meaningful to that other.

11. People understand village creation to involve a partial suspension of landownership principles, such that any person can live in the village space without prejudice. In the midst of conflicts, owners of the particular place where a village is sited sometimes raise differences of ownership as an issue, but this is unusual.

12. Compare Hill's (2005) account of how English speakers' avowedly nonracist uses of mock Spanish in the United States depend for their indexical value ("easygoing persona") on intertextual relations with overtly racist uses.

CHAPTER 2. PAIRING AND AVOIDANCE

1. Many children lose their mothers and are raised by a foster mother, but nobody is called matronymically except by the name of a birth mother. Yet parturition is not all that goes into a matronymic designation. Children who die before growing into social personhood are not assigned birth order designations: a matronymic's use is rooted in an accumulated history of habitual application of that expression to the person, a mediating layer of social recognition of the original event of birth. More generally, people's use of matronymics and other dyad-based referring forms depends on contingencies of habit, euphony, and historical chaining of usages. Some people come to be known more by a teknonym than by a matronymic. Speakers form teknonyms using the names of all different types of children: sometimes a firstborn, sometimes a last born, and sometimes a child in between. An early-deceased child might continue to hold the position of "firstborn" of a particular woman, or it might be forgotten, with a later child coming to be called by the matronymic "firstborn" expression. And so forth.

2. This genre is analyzed in detail in Stasch 2002. Other topics discussed in this chapter are interpreted in more depth in Stasch 2003b, 2008b.

3. This pattern is similar in figurative organization to the use of plural pronouns in European T/V systems (e.g., French *tu* vs. *vous*). The pattern of wife's mother and daughter's husband avoiding singular forms in reference to each other is cross-linguistically common.

4. People's concern with name avoidance colored their experiences of my interview practices. I learned to speak in ways sensitive to name-avoidance etiquette, but nonetheless people understood interviews with me to involve indiscriminate saying of names. Once a woman who turned down my request for an interview cited the fact that she had a small, vulnerable son. She feared that all the mentioning of people's names in our conversation would lead to one of us accidentally uttering her boy's *xoxulop*.

5. The topography of invisible people's existence is conveyed well by many old people's reputed response to seeing television sets for the first time, namely, the statement, "They're visible, not on the other side *[xan]*!" Figures on the screen were interpreted as invisible people made visible, instead of staying spatially present but invisible as normally would be the case.

6. Other deictics altogether are used to express "here" versus "there," or "this side" versus "that side," when the spatial relations under discussion involve only a linear boundary, not an enclosing one.

7. Parkin (2003: 28–39, 55–59, 110–15) usefully catalogs some of the diverse kinds of relations of pairing that have been distinguished or conflated in just the anthropological literature on "oppositions." On the same point, see also Reuter (2002), who demonstrates that labeling a pattern of representations as "dualism" can be the beginning of an important analysis, or the opening of a field of questions, but is not a very meaningful finding by itself. He aptly calls for "study of cross-cultural variations in the ways the relationship between conceptual opposites (and, if they are social categories, the relationship between

their human representatives) is structured" (p. 151). See also Rumsey 2002: 282 on poetic parallelism; and Ogden 1967 [1932] on lexical semantics.

CHAPTER 3. STRANGE KIN

1. A focus on otherness has important precedents in the kinship literature. Peletz (2001) specifically reviews emotional ambivalence as a theme in kinship studies. The emotional otherness of kin, though, is often part and parcel of their structural, categorial otherness at broader levels of cultural evaluation. Anthropologists are quite used to analyzing marriage as a core social site of intimate reckoning with distance, whether following Lévi-Strauss's (1969 [1949]) portrayal of in-law relations as a problem of involvement with social others or following a range of available ethnographies of the racial, class, gender, and sexual politics of intimate unions. Even so, Lepri's (2005) study of kinship processes in a western Amazonian society is a relatively rare example of a work documenting directly how otherness is the core problematic of social relating across all areas of certain people's kinship lives. The Esa Ejja people about whom Lepri writes divide the speakers of their language into "those who live elsewhere" (lit., "other sleeping") and "those who live with me." They then divide this second category into "nonothers" and "others" (centered on cross-relatives). "Other" and "nonother" are major terms of kinship analysis, and "other" is the linguistically unmarked category against the background of which the idea of close belonging, or being "nonother," is brought into definition (Lepri 2005: 711). Other studies contain similar indications that questions of otherness saturate people's kinship acts and experiences, in numerous human locations (e.g., Storrie 2003: 152).

2. See also Agha 2007: 340–85 on the crucial point that even the strictly linguistic aspects of kin categorization cannot accurately be studied as primarily a matter of a codelike structure of categories that exists independently of use. Rather, kin term *use* in a context of speaking, accompanied by cotextual indexical cues, is the elementary form of kinship language.

3. Works by Myers (1986), Overing and Passes (2000), and Carsten (1997) are representative here.

4. The idea that action makes or breaks relations and that kinship centrally rests in people's ethical manners of action toward one another is again a major leitmotif of the ethnography of kinship in recent decades. See, e.g., Samson 1988 on "performative kinship," Overing 2003 on "generative cultures," Weston 1991 on "families we choose," the turn toward study of adoption and technologically assisted reproduction in Western industrialized societies, and countless ethnographies documenting the importance of food-giving in kin bonds.

5. The child-generation terms *salal* "niece" and *sabül* "nephew" are analyzable into a prefix *sa-* and the words *abül* "son" and *lal* "daughter." The morpheme *sa-* has no meaning independent of these usages. Its only other occurrence is as a prefix to the plural, gender-neutral word *mabün* "children," forming the term *sa-mabün* "sister's children." The morpheme is semantically empty, except as a marker of difference setting the parental cross-siblinghood categories apart as the special case.

6. These and other aspects of Korowai kin categorization are discussed in more detail in van Enk and de Vries 1997: 139–53; and Stasch 2001a: 183–243.

7. So too they have trouble making compound words out of other cross-sex pairs of reciprocal consanguineal kinship terms, such as "elder sister" and "younger brother" (whereas "elder sister–younger sister" is a routine expression). The only cross-sex compounds speakers readily form out of reciprocal kinship terms are nonconsanguineal ones, designating spousal pairs or mother-in-law and son-in-law pairs. Gender difference is perhaps felt to be too awkward in consanguineal kinship for Korowai to be able to bend it to the compact relational unity expressed in a pairing compound.

8. Ngengel's statement is a variation on a standard theme. Another man put the generalization this way: "Children's father's side's territory habitually/conventionally becomes their own territory. Their mother's side habitually/conventionally becomes their uncles-and-mothers." See Rumsey 1981 for an account of a similar practice of applying kin terms to patrigroups by Ngarinyin of northwestern Australia.

9. Symmetrically, speakers also often playfully address an aunt (i.e., father's sister) as "father." The principle of these figurative uses is thus that a parental-generation relative's gender category is more a matter of being a relative *through* the speaker's mother or father than a matter of the relative's own bodily attributes.

10. The unity of a patriclan also seems to be emphasized by certain details of how Korowai women categorize their child-generation kin, at variance with the canonical Omaha pattern. As represented in figure 10, a father's sister is called *mul* "aunt," making her a marked parental cross-relative in a manner analogous to a mother's brother. But such a woman does not call her brother's child "nephew" or "niece" (as an uncle would call his sister's child). Rather, she calls these children "son" or "daughter." In doing so, she effectively speaks from the position of her brother himself, and from the position of patriclan affiliation. Given that clans are exogamous, one element of the markedness of the relation between maternal uncle and sister's child is that the two persons so related are members of different clans, as I have already underlined. For a woman, though, the sons and daughters of her cross-sex sibling belong to her own patriclan. Same-patriclan collateral descendants are always "children" rather than "nieces" or "nephews," regardless of speaker's sex. While relations to a father's mother can be emotionally important, this pattern of kin categorization nonetheless mutes the possibility of a full female counterpart, on the paternal side, to the distinctive figure of the mother's brother. On the maternal side, a mother's sister, called *ni* "mother," most often calls her sister's child "son" or "daughter," but sometimes also or instead calls her sister's child "nephew" or "niece." This too departs from the marking of cross-sex links and again has women speaking from the point of view of a patriclan. The children of a clan's (or sibling set's) women are that clan's (or sibling set's) "nephews" and "nieces."

11. Women's association with geographic displacement is also apparent in people's use of the idiom "her youths/bachelors" (*yaxofel*; also *naxofel* "my youths/bachelors") to refer collectively to a married woman's natal clan, figuring that clan as composed of her unmarried younger brothers. Often speakers

say who a woman's "bachelors" are, as a spontaneous sequitur to saying who her "uncles" are. Where a man has a single clan of "uncles" that he is external to but that anchors who he is, a married woman can also be felt to be similarly external (in geography of life participation, though not in membership) to her own clan of origin. When saying who she is, it is relevant to identify the clan she originated from before marital displacement, in a way that is not true of men.

12. Notably, the same is true of clan membership, even though clanship is in the first instance automatically determined by paternity. When describing clan membership, people often do not speak of a child simply being a member of its father's clan but speak instead of people "uttering" (filo-) the name of the father's clan as the child's clan.

13. People are restrained in how widely they perform this ritual of happiness. A common refrain is that if one were to try to shake hands with a person to whom one is not really socially linked, "He/she will say, 'Who's your relative?'" (gəlambil yaxop daxe).

14. The reflexive emphasis on action can be seen even in one pattern of talk about kinship I have already mentioned: speakers' use of the expression amomate "habitually so" (lit., "they habitually do thusly") as a kinship category modifier that contrasts with categories like "proper" or "true." In this expression, the verb stem "do thus" (a-mo-) consists of the verbalizing form -mo- "do" added to the deictic a- "thus, there." (In the use of amomate in kinship discourse, the deictic element a- "thus" occurs without an explicit antecedent. "Thus" just refers to the general fact of being in the kin relation under discussion.) I emphasized above that the expression "just so, done thusly" is a way to compare a relation unfavorably to more steadfast, direct kin relations. On the other hand, the category is kinship; it has an affirmative side. With this label, Korowai recognize affirmatively that one basis of kin relations is "doing thus." Habitually representing it to be so, just saying it in situated speech, is an action that makes people relatives.

15. So too when I asked Korowai friends open-endedly what other people in some particular place on the land said about me, I was often told that I had become a relative in that place by giving objects like fishing tackle to people, or that people anticipated that if I came to their place, then I would "become a relative" in this gift-based way.

16. The myth-ending formula also matches Wagner's model of New Guinean social ontologies (e.g., 1981 [1975], 1977), according to which social action unfolds against a plenitude of relatedness, and it is differentiation and disconnection that action seeks to achieve. Being a person in a world of kinship is a problem of knowing who your others are, including the others who are so strange as to be not of the same species.

CHAPTER 4. CHILDREN AND
THE CONTINGENCY OF ATTACHMENT

1. On the side of parent-child identification (rather than disparity), a characteristic if idiosyncratic expression of how much adults see themselves in children was one woman's Freudian slip in conversation with me: at one point she said, "Then later I died," when she meant to say that later her child died. (She

changed her statement to the intended description as we continued talking.) Another, more conventional linguistic pattern of parent-child identification is men's occasional "address inversion" when speaking to young sons. A man addresses his son as "father" or "my father." This is a poignant statement of equality and identification, through the portrayal of the father-son relation as the reverse of its appearance.

2. Other studies similarly document how the possibility of infanticide is shaped by newborns' culturally particular categorial status. See Scrimshaw 1984; Sargent 1988; Scheper-Hughes 1992: 432–33; and Schulte 1994.

3. This awareness is patent, for example, in the fact that speakers use several synonymous terms for "pandanus" interchangeably in the kinship expressions, including *laün, bamun, xafün, sapuan,* and *maüan.*

4. Identification of breast milk with sago starch is also supported by actual child-feeding practice. Raw starch in water and the squishy innards of sago grubs are used as breast milk substitutes when a nursing infant's mother dies. These are also among the first nonmilk foods all babies eat.

5. Once when I asked Fenelun whether he liked having children, he said no, because the experience of having children consists entirely of feeling grief for them when they are sick and being angry at them the rest of the time for being mischievous. This pessimistic statement was not representative of Fenelun's actual total bond with his children, but it indicates how prominently parents experience their children as autonomous violators' of parents' desires and how much parents experience relations with children in terms of disparities between how things are and how parents wish them to be. As in so many other areas, this experience of social contradiction is lived and expressed as emotional distress.

CHAPTER 5. MARRIAGE AS DISRUPTION
AND CREATION OF BELONGING

1. My argument parallels Harrison's (1993b) study of how some New Guinea peoples understand violation to be in certain contexts integral to social life and socially generative. Harrison's subject is warfare, or actions of extreme bodily violence, whereas this chapter extends the question of the possible social generativeness of violation to more mundane processes of kinship. My account of disruption and impingement runs parallel also to Rutherford (2003: 73–108) on "surprise" and Viveiros de Castro (2004) on "predation." See too Greenblatt 1991: 19–20, summarizing discourses of "wonder" in Spinoza and Descartes.

2. To have illicit sex is to "screw stealthily" *(nanem gomo-),* and an infant gestated from nonmarital sex is a "stealth child" *(nanem-mbam).*

3. This aspect of Korowai marriage parallels the salience of narratives of meeting, courtship, and proposing in U.S. marriages, in which a history of events by which two people came together is taken as the relation's compelling image and definition. The history is a signifier for fixing an otherwise indefinite signified, the marital bond.

4. I touch below on norms of sororal polygyny and fraternal widow inheritance. Widow inheritance is serial marriage of one woman to a plurality of brothers, and sororal polygyny is concurrent marriage of one man to a plurality

of sisters. Both are based on a notion of sibling identity. Here too Korowai bring sibling and spousal ties into close contact, as if the two bonds are more fully themselves when closely compared.

5. Many joking avoidance partnerships commemorate transgressive accidents of same-sex bodily contact (Stasch 2002: 341). An extreme in the association of clasping with violated autonomy is the historical practice of seizing men accused of witchcraft and leading them away to be killed. This traumatic possibility sits in the background, in support of people's sense that to grab people is to impinge on them.

6. Compare Cannell's (1999) account of women's marriage stories in the Bicol region of the Philippines, where many marriages have a complexly temporal moral logic: women are initially shocked by marriages their parents arrange for them, then grow to approve of the marriages over time, but also preserve the story of their own reluctant submission to parental coercion as a gift they have given to those around them. While differing in details, Bicol marriages recall several Korowai patterns: the way the story of a marriage's process of coming into existence *is* the marriage; the developmental cycle of spousal emotions, based on histories of practice; and the pattern of systematic violation of persons being in some respects a site of value making.

7. The grandparent terms imply nothing about the bodily maturity of the two spouses: they could be the same ages. In this discussion I also take for granted the further point explained in chapter 3 that grandparenthood is a *reciprocal* relation in face-to-face categorization, even while people distinguish "grandparent" and "grandchild" categories when narrating genealogical relations outside of the grandchild's presence.

8. Though I have stated as a matter of descriptive fact that to a given ego, members of his or her mother's clan (the "uncles") are taboo to marry, there is at least one geographic pocket in the Korowai region, around Sinimburu village, where no such taboo is recognized and where marriage to a mother's clanmate is quite common. I have not learned any specific, obvious reasons that people in this region do not share the rule against marrying a maternal clansperson that Korowai elsewhere find very compelling. The many persons I have asked about the disparity generally said that they themselves do not have an explanation for it. But it is interesting that in discussing marriages to a man or a woman of one's mother's clan, Korowai in this geographic area very frequently praise such marriages in the same way that "grandparent" marriages are more widely praised: the "uncle" or "mother" (and linked affinal relatives) is not a stranger.

9. About marriages in Bristol between Pakistani nationals and British-born descendants of Pakistani immigrants, Charsley (2005: 86) reports similar motives for cousin unions:

> The marriage of a child presents an opportunity to strengthen connections between much-missed kin separated by migration decades earlier. Parental exegeses also stress the need to protect daughters, conceptualized as vulnerable to mistreatment by in-laws. For some, the marriage of a daughter in Britain to a trusted relative who has been raised in an Islamic society is one response to this risk.

Charsley documents a general marital problematic of otherness and belonging in relation to social spaces strikingly similar to Korowai marriage processes, except that in Bristol it is immigrant *grooms,* rather than brides, who bear the heaviest burdens of marriage's mismatches of physical presence and social vulnerability.

10. The action is described by the idiom *aup laxabe-* "pluck [the victim's] voice." I referred to this idiom briefly in chapter 4 when discussing fear of newborns. The curser expresses internally the idea that the person will die, and this causes death.

CHAPTER 6. DIALECTICS OF CONTACT
AND SEPARATION IN MOURNING

1. The only other cases of historically or ethnographically documented society-internal capital punishment at frequencies as high as past Korowai practice are other New Guinea societies in which people held similar beliefs about death-causing witches (Steadman 1972; Schieffelin 1976; Knauft 1985).

2. Greater security from nighttime attacks by witches is one reason that women and men alike regularly give in support of polygynous marriage.

3. Given the corporeal emphasis of *laleo* imagery I describe momentarily, "zombie" is also a fitting possible translation; "spirit" is inappropriate. "Demon" has the advantage of its association with ancient Greek imagery of *daimon* beings who are unpredictable, intrusive, incomprehensible powers but who are also (after Plato) intermediate between humanity and divinity, akin to Korowai monsters' contradictory status as both humanlike and beyond the pale of humanity. The adjectival potential of "demon" (and quick link to more unambiguously adjectival "demonic") is also appropriate to *laleo*'s simultaneous signification of both a being and a quality of being.

4. Korowai categorization of new technological objects as so many "demon" articles, parallel to Korowai people's own "human" counterpart items of material culture, is another expression of this understanding of demons as standing to humans in a relation of close deformation. I discussed this pattern briefly in chapter 1.

5. Occasionally people do consume objects of unknown origin. If two people share such an object, they might joke uncomfortably about it having probably been *lumbel* and then decide to call each other "my *lumbel*" as a joking avoidance term, of the sort described in chapter 2.

6. Destroying cultigens and renouncing specific food species are common mourning observances all across New Guinea. On the worldwide occurrence of personalistic, private acts of mournful renunciation, and these acts' relative invisibility in anthropology, see Williams 2003 [1993]: 83.

7. In her discussion of Kaluli *gisalo* performances, Munn identifies "now alone, once together with [so-and-so] at [such-and-such place]" as a recurrent frame of memory construction, a "basic spatiotemporal structure of Kaluli remembering" (1995: 92). The Korowai analog in the matter of species renunciations would be "now alone, once together with so-and-so eating such-and-such food."

8. Often when people choose not to fell mortuary sago they are motivated by the same ambivalences that color performance of the meals. The survivors do

not want to eat sago without the person who saw and grew it, or their grief is so great that they have no desire for food or no strength to do any work.

9. Throughout this book I have cited *lelip* "together" as a major Korowai term of social description, but an allied category often used to describe inter-local concord or discord is the verb *xolfu-* "be unitary, be reconciled, mix freely, associate."

10. That payments are made in recognition of a loss (the disappearance of a consociate from the world) is what prompts me to call the transactions "indemnities." "Compensation" would more strongly imply culpability of the compensating party and equivalence of what is given to what is lost. Such implications are not appropriate here. I treat later the questions of payers' accountability and the substitutive relation between payment and dead person. Main Korowai expressions by which people speak of death indemnification are "give articles" *(misafi fedo-)*, "pay articles" *(misafi abolo-)*, "speak demands" *(guf u-)*, and "demand talk, demand politics" *(guf-aup)*. In talk about the indemnity pattern, coresidents are often referred to using such terms as *xaimanop* "house people" and *xaimlelipanop* "same house people." Demanders are often referred to by expressions like *xosüanop* "yonder people," *yanibolüpanop* "elsewhere people," or simply *lambil* "relatives."

11. Usually it is amicable interaction that is a basis for indemnity claims, but histories of antagonism can also lead to demands. A woman named Ya frequently announced her intention to demand when her sister's daughter or sister's daughter's husband died, because the sister's daughter's husband had once furtively killed her pig during an unrelated indemnity dispute and then paid compensation. When Ya fell ill during my fieldwork, her sister's daughter turned the tables, by telling many people that *she* would be owed an indemnity if Ya died, based on Ya's announcements of a prospective indemnity demand in the opposite direction. These events are characteristic of the improvisatory, self-propelling character of indemnity processes, the improbability of many demands, and the contingent unfolding of efforts of persuasion.

12. Explicit comparisons of residential separation to death are common in other contexts, as described in my account of marriage. If a married woman lives far away from her relatives and does not visit regularly, those relatives will typically complain of their longed-for bond that it is as though the woman has died. If coresident kin fight and one of them moves away, when their anger subsides the one at home is likely to urge the other one to come back with remarks like "If you die and I'm living alone, I'll be sorrowful. Come quickly."

CONCLUSION

1. An anthropologically traditional way in which parts of this study could be seen as going together is that they treat phases in a personal and social "life cycle." Korowai are indeed sensitively attuned to temporalities of the human life course. They are preoccupied with ways in which a person in one transitional moment of life is involved in longer developmental trajectories, such that the meaning of the person's acts and experiences at that moment is heavily defined by the moment's vivid, complex relations with other pasts and futures

of the person's existence. Major developmental events and processes are also prime foci of feeling and attention around which Korowai envision their world and people's relational places in it. However, their concern is with *relational* life courses: Korowai tend to apprehend persons and events not as self-standing entities but as signs of relationships. In addition, the links between different life-stage processes are bidirectional and plural, as just outlined, whereas the idea of a "life course" or "life cycle" (as an organizing unit of anthropological description) could erroneously be taken to imply a unidirectional mode of interconnection between these processes. Finally, the "life cycle" idea could be mistaken for a purely temporal entity, whereas, as we have seen, all these kinds of developmental processes that Korowai focus on are irreducibly spatial as well as temporal. These are all perhaps reasons to favor "field of otherness" as a synoptic organizing image of this book's subject, if one is needed.

2. Ideas to the effect that relations are made in actions have been proposed previously by many anthropologists, including those influenced specifically by New Guinea fieldwork. Wagner (1974) describes exchange events as creating the existence of groups among Daribi and other New Guineans, instead of groups preceding the exchanges they enter into. He also typifies whole societies as creating their order of cultural conventions "by constantly trying to change, readjust, and impinge upon it. . . . Their concern might be thought of as an effort to 'knock the conventional off balance.' . . . [Their conventions] are not intended to be 'performed' or followed as a 'code,' *but rather used as the basis of inventive improvisation*" (Wagner 1981 [1975]: 87–88; original emphasis). Merlan and Rumsey (1991: 215) similarly show how, among Ku Waru speakers of highland Papua New Guinea, "social identities are constructed in the actual practice of exchange." Sahlins's (1985) discussion of "performative structures" is also in this family of theoretical formulations.

References

Abbott, Andrew. 1995. "Things of Boundaries." *Social Research* 62 (4): 857–82.

Agha, Asif. 2007. *Language and Social Relations*. Cambridge: Cambridge University Press.

Anderson, Benedict. 1991. *Imagined Communities: Reflections on the Origin and Spread of Nationalism*. London: Verso.

Århem, Kaj. 1981a. "Bride Capture, Sister Exchange, and Gift Marriage among the Makuna: A Model of Marriage Exchange." *Ethnos* 46 (1–2): 47–63.

———. 1981b. *Makuna Social Organization: A Study of Descent, Alliance and the Formation of Corporate Groups in the North-Western Amazon*. Stockholm: Almqvist & Wiksell International.

———. 1998. "Powers of Place: Landscape, Territory, and Local Belonging in Northwest Amazonia." In *Locality and Belonging*, ed. N. Lovell, 78–102. London: Routledge.

Ash, Juliet. 1996. "Memory and Objects." In *The Gendered Object*, ed. P. Kirkham, 219–24. Manchester: Manchester University Press.

Bakker, Sybe, ed. 1996. *Op weg naar het licht*. Groningen: Boon Uitgever.

Barnard, Alan. 1978. "Universal Systems of Kin Categorization." *African Studies* 37: 69–81.

Barth, Fredrik. 1969. "Ethnic Groups and Boundaries: The Social Organization of Cultural Difference." In *Ethnic Groups and Boundaries*, ed. F. Barth, 9–38. Bergen: Universitetsforlaget.

Bashkow, Ira. 2004. "A Neo-Boasian Conception of Cultural Boundaries." *American Anthropologist* 106 (3): 443–58.

———. 2006. *The Meaning of Whitemen: Race and Modernity in the Orokaiva Cultural World*. Chicago: University of Chicago Press.

Bateson, Gregory. 1958 [1936]. *Naven: A Survey of the Problems Suggested by a Composite Picture of the Culture of a New Guinea Tribe Drawn from Three Points of View*. Stanford: Stanford University Press.

Battaglia, Debora. 1990. *On the Bones of the Serpent: Person, Memory, and Mortality in Sabarl Island Society*. Chicago: University of Chicago Press.

———. 1992. "The Body in the Gift: Memory and Forgetting in Sabarl Mortuary Exchange." *American Ethnologist* 19: 3–18.

Benveniste, Émile. 1971 [1956]. "The Nature of Pronouns." In *Problems in General Linguistics*, 217–22. Miami: University of Miami Press.

———. 1971 [1958]. "Subjectivity in Language." In *Problems in General Linguistics*, 223–30. Miami: University of Miami Press.

Biersack, Aletta. 1987. "Moonlight: Negative Images of Transcendence in Paiela Pollution." *Oceania* 57: 178–94.

Bird-David, Nurit. 1999. "'Animism' Revisited: Personhood, Environment, and Relational Epistemology." *Current Anthropology* 40 (Suppl.): 67–91.

Boellstorff, Tom. 2002. "Ethnolocality." *Asia Pacific Journal of Anthropology* 3 (1): 24–48.

Borneman, John. 1997. "Caring and Being Cared For: Displacing Marriage, Kinship, Gender, and Sexuality." *International Journal of Social Science* 154: 623–35.

Bulmer, Ralph. 1967. "Why Is the Cassowary Not a Bird? A Problem of Zoological Taxonomy among the Karam of the New Guinea Highlands." *Man*, n.s., 2: 5–25.

Burridge, K. O. L. 1975. "The Melanesian Manager." In *Studies in Social Anthropology*, ed. J. H. M. Beattie and R. G. Lienhardt, 86–104. Oxford: Clarendon Press.

Busse, Mark. 1987. "Sister Exchange among the Wamek of the Middle Fly." Ph.D. dissertation, University of California, San Diego.

Cahnman, Werner J. 1973. *Ferdinand Tönnies: A New Evaluation. Essays and Documents*. Leiden: Brill.

Cannell, Fenella. 1999. *Power and Intimacy in the Christian Philippines*. Cambridge: Cambridge University Press.

Carneiro da Cunha, Manuela. 1981. "Eschatology among the Krahó: Reflection upon Society, Free Field of Fabulation." In *Mortality and Immortality: The Anthropology and Archaeology of Death*, ed. S. C. Humphreys and H. King, 161–74. London: Academic Press.

Carsten, Janet. 1997. *The Heat of the Hearth: The Process of Kinship in a Malay Fishing Community*. Oxford: Clarendon Press.

———. 2004. *After Kinship*. Cambridge: Cambridge University Press.

Certeau, Michel de. 1984. *The Practice of Everyday Life*. Trans. S. Randall. Berkeley: University of California Press.

Charsley, Katharine. 2005. "Unhappy Husbands: Masculinity and Migration in Transnational Pakistani Marriages." *Journal of the Royal Anthropological Institute* 11 (1): 85–105.

Clark, Jeffrey, and Jenny Hughes. 1995. "A History of Sexuality and Gender in Tari." In *Papuan Borderlands: Huli, Duna, and Ipili Perspectives on the Papua New Guinea Highlands,* ed. A. Biersack, 315–40. Ann Arbor: University of Michigan Press.

Conklin, Beth. 2001. *Consuming Grief: Compassionate Cannibalism in an Amazonian Society.* Austin: University of Texas Press.

Cresswell, Tim. 1997. "Imagining the Nomad: Mobility and the Postmodern Primitive." In *Space and Social Theory: Interpreting Modernity and Postmodernity,* ed. G. Benko and U. Strohmayer, 360–79. Oxford: Blackwell.

Danziger, Eve. 2001. *Relatively Speaking: Language, Thought, and Kinship among the Mopan Maya.* Oxford: Oxford University Press.

Dastur, Françoise. 1996. *Death: An Essay on Finitude.* London: Athlone.

Dening, Greg. 1992. *Mr. Bligh's Bad Language: Passion, Power, and Theatre on the Bounty.* Cambridge: Cambridge University Press.

de Vries, Tj. S. 1983. *Een open plek in het oerwoud: Evangelieverkondiging aan het volk van Irian Jaya.* Groningen: De Vuurbaak.

Eco, Umberto. 1995. *The Search for the Perfect Language.* Oxford: Blackwell.

Ellen, Roy. 2006. "Local Knowledge and Management of Sago Palm *(Metroxylon sagu Rottboell)* Diversity in South Central Seram, Maluku, Eastern Indonesia." *Journal of Ethnobiology* 26 (2): 258–98.

Evans-Pritchard, E. E. 1940. "The Nuer of the Southern Sudan." In *African Political Systems,* ed. M. Fortes and E. E. Evans-Pritchard, 272–96. Oxford: Oxford University Press.

Fabian, Johannes. 1983. *Time and the Other: How Anthropology Makes Its Object.* New York: Columbia University Press.

———. 2006. "The Other Revisited: Critical Afterthoughts." *Anthropological Theory* 6 (2): 139–52.

Faubion, James D. 2001. "Introduction: Toward an Anthropology of the Ethics of Kinship." In *The Ethics of Kinship: Ethnographic Inquiries,* ed. J. D. Faubion, 1–28. Lanham, MD: Rowman & Littlefield.

Flach, Michiel. 1997. *Sago Palm: Metroxylon Sagu Rottb.* Rome: International Plant Genetics Resources Institute.

Ford, Richard. 2004. "My Mother, in Memory." In *Vintage Ford,* 167–97. New York: Vintage Books.

Fortes, Meyer. 1969. *Kinship and the Social Order: The Legacy of Lewis Henry Morgan.* Chicago: Aldine.

Foucault, Michel. 1986. "Of Other Spaces." *Diacritics* 16 (1): 22–27.

Fox, James J. 1997. "Place and Landscape in Comparative Austronesian Perspective." In *The Poetic Power of Place: Comparative Perspectives on Austronesian Ideas of Locality,* ed. J. J. Fox, 1–21. Canberra: Department of Anthropology, Research School of Pacific and Asian Studies, Australian National University.

Freud, Sigmund. 1955 [1919]. "The 'Uncanny.'" In *An Infantile Neurosis and Other Works. The Standard Edition of the Complete Psychological Works of Sigmund Freud, Vol. 17 (1917–1919),* ed. J. Strachey, 219–52. London: Hogarth Press.

Geertz, Clifford. 1973. "Person, Time, and Conduct in Bali." In *The Interpretation of Cultures*, 412–53. New York: Basic Books.

Gell, Alfred. 1992. "Intertribal Commodity Barter and Reproductive Gift Exchange in Old Melanesia." In *Barter, Exchange, and Value: An Anthropological Approach*, ed. S. Hugh-Jones and C. Humphrey, 142–68. Cambridge: Cambridge University Press.

Gibson, Margaret. 2004. "Melancholy Objects." *Mortality* 9 (4): 285–99.

Goldman, Laurence R. 1998. *Child's Play: Myth, Mimesis and Make-Believe*. Oxford: Berg.

Greenblatt, Stephen. 1991. *Marvelous Possessions: The Wonder of the New World*. Chicago: University of Chicago Press.

Gunn, B. V., P. Stevens, M. Singadan, L. Sunari, and P. Chatterton. 2004. *Eaglewood in Papua New Guinea*. Resource Management in Asia-Pacific Working Paper No. 51. Canberra: Resource Management in Asia-Pacific Program, Research School of Pacific and Asian Studies, Australian National University.

Gupta, Akhil, and James Ferguson. 1992. "Beyond 'Culture': Space, Identity and the Politics of Difference." *Cultural Anthropology* 7 (1): 6–23.

Hallam, Elizabeth, and Jenny Hockey. 2001. *Death, Memory, and Material Culture*. Oxford: Berg.

Hallowell, A. Irving. 1955. "The Nature and Function of Property as a Social Institution." In *Culture and Experience*, 236–49. Philadelphia: University of Pennsylvania Press.

Hanks, William. 1990. *Referential Practice: Language and Lived Space among the Maya*. Chicago: University of Chicago Press.

Harris, Jose. 2001. "General Introduction." In *Community and Civil Society*, by Ferdinand Tonnies, ix–xxx. Cambridge: Cambridge University Press.

Harrison, Simon. 1993a. "The Commerce of Cultures in Melanesia." *Man* 28: 139–58.

———. 1993b. *The Mask of War: Violence, Ritual, and the Self in Melanesia*. Manchester: Manchester University Press.

Hill, Jane H. 2005. "Intertextuality as Source and Evidence for Indirect Indexical Meanings." *Journal of Linguistic Anthropology* 15 (1): 113–24.

Hirsch, Jennifer S. 2003. *A Courtship after Marriage: Sexuality and Love in Mexican Transnational Families*. Berkeley: University of California Press.

Hogbin, H. Ian, and Camilla Wedgwood. 1953. "Local Grouping in Melanesia." *Oceania* 23: 241–76.

Inoue, Miyako. 2004. "What Does Language Remember? Indexical Inversion and the Naturalized History of Japanese Women." *Journal of Linguistic Anthropology* 14 (1): 39–56.

Jespersen, Otto. 1922. *Language: Its Nature, Development, and Origin*. New York: Henry Holt & Company.

Keane, Webb. 1997. *Signs of Recognition: Powers and Hazards of Representation in an Indonesian Society*. Berkeley: University of California Press.

———. 2003. "Self-Interpretation, Agency, and the Objects of Anthropology: Reflections on a Genealogy." *Comparative Studies in Society and History* 45 (2): 222–48.

Kearney, Richard. 2003. *Strangers, Gods, and Monsters: Interpreting Otherness.* London: Routledge.

Keen, Ian. 2004. *Aboriginal Economy and Society: Australia at the Threshold of Colonisation.* Oxford: Oxford University Press.

Knauft, Bruce M. 1985. *Good Company and Violence: Sorcery and Social Action in a Lowland New Guinea Society.* Berkeley: University of California Press.

Kripke, Saul. 1980. *Naming and Necessity.* Oxford: Basil Blackwell.

Lepri, Isabella. 2005. "The Meanings of Kinship among the Ese Ejja of Northern Bolivia." *Journal of the Royal Anthropological Institute* 11 (4): 703–24.

LeRoy, John. 1985. *Fabricated World: An Interpretation of Kewa Tales.* Vancouver: University of British Columbia Press.

Lévi-Strauss, Claude. 1969 [1949]. *The Elementary Structures of Kinship.* Trans. J. H. Bell, J. R. Sturmer, and R. Needham. Boston: Beacon Press.

———. 1976 [1971]. "Relations of Symmetry Between Rituals and Myths of Neighboring Peoples." In *Structural Anthropology*, vol. 2, 238–55. New York: Basic Books.

Levinson, Stephen. 2003. *Space in Language and Cognition: Explorations in Cognitive Diversity.* Cambridge: Cambridge University Press.

Liebersohn, Harry. 1988. *Fate and Utopia in German Sociology, 1870–1923.* Cambridge, MA: MIT Press.

Lowe, Celia. 2003. "The Magic of Place: Sama at Sea and on Land in Sulawesi, Indonesia." *Bijdragen tot de Taal-, Land- en Volkenkunde* 159 (1): 109–33.

Maine, Henry Sumner. 1861. *Ancient Law: Its Connections with the Early History of Society, and Its Relation to Modern Ideas.* London: J. Murray.

———. 1871. *Village-Communities in the East and West: Six Lectures Delivered at Oxford.* London: J. Murray.

Majnep, Ian Saem, and Ralph Bulmer. 1977. *Birds of My Kalam Country.* Auckland: University of Auckland Press.

McDowell, Nancy. 1978. "The Flexibility of Sister Exchange in Bun." *Oceania* 48: 207–31.

———. 1988. "Reproductive Decision Making and the Value of Children in Traditional Papua New Guinea." In *Reproductive Decision Making and the Value of Children in Traditional Papua New Guinea*, vol. 27, ed. N. McDowell, 9–43. IASER Monograph. Boroko: Institute of Applied Social and Economic Research.

———. 1990. "Person, Reciprocity, and Change: Explorations of Burridge in Bun." In *Sepik Heritage: Tradition and Change in Papua New Guinea*, ed. N. Lutkehaus, C. Kaufmann, W. Mitchell, D. Newton, L. Osmundsen, and M. Schuster, 343–50. Durham, NC: Carolina Academic Press.

McKinley, Robert. 1971. "A Critique of the Reflectionist Theory of Kinship Terminology: The Crow-Omaha Case." *Man* 6: 228–47.

———. 2001. "The Philosophy of Kinship: A Reply to Schneider's *Critique of the Study of Kinship.*" In *The Cultural Analysis of Kinship: The Legacy of David M. Schneider*, ed. R. Feinberg and M. Oppenheimer, 131–67. Urbana: University of Illinois Press.

Merlan, Francesca. 1997. "The Mother-in-Law Taboo: Avoidance and Obligation in Aboriginal Australian Society." In *Scholar and Sceptic: Australian Aboriginal Studies in Honour of L. R. Hiatt*, ed. F. Merlan, J. Morton, and A. Rumsey, 95–22, 266–71. Canberra: Aboriginal Studies Press.

———. 2005. "Explorations towards Intercultural Accounts of Socio-Cultural Reproduction and Change." *Oceania* 75 (3): 167–82.

Merlan, Francesca, and Jeffrey Heath. 1982. "Dyadic Kinship Terms." In *The Languages of Kinship in Aboriginal Australia*, ed. J. Heath, F. Merlan, and A. Rumsey, 107–24. Oceania Linguistic Monograph No. 24. Sydney: University of Sydney.

Merlan, Francesca, and Alan Rumsey. 1991. *Ku Waru: Language and Segmentary Politics in the Western Nebilyer Valley, Papua New Guinea*. Cambridge: Cambridge University Press.

Middleton, John. 1960. *Lugbara Religion: Ritual and Authority among an East African People*. London: Oxford University Press.

Mitzman, Arthur. 1973. *Sociology and Estrangement: Three Sociologists of Imperial Germany*. New York: Knopf.

Momberg, Frank, Rajindra Puri, and Timothy Jessup. 2000. "Exploitation of Gaharu, and Forest Conservation Efforts in the Kayan Mentarang National Park, East Kalimantan, Indonesia." In *People, Plants, and Justice: The Politics of Nature Conservation*, ed. C. Zerner, 259–84. New York: Columbia University Press.

Munn, Nancy D. 1986. *The Fame of Gawa: A Symbolic Study of Value Transformation in a Massim (Papua New Guinea) Society*. Cambridge: Cambridge University Press.

———. 1995. "An Essay on the Symbolic Construction of Memory in the Kaluli Gisalo." In *Cosmos and Society in Oceania*, ed. D. de Coppet and A. Iteanu, 83–104. Oxford: Berg.

Myers, Fred. 1986. *Pintupi Country, Pintupi Self: Sentiment, Place, and Politics among Western Desert Aborigines*. Washington, DC: Smithsonian Institution Press.

Nourse, Jennifer W. 1999. *Conceiving Spirits: Birth Rituals and Contested Identities among Laujé of Indonesia*. Washington, DC: Smithsonian Institution Press.

Ogden, C. K. 1967 [1932]. *Opposition: A Linguistic and Psychological Analysis*. Bloomington: Indiana University Press.

Overing, Joanna. 2003. "In Praise of the Everyday: Trust and the Art of Social Living in an Amazonian Community." *Ethnos* 68 (3): 293–316.

Overing, Joanna, and Alan Passes. 2000. *The Anthropology of Love and Anger: The Aesthetics of Conviviality in Native Amazonia*. London: Routledge.

Parkin, Robert. 2003. *Louis Dumont and Hierarchical Opposition*. Oxford: Berghahn.

Peletz, Michael G. 2001. "Ambivalence in Kinship since the 1940s." In *Relative Values: Reconfiguring Kinship Studies*, ed. S. Franklin and S. McKinnon, 413–44. Durham, NC: Duke University Press.

Pitt-Rivers, Julian. 1977. "The Law of Hospitality." In *The Fate of Shechem, or the Politics of Sex: Essays in the Anthropology of the Mediterranean,* 94–112. Cambridge: Cambridge University Press.

Pratt, Mary Louise. 1992. *Imperial Eyes: Travel Writing and Transculturation.* London: Routledge.

Quanchi, Max. 1994. "Photography, Representation, and Cross-Cultural Encounters: Seeking Reality in Papua 1880–1930." Ph.D dissertation, University of Queensland, Brisbane.

———.1999. "Tree-Houses, Representation, and Photography on the Papuan Coast, 1880 to 1930." In *Art and Performance in Oceania,* ed. B. Craig, B. Kernot, and C. Anderson, 218–30. Honolulu: University of Hawai'i Press.

Radcliffe-Brown, A. R. 1952. "The Mother's Brother in South Africa." In *Structure and Function in Primitive Society,* 15–31. New York: Free Press.

Ramos, Alcida R. 1995. *Sanumá Memories: Yanomami Ethnography in Times of Crisis.* Madison: University of Wisconsin Press.

Redfield, Robert. 1940. "The Folk Society and Culture." *American Journal of Sociology* 45 (5): 731–42.

Reed, Adam. 2003. *Papua New Guinea's Last Place: Experiences of Constraint in a Postcolonial Prison.* Oxford: Berghahn.

Reuter, Thomas. 2002. *The House of Our Ancestors: Precedence and Dualism in Highland Balinese Society.* Leiden: KITLV.

Ricoeur, Paul. 1992. *Oneself as Another.* Trans. K. Blamey. Chicago: University of Chicago Press.

Rigsby, Bruce. 1998. "A Survey of Property Theory and Tenure Types." In *Customary Marine Tenure in Australia,* ed. N. Peterson and B. Rigsby, 22–46. Oceania Monograph 48. Sydney: Oceania Publications, University of Sydney.

Robbins, Joel. 1994. "Equality as a Value: Ideology in Dumont, Melanesia, and the West." *Social Analysis* 36: 21–70.

———. 2003. "Properties of Nature, Properties of Culture: Possession, Recognition, and the Substance of Politics in a Papua New Guinea Society." *Journal of the Finnish Anthropological Society* 28 (1): 9–28.

———. 2004. *Becoming Sinners: Christianity and Moral Torment in a Papua New Guinea Society.* Berkeley: University of California Press.

———. 2007. "Morality, Politics, and the Melanesian Big Man: On *The Melanesian Manager* and the Transformation of Political Anthropology." In *The Anthropology of Morality in Melanesia and Beyond,* ed. J. Barker, 25–37. Aldershot: Ashgate.

Robbins, Joel, and Alan Rumsey. 2008. "Introduction: Cultural and Linguistic Anthropology and the Opacity of Other Minds." *Anthropological Quarterly* 81 (2): 407–20.

Rosaldo, Michelle Z. 1982. "The Things We Do with Words: Ilongot Speech Acts and Speech Act Theory in Philosophy." *Language in Society* 11 (2): 203–37.

Rosaldo, Renato. 1980. *Ilongot Headhunting, 1883–1974: A Study in Society and History.* Stanford: Stanford University Press.

Rumsey, Alan. 1981. "Kinship and Context among the Ngarinyin." *Oceania* 51 (3):181–92.

———. 2002. "Aspects of Ku Waru Ethnosyntax and Social Life." In *Ethnosyntax: Explorations in Grammar and Culture,* ed. N. J. Enfield, 259–86. Oxford: Oxford University Press.

———. 2003. "Language, Desire, and the Ontogenesis of Intersubjectivity." *Language & Communication* 23 (2): 169–87.

———. 2006. "The Articulation of Indigenous and Exogenous Orders in Highland New Guinea and Beyond." *Australian Journal of Anthropology* 17 (1): 47–69.

Rutherford, Danilyn. 2003. *Raiding the Land of the Foreigners: The Limits of the Nation on an Indonesian Frontier.* Princeton: Princeton University Press.

Sahlins, Marshall. 1972 [1965]. "On the Sociology of Primitive Exchange." In *Stone Age Economics,* 185–275. New York: Aldine de Gruyter.

———. 1985. *Islands of History.* Chicago: University of Chicago Press.

Samson, Basil. 1988. "A Grammar of Exchange." In *Being Black: Aboriginal Cultures in Settled Australia,* ed. I. Keen, 159–77. Canberra: Aboriginal Studies Press.

Santner, Eric L. 2001. *On the Psychotheology of Everyday Life: Reflections on Freud and Rosenzweig.* Chicago: University of Chicago Press.

Sargent, Carolyn. 1988. "Born to Die: Witchcraft and Infanticide in Bariba Culture." *Ethnology* 27: 79–95.

Scheper-Hughes, Nancy. 1992. *Death without Weeping: The Violence of Everyday Life in Brazil.* Berkeley: University of California Press.

Schieffelin, Bambi B. 1990. *The Give and Take of Everyday Life: Language Socialization of Kaluli Children.* Cambridge: Cambridge University Press.

Schieffelin, Edward L. 1976. *The Sorrow of the Lonely and the Burning of the Dancers.* New York: St. Martin's Press.

Schneider, David M. 1980 [1968]. *American Kinship: A Cultural Account.* Chicago: University of Chicago Press.

———. 1984. *A Critique of the Study of Kinship.* Ann Arbor: University of Michigan Press.

Schuiling, D. L., and M. Flach. 1985. *Guidelines for the Cultivation of Sago Palm.* Wageningen: Department of Tropical Crop Science, Agricultural University Wageningen.

Schulte, Regina. 1994. *The Village in Court: Arson, Infanticide, and Poaching in the Court Records of Upper Bavaria, 1848–1910.* Trans. B. Selman. Cambridge: Cambridge University Press.

Schutz, Alfred. 1944. "The Stranger: An Essay in Social Psychology." *American Journal of Sociology* 49: 499–507.

———. 1945."The Homecomer." *American Journal of Sociology* 50 (5): 369–76.

———. 1967 [1932]. *The Phenomenology of the Social World.* Trans. G. Walsh and F. Lehnert. Evanston, IL: Northwestern University Press.

Scrimshaw, Susan C. M. 1984. "Infanticide in Human Populations: Societal and Individual Concerns." In *Infanticide: Comparative and Evolutionary Perspectives,* ed. G. Hausfater and S. B. Hrdy, 439–62. New York: Aldine.

Sekretariat Keadilan dan Perdamaian, Keuskupan Agung Merauke. 2004. *Bisnis Gaharu dan Dampaknya Terhadap Kehidupan Orang Awyu dan Wiyagar di Distrik Assue, Kabupaten Mappi—Papua Selatan* (The Gaharu Business and Its

Impact on the Lives of Awyu and Wiyagar People in Assue District, Mappi Regency, South Papua). Merauke: Office of Justice and Peace, Archdiocese of Merauke. www.hampapua.org/skp/indexe.html. Accessed November 16, 2004.

Shils, Edward. 1957. "Primordial, Personal, Sacred, and Civil Ties: Some Particular Observations on the Relationships of Sociological Research and Theory." *British Journal of Sociology* 8 (2): 130–45.

Shryock, Andrew. 2004. "The New Jordanian Hospitality: House, Host, and Guest in the Culture of Public Display." *Comparative Studies in Society and History* 46 (1): 35–62.

Silverstein, Michael. 1976. "Shifters, Linguistic Categories, and Cultural Description." In *Meaning in Anthropology,* ed. K. H. Basso and H. A. Selby, 11–55. Albuquerque: University of New Mexico Press.

———. 1993. "Metapragmatic Discourse and Metapragmatic Function." In *Reflexive Language: Reported Speech and Metapragmatics,* ed. J. A. Lucy, 33–58. Cambridge: Cambridge University Press.

Simmel, Georg. 1950 [1908]. "The Stranger." In *The Sociology of Georg Simmel,* ed. K. H. Wolff, 402–8. New York: Free Press.

———. 1955 [1908]. "Conflict." In *Conflict and the Web of Group Affiliations,* 11–123. New York: Free Press.

———. 1971 [1918]. "The Transcendent Character of Life." In *Georg Simmel on Individuality and Social Forms: Selected Writings,* ed. D. N. Levine, 353–74. Chicago: University of Chicago Press.

———. 1997 [1909]. "Bridge and Door." In *Simmel on Culture: Selected Writings,* ed. D. Frisby and M. Featherstone, 170–74. London: Sage.

Spyer, Patricia. 2000. *The Memory of Trade: Modernity's Entanglements on an Eastern Indonesian Island.* Durham, NC: Duke University Press.

Stasch, Rupert. 1996. "Killing as Reproductive Agency: Dugong, Pigs, and Humanity among the Kiwai, circa 1900." *Anthropos* 91: 359–79.

———. 2001a. "Figures of Alterity among Korowai of Irian Jaya: Kinship, Mourning, and Festivity in a Dispersed Society." Ph.D. dissertation, University of Chicago.

———. 2001b. "Giving up Homicide: Korowai Experience of Witches and Police (West Papua)." *Oceania* 72 (1): 33–55.

———. 2002. "Joking Avoidance: A Korowai Pragmatics of Being Two." *American Ethnologist* 29 (2): 335–65.

———. 2003a. "The Semiotics of World-Making in Korowai Feast Longhouses." *Language & Communication* 23 (3–4): 359–83.

———. 2003b. "Separateness as a Relation: The Iconicity, Univocality, and Creativity of Korowai Mother-in-law Avoidance." *Journal of the Royal Anthropological Institute* 9 (2): 311–29.

———. 2007. "Demon Language: The Otherness of Indonesian in a Papuan Community." In *Consequences of Contact: Language Ideologies and Sociocultural Transformations in Pacific Societies,* ed. M. Makihara and B. B. Schieffelin, 96–124. Oxford: Oxford University Press.

———. 2008a. "Knowing Minds Is a Matter of Authority: Political Dimensions of Opacity Statements in Korowai Moral Psychology." *Anthropological Quarterly* 81 (2): 443–53.

———. 2008b. "Referent-Wrecking in Korowai: A New Guinea Abuse Register as Ethnosemiotic Protest." *Language in Society* 37 (1): 1–25.

Steadman, Lyle. 1972. "Neighbors and Killers: Residence and Dominance among the Hewa of New Guinea." Ph.D. dissertation, Australia National University.

Steinmetz, George. 1996. "Irian Jaya's People of the Trees." *National Geographic* 189 (2): 34–43.

Storrie, Robert. 2003. "Equivalence, Personhood, and Relationality: Processes of Relatedness among the Hoti of Venezuelan Guiana." *Journal of the Royal Anthropological Institute* 9 (3): 409–28.

Stråth, Bo. 2001. "Community/Society: History of the Concept." In *International Encyclopedia of the Social & Behavioral Sciences,* ed. N. Smelser and P. Baltes, 2378–83. Oxford: Elsevier.

Strathern, Marilyn. 1987. "Producing Difference: Connections and Disconnections in Two New Guinea Highland Kinship Systems." In *Gender and Kinship: Essays Toward a Unified Analysis,* ed. J. Collier and S. Yanagisako, 271–300. Stanford: Stanford University Press.

———. 1988. *The Gender of the Gift: Problems with Women and Problems with Society in Melanesia.* Berkeley: University of California Press.

Taylor, Anne-Christine. 1985. "L'Art de la réduction: La guerre et les mécanismes de la différenciation tribale dans la culture Jivaro." *Journal de la Société des Américanistes* 71: 159–73.

———. 1993. "Remembering to Forget: Identity, Mourning, and Memory among the Jivaro." *Man* 28: 653–78.

Titiev, Mischa. 1956. "The Importance of Space in Primitive Kinship." *American Anthropologist* 58: 854–65.

Todorov, Tzvetan. 1984. *The Conquest of America: The Question of the Other.* Trans. R. Howard. New York: Harper and Row.

Tönnies, Ferdinand. 1957 [1887]. *Community and Society.* Trans. C. Loomis. East Lansing: Michigan State University Press.

———. 1971 [1912]. "Preface to the Second Edition of *Gemeinschaft und Gesellschaft.*" In *Ferdinand Tönnies on Sociology: Pure, Applied, and Empirical. Selected Writings,* ed. W. J. Cahnman and R. Heberle, 24–36. Chicago: University of Chicago Press.

Trawick, Margaret. 1990. *Notes on Love in a Tamil Family.* Berkeley: University of California Press.

Tsing, Anna. 1993. *In the Realm of the Diamond Queen: Marginality in an Out-of-the-Way Place.* Princeton: Princeton University Press.

———. 2005. *Friction: An Ethnography of Global Connection.* Princeton: Princeton University Press.

Valeri, Valerio. 1990. "Both Nature and Culture: Reflections on Menstrual and Parturitional Taboos in Huaulu (Seram)." In *Power and Difference: Gender in Island Southeast Asia,* ed. J. Atkinson and S. Errington, 235–72. Stanford: Stanford University Press.

———. 1994. "Buying Women but Not Selling Them: Gift and Commodity Exchange in Huaulu Alliance." *Man* 29 (1): 1–26.

———. 2000. *The Forest of Taboos: Morality, Hunting, and Identity among the Huaulu of the Moluccas.* Madison: University of Wisconsin Press.

van Enk, Gerrit J., and Lourens de Vries. 1997. *The Korowai of Irian Jaya: Their Language in Its Cultural Context.* Oxford: Oxford University Press.

Viveiros de Castro, Eduardo. 1998. "Cosmological Deixis and Amazonian Perspectivism." *Journal of the Royal Anthropological Institute* 4: 469–88.

———. 2001. "GUT Feelings about Amazonia: Potential Affinity and the Construction of Sociality." In *Beyond the Visible and the Material: The Amerindianization of Society in the Work of Peter Rivière,* ed. L. M. Rival and N. L. Whitehead, 19–43. Oxford: Oxford University Press.

———. 2004. "Exchanging Perspectives: The Transformation of Objects into Subjects in Amerindian Ontologies." *Common Knowledge* 10 (3): 463–84.

———. forthcoming. "Intensive Filiation and Demonic Alliance." In *Deleuzian Intersections in Science, Technology, and Anthropology,* ed. C. B. Jensen and K. Rödje. Oxford: Benghahn.

Vlasblom, Dirk. 2004. *Papoea: Een Geschiedenis.* Amsterdam: Mets & Schilt.

Wagner, Roy. 1967. *The Curse of Souw: Principles of Daribi Clan Definition and Alliance.* Chicago: University of Chicago Press.

———. 1974. "Are There Social Groups in the New Guinea Highlands?" In *Frontiers of Anthropology,* ed. M. Leaf, 95–122. New York: Van Nostrand.

———. 1977. "Analogic Kinship: A Daribi Example." *American Ethnologist* 4: 623–42.

———. 1981 [1975]. *The Invention of Culture.* Chicago: University of Chicago Press.

———. 1986. *Symbols That Stand for Themselves.* Chicago: University of Chicago Press.

Welsch, Robert L. 1994. "Pig Feasts and Expanding Networks of Cultural Influence in the Upper Fly-Digul Plain." In *Migration and Transformations: Regional Perspectives on New Guinea,* ed. A. J. Strathern and G. Stürzenhofecker, 85–119. Pittsburgh: University of Pittsburgh Press.

Weston, Kath. 1991. *Families We Choose: Lesbians, Gays, Kinship.* New York: Columbia University Press.

Williams, Patrick. 2003 [1993]. *Gypsy World: The Silence of the Living and the Voices of the Dead.* Trans. C. Tihanyi. Chicago: University of Chicago Press.

Index

Text : 10/13 Sabon
Display: Sabon
Compositor : BookComp, Inc.
Printer and binder: Thomson-Shore, Inc.